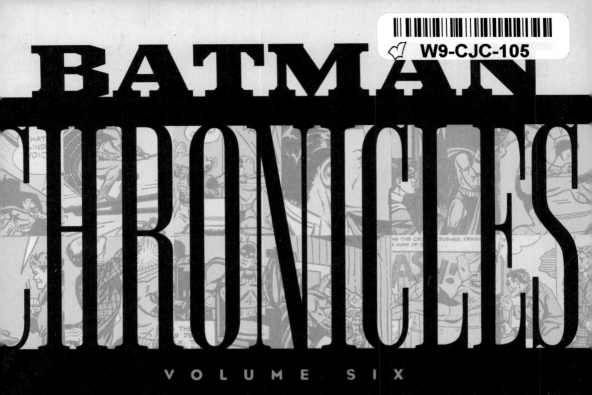

BATMAN CHRONICLES

VOLUME SIX

BATMAN CREATED BY BOB KANE

ALL STORIES WRITTEN BY BILL FINGER. ALL COVERS AND STORIES PENCILLED BY BOB KANE
AND INKED BY JERRY ROBINSON UNLESS OTHERWISE NOTED.

**These stories were originally untitled and are
titled here for reader convenience.*

THE BATMAN CHRONICLES VOLUME 6. Published by DC Comics. Cover and compilation Copyright © 2008 DC Comics.
All Rights Reserved. Originally published in single magazine form in BATMAN 10-11, DETECTIVE COMICS 62-65, and WORLD'S FINEST COMICS
5 and 6. Copyright 1941 DC Comics. All Rights Reserved. All characters, their distinctive likenesses and related elements featured in this publication
are trademarks of DC Comics. The stories, characters and incidents featured in this publication are entirely fictional.
DC Comics does not read or accept unsolicited submissions of ideas, stories or artwork.

DC Comics, 1700 Broadway, New York, NY 10019
A Warner Bros. Entertainment Company
Printed in Canada. First Printing.
ISBN: 978-1-4012-1961-1

Cover art by Fred Ray.

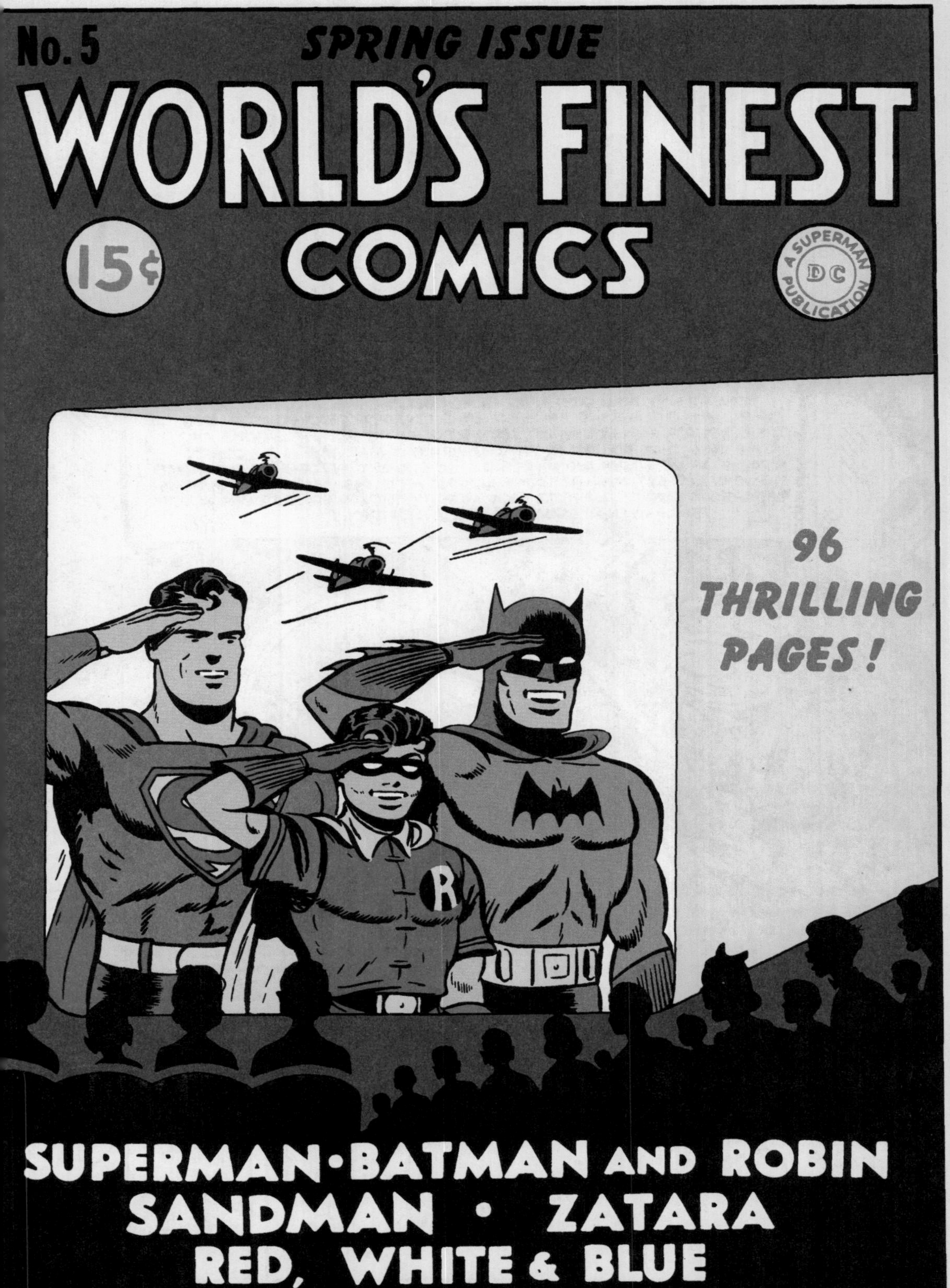
No. 5
SPRING ISSUE
WORLD'S FINEST COMICS
15¢
A SUPERMAN DC PUBLICATION
96 THRILLING PAGES!
R
SUPERMAN · BATMAN AND ROBIN
SANDMAN · ZATARA
RED, WHITE & BLUE

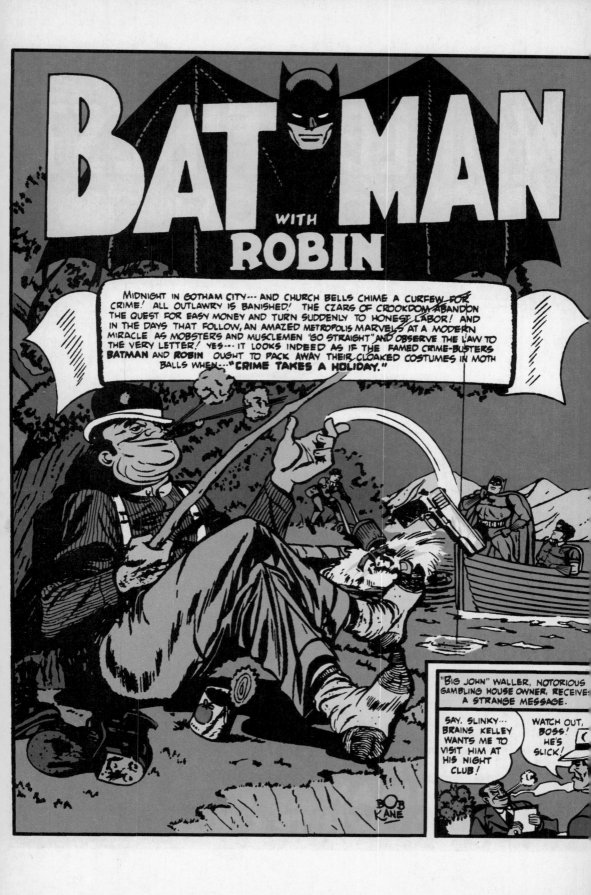

BAT MAN
WITH ROBIN

MIDNIGHT IN GOTHAM CITY··· AND CHURCH BELLS CHIME A CURFEW FOR CRIME! ALL OUTLAWRY IS BANISHED! THE CZARS OF CROOKDOM ABANDON THE QUEST FOR EASY MONEY AND TURN SUDDENLY TO HONEST LABOR! AND IN THE DAYS THAT FOLLOW, AN AMAZED METROPOLIS MARVELS AT A MODERN MIRACLE AS MOBSTERS AND MUSCLEMEN "GO STRAIGHT" AND OBSERVE THE LAW TO THE VERY LETTER! YES··· IT LOOKS INDEED AS IF THE FAMED CRIME-BUSTERS BATMAN AND ROBIN OUGHT TO PACK AWAY THEIR CLOAKED COSTUMES IN MOTH BALLS WHEN···"CRIME TAKES A HOLIDAY."

BOB KANE

"BIG JOHN" WALLER, NOTORIOUS GAMBLING HOUSE OWNER, RECEIVES A STRANGE MESSAGE.

SAY, SLINKY··· BRAINS KELLEY WANTS ME TO VISIT HIM AT HIS NIGHT CLUB!

WATCH OUT, BOSS! HE'S SLICK!

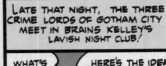

AND IN AN ELABORATE POOLROOM IN ANOTHER PART OF THE CITY, HEADQUARTERS OF DUDE DAVIS...

WELL, WELL! SO BRAINS KELLEY WANTS TO SEE ME TONIGHT! MAYBE HE WANTS TO CUT ME IN ON SOMETHING!

HE'S GETTING WISE TO HIMSELF, DUDE!

LATE THAT NIGHT, THE THREE CRIME LORDS OF GOTHAM CITY MEET IN BRAINS KELLEY'S LAVISH NIGHT CLUB!

WHAT'S UP, BRAINS?

SOMETHING BIG COOKING?

HERE'S THE IDEA, GENTLEMEN... I WANT YOU TO INSTRUCT YOUR MEN TO STOP ALL CRIMINAL ACTIVITIES IN GOTHAM CITY, BEGINNING AT MIDNIGHT TOMORROW!

TRYING TO PULL A FAST ONE, HUH? THINK WE'RE CRAZY?

I THOUGHT YOU WANTED TO CUT US IN ON SOME JOB! BUT YOU WANT TO CUT OUR OWN THROATS!

SIT DOWN, BOYS...I'M NOT CRAZY.. LISTEN...

AND AT THE STROKE OF MIDNIGHT THE NEXT DAY, A UNIQUE REFORM WAVE SWEEPS GOTHAM CITY...

HERE, MISTER-- I JUST TOOK THIS OUTTA YOUR POCKET! BUT DUDE DAVIS SAYS NO MORE CRIME FROM NOW ON!

HUH... NO MORE CRIME?

SORRY, MISTER. I CAN'T TAKE THIS FROM YOU! I GOT ORDERS TO KNOCK OFF ----CAN'T DO ANY MORE ROBBING!

GO RIGHT BACK TO SLEEP, FOLKS! WE'LL PUT EVERYTHING BACK WHERE IT BELONGS!

YEAH, IT'S MIDNIGHT, AND BIG JOHN SAYS WE GOTTA BE HONEST MEN FROM NOW ON!

CRIME TAKES A HOLIDAY IN GOTHAM CITY! IN THE DAYS THAT FOLLOW, UNDERWORLD ROGUES CONTINUE TO BEWILDER THE METROPOLIS---

WAIT FOR THE GREEN LIGHT! WE ALL GOTTA OBEY THE LAW!

PRESENT FROM THE BOYS, OFFICER! A PAIR OF RUBBERS FOR RAINY WEATHER. CAN'T HAVE YOU CATCHING COLD!

2

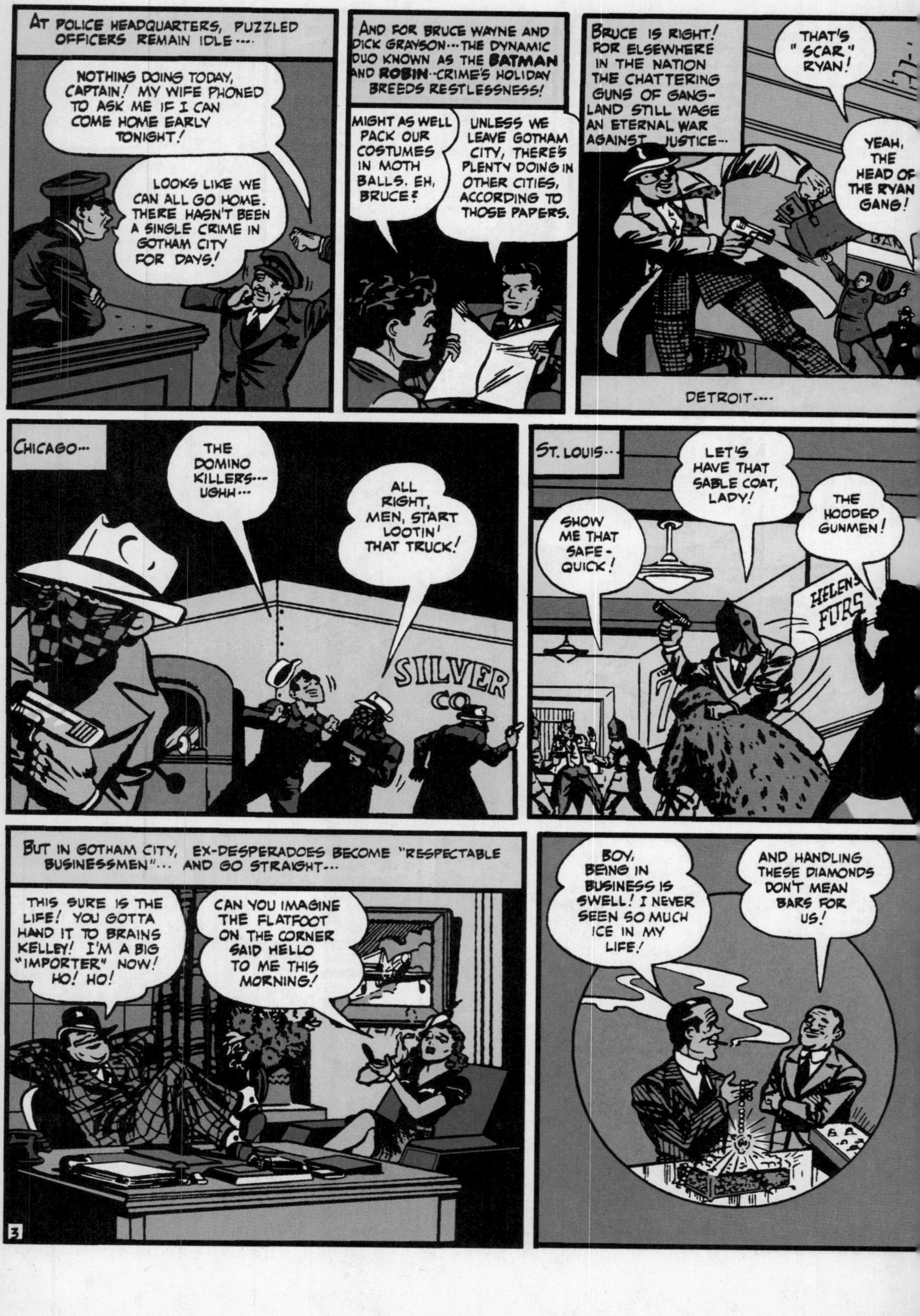
AT POLICE HEADQUARTERS, PUZZLED OFFICERS REMAIN IDLE....
NOTHING DOING TODAY, CAPTAIN! MY WIFE PHONED TO ASK ME IF I CAN COME HOME EARLY TONIGHT!
LOOKS LIKE WE CAN ALL GO HOME. THERE HASN'T BEEN A SINGLE CRIME IN GOTHAM CITY FOR DAYS!
AND FOR BRUCE WAYNE AND DICK GRAYSON...THE DYNAMIC DUO KNOWN AS THE BATMAN AND ROBIN--CRIME'S HOLIDAY BREEDS RESTLESSNESS!
MIGHT AS WELL PACK OUR COSTUMES IN MOTH BALLS. EH, BRUCE?
UNLESS WE LEAVE GOTHAM CITY, THERE'S PLENTY DOING IN OTHER CITIES, ACCORDING TO THOSE PAPERS.
BRUCE IS RIGHT! FOR ELSEWHERE IN THE NATION THE CHATTERING GUNS OF GANG-LAND STILL WAGE AN ETERNAL WAR AGAINST JUSTICE--
THAT'S "SCAR" RYAN!
YEAH, THE HEAD OF THE RYAN GANG!
DETROIT....
CHICAGO...
THE DOMINO KILLERS--- UGHH...
ALL RIGHT, MEN, START LOOTIN' THAT TRUCK!
SILVER CO
ST. LOUIS...
LET'S HAVE THAT SABLE COAT, LADY!
SHOW ME THAT SAFE-QUICK!
THE HOODED GUNMEN!
HELEN'S FURS
BUT IN GOTHAM CITY, EX-DESPERADOES BECOME "RESPECTABLE BUSINESSMEN"... AND GO STRAIGHT...
THIS SURE IS THE LIFE! YOU GOTTA HAND IT TO BRAINS KELLEY! I'M A BIG "IMPORTER" NOW! HO! HO!
CAN YOU IMAGINE THE FLATFOOT ON THE CORNER SAID HELLO TO ME THIS MORNING!
3
BOY, BEING IN BUSINESS IS SWELL! I NEVER SEEN SO MUCH ICE IN MY LIFE!
AND HANDLING THESE DIAMONDS DON'T MEAN BARS FOR US!

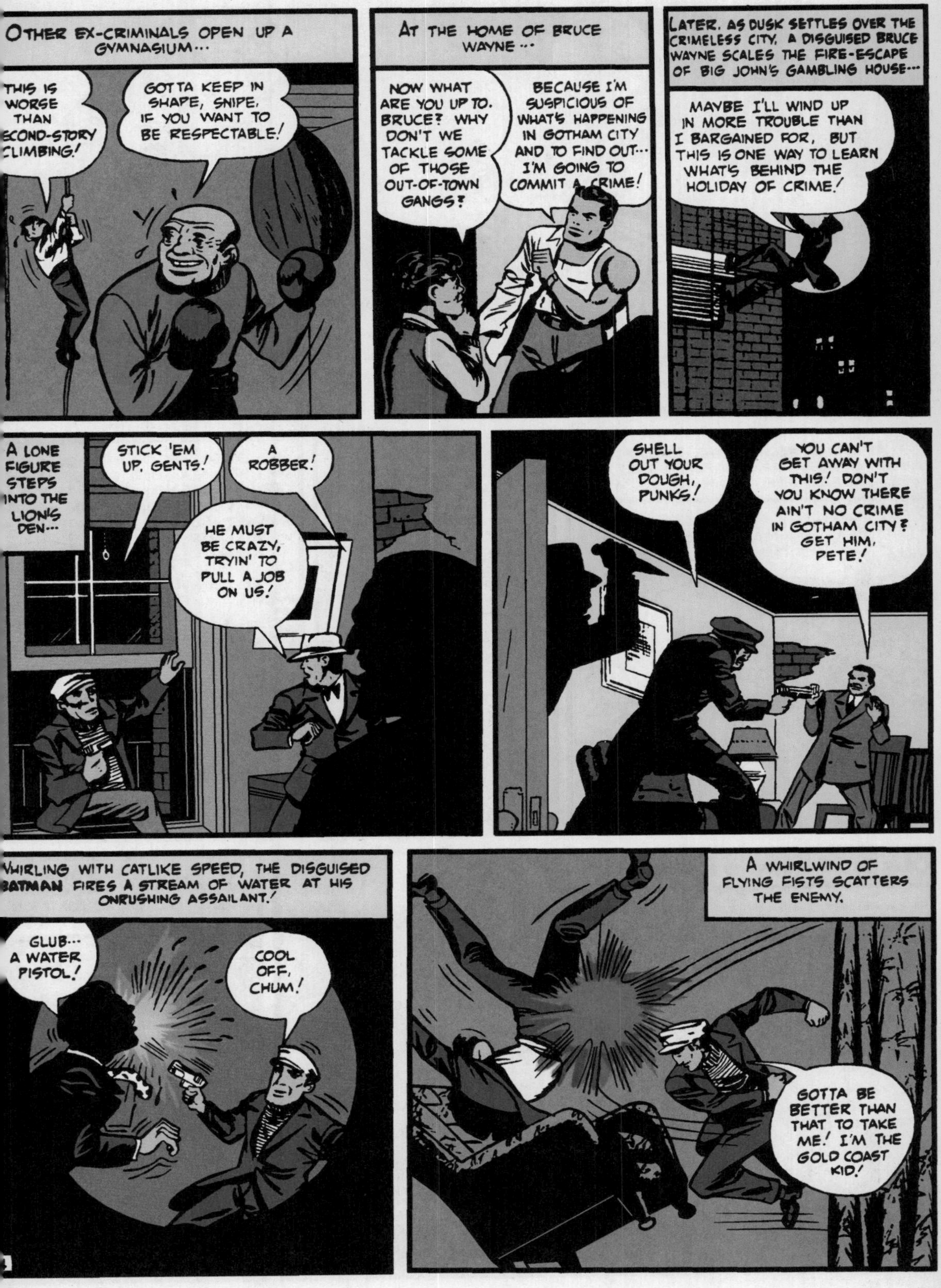

OTHER EX-CRIMINALS OPEN UP A GYMNASIUM...
THIS IS WORSE THAN ECOND-STORY CLIMBING!
GOTTA KEEP IN SHAPE, SNIPE, IF YOU WANT TO BE RESPECTABLE!
AT THE HOME OF BRUCE WAYNE...
NOW WHAT ARE YOU UP TO, BRUCE? WHY DON'T WE TACKLE SOME OF THOSE OUT-OF-TOWN GANGS?
BECAUSE I'M SUSPICIOUS OF WHAT'S HAPPENING IN GOTHAM CITY AND TO FIND OUT... I'M GOING TO COMMIT A CRIME!
LATER, AS DUSK SETTLES OVER THE CRIMELESS CITY, A DISGUISED BRUCE WAYNE SCALES THE FIRE-ESCAPE OF BIG JOHN'S GAMBLING HOUSE...
MAYBE I'LL WIND UP IN MORE TROUBLE THAN I BARGAINED FOR, BUT THIS IS ONE WAY TO LEARN WHAT'S BEHIND THE HOLIDAY OF CRIME!
A LONE FIGURE STEPS INTO THE LION'S DEN...
STICK 'EM UP, GENTS!
A ROBBER!
HE MUST BE CRAZY, TRYIN' TO PULL A JOB ON US!
SHELL OUT YOUR DOUGH, PUNKS!
YOU CAN'T GET AWAY WITH THIS! DON'T YOU KNOW THERE AIN'T NO CRIME IN GOTHAM CITY? GET HIM, PETE!
VHIRLING WITH CATLIKE SPEED, THE DISGUISED BATMAN FIRES A STREAM OF WATER AT HIS ONRUSHING ASSAILANT!
GLUB... A WATER PISTOL!
COOL OFF, CHUM!
A WHIRLWIND OF FLYING FISTS SCATTERS THE ENEMY.
GOTTA BE BETTER THAN THAT TO TAKE ME! I'M THE GOLD COAST KID!

I AM A TOUGH GUY, I AM!

YOU MEAN-- YOU WERE!

HAD BRUCE BROUGHT THE POWERFUL MUSCLES OF THE **BATMAN** INTO PLAY, HE COULD EASILY HAVE HURLED BIG JOHN ACROSS THE ROOM...

WE OUGHTTA TURN HIM OVER TO THE COPS!

YEAH! HE'S DISTURBING THE PEACE!

BUT DELIBERATELY HE ALLOWS HIMSELF TO BE CAPTURED!

WAIT A MINUTE! THIS GUY HAD ENOUGH NERVE TO HOLD ME UP WITH A WATER PISTOL AND THEN PUT UP A GOOD FIGHT! MAYBE WE CAN USE HIM!

JUST WHAT I HOPED HE'D THINK! MY PLAN IS WORKING!

THE GOLD COAST KID, EH? YOU MUST BE A STRANGER, OR YOU'D KNOW THERE'S NO MORE CRIME IN GOTHAM CITY. BUT I NEED ANOTHER MAN ON A CERTAIN JOB. LISTEN, KID...

SURE, IF IT MEANS DOUGH. COUNT ME IN!

I'M IN WITH THE GANG!

LATER, BRUCE IS TAKEN TO A RESTAURANT...

I CAN'T GET OVER IT--A WATER PISTOL! BOY, I BET THIS KID'D TACKLE THE **BATMAN** HIMSELF!

THE BATMAN! WE DON'T HAVE TO WORRY ABOUT THAT GUY, NO MORE HUH, BOSS?

YEAH, WE TIED HIS HANDS WITH THIS HOLIDAY CRIME'S SUPPOSED TO BE TAKING. FINISH UP YOUR MEAL, KID. WE'LL MEET YOU OUTSIDE.

I'LL BE WITH YA IN A SECOND!

LEFT ALONE FOR A MOMENT, BRUCE SWIFTLY MAKES AN URGENT CALL ON HIS PORTABLE WIRELESS...

BRUCE, ANY NEWS?

HAVE TO TALK FAST...I'M IN WITH BIG JOHN'S GANG! WE'RE GOING TO ROB THE CURTIS SILK WAREHOUSE IN PHILADELPHIA. TIP OFF THE POLICE!

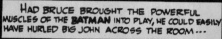

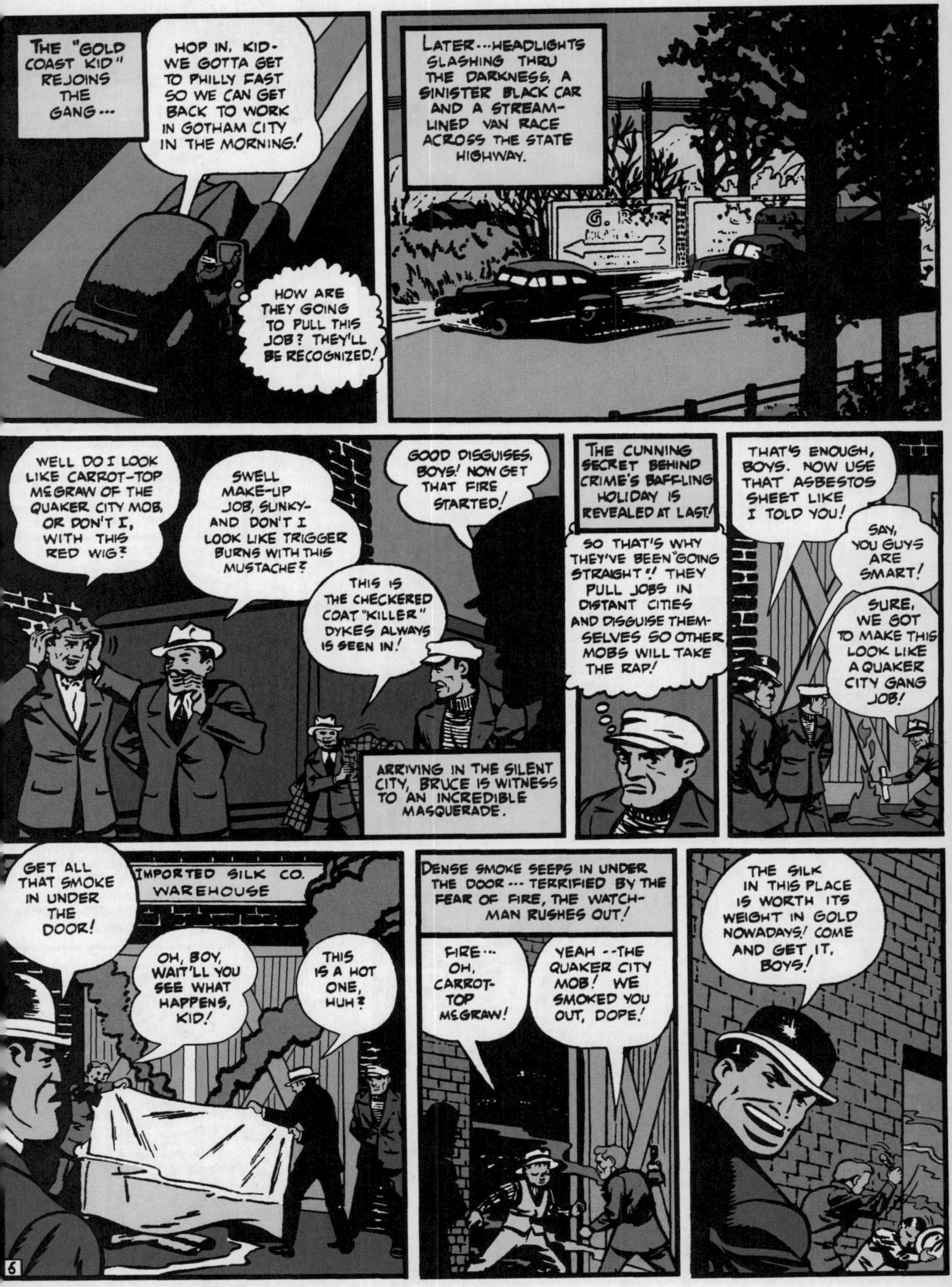
THE "GOLD COAST KID" REJOINS THE GANG...
HOP IN, KID- WE GOTTA GET TO PHILLY FAST SO WE CAN GET BACK TO WORK IN GOTHAM CITY IN THE MORNING!
HOW ARE THEY GOING TO PULL THIS JOB? THEY'LL BE RECOGNIZED!
LATER...HEADLIGHTS SLASHING THRU THE DARKNESS, A SINISTER BLACK CAR AND A STREAM-LINED VAN RACE ACROSS THE STATE HIGHWAY.
WELL DO I LOOK LIKE CARROT-TOP McGRAW OF THE QUAKER CITY MOB, OR DON'T I, WITH THIS RED WIG?
SWELL MAKE-UP JOB, SUNKY- AND DON'T I LOOK LIKE TRIGGER BURNS WITH THIS MUSTACHE?
GOOD DISGUISES, BOYS! NOW GET THAT FIRE STARTED!
THIS IS THE CHECKERED COAT "KILLER" DYKES ALWAYS IS SEEN IN!
ARRIVING IN THE SILENT CITY, BRUCE IS WITNESS TO AN INCREDIBLE MASQUERADE.
THE CUNNING SECRET BEHIND CRIME'S BAFFLING HOLIDAY IS REVEALED AT LAST!
SO THAT'S WHY THEY'VE BEEN "GOING STRAIGHT"! THEY PULL JOBS IN DISTANT CITIES AND DISGUISE THEM-SELVES SO OTHER MOBS WILL TAKE THE RAP!
THAT'S ENOUGH, BOYS. NOW USE THAT ASBESTOS SHEET LIKE I TOLD YOU!
SAY, YOU GUYS ARE SMART!
SURE, WE GOT TO MAKE THIS LOOK LIKE A QUAKER CITY GANG JOB!
GET ALL THAT SMOKE IN UNDER THE DOOR!
IMPORTED SILK CO. WAREHOUSE
OH, BOY, WAIT'LL YOU SEE WHAT HAPPENS, KID!
THIS IS A HOT ONE, HUH?
6
DENSE SMOKE SEEPS IN UNDER THE DOOR --- TERRIFIED BY THE FEAR OF FIRE, THE WATCH-MAN RUSHES OUT!
FIRE... OH, CARROT-TOP McGRAW!
YEAH --THE QUAKER CITY MOB! WE SMOKED YOU OUT, DOPE!
THE SILK IN THIS PLACE IS WORTH ITS WEIGHT IN GOLD NOWADAYS! COME AND GET IT, BOYS!

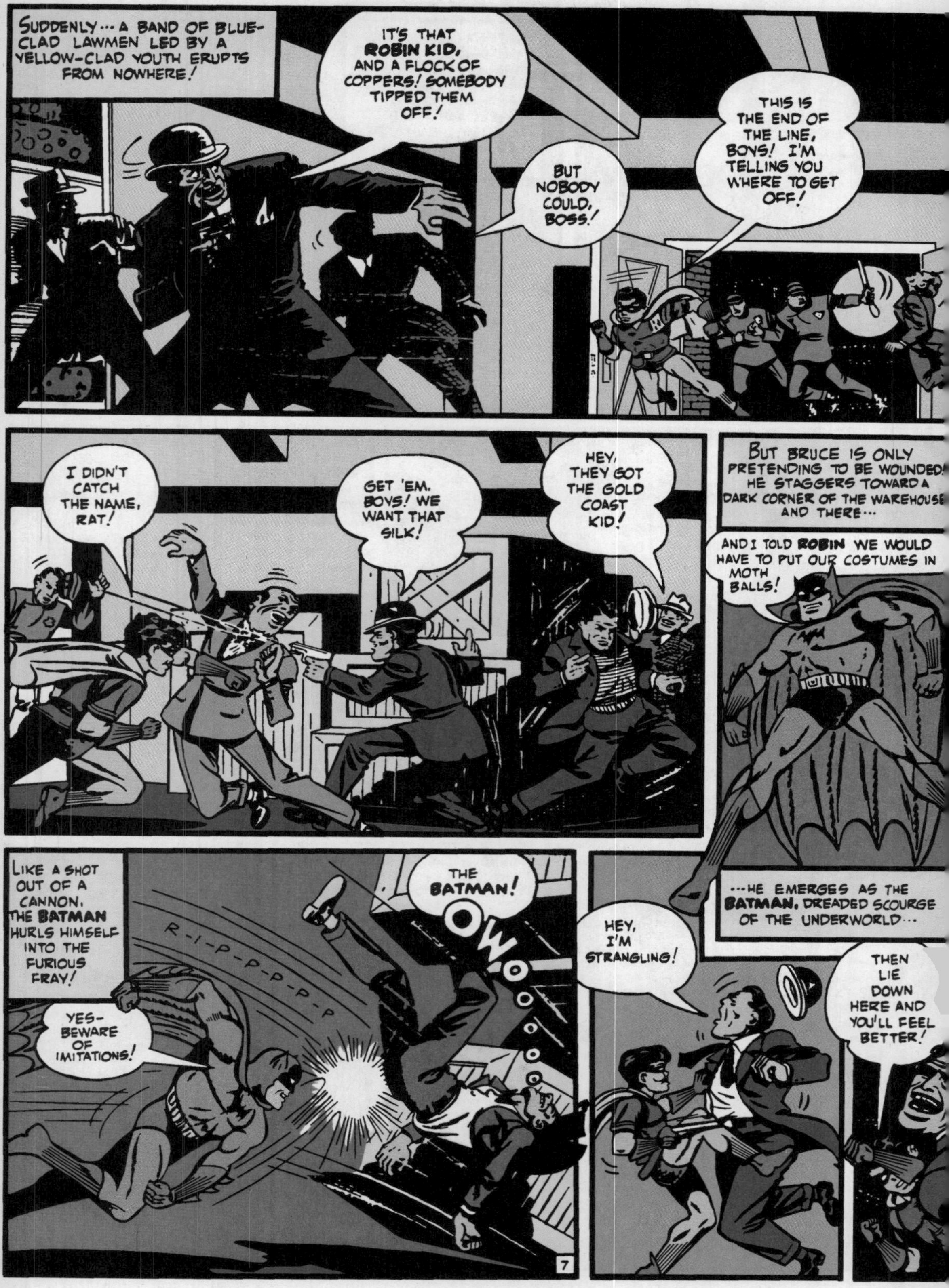
SUDDENLY... A BAND OF BLUE-CLAD LAWMEN LED BY A YELLOW-CLAD YOUTH ERUPTS FROM NOWHERE!
IT'S THAT **ROBIN KID,** AND A FLOCK OF COPPERS! SOMEBODY TIPPED THEM OFF!
BUT NOBODY COULD, BOSS!
THIS IS THE END OF THE LINE, BOYS! I'M TELLING YOU WHERE TO GET OFF!
I DIDN'T CATCH THE NAME, RAT!
GET 'EM, BOYS! WE WANT THAT SILK!
HEY, THEY GOT THE GOLD COAST KID!
BUT BRUCE IS ONLY PRETENDING TO BE WOUNDED! HE STAGGERS TOWARD A DARK CORNER OF THE WAREHOUSE AND THERE...
AND I TOLD **ROBIN** WE WOULD HAVE TO PUT OUR COSTUMES IN MOTH BALLS!
...HE EMERGES AS THE **BATMAN,** DREADED SCOURGE OF THE UNDERWORLD...
LIKE A SHOT OUT OF A CANNON, THE **BATMAN** HURLS HIMSELF INTO THE FURIOUS FRAY!
R-I-P-P-P-P-P-P
THE **BATMAN!**
OWOOOOOO
YES-BEWARE OF IMITATIONS!
7
HEY, I'M STRANGLING!
THEN LIE DOWN HERE AND YOU'LL FEEL BETTER!

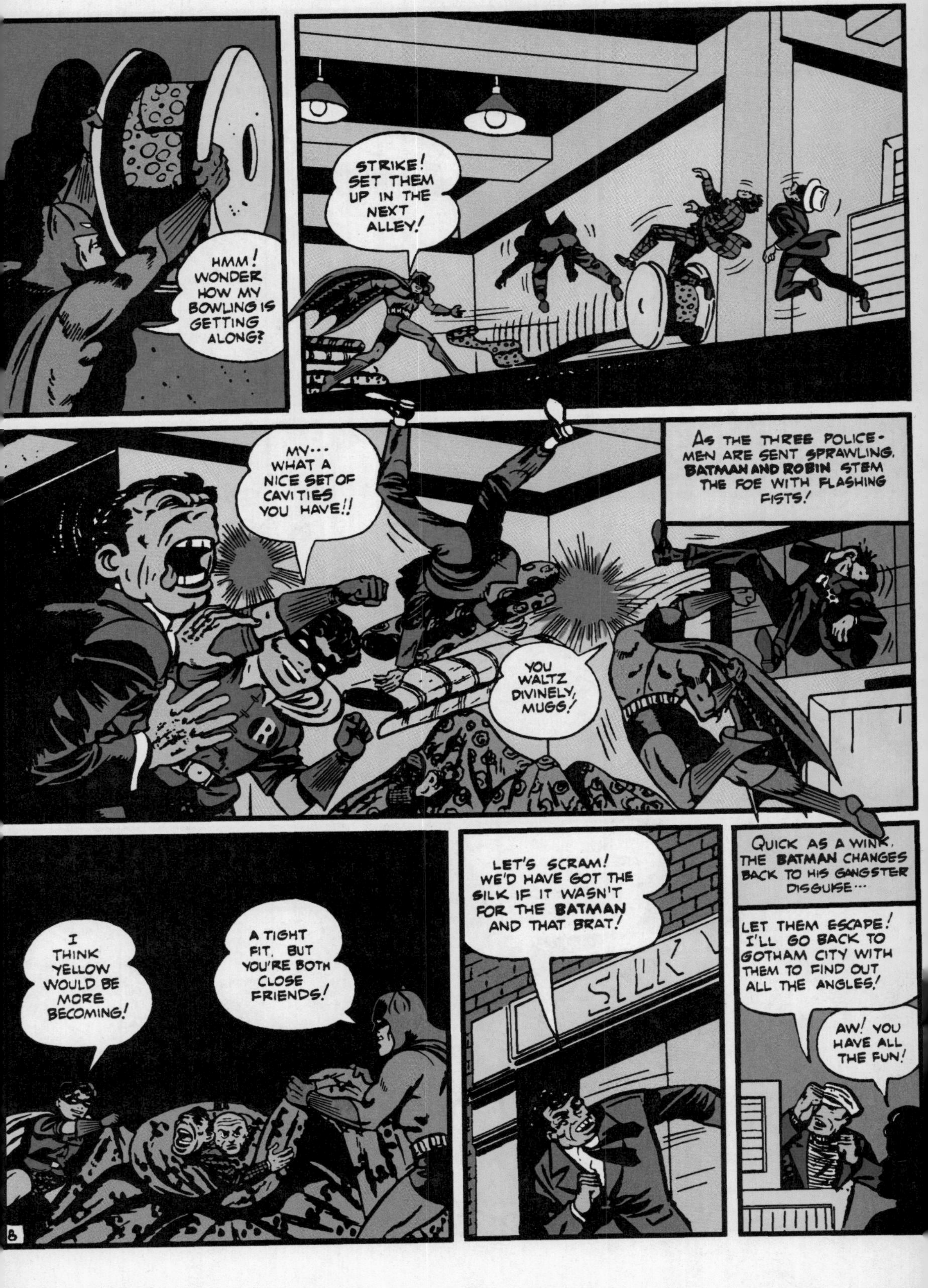
HMM! WONDER HOW MY BOWLING IS GETTING ALONG?
STRIKE! SET THEM UP IN THE NEXT ALLEY!
MY··· WHAT A NICE SET OF CAVITIES YOU HAVE!!
AS THE THREE POLICEMEN ARE SENT SPRAWLING, BATMAN AND ROBIN STEM THE FOE WITH FLASHING FISTS!
YOU WALTZ DIVINELY, MUGG!
I THINK YELLOW WOULD BE MORE BECOMING!
A TIGHT FIT, BUT YOU'RE BOTH CLOSE FRIENDS!
LET'S SCRAM! WE'D HAVE GOT THE SILK IF IT WASN'T FOR THE BATMAN AND THAT BRAT!
SILK
QUICK AS A WINK, THE BATMAN CHANGES BACK TO HIS GANGSTER DISGUISE···
LET THEM ESCAPE! I'LL GO BACK TO GOTHAM CITY WITH THEM TO FIND OUT ALL THE ANGLES!
AW! YOU HAVE ALL THE FUN!
8

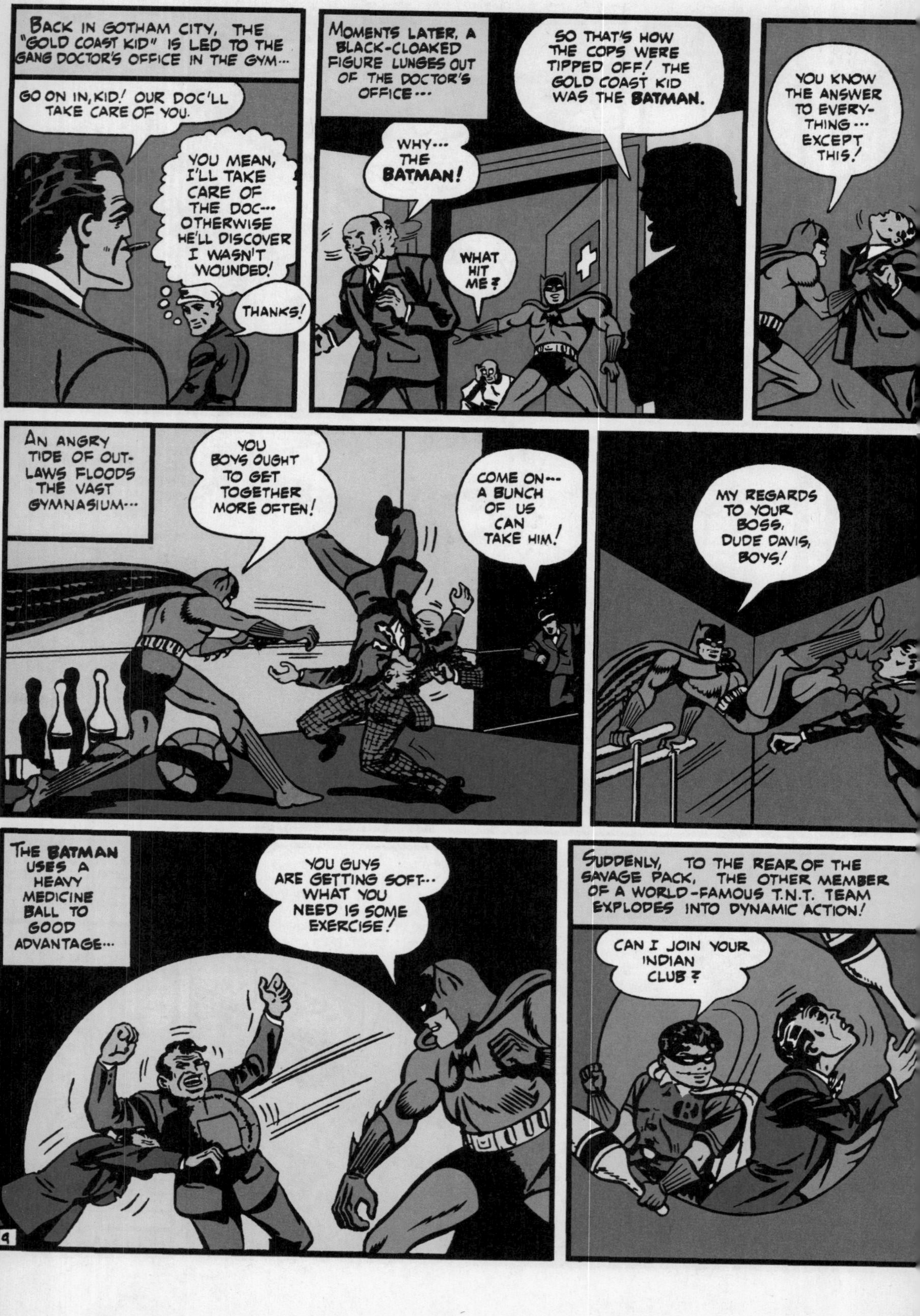
BACK IN GOTHAM CITY, THE "GOLD COAST KID" IS LED TO THE GANG DOCTOR'S OFFICE IN THE GYM...
GO ON IN, KID! OUR DOC'LL TAKE CARE OF YOU.
YOU MEAN, I'LL TAKE CARE OF THE DOC--- OTHERWISE HE'LL DISCOVER I WASN'T WOUNDED!
THANKS!
MOMENTS LATER, A BLACK-CLOAKED FIGURE LUNGES OUT OF THE DOCTOR'S OFFICE---
SO THAT'S HOW THE COPS WERE TIPPED OFF! THE GOLD COAST KID WAS THE BATMAN.
WHY--- THE BATMAN!
WHAT HIT ME?
YOU KNOW THE ANSWER TO EVERY-THING--- EXCEPT THIS!
AN ANGRY TIDE OF OUT-LAWS FLOODS THE VAST GYMNASIUM---
YOU BOYS OUGHT TO GET TOGETHER MORE OFTEN!
COME ON--- A BUNCH OF US CAN TAKE HIM!
MY REGARDS TO YOUR BOSS, DUDE DAVIS, BOYS!
THE BATMAN USES A HEAVY MEDICINE BALL TO GOOD ADVANTAGE---
YOU GUYS ARE GETTING SOFT--- WHAT YOU NEED IS SOME EXERCISE!
9
SUDDENLY, TO THE REAR OF THE SAVAGE PACK, THE OTHER MEMBER OF A WORLD-FAMOUS T.N.T. TEAM EXPLODES INTO DYNAMIC ACTION!
CAN I JOIN YOUR INDIAN CLUB?

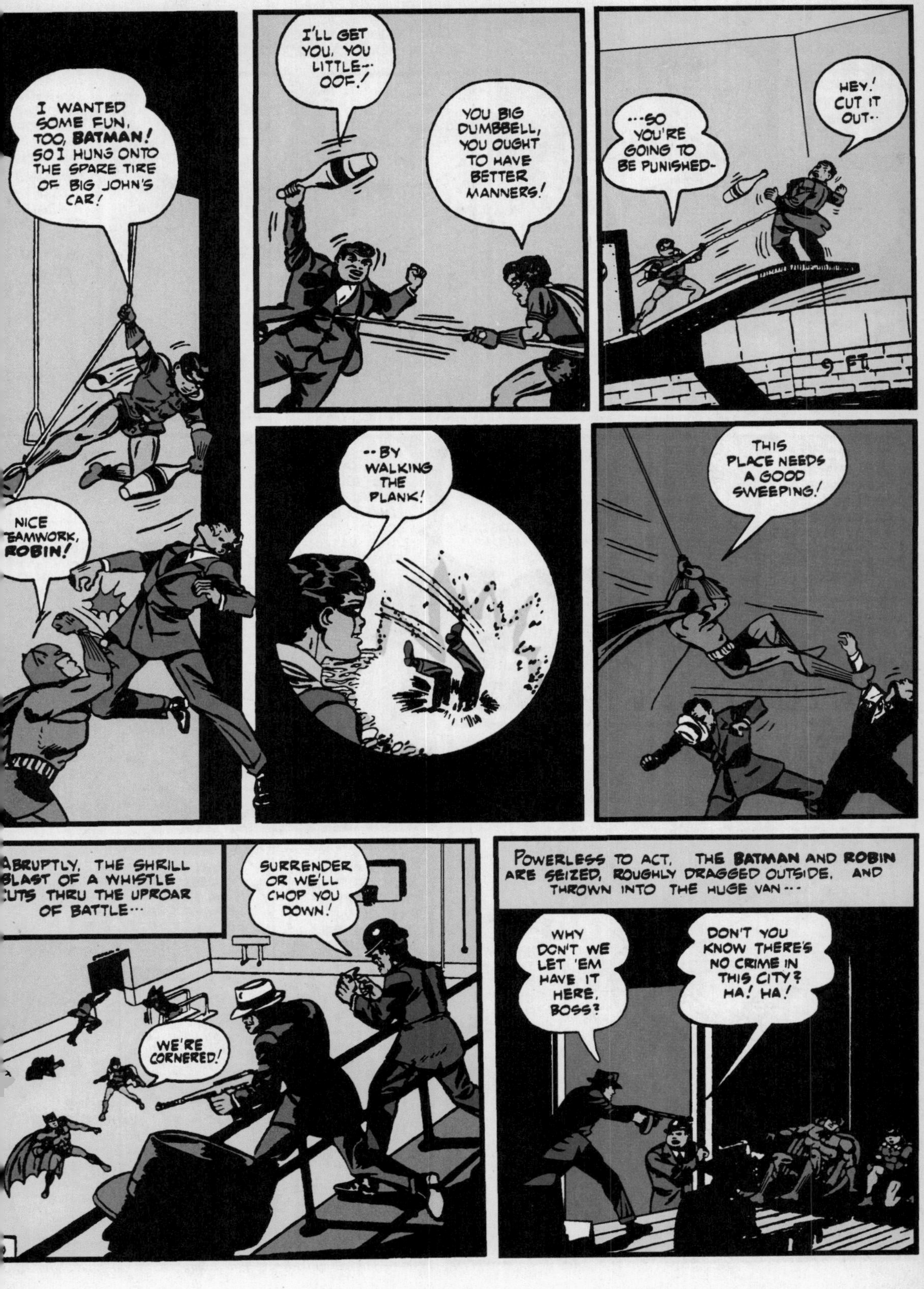
I WANTED SOME FUN, TOO, BATMAN! SO I HUNG ONTO THE SPARE TIRE OF BIG JOHN'S CAR!
NICE TEAMWORK, ROBIN!
I'LL GET YOU, YOU LITTLE-- OOF!
YOU BIG DUMBBELL, YOU OUGHT TO HAVE BETTER MANNERS!
HEY! CUT IT OUT--
---SO YOU'RE GOING TO BE PUNISHED-
9 FT.
--BY WALKING THE PLANK!
THIS PLACE NEEDS A GOOD SWEEPING!
ABRUPTLY, THE SHRILL BLAST OF A WHISTLE CUTS THRU THE UPROAR OF BATTLE---
SURRENDER OR WE'LL CHOP YOU DOWN!
WE'RE CORNERED!
POWERLESS TO ACT, THE BATMAN AND ROBIN ARE SEIZED, ROUGHLY DRAGGED OUTSIDE, AND THROWN INTO THE HUGE VAN---
WHY DON'T WE LET 'EM HAVE IT HERE, BOSS?
DON'T YOU KNOW THERE'S NO CRIME IN THIS CITY? HA! HA!

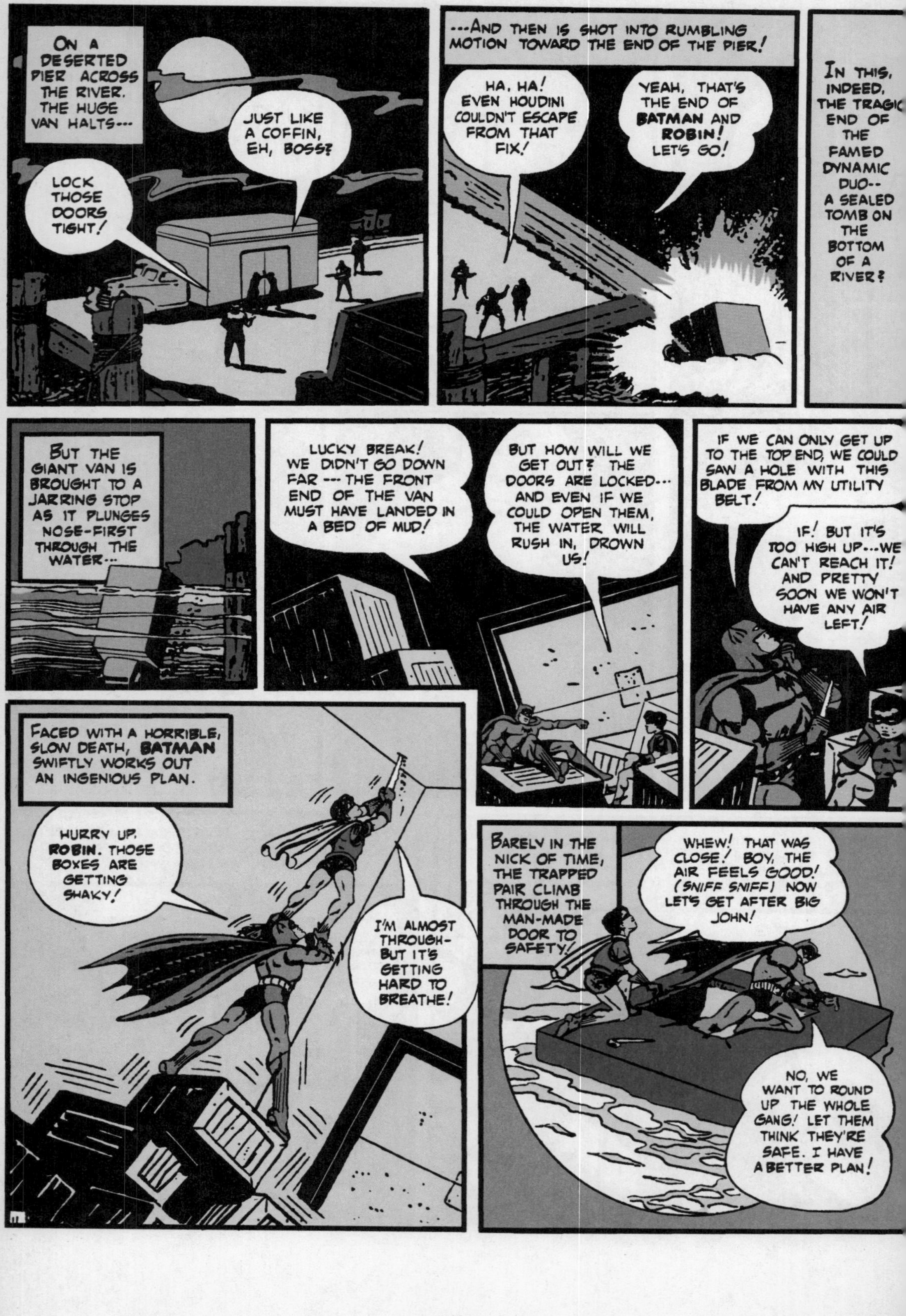
ON A DESERTED PIER ACROSS THE RIVER. THE HUGE VAN HALTS---
LOCK THOSE DOORS TIGHT!
JUST LIKE A COFFIN, EH, BOSS?
---AND THEN IS SHOT INTO RUMBLING MOTION TOWARD THE END OF THE PIER!
HA, HA! EVEN HOUDINI COULDN'T ESCAPE FROM THAT FIX!
YEAH, THAT'S THE END OF BATMAN AND ROBIN! LET'S GO!
IN THIS, INDEED, THE TRAGIC END OF THE FAMED DYNAMIC DUO-- A SEALED TOMB ON THE BOTTOM OF A RIVER?
BUT THE GIANT VAN IS BROUGHT TO A JARRING STOP AS IT PLUNGES NOSE-FIRST THROUGH THE WATER---
LUCKY BREAK! WE DIDN'T GO DOWN FAR --- THE FRONT END OF THE VAN MUST HAVE LANDED IN A BED OF MUD!
BUT HOW WILL WE GET OUT? THE DOORS ARE LOCKED--- AND EVEN IF WE COULD OPEN THEM, THE WATER WILL RUSH IN, DROWN US!
IF WE CAN ONLY GET UP TO THE TOP END, WE COULD SAW A HOLE WITH THIS BLADE FROM MY UTILITY BELT!
IF! BUT IT'S TOO HIGH UP---WE CAN'T REACH IT! AND PRETTY SOON WE WON'T HAVE ANY AIR LEFT!
FACED WITH A HORRIBLE, SLOW DEATH, BATMAN SWIFTLY WORKS OUT AN INGENIOUS PLAN.
HURRY UP, ROBIN. THOSE BOXES ARE GETTING SHAKY!
I'M ALMOST THROUGH- BUT IT'S GETTING HARD TO BREATHE!
BARELY IN THE NICK OF TIME, THE TRAPPED PAIR CLIMB THROUGH THE MAN-MADE DOOR TO SAFETY!
WHEW! THAT WAS CLOSE! BOY, THE AIR FEELS GOOD! (SNIFF SNIFF) NOW LET'S GET AFTER BIG JOHN!
NO, WE WANT TO ROUND UP THE WHOLE GANG! LET THEM THINK THEY'RE SAFE. I HAVE A BETTER PLAN!
11

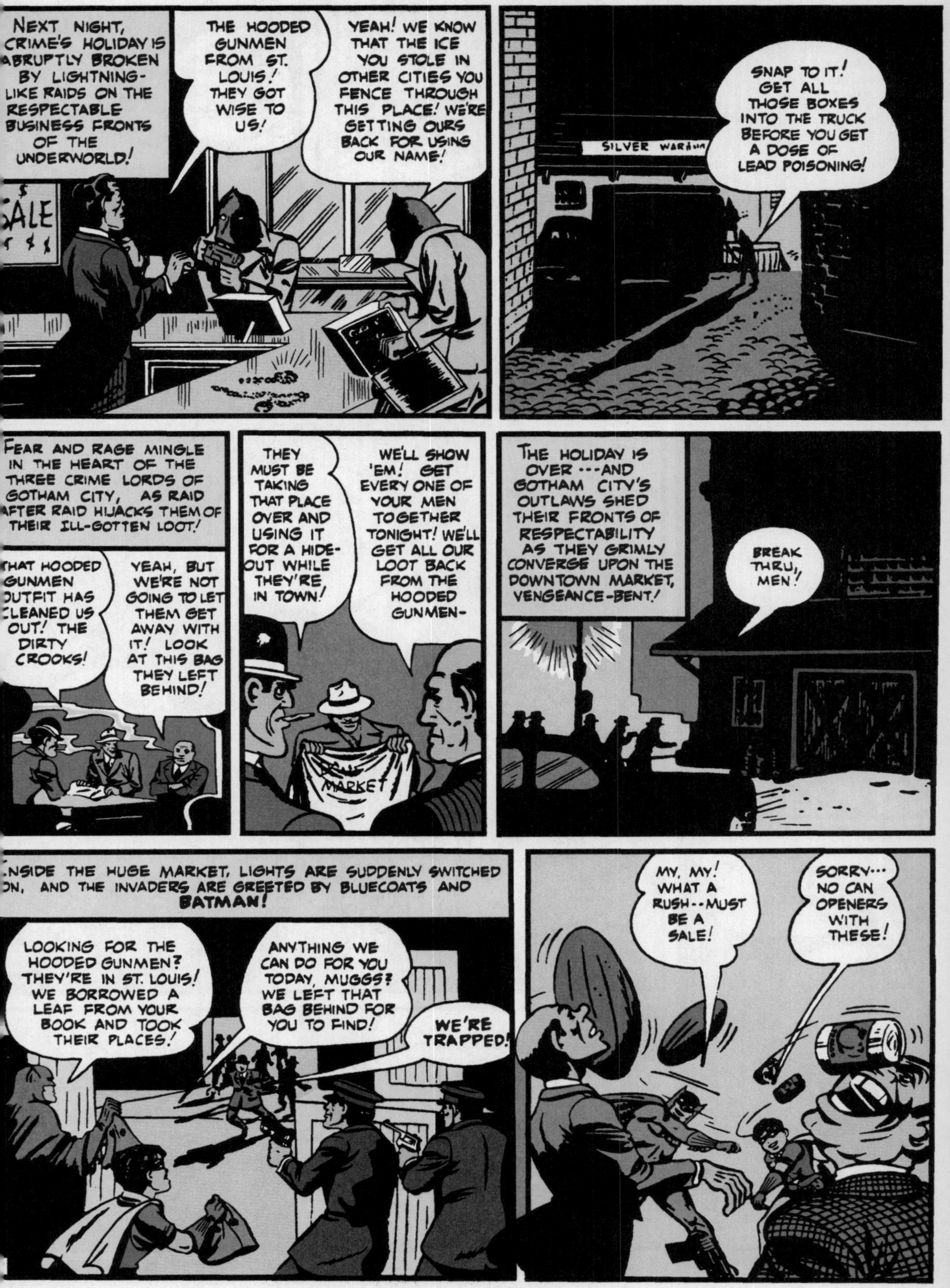

NEXT NIGHT, CRIME'S HOLIDAY IS ABRUPTLY BROKEN BY LIGHTNING-LIKE RAIDS ON THE RESPECTABLE BUSINESS FRONTS OF THE UNDERWORLD!
THE HOODED GUNMEN FROM ST. LOUIS! THEY GOT WISE TO US!
YEAH! WE KNOW THAT THE ICE YOU STOLE IN OTHER CITIES YOU FENCE THROUGH THIS PLACE! WE'RE GETTING OURS BACK FOR USING OUR NAME!
SALE
SILVER
SNAP TO IT! GET ALL THOSE BOXES INTO THE TRUCK BEFORE YOU GET A DOSE OF LEAD POISONING!
FEAR AND RAGE MINGLE IN THE HEART OF THE THREE CRIME LORDS OF GOTHAM CITY, AS RAID AFTER RAID HIJACKS THEM OF THEIR ILL-GOTTEN LOOT!
THAT HOODED GUNMEN OUTFIT HAS CLEANED US OUT! THE DIRTY CROOKS!
YEAH, BUT WE'RE NOT GOING TO LET THEM GET AWAY WITH IT! LOOK AT THIS BAG THEY LEFT BEHIND!
THEY MUST BE TAKING THAT PLACE OVER AND USING IT FOR A HIDE-OUT WHILE THEY'RE IN TOWN!
WE'LL SHOW 'EM! GET EVERY ONE OF YOUR MEN TOGETHER TONIGHT! WE'LL GET ALL OUR LOOT BACK FROM THE HOODED GUNMEN-
MARKET
THE HOLIDAY IS OVER --- AND GOTHAM CITY'S OUTLAWS SHED THEIR FRONTS OF RESPECTABILITY AS THEY GRIMLY CONVERGE UPON THE DOWNTOWN MARKET, VENGEANCE-BENT!
BREAK THRU, MEN!
INSIDE THE HUGE MARKET, LIGHTS ARE SUDDENLY SWITCHED ON, AND THE INVADERS ARE GREETED BY BLUECOATS AND BATMAN!
LOOKING FOR THE HOODED GUNMEN? THEY'RE IN ST. LOUIS! WE BORROWED A LEAF FROM YOUR BOOK AND TOOK THEIR PLACES!
ANYTHING WE CAN DO FOR YOU TODAY, MUGGS? WE LEFT THAT BAG BEHIND FOR YOU TO FIND!
WE'RE TRAPPED!
MY, MY! WHAT A RUSH--MUST BE A SALE!
SORRY... NO CAN OPENERS WITH THESE!

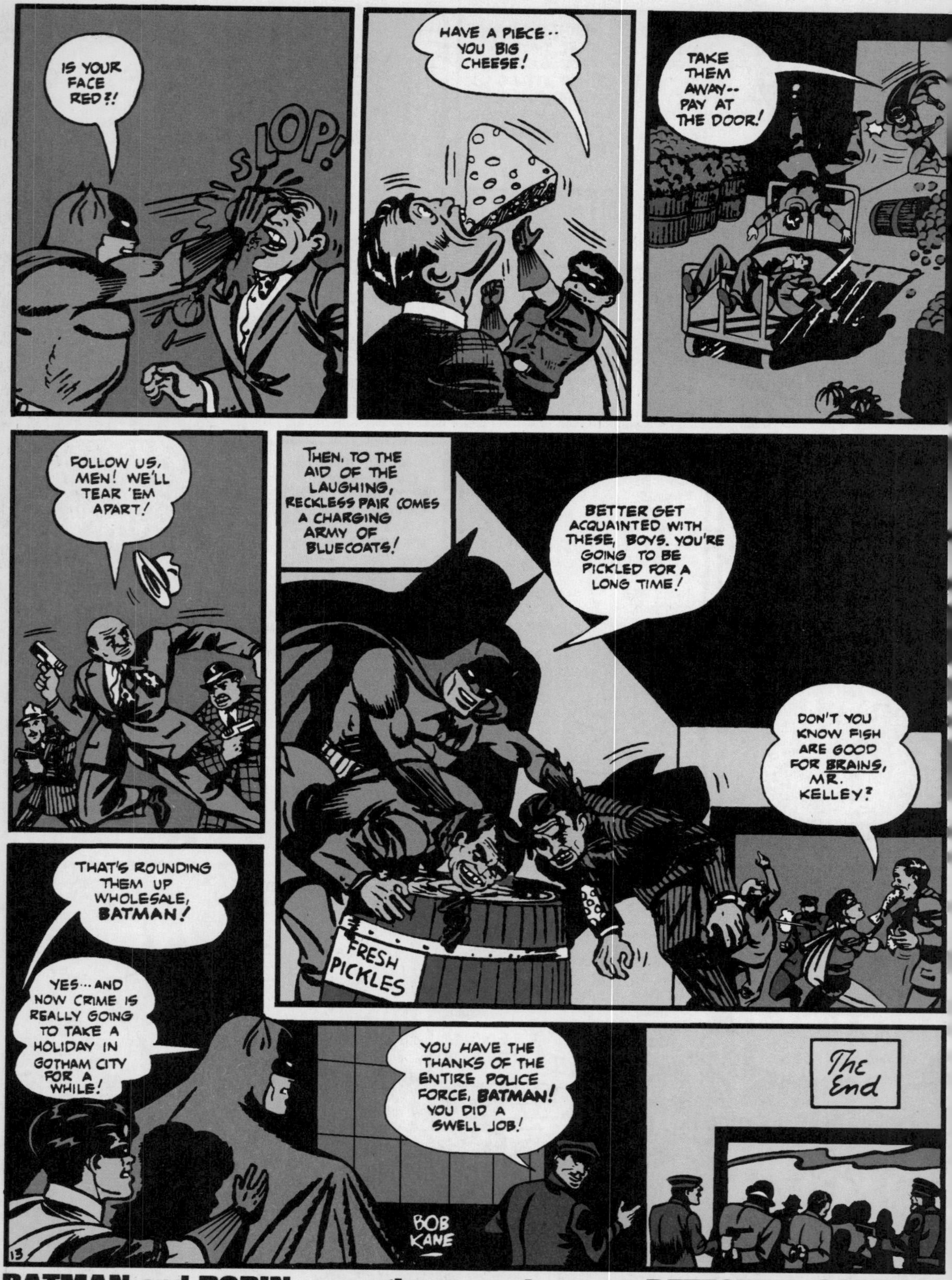
IS YOUR FACE RED?!
SLOP!
HAVE A PIECE.. YOU BIG CHEESE!
TAKE THEM AWAY-- PAY AT THE DOOR!
FOLLOW US, MEN! WE'LL TEAR 'EM APART!
THEN, TO THE AID OF THE LAUGHING, RECKLESS PAIR COMES A CHARGING ARMY OF BLUECOATS!
BETTER GET ACQUAINTED WITH THESE, BOYS. YOU'RE GOING TO BE PICKLED FOR A LONG TIME!
DON'T YOU KNOW FISH ARE GOOD FOR BRAINS, MR. KELLEY?
FRESH PICKLES
THAT'S ROUNDING THEM UP WHOLESALE, BATMAN!
YES... AND NOW CRIME IS REALLY GOING TO TAKE A HOLIDAY IN GOTHAM CITY FOR A WHILE!
YOU HAVE THE THANKS OF THE ENTIRE POLICE FORCE, BATMAN! YOU DID A SWELL JOB!
BOB KANE
The End
13

BATMAN and ROBIN zoom thru every issue of DETECTIVE COMICS!

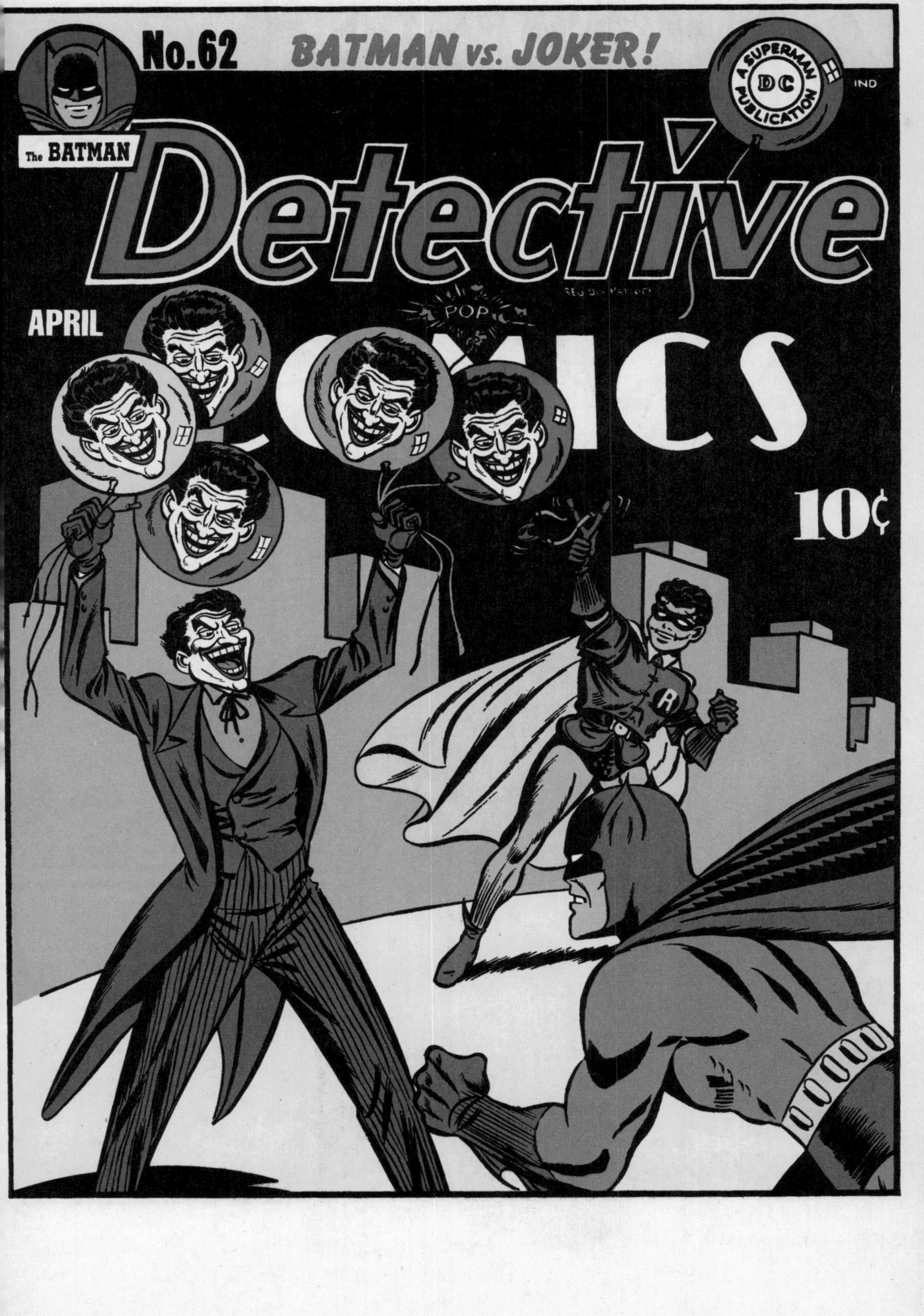
No. 62
BATMAN vs. JOKER!
A SUPERMAN DC PUBLICATION
IND
The BATMAN
Detective
REG. U.S. PAT. OFF.
APRIL
POP
COMICS
10¢

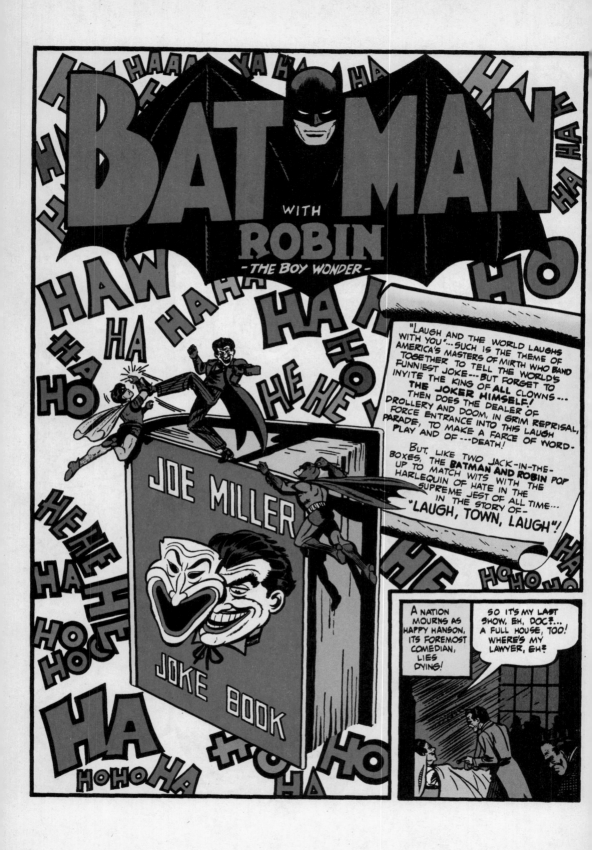

BAT MAN

WITH

ROBIN

—THE BOY WONDER—

"LAUGH AND THE WORLD LAUGHS WITH YOU"...SUCH IS THE THEME OF AMERICA'S MASTERS OF MIRTH WHO BAND TOGETHER TO TELL THE WORLD'S FUNNIEST JOKE---BUT FORGET TO INVITE THE KING OF ALL CLOWNS... **THE JOKER HIMSELF!** THEN DOES THE DEALER OF DROLLERY AND DOOM, IN GRIM REPRISAL, FORCE ENTRANCE INTO THIS LAUGH PARADE, TO MAKE A FARCE OF WORD-PLAY AND OF---DEATH!

BUT, LIKE TWO JACK-IN-THE-BOXES, THE **BATMAN AND ROBIN** POP UP TO MATCH WITS WITH THE HARLEQUIN OF HATE IN THE SUPREME JEST OF ALL TIME... IN THE STORY OF— **"LAUGH, TOWN, LAUGH"!**

JOE MILLER JOKE BOOK

A NATION MOURNS AS HAPPY HANSON, ITS FOREMOST COMEDIAN, LIES DYING!

SO IT'S MY LAST SHOW, EH, DOC?... A FULL HOUSE, TOO! WHERE'S MY LAWYER, EH?

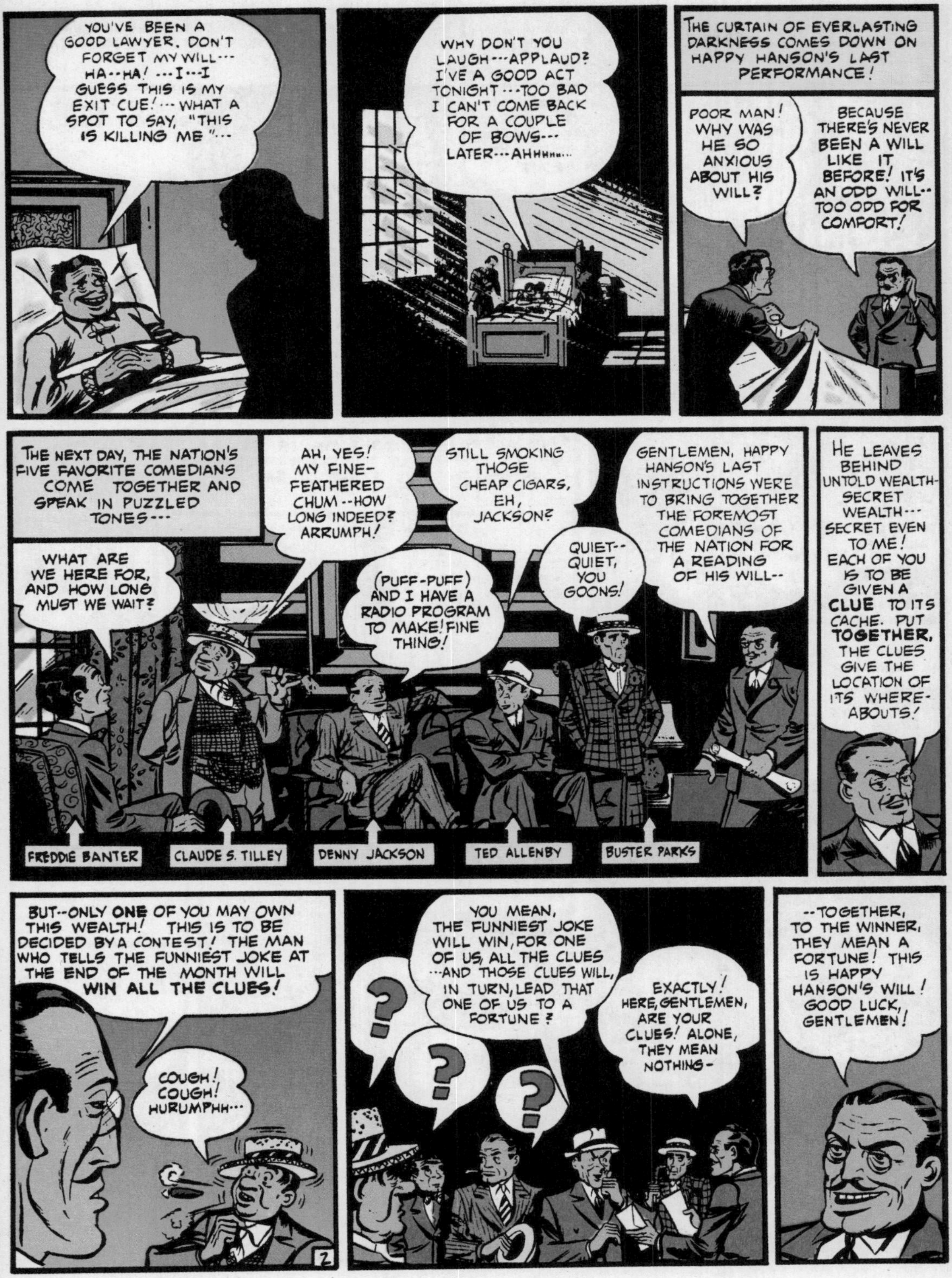

YOU'VE BEEN A GOOD LAWYER. DON'T FORGET MY WILL--- HA--HA! ---I---I GUESS THIS IS MY EXIT CUE! --- WHAT A SPOT TO SAY, "THIS IS KILLING ME"---
WHY DON'T YOU LAUGH---APPLAUD? I'VE A GOOD ACT TONIGHT---TOO BAD I CAN'T COME BACK FOR A COUPLE OF BOWS--- LATER---AHHHH....
THE CURTAIN OF EVERLASTING DARKNESS COMES DOWN ON HAPPY HANSON'S LAST PERFORMANCE!
POOR MAN! WHY WAS HE SO ANXIOUS ABOUT HIS WILL?
BECAUSE THERE'S NEVER BEEN A WILL LIKE IT BEFORE! IT'S AN ODD WILL-- TOO ODD FOR COMFORT!
THE NEXT DAY, THE NATION'S FIVE FAVORITE COMEDIANS COME TOGETHER AND SPEAK IN PUZZLED TONES---
WHAT ARE WE HERE FOR, AND HOW LONG MUST WE WAIT?
AH, YES! MY FINE-FEATHERED CHUM--HOW LONG INDEED? ARRUMPH!
STILL SMOKING THOSE CHEAP CIGARS, EH, JACKSON?
(PUFF-PUFF) AND I HAVE A RADIO PROGRAM TO MAKE! FINE THING!
QUIET--QUIET, YOU GOONS!
GENTLEMEN, HAPPY HANSON'S LAST INSTRUCTIONS WERE TO BRING TOGETHER THE FOREMOST COMEDIANS OF THE NATION FOR A READING OF HIS WILL--
FREDDIE BANTER
CLAUDE S. TILLEY
DENNY JACKSON
TED ALLENBY
BUSTER PARKS
HE LEAVES BEHIND UNTOLD WEALTH-SECRET WEALTH---SECRET EVEN TO ME! EACH OF YOU IS TO BE GIVEN A CLUE TO ITS CACHE. PUT TOGETHER, THE CLUES GIVE THE LOCATION OF ITS WHERE-ABOUTS!
BUT--ONLY ONE OF YOU MAY OWN THIS WEALTH! THIS IS TO BE DECIDED BY A CONTEST! THE MAN WHO TELLS THE FUNNIEST JOKE AT THE END OF THE MONTH WILL WIN ALL THE CLUES!
COUGH! COUGH! HURUMPHH---
2
YOU MEAN, THE FUNNIEST JOKE WILL WIN, FOR ONE OF US, ALL THE CLUES ---AND THOSE CLUES WILL, IN TURN, LEAD THAT ONE OF US TO A FORTUNE?
?
?
?
EXACTLY! HERE, GENTLEMEN, ARE YOUR CLUES! ALONE, THEY MEAN NOTHING-
--TOGETHER, TO THE WINNER, THEY MEAN A FORTUNE! THIS IS HAPPY HANSON'S WILL! GOOD LUCK, GENTLEMEN!

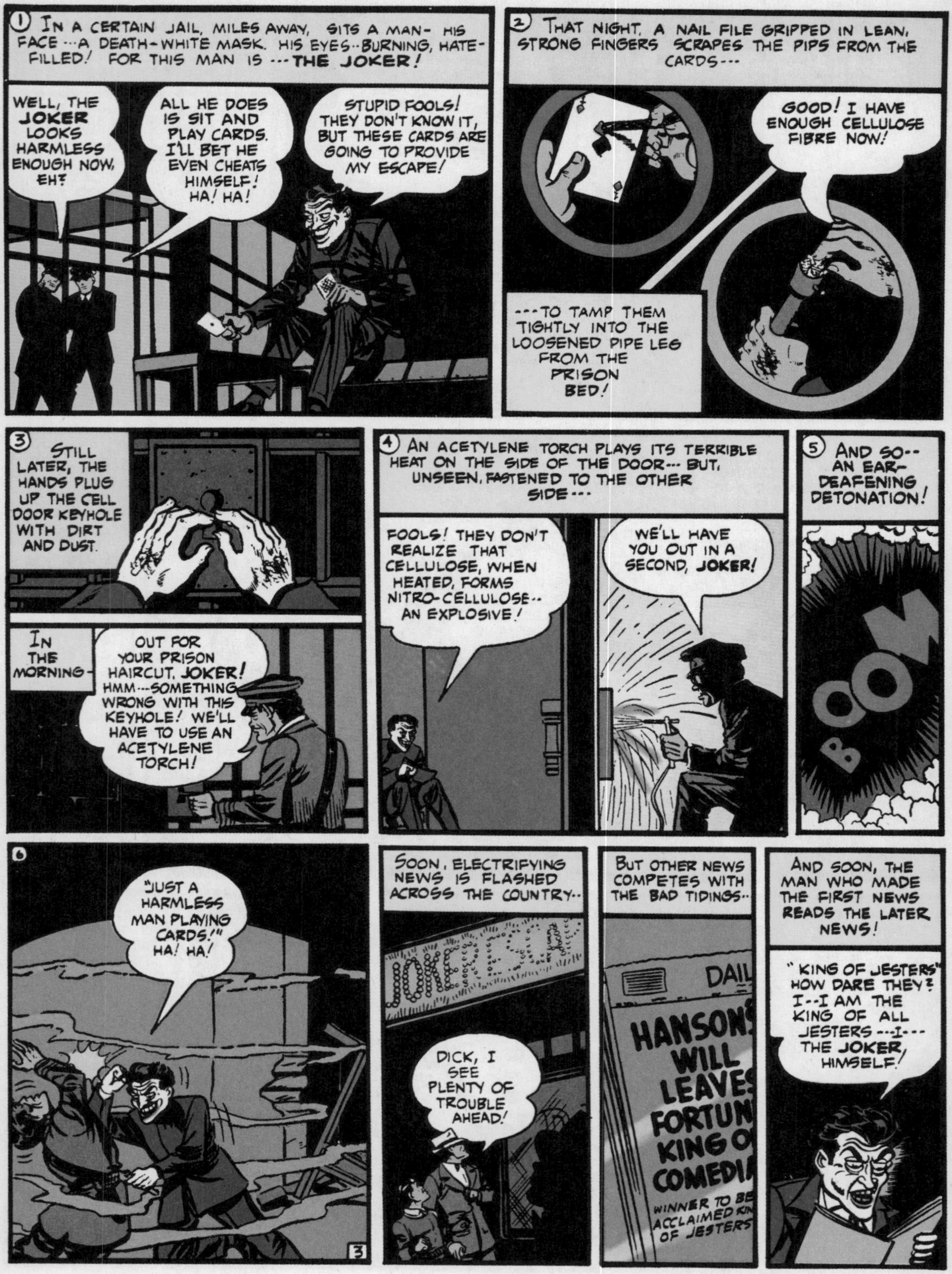

1 IN A CERTAIN JAIL, MILES AWAY, SITS A MAN- HIS FACE ---A DEATH-WHITE MASK. HIS EYES--BURNING, HATE-FILLED! FOR THIS MAN IS ---THE JOKER!
WELL, THE JOKER LOOKS HARMLESS ENOUGH NOW, EH?
ALL HE DOES IS SIT AND PLAY CARDS. I'LL BET HE EVEN CHEATS HIMSELF! HA! HA!
STUPID FOOLS! THEY DON'T KNOW IT, BUT THESE CARDS ARE GOING TO PROVIDE MY ESCAPE!
2 THAT NIGHT, A NAIL FILE GRIPPED IN LEAN, STRONG FINGERS SCRAPES THE PIPS FROM THE CARDS---
GOOD! I HAVE ENOUGH CELLULOSE FIBRE NOW!
---TO TAMP THEM TIGHTLY INTO THE LOOSENED PIPE LEG FROM THE PRISON BED!
3 STILL LATER, THE HANDS PLUG UP THE CELL DOOR KEYHOLE WITH DIRT AND DUST.
IN THE MORNING-
OUT FOR YOUR PRISON HAIRCUT, JOKER! HMM---SOMETHING WRONG WITH THIS KEYHOLE! WE'LL HAVE TO USE AN ACETYLENE TORCH!
4 AN ACETYLENE TORCH PLAYS ITS TERRIBLE HEAT ON THE SIDE OF THE DOOR--- BUT, UNSEEN, FASTENED TO THE OTHER SIDE---
FOOLS! THEY DON'T REALIZE THAT CELLULOSE, WHEN HEATED, FORMS NITRO-CELLULOSE-- AN EXPLOSIVE!
WE'LL HAVE YOU OUT IN A SECOND, JOKER!
5 AND SO-- AN EAR-DEAFENING DETONATION!
BOOM
6
"JUST A HARMLESS MAN PLAYING CARDS!" HA! HA!
3
SOON, ELECTRIFYING NEWS IS FLASHED ACROSS THE COUNTRY--
DICK, I SEE PLENTY OF TROUBLE AHEAD!
BUT OTHER NEWS COMPETES WITH THE BAD TIDINGS--
DAIL
HANSONS WILL LEAVES FORTUN KING O COMEDIA
WINNER TO BE ACCLAIMED KIN OF JESTERS
AND SOON, THE MAN WHO MADE THE FIRST NEWS READS THE LATER NEWS!
"KING OF JESTERS" HOW DARE THEY? I--I AM THE KING OF ALL JESTERS ---I--- THE JOKER, HIMSELF!

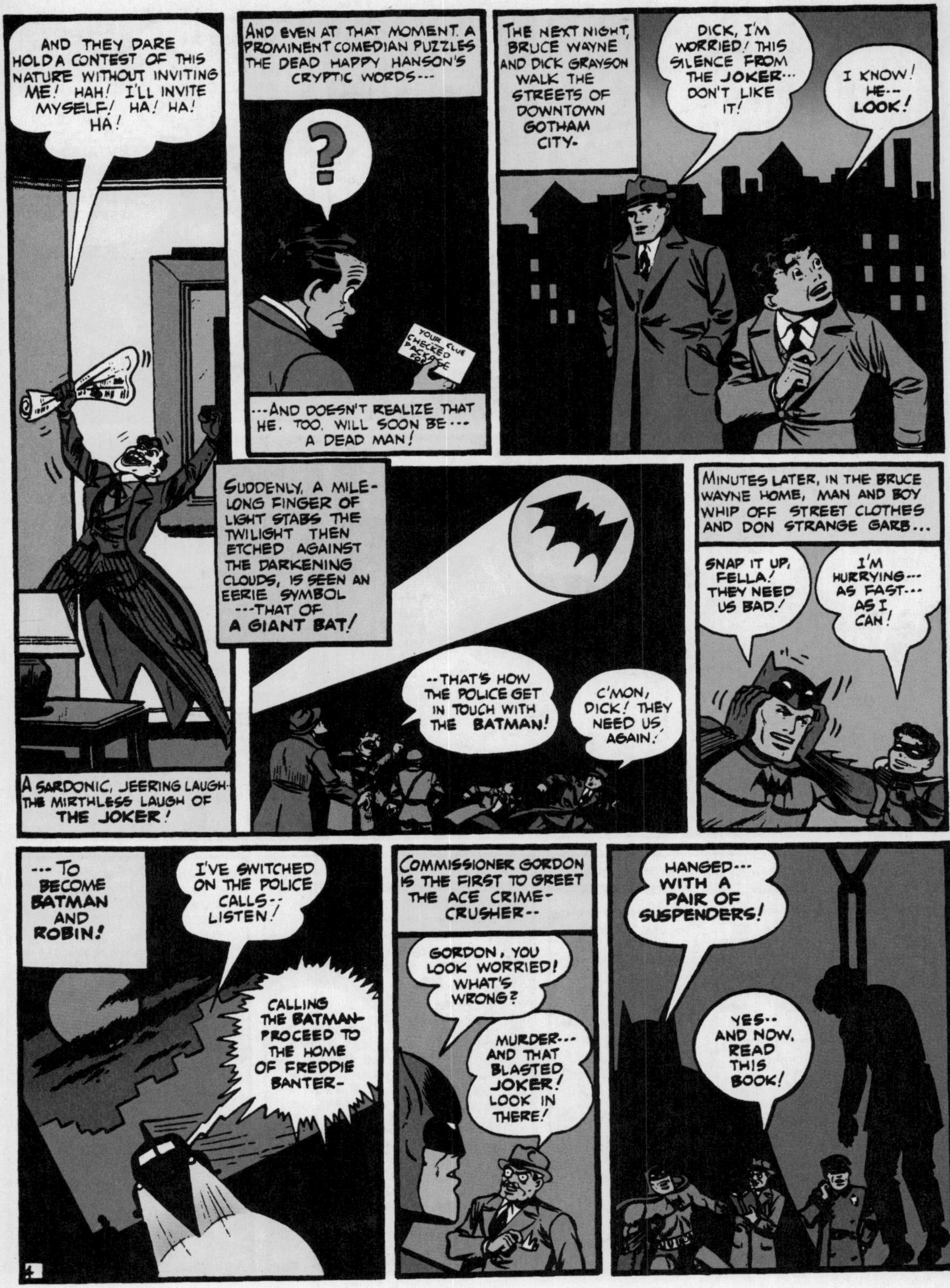
AND THEY DARE HOLD A CONTEST OF THIS NATURE WITHOUT INVITING ME! HAH! I'LL INVITE MYSELF! HA! HA! HA!
A SARDONIC, JEERING LAUGH-THE MIRTHLESS LAUGH OF THE JOKER!
AND EVEN AT THAT MOMENT, A PROMINENT COMEDIAN PUZZLES THE DEAD HAPPY HANSON'S CRYPTIC WORDS---
?
---AND DOESN'T REALIZE THAT HE, TOO, WILL SOON BE--- A DEAD MAN!
THE NEXT NIGHT, BRUCE WAYNE AND DICK GRAYSON WALK THE STREETS OF DOWNTOWN GOTHAM CITY-
DICK, I'M WORRIED! THIS SILENCE FROM THE JOKER--- DON'T LIKE IT!
I KNOW! HE-- LOOK!
SUDDENLY, A MILE-LONG FINGER OF LIGHT STABS THE TWILIGHT THEN ETCHED AGAINST THE DARKENING CLOUDS, IS SEEN AN EERIE SYMBOL ---THAT OF A GIANT BAT!
--THAT'S HOW THE POLICE GET IN TOUCH WITH THE BATMAN!
C'MON, DICK! THEY NEED US AGAIN!
MINUTES LATER, IN THE BRUCE WAYNE HOME, MAN AND BOY WHIP OFF STREET CLOTHES AND DON STRANGE GARB...
SNAP IT UP, FELLA! THEY NEED US BAD!
I'M HURRYING--- AS FAST--- AS I CAN!
--- TO BECOME BATMAN AND ROBIN!
I'VE SWITCHED ON THE POLICE CALLS-- LISTEN!
CALLING THE BATMAN-PROCEED TO THE HOME OF FREDDIE BANTER-
COMMISSIONER GORDON IS THE FIRST TO GREET THE ACE CRIME-CRUSHER--
GORDON, YOU LOOK WORRIED! WHAT'S WRONG?
MURDER--- AND THAT BLASTED JOKER! LOOK IN THERE!
HANGED--- WITH A PAIR OF SUSPENDERS!
YES-- AND NOW, READ THIS BOOK!

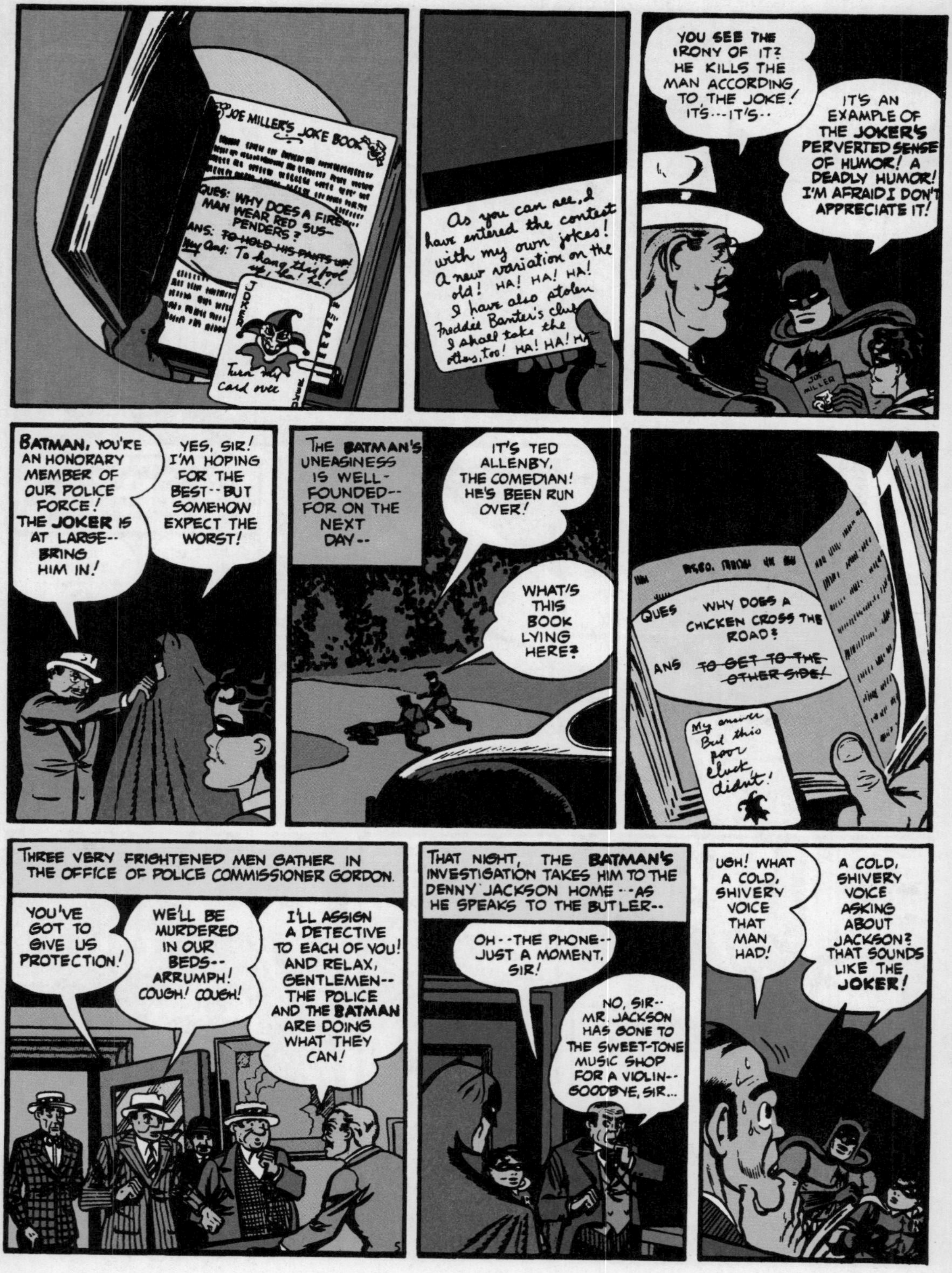
JOE MILLER'S JOKE BOOK
QUES: WHY DOES A FIREMAN WEAR RED SUSPENDERS?
ANS: TO HOLD HIS PANTS UP!
My Ans: To hang this fool up, ha! ha!
JOKER
Turn my card over
As you can see, I have entered the contest with my own jokes! A new variation on the old! HA! HA! HA! I have also stolen Freddie Banter's club. I shall take the others, too! HA! HA! HA
YOU SEE THE IRONY OF IT? HE KILLS THE MAN ACCORDING TO THE JOKE! IT'S---IT'S--
IT'S AN EXAMPLE OF THE JOKER'S PERVERTED SENSE OF HUMOR! A DEADLY HUMOR! I'M AFRAID I DON'T APPRECIATE IT!
JOE MILLER
BATMAN, YOU'RE AN HONORARY MEMBER OF OUR POLICE FORCE! THE JOKER IS AT LARGE-- BRING HIM IN!
YES, SIR! I'M HOPING FOR THE BEST--BUT SOMEHOW EXPECT THE WORST!
THE BATMAN'S UNEASINESS IS WELL-FOUNDED--FOR ON THE NEXT DAY--
IT'S TED ALLENBY, THE COMEDIAN! HE'S BEEN RUN OVER!
WHAT'S THIS BOOK LYING HERE?
QUES WHY DOES A CHICKEN CROSS THE ROAD?
ANS TO GET TO THE OTHER SIDE!
My answer But this poor cluck didn't!
THREE VERY FRIGHTENED MEN GATHER IN THE OFFICE OF POLICE COMMISSIONER GORDON.
YOU'VE GOT TO GIVE US PROTECTION!
WE'LL BE MURDERED IN OUR BEDS-- ARRUMPH! COUGH! COUGH!
I'LL ASSIGN A DETECTIVE TO EACH OF YOU! AND RELAX, GENTLEMEN-- THE POLICE AND THE BATMAN ARE DOING WHAT THEY CAN!
THAT NIGHT, THE BATMAN'S INVESTIGATION TAKES HIM TO THE DENNY JACKSON HOME --AS HE SPEAKS TO THE BUTLER--
OH--THE PHONE-- JUST A MOMENT, SIR!
NO, SIR-- MR. JACKSON HAS GONE TO THE SWEET-TONE MUSIC SHOP FOR A VIOLIN-- GOODBYE, SIR...
UGH! WHAT A COLD, SHIVERY VOICE THAT MAN HAD!
A COLD, SHIVERY VOICE ASKING ABOUT JACKSON? THAT SOUNDS LIKE THE JOKER!

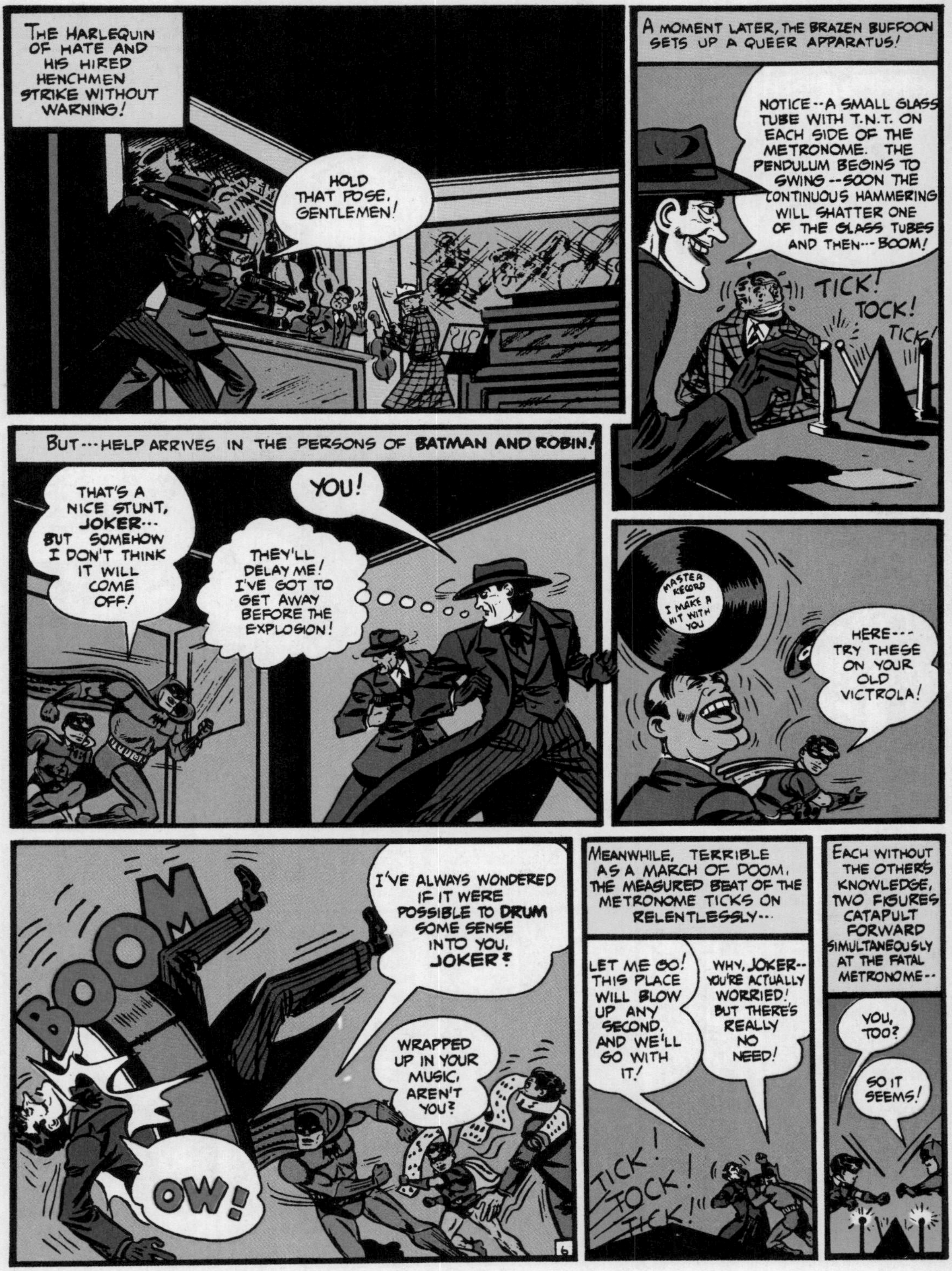

THE HARLEQUIN OF HATE AND HIS HIRED HENCHMEN STRIKE WITHOUT WARNING!
HOLD THAT POSE, GENTLEMEN!
A MOMENT LATER, THE BRAZEN BUFFOON SETS UP A QUEER APPARATUS!
NOTICE--A SMALL GLASS TUBE WITH T.N.T. ON EACH SIDE OF THE METRONOME. THE PENDULUM BEGINS TO SWING--SOON THE CONTINUOUS HAMMERING WILL SHATTER ONE OF THE GLASS TUBES AND THEN---BOOM!
TICK! TOCK! TICK!
BUT---HELP ARRIVES IN THE PERSONS OF BATMAN AND ROBIN!
THAT'S A NICE STUNT, JOKER---BUT SOMEHOW I DON'T THINK IT WILL COME OFF!
YOU!
THEY'LL DELAY ME! I'VE GOT TO GET AWAY BEFORE THE EXPLOSION!
MASTER RECORD — I MAKE A HIT WITH YOU
HERE--- TRY THESE ON YOUR OLD VICTROLA!
BOOM
I'VE ALWAYS WONDERED IF IT WERE POSSIBLE TO DRUM SOME SENSE INTO YOU, JOKER?
WRAPPED UP IN YOUR MUSIC, AREN'T YOU?
OW!
6
MEANWHILE, TERRIBLE AS A MARCH OF DOOM, THE MEASURED BEAT OF THE METRONOME TICKS ON RELENTLESSLY---
LET ME GO! THIS PLACE WILL BLOW UP ANY SECOND, AND WE'LL GO WITH IT!
WHY, JOKER--YOU'RE ACTUALLY WORRIED! BUT THERE'S REALLY NO NEED!
TICK! TOCK! TICK!
EACH WITHOUT THE OTHER'S KNOWLEDGE, TWO FIGURES CATAPULT FORWARD SIMULTANEOUSLY AT THE FATAL METRONOME--
YOU, TOO?
SO IT SEEMS!

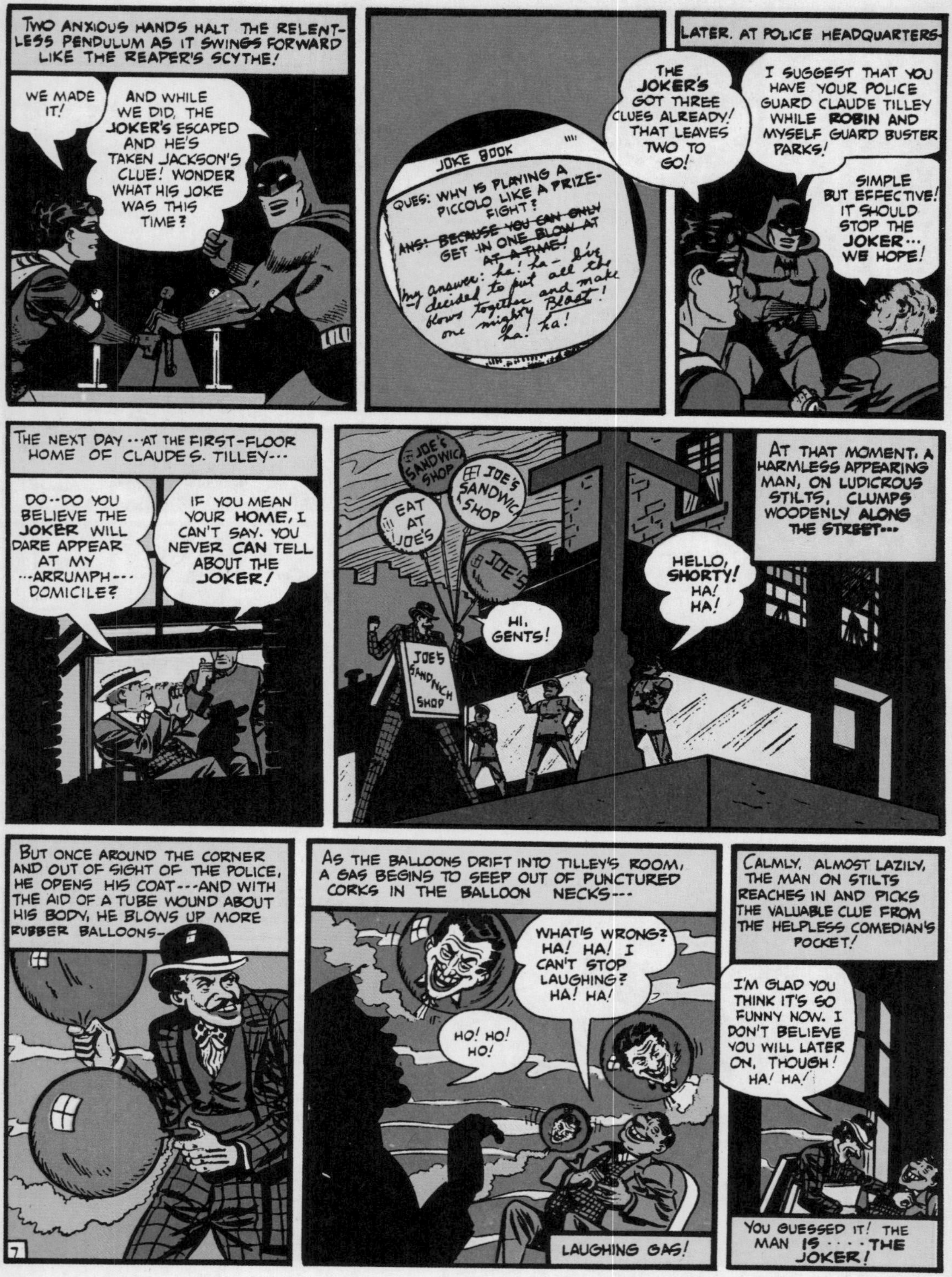
TWO ANXIOUS HANDS HALT THE RELENTLESS PENDULUM AS IT SWINGS FORWARD LIKE THE REAPER'S SCYTHE!
WE MADE IT!
AND WHILE WE DID, THE JOKER'S ESCAPED AND HE'S TAKEN JACKSON'S CLUE! WONDER WHAT HIS JOKE WAS THIS TIME?
JOKE BOOK
QUES: WHY IS PLAYING A PICCOLO LIKE A PRIZE-FIGHT?
ANS: BECAUSE YOU CAN ONLY GET IN ONE BLOW AT A TIME!
my answer: ha! ha- I've decided to put all the blows together and make one mighty Blast! ha! ha!
LATER. AT POLICE HEADQUARTERS-
THE JOKER'S GOT THREE CLUES ALREADY! THAT LEAVES TWO TO GO!
I SUGGEST THAT YOU HAVE YOUR POLICE GUARD CLAUDE TILLEY WHILE ROBIN AND MYSELF GUARD BUSTER PARKS!
SIMPLE BUT EFFECTIVE! IT SHOULD STOP THE JOKER... WE HOPE!
THE NEXT DAY...AT THE FIRST-FLOOR HOME OF CLAUDE S. TILLEY...
DO--DO YOU BELIEVE THE JOKER WILL DARE APPEAR AT MY ...ARRUMPH... DOMICILE?
IF YOU MEAN YOUR HOME, I CAN'T SAY. YOU NEVER CAN TELL ABOUT THE JOKER!
JOE'S SANDWICH SHOP
JOE'S SANDWICH SHOP
EAT AT JOE'S
JOE'S
JOE'S SANDWICH SHOP
HI, GENTS!
AT THAT MOMENT, A HARMLESS APPEARING MAN, ON LUDICROUS STILTS, CLUMPS WOODENLY ALONG THE STREET...
HELLO, SHORTY! HA! HA!
BUT ONCE AROUND THE CORNER AND OUT OF SIGHT OF THE POLICE, HE OPENS HIS COAT---AND WITH THE AID OF A TUBE WOUND ABOUT HIS BODY, HE BLOWS UP MORE RUBBER BALLOONS-
7
AS THE BALLOONS DRIFT INTO TILLEY'S ROOM, A GAS BEGINS TO SEEP OUT OF PUNCTURED CORKS IN THE BALLOON NECKS---
WHAT'S WRONG? HA! HA! I CAN'T STOP LAUGHING? HA! HA!
HO! HO! HO!
LAUGHING GAS!
CALMLY, ALMOST LAZILY, THE MAN ON STILTS REACHES IN AND PICKS THE VALUABLE CLUE FROM THE HELPLESS COMEDIAN'S POCKET!
I'M GLAD YOU THINK IT'S SO FUNNY NOW. I DON'T BELIEVE YOU WILL LATER ON, THOUGH! HA! HA!
YOU GUESSED IT! THE MAN IS.... THE JOKER!

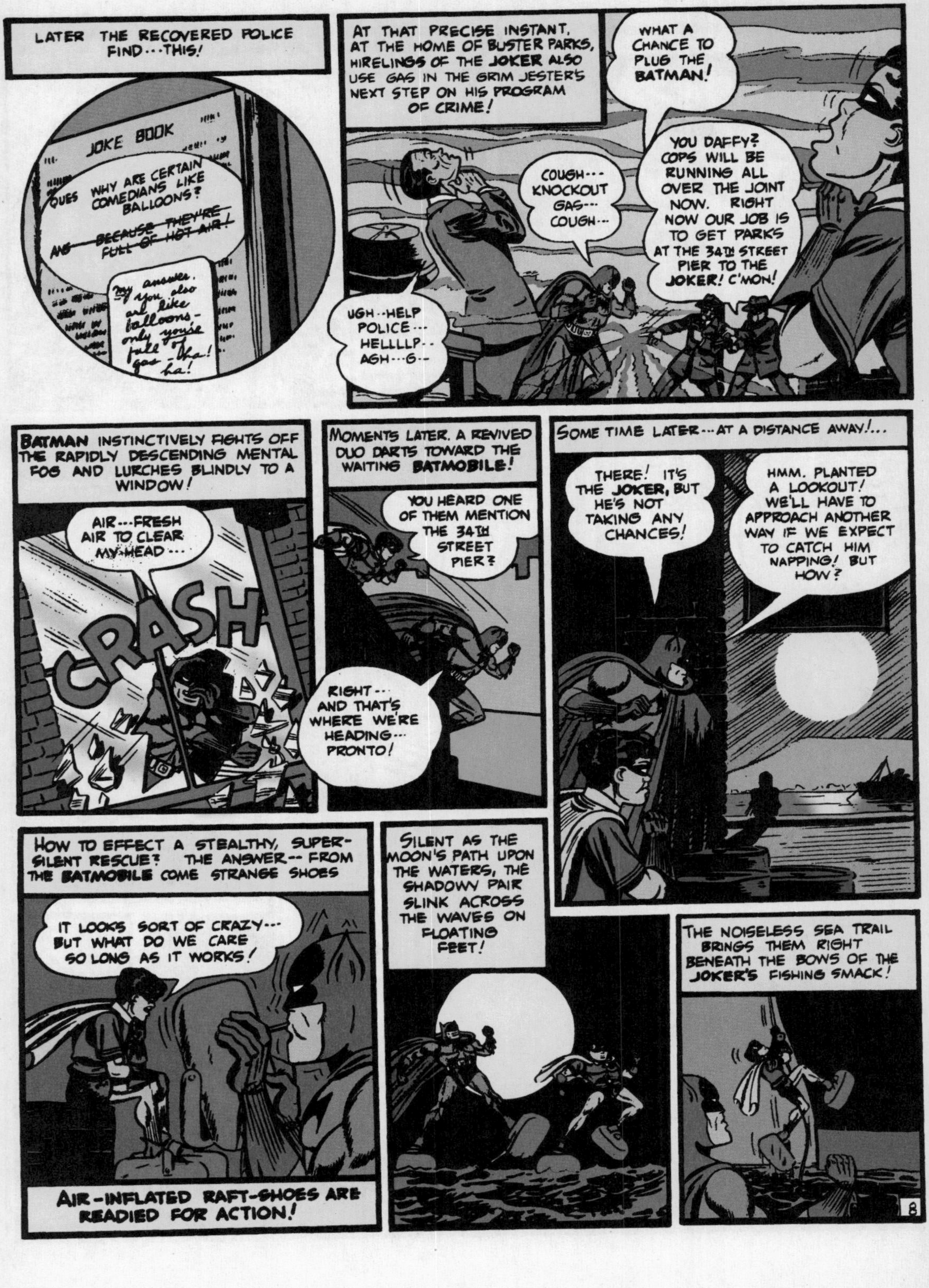

LATER THE RECOVERED POLICE FIND---THIS!
JOKE BOOK
QUES WHY ARE CERTAIN COMEDIANS LIKE BALLOONS?
ANS BECAUSE THEY'RE FULL OF HOT AIR!
my answer. you also are like balloons - only you're full of gas - ha! ha!
AT THAT PRECISE INSTANT, AT THE HOME OF BUSTER PARKS, HIRELINGS OF THE JOKER ALSO USE GAS IN THE GRIM JESTER'S NEXT STEP ON HIS PROGRAM OF CRIME!
WHAT A CHANCE TO PLUG THE BATMAN!
COUGH--- KNOCKOUT GAS--- COUGH---
YOU DAFFY? COPS WILL BE RUNNING ALL OVER THE JOINT NOW. RIGHT NOW OUR JOB IS TO GET PARKS AT THE 34TH STREET PIER TO THE JOKER! C'MON!
UGH--HELP POLICE--- HELLLLP-- AGH---G--
BATMAN INSTINCTIVELY FIGHTS OFF THE RAPIDLY DESCENDING MENTAL FOG AND LURCHES BLINDLY TO A WINDOW!
AIR---FRESH AIR TO CLEAR MY HEAD---
CRASH
MOMENTS LATER. A REVIVED DUO DARTS TOWARD THE WAITING BATMOBILE!
YOU HEARD ONE OF THEM MENTION THE 34TH STREET PIER?
RIGHT--- AND THAT'S WHERE WE'RE HEADING--- PRONTO!
SOME TIME LATER---AT A DISTANCE AWAY!...
THERE! IT'S THE JOKER, BUT HE'S NOT TAKING ANY CHANCES!
HMM. PLANTED A LOOKOUT! WE'LL HAVE TO APPROACH ANOTHER WAY IF WE EXPECT TO CATCH HIM NAPPING! BUT HOW?
HOW TO EFFECT A STEALTHY, SUPER-SILENT RESCUE? THE ANSWER-- FROM THE BATMOBILE COME STRANGE SHOES
IT LOOKS SORT OF CRAZY--- BUT WHAT DO WE CARE SO LONG AS IT WORKS!
AIR-INFLATED RAFT-SHOES ARE READIED FOR ACTION!
SILENT AS THE MOON'S PATH UPON THE WATERS, THE SHADOWY PAIR SLINK ACROSS THE WAVES ON FLOATING FEET!
THE NOISELESS SEA TRAIL BRINGS THEM RIGHT BENEATH THE BOWS OF THE JOKER'S FISHING SMACK!
8

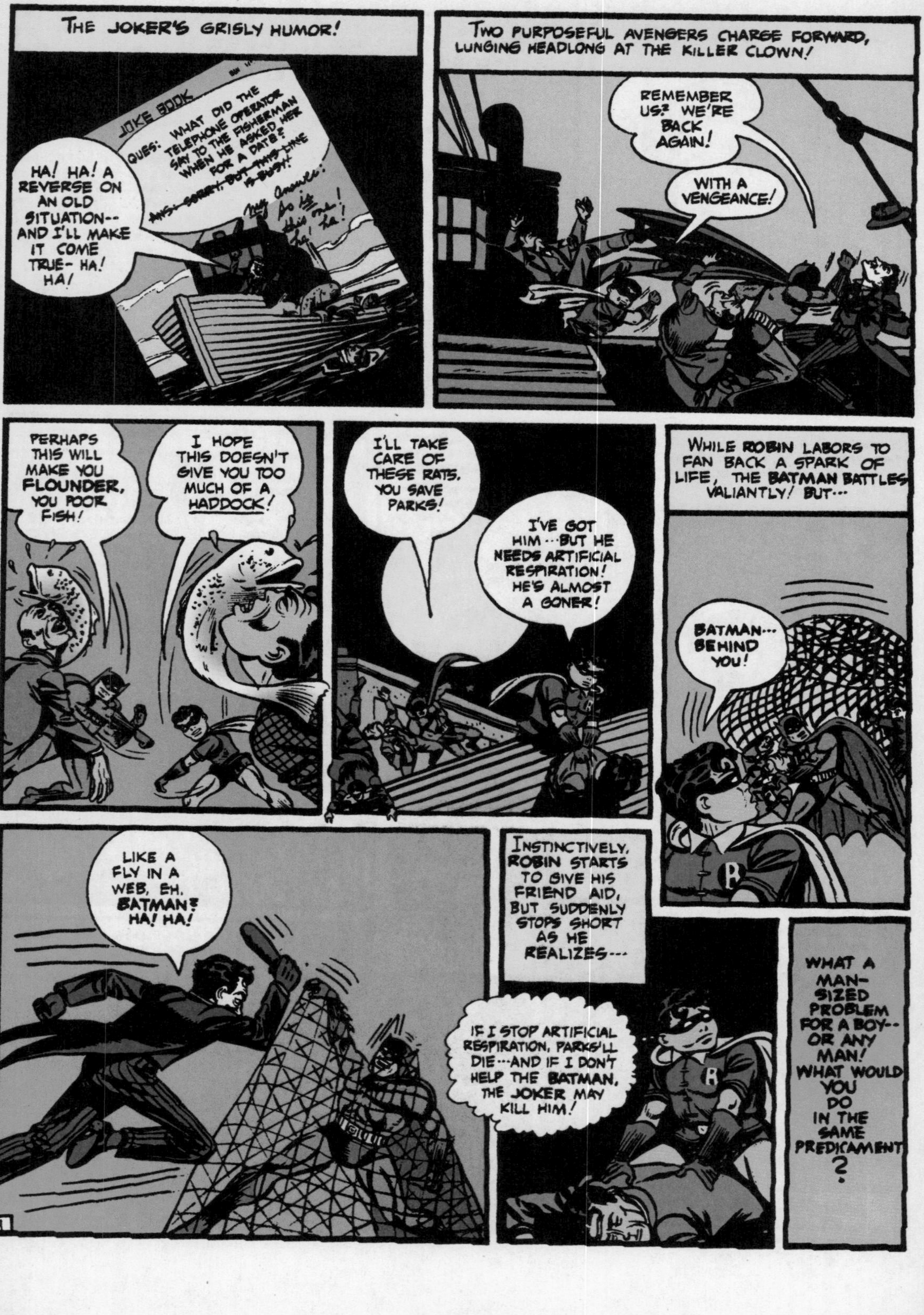
THE JOKER'S GRISLY HUMOR!
JOKE BOOK
QUES: WHAT DID THE TELEPHONE OPERATOR SAY TO THE FISHERMAN WHEN HE ASKED HER FOR A DATE?
ANS: SORRY, BUT THIS LINE IS BUSY!
New answer: So is this one! Ha! Ha!
HA! HA! A REVERSE ON AN OLD SITUATION-- AND I'LL MAKE IT COME TRUE- HA! HA!
TWO PURPOSEFUL AVENGERS CHARGE FORWARD, LUNGING HEADLONG AT THE KILLER CLOWN!
REMEMBER US? WE'RE BACK AGAIN!
WITH A VENGEANCE!
PERHAPS THIS WILL MAKE YOU FLOUNDER, YOU POOR FISH!
I HOPE THIS DOESN'T GIVE YOU TOO MUCH OF A HADDOCK!
I'LL TAKE CARE OF THESE RATS. YOU SAVE PARKS!
I'VE GOT HIM ··· BUT HE NEEDS ARTIFICIAL RESPIRATION! HE'S ALMOST A GONER!
WHILE ROBIN LABORS TO FAN BACK A SPARK OF LIFE, THE BATMAN BATTLES VALIANTLY! BUT···
BATMAN··· BEHIND YOU!
LIKE A FLY IN A WEB, EH, BATMAN? HA! HA!
INSTINCTIVELY, ROBIN STARTS TO GIVE HIS FRIEND AID, BUT SUDDENLY STOPS SHORT AS HE REALIZES···
IF I STOP ARTIFICIAL RESPIRATION, PARKS'LL DIE···AND IF I DON'T HELP THE BATMAN, THE JOKER MAY KILL HIM!
WHAT A MAN-SIZED PROBLEM FOR A BOY-- OR ANY MAN! WHAT WOULD YOU DO IN THE SAME PREDICAMENT?

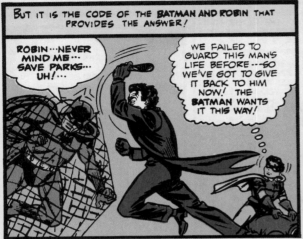

BUT IT IS THE CODE OF THE BATMAN AND ROBIN THAT PROVIDES THE ANSWER!
ROBIN---NEVER MIND ME--- SAVE PARKS--- UH!---
WE FAILED TO GUARD THIS MAN'S LIFE BEFORE---SO WE'VE GOT TO GIVE IT BACK TO HIM NOW! THE BATMAN WANTS IT THIS WAY!
AND SO WE HAVE AN ODD SITUATION---ROBIN UNABLE TO AID HIS BEST FRIEND IN THE GRIP OF THEIR WORST ENEMY!
BATMAN--- BATMAN---
I'M GONNA BLAST THAT KID ONCE AND FOR ALL!
NO! HIS MENTAL TORTURE AT THE MOMENT IS WORSE THAN ANY BULLET COULD POSSIBLY BE. HA! HA! LET'S GO! HA! HA!
LATER, IN HIS SECRET HIDEOUT, THE JOKER STUDIES THE COLLECTED CLUES!
YOUR CLUE ASK FOR
YOUR CLUE CHECKED PACKAGE FOR
YOUR CLUE M. WINNER
YOUR CLUE AT HOTEL
YOUR CLUE GRAND
THE FORTUNE IS IN THE PACKAGE! HA! HA! AH, AWAKE, ARE YOU, BATMAN?? HA! HA! IN SPITE OF YOU, I'VE WON, I'VE WON!
I'VE PREPARED FOR THIS DAY, BATMAN! LOOK! SEE THOSE TWO DOORS? ONE OF THEM LEADS TO SAFETY---
---THE OTHER LEADS TO YOUR DOOM! YOU HAVE YOUR CHOICE! CHOOSE WELL, BATMAN! IT'S WIN OR LOSE NOW.
10
SUDDENLY, A CURIOUS LOOK LEAPS TO THE JOKER'S MOCKING EYES!
YOU KNOW---I DON'T KNOW WHY I GO TO SUCH LENGTHS TO DISPOSE OF YOU---WHEN ALL I NEED DO IS RIP OFF YOUR MASK---REVEAL YOUR NAME TO THE UNDERWORLD--
THANKS FOR THE ADVICE. YOU'RE TOO KIND! I'LL BET YOU GIVE AWAY ICE IN THE WINTER TIME!
--AND END THE CAREER OF THE BATMAN FOREVER!
ONCE IT IS REVEALED THAT BATMAN IS REALLY BRUCE WAYNE, THE SOCIETY PLAYBOY, HIS ROLE AS THE NATION'S LEADING CRIME-FIGHTER IS ENDED FOR ALL TIME! WILL THE COWL BE REMOVED?? IS THIS THE BATMAN'S LAST CASE!

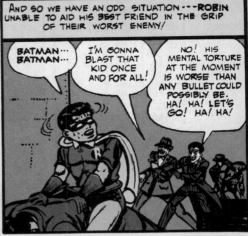

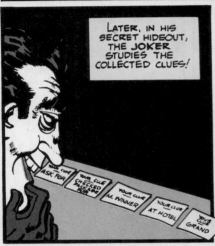

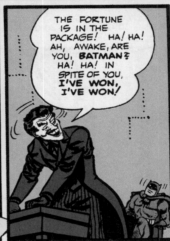

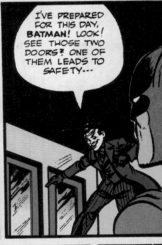

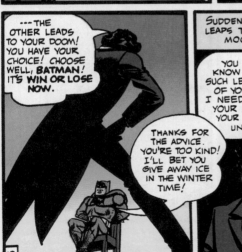

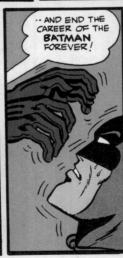

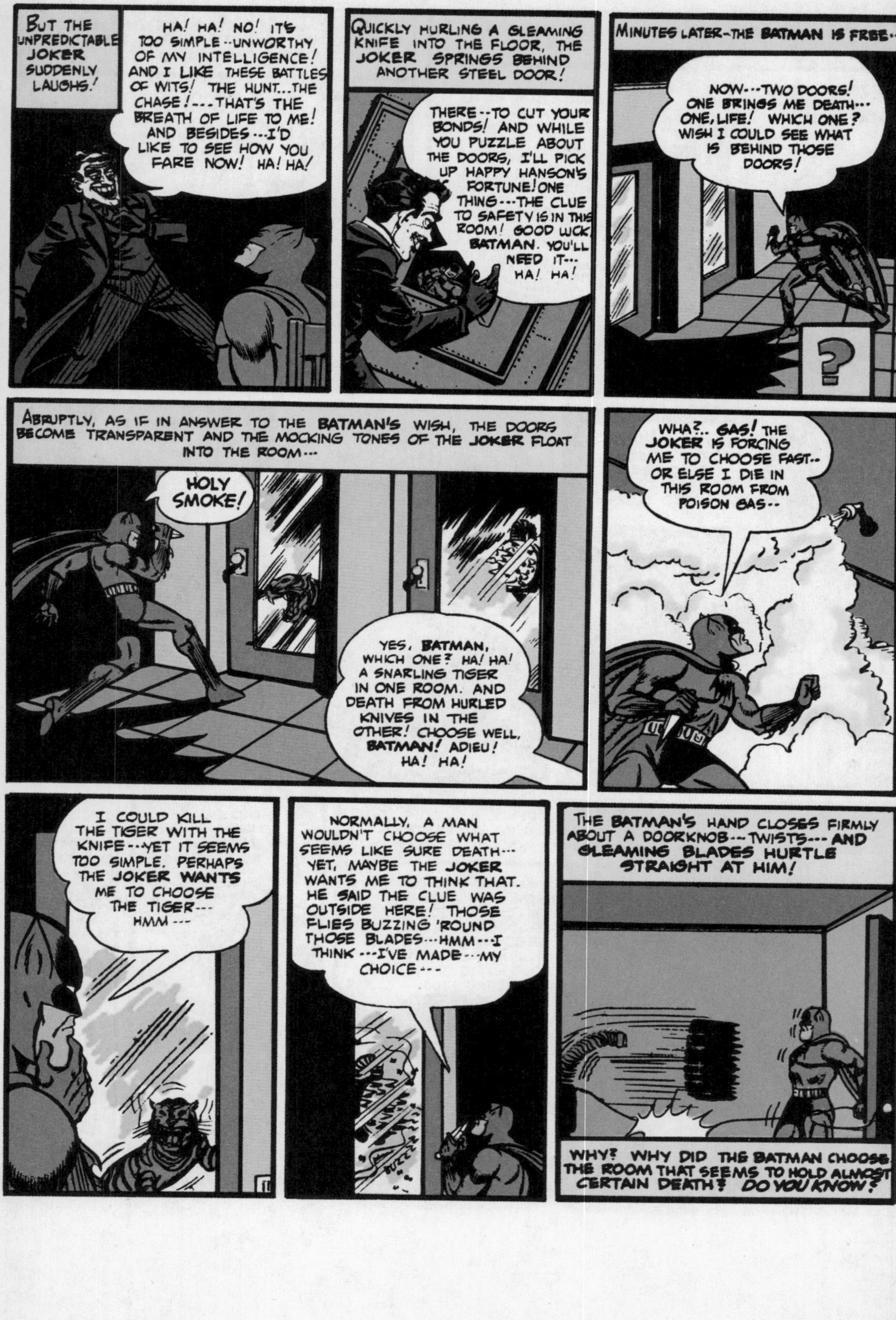

BUT THE UNPREDICTABLE JOKER SUDDENLY LAUGHS!
HA! HA! NO! IT'S TOO SIMPLE--UNWORTHY OF MY INTELLIGENCE! AND I LIKE THESE BATTLES OF WITS! THE HUNT...THE CHASE!---THAT'S THE BREATH OF LIFE TO ME! AND BESIDES---I'D LIKE TO SEE HOW YOU FARE NOW! HA! HA!
QUICKLY HURLING A GLEAMING KNIFE INTO THE FLOOR, THE JOKER SPRINGS BEHIND ANOTHER STEEL DOOR!
THERE--TO CUT YOUR BONDS! AND WHILE YOU PUZZLE ABOUT THE DOORS, I'LL PICK UP HAPPY HANSON'S FORTUNE! ONE THING---THE CLUE TO SAFETY IS IN THIS ROOM! GOOD LUCK BATMAN. YOU'LL NEED IT--- HA! HA!
MINUTES LATER--THE BATMAN IS FREE---
NOW---TWO DOORS! ONE BRINGS ME DEATH--- ONE, LIFE! WHICH ONE? WISH I COULD SEE WHAT IS BEHIND THOSE DOORS!
?
ABRUPTLY, AS IF IN ANSWER TO THE BATMAN'S WISH, THE DOORS BECOME TRANSPARENT AND THE MOCKING TONES OF THE JOKER FLOAT INTO THE ROOM---
HOLY SMOKE!
YES, BATMAN, WHICH ONE? HA! HA! A SNARLING TIGER IN ONE ROOM. AND DEATH FROM HURLED KNIVES IN THE OTHER! CHOOSE WELL, BATMAN! ADIEU! HA! HA!
WHA?.. GAS! THE JOKER IS FORCING ME TO CHOOSE FAST-- OR ELSE I DIE IN THIS ROOM FROM POISON GAS--
I COULD KILL THE TIGER WITH THE KNIFE---YET IT SEEMS TOO SIMPLE. PERHAPS THE JOKER WANTS ME TO CHOOSE THE TIGER--- HMM ---
NORMALLY, A MAN WOULDN'T CHOOSE WHAT SEEMS LIKE SURE DEATH--- YET, MAYBE THE JOKER WANTS ME TO THINK THAT. HE SAID THE CLUE WAS OUTSIDE HERE! THOSE FLIES BUZZING 'ROUND THOSE BLADES---HMM---I THINK---I'VE MADE---MY CHOICE---
BUZZZZ
THE BATMAN'S HAND CLOSES FIRMLY ABOUT A DOORKNOB---TWISTS--- AND GLEAMING BLADES HURTLE STRAIGHT AT HIM!
WHY? WHY DID THE BATMAN CHOOSE THE ROOM THAT SEEMS TO HOLD ALMOST CERTAIN DEATH? DO YOU KNOW?

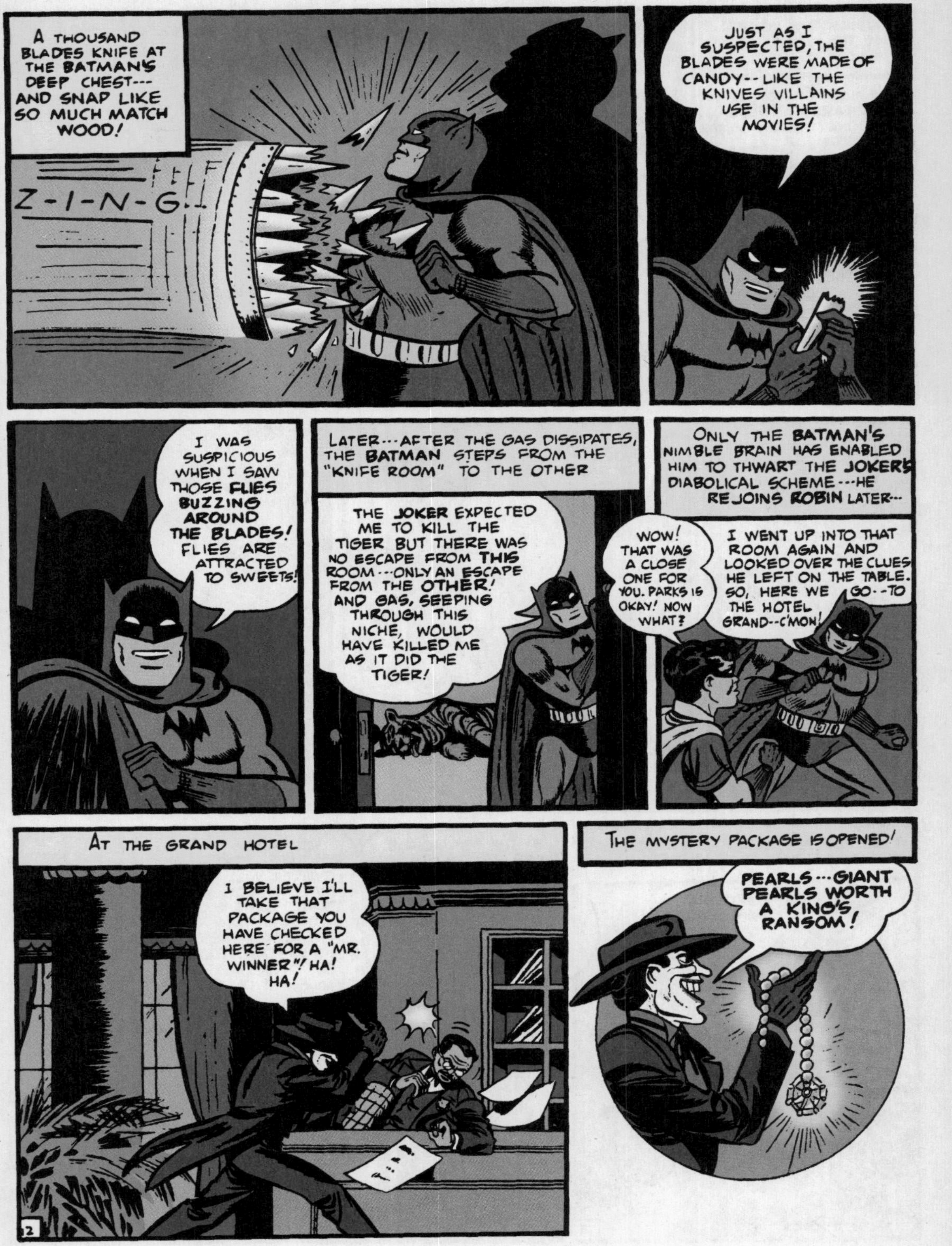
A THOUSAND BLADES KNIFE AT THE BATMAN'S DEEP CHEST--- AND SNAP LIKE SO MUCH MATCH WOOD!
Z-I-N-G
JUST AS I SUSPECTED, THE BLADES WERE MADE OF CANDY--LIKE THE KNIVES VILLAINS USE IN THE MOVIES!
I WAS SUSPICIOUS WHEN I SAW THOSE FLIES BUZZING AROUND THE BLADES! FLIES ARE ATTRACTED TO SWEETS!
LATER---AFTER THE GAS DISSIPATES, THE BATMAN STEPS FROM THE "KNIFE ROOM" TO THE OTHER
THE JOKER EXPECTED ME TO KILL THE TIGER BUT THERE WAS NO ESCAPE FROM THIS ROOM---ONLY AN ESCAPE FROM THE OTHER! AND GAS, SEEPING THROUGH THIS NICHE, WOULD HAVE KILLED ME AS IT DID THE TIGER!
ONLY THE BATMAN'S NIMBLE BRAIN HAS ENABLED HIM TO THWART THE JOKER'S DIABOLICAL SCHEME---HE REJOINS ROBIN LATER---
WOW! THAT WAS A CLOSE ONE FOR YOU. PARKS IS OKAY! NOW WHAT?
I WENT UP INTO THAT ROOM AGAIN AND LOOKED OVER THE CLUES HE LEFT ON THE TABLE. SO, HERE WE GO--TO THE HOTEL GRAND--C'MON!
AT THE GRAND HOTEL
I BELIEVE I'LL TAKE THAT PACKAGE YOU HAVE CHECKED HERE FOR A "MR. WINNER"! HA! HA!
THE MYSTERY PACKAGE IS OPENED!
PEARLS---GIANT PEARLS WORTH A KING'S RANSOM!

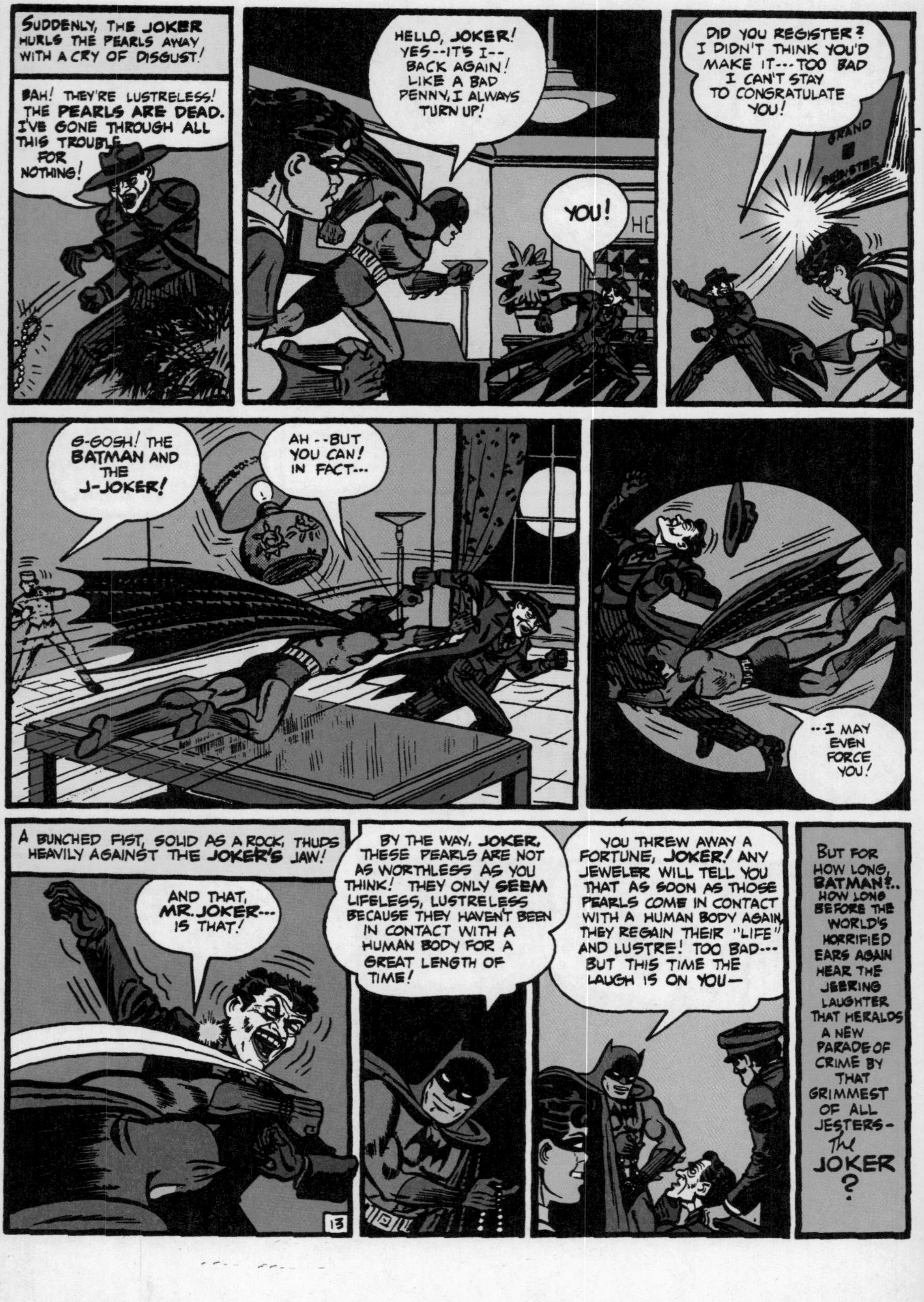
SUDDENLY, THE JOKER HURLS THE PEARLS AWAY WITH A CRY OF DISGUST!
BAH! THEY'RE LUSTRELESS! THE PEARLS ARE DEAD. I'VE GONE THROUGH ALL THIS TROUBLE FOR NOTHING!
HELLO, JOKER! YES--IT'S I--BACK AGAIN! LIKE A BAD PENNY, I ALWAYS TURN UP!
YOU!
DID YOU REGISTER? I DIDN'T THINK YOU'D MAKE IT---TOO BAD I CAN'T STAY TO CONGRATULATE YOU!
G-GOSH! THE BATMAN AND THE J-JOKER!
AH--BUT YOU CAN! IN FACT---
--I MAY EVEN FORCE YOU!
A BUNCHED FIST, SOLID AS A ROCK, THUDS HEAVILY AGAINST THE JOKER'S JAW!
AND THAT, MR. JOKER--- IS THAT!
13
BY THE WAY, JOKER, THESE PEARLS ARE NOT AS WORTHLESS AS YOU THINK! THEY ONLY SEEM LIFELESS, LUSTRELESS BECAUSE THEY HAVEN'T BEEN IN CONTACT WITH A HUMAN BODY FOR A GREAT LENGTH OF TIME!
YOU THREW AWAY A FORTUNE, JOKER! ANY JEWELER WILL TELL YOU THAT AS SOON AS THOSE PEARLS COME IN CONTACT WITH A HUMAN BODY AGAIN, THEY REGAIN THEIR "LIFE" AND LUSTRE! TOO BAD--- BUT THIS TIME THE LAUGH IS ON YOU—
BUT FOR HOW LONG, BATMAN?.. HOW LONG BEFORE THE WORLD'S HORRIFIED EARS AGAIN HEAR THE JEERING LAUGHTER THAT HERALDS A NEW PARADE OF CRIME BY THAT GRIMMEST OF ALL JESTERS- The JOKER?

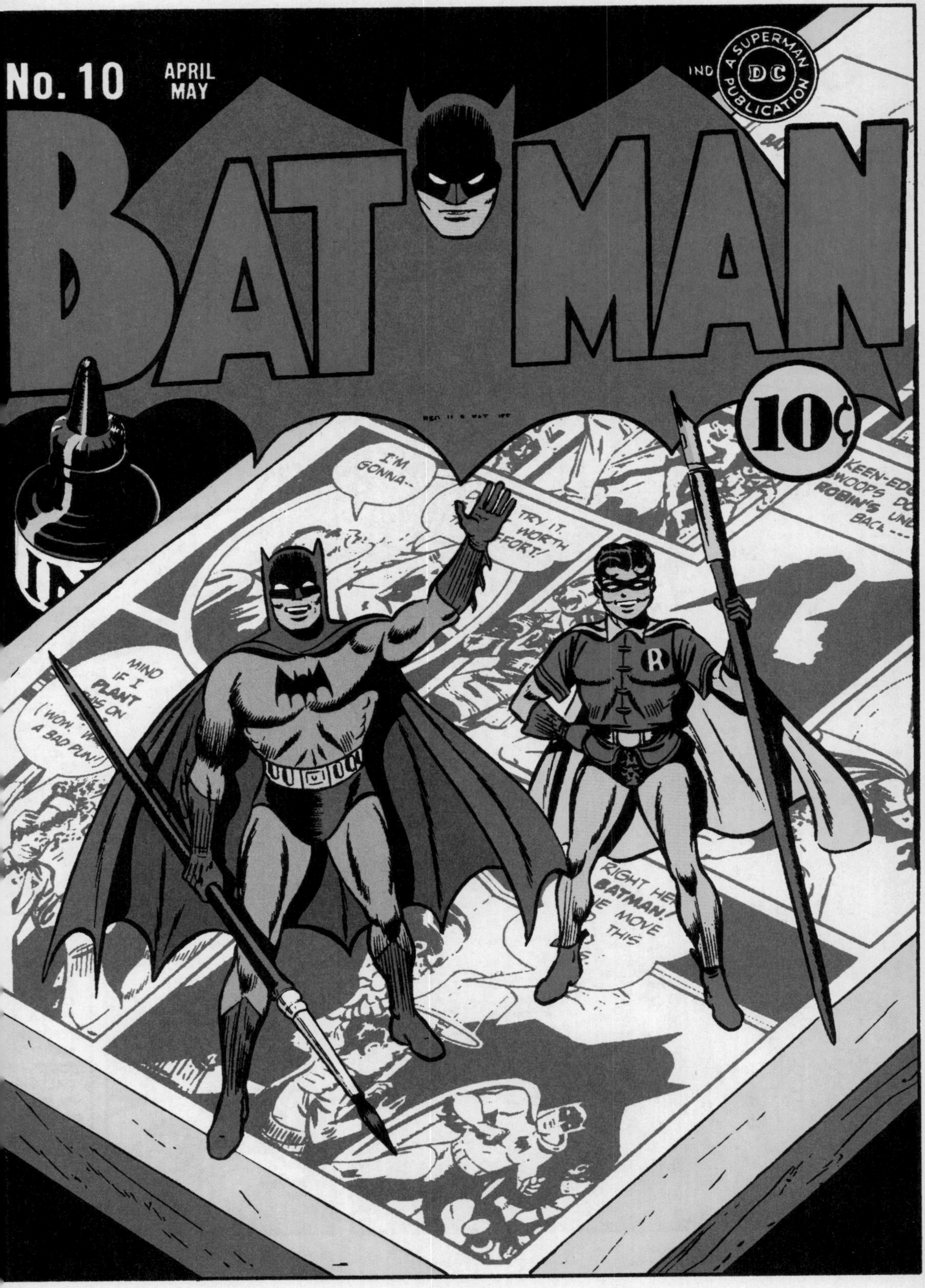

No. 10
APRIL
MAY
IND
A SUPERMAN
DC
PUBLICATION
BATMAN
10¢
I'M GONNA--
TRY IT. WORTH
MIND IF I PLANT
A BAD PUN!
ROBIN'S
BATMAN!
MOVE THIS

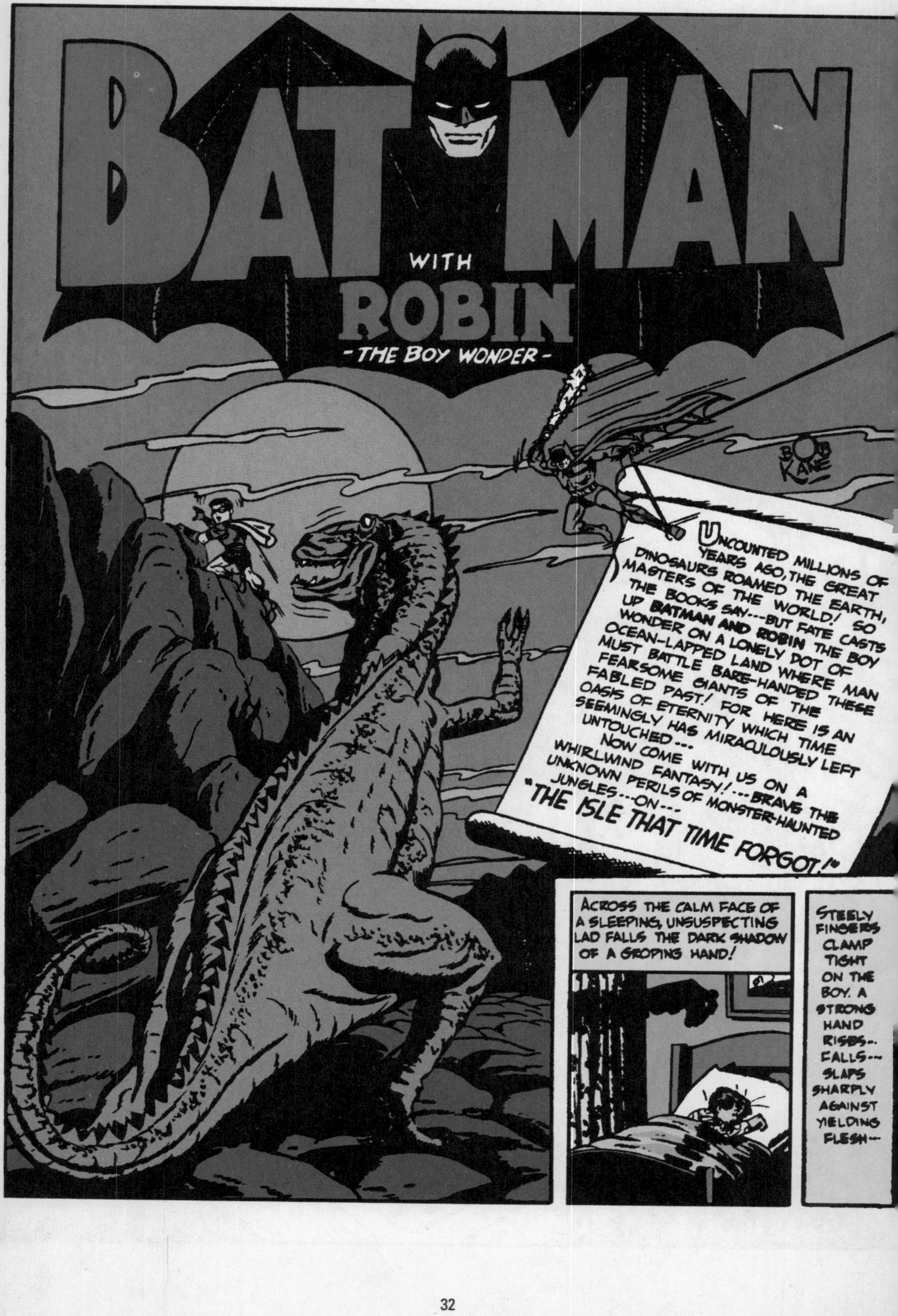
BATMAN
WITH
ROBIN
-THE BOY WONDER-
BOB KANE
UNCOUNTED MILLIONS OF YEARS AGO, THE GREAT DINOSAURS ROAMED THE EARTH, MASTERS OF THE WORLD! SO THE BOOKS SAY---BUT FATE CASTS UP BATMAN AND ROBIN THE BOY WONDER ON A LONELY DOT OF OCEAN-LAPPED LAND WHERE MAN MUST BATTLE BARE-HANDED THESE FEARSOME GIANTS OF THE FABLED PAST! FOR HERE IS AN OASIS OF ETERNITY WHICH TIME SEEMINGLY HAS MIRACULOUSLY LEFT UNTOUCHED---
NOW COME WITH US ON A WHIRLWIND FANTASY!---BRAVE THE UNKNOWN PERILS OF MONSTER-HAUNTED JUNGLES---ON---
"THE ISLE THAT TIME FORGOT!"
ACROSS THE CALM FACE OF A SLEEPING, UNSUSPECTING LAD FALLS THE DARK SHADOW OF A GROPING HAND!
STEELY FINGERS CLAMP TIGHT ON THE BOY. A STRONG HAND RISES-- FALLS-- SLAPS SHARPLY AGAINST YIELDING FLESH--

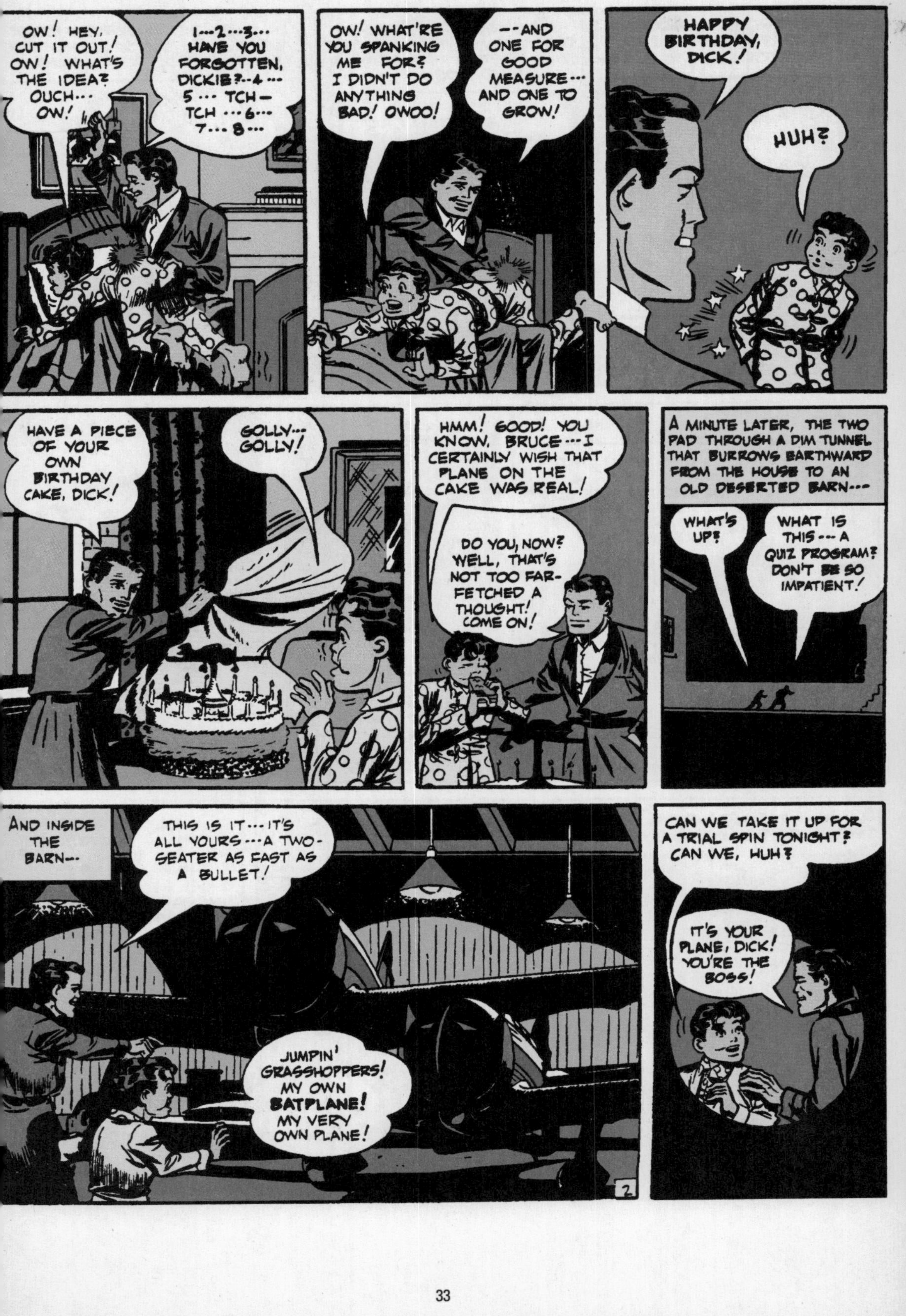
OW! HEY, CUT IT OUT! OW! WHAT'S THE IDEA? OUCH--- OW!
1---2---3--- HAVE YOU FORGOTTEN, DICKIE?--4--- 5--- TCH-TCH ---6--- 7--- 8---
OW! WHAT'RE YOU SPANKING ME FOR? I DIDN'T DO ANYTHING BAD! OWOO!
--AND ONE FOR GOOD MEASURE--- AND ONE TO GROW!
HAPPY BIRTHDAY, DICK!
HUH?
HAVE A PIECE OF YOUR OWN BIRTHDAY CAKE, DICK!
GOLLY--- GOLLY!
HMM! GOOD! YOU KNOW, BRUCE---I CERTAINLY WISH THAT PLANE ON THE CAKE WAS REAL!
DO YOU, NOW? WELL, THAT'S NOT TOO FAR-FETCHED A THOUGHT! COME ON!
A MINUTE LATER, THE TWO PAD THROUGH A DIM TUNNEL THAT BURROWS EARTHWARD FROM THE HOUSE TO AN OLD DESERTED BARN---
WHAT'S UP?
WHAT IS THIS--- A QUIZ PROGRAM? DON'T BE SO IMPATIENT!
AND INSIDE THE BARN--
THIS IS IT---IT'S ALL YOURS---A TWO-SEATER AS FAST AS A BULLET!
JUMPIN' GRASSHOPPERS! MY OWN BATPLANE! MY VERY OWN PLANE!
2
CAN WE TAKE IT UP FOR A TRIAL SPIN TONIGHT? CAN WE, HUH?
IT'S YOUR PLANE, DICK! YOU'RE THE BOSS!

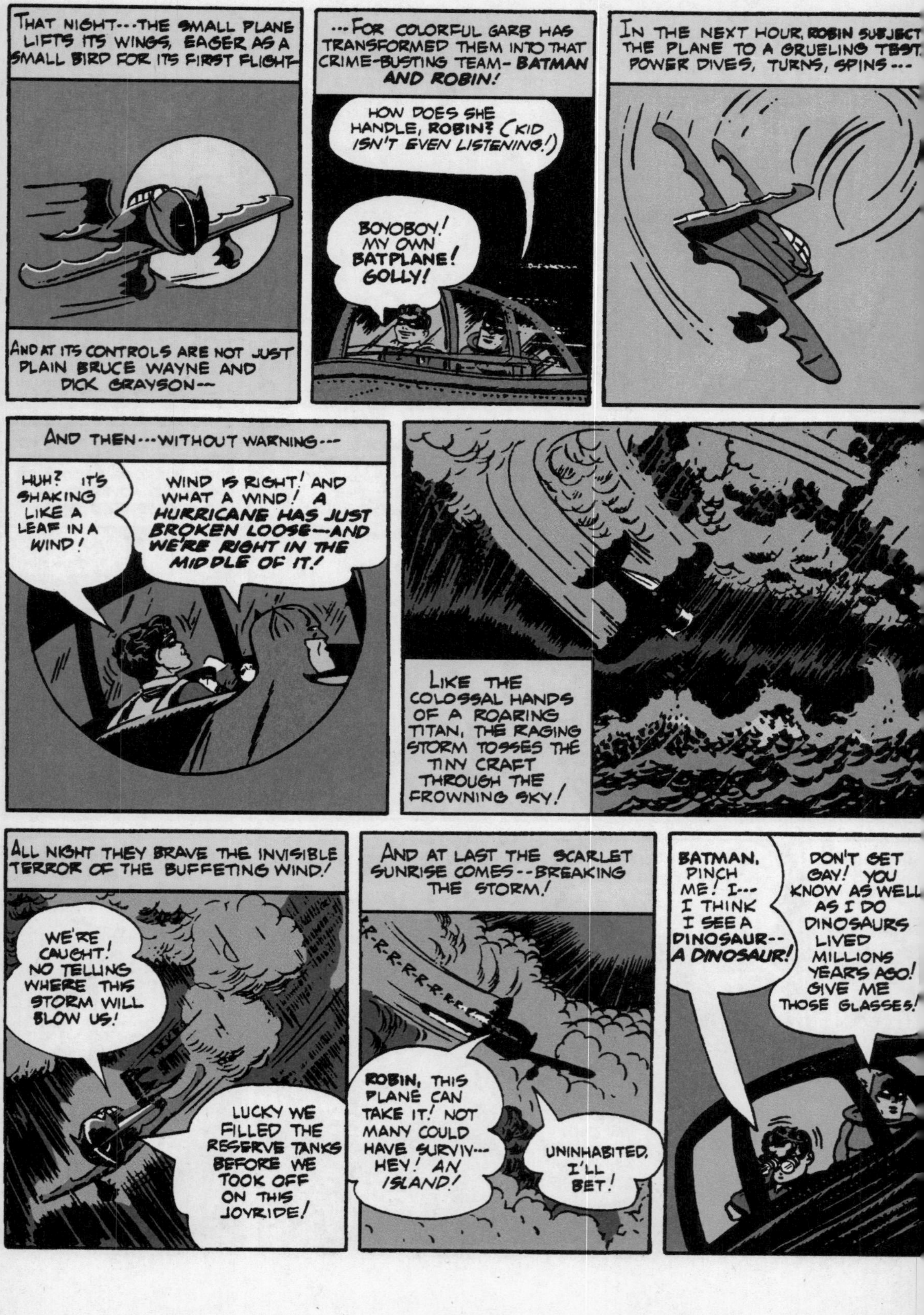
THAT NIGHT---THE SMALL PLANE LIFTS ITS WINGS, EAGER AS A SMALL BIRD FOR ITS FIRST FLIGHT--
AND AT ITS CONTROLS ARE NOT JUST PLAIN BRUCE WAYNE AND DICK GRAYSON--
---FOR COLORFUL GARB HAS TRANSFORMED THEM INTO THAT CRIME-BUSTING TEAM- BATMAN AND ROBIN!
HOW DOES SHE HANDLE, ROBIN? (KID ISN'T EVEN LISTENING!)
BOYOBOY! MY OWN BATPLANE! GOLLY!
IN THE NEXT HOUR, ROBIN SUBJECT THE PLANE TO A GRUELING TEST. POWER DIVES, TURNS, SPINS---
AND THEN---WITHOUT WARNING---
HUH? IT'S SHAKING LIKE A LEAF IN A WIND!
WIND IS RIGHT! AND WHAT A WIND! A HURRICANE HAS JUST BROKEN LOOSE--AND WE'RE RIGHT IN THE MIDDLE OF IT!
LIKE THE COLOSSAL HANDS OF A ROARING TITAN, THE RAGING STORM TOSSES THE TINY CRAFT THROUGH THE FROWNING SKY!
ALL NIGHT THEY BRAVE THE INVISIBLE TERROR OF THE BUFFETING WIND!
WE'RE CAUGHT! NO TELLING WHERE THIS STORM WILL BLOW US!
LUCKY WE FILLED THE RESERVE TANKS BEFORE WE TOOK OFF ON THIS JOYRIDE!
AND AT LAST THE SCARLET SUNRISE COMES--BREAKING THE STORM!
R-R-R-R-R-R-R-R
ROBIN, THIS PLANE CAN TAKE IT! NOT MANY COULD HAVE SURVIV--- HEY! AN ISLAND!
UNINHABITED, I'LL BET!
BATMAN, PINCH ME! I--- I THINK I SEE A DINOSAUR-- A DINOSAUR!
DON'T GET GAY! YOU KNOW AS WELL AS I DO DINOSAURS LIVED MILLIONS YEARS AGO! GIVE ME THOSE GLASSES!

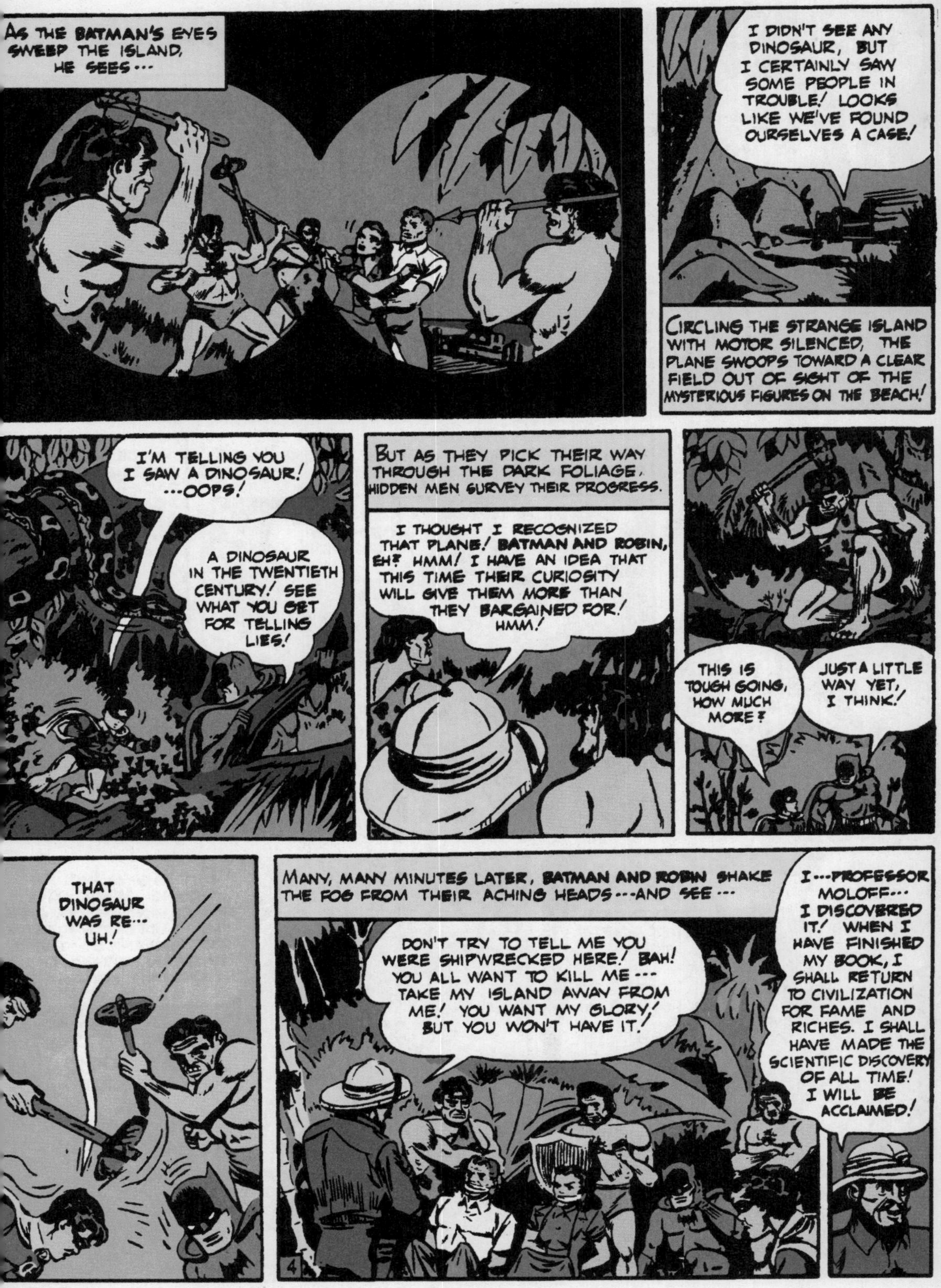

AS THE BATMAN'S EYES SWEEP THE ISLAND, HE SEES ---
I DIDN'T SEE ANY DINOSAUR, BUT I CERTAINLY SAW SOME PEOPLE IN TROUBLE! LOOKS LIKE WE'VE FOUND OURSELVES A CASE!
CIRCLING THE STRANGE ISLAND WITH MOTOR SILENCED, THE PLANE SWOOPS TOWARD A CLEAR FIELD OUT OF SIGHT OF THE MYSTERIOUS FIGURES ON THE BEACH!
I'M TELLING YOU I SAW A DINOSAUR! ---OOPS!
A DINOSAUR IN THE TWENTIETH CENTURY! SEE WHAT YOU GET FOR TELLING LIES!
BUT AS THEY PICK THEIR WAY THROUGH THE DARK FOLIAGE, HIDDEN MEN SURVEY THEIR PROGRESS.
I THOUGHT I RECOGNIZED THAT PLANE! BATMAN AND ROBIN, EH? HMM! I HAVE AN IDEA THAT THIS TIME THEIR CURIOSITY WILL GIVE THEM MORE THAN THEY BARGAINED FOR! HMM!
THIS IS TOUGH GOING, HOW MUCH MORE?
JUST A LITTLE WAY YET, I THINK!
THAT DINOSAUR WAS RE--- UH!
MANY, MANY MINUTES LATER, BATMAN AND ROBIN SHAKE THE FOG FROM THEIR ACHING HEADS---AND SEE ---
DON'T TRY TO TELL ME YOU WERE SHIPWRECKED HERE! BAH! YOU ALL WANT TO KILL ME --- TAKE MY ISLAND AWAY FROM ME! YOU WANT MY GLORY! BUT YOU WON'T HAVE IT!
4
I ---PROFESSOR MOLOFF--- I DISCOVERED IT! WHEN I HAVE FINISHED MY BOOK, I SHALL RETURN TO CIVILIZATION FOR FAME AND RICHES. I SHALL HAVE MADE THE SCIENTIFIC DISCOVERY OF ALL TIME! I WILL BE ACCLAIMED!

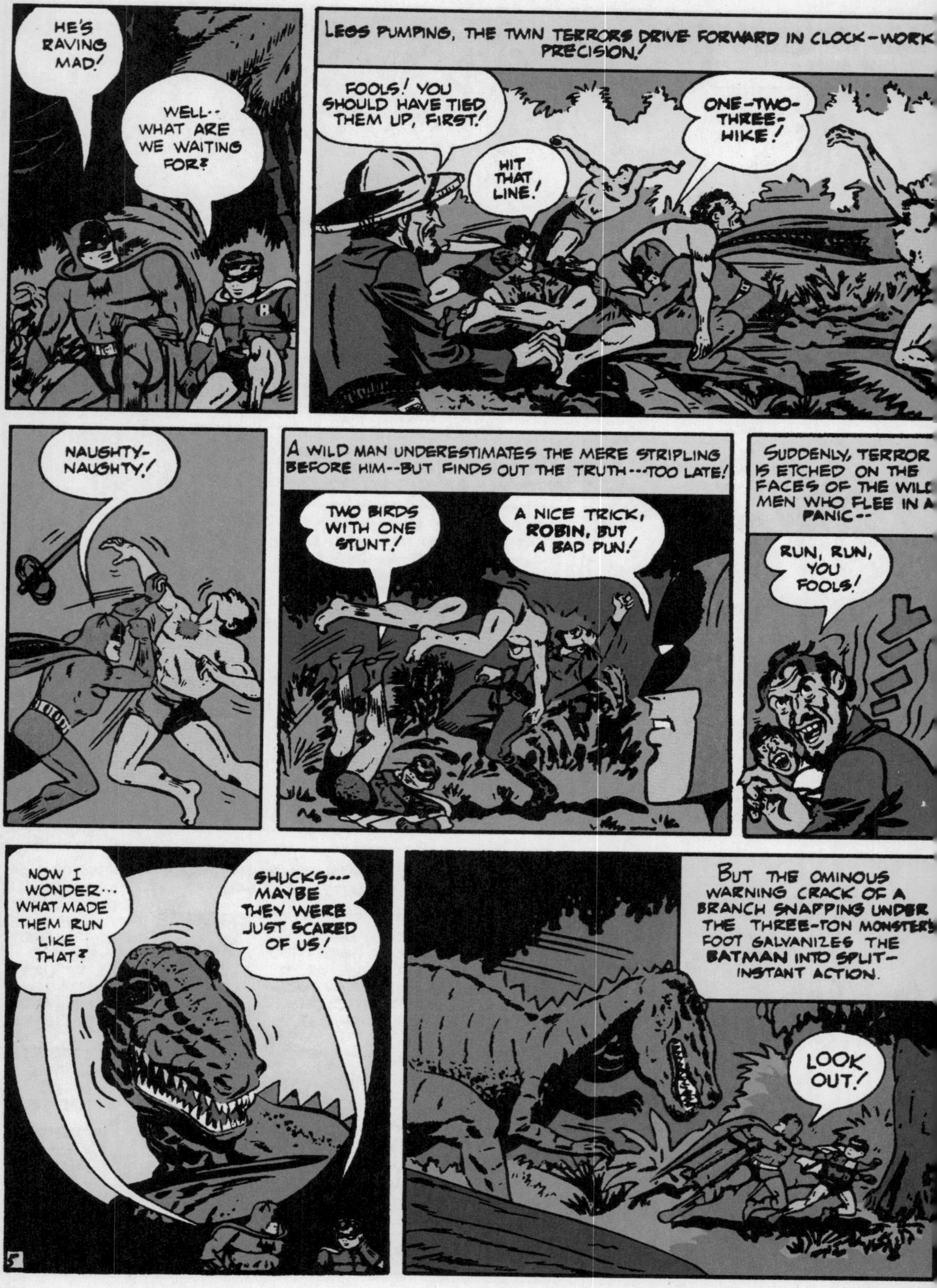
HE'S RAVING MAD!
WELL--WHAT ARE WE WAITING FOR?
LEGS PUMPING, THE TWIN TERRORS DRIVE FORWARD IN CLOCK-WORK PRECISION!
FOOLS! YOU SHOULD HAVE TIED THEM UP, FIRST!
HIT THAT LINE!
ONE-TWO-THREE-HIKE!
NAUGHTY-NAUGHTY!
A WILD MAN UNDERESTIMATES THE MERE STRIPLING BEFORE HIM--BUT FINDS OUT THE TRUTH---TOO LATE!
TWO BIRDS WITH ONE STUNT!
A NICE TRICK, ROBIN, BUT A BAD PUN!
SUDDENLY, TERROR IS ETCHED ON THE FACES OF THE WILD MEN WHO FLEE IN A PANIC--
RUN, RUN, YOU FOOLS!
NOW I WONDER... WHAT MADE THEM RUN LIKE THAT?
SHUCKS--- MAYBE THEY WERE JUST SCARED OF US!
5
BUT THE OMINOUS WARNING CRACK OF A BRANCH SNAPPING UNDER THE THREE-TON MONSTER'S FOOT GALVANIZES THE BATMAN INTO SPLIT-INSTANT ACTION.
LOOK OUT!

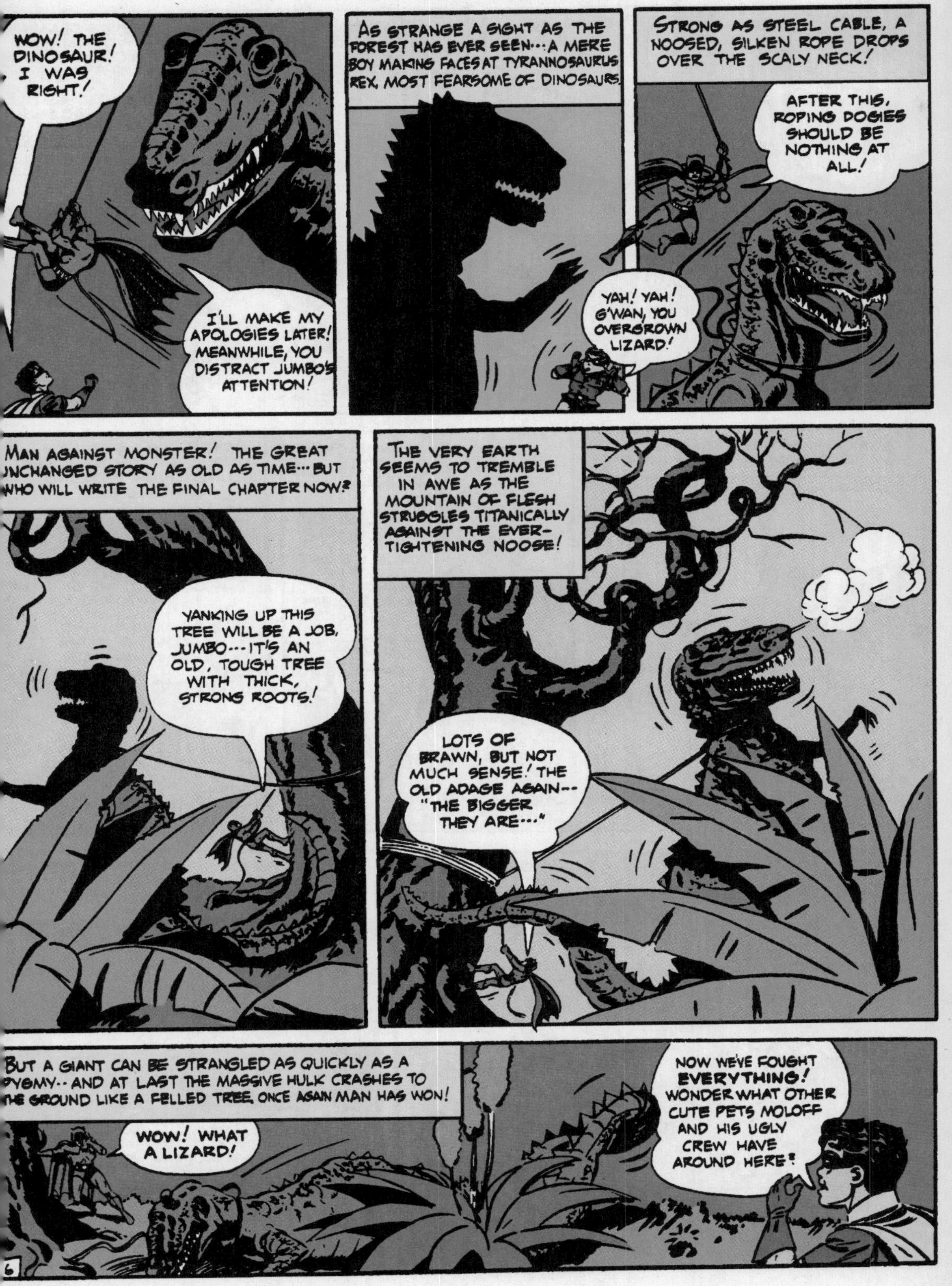
WOW! THE DINOSAUR! I WAS RIGHT!
I'LL MAKE MY APOLOGIES LATER! MEANWHILE, YOU DISTRACT JUMBO'S ATTENTION!
AS STRANGE A SIGHT AS THE FOREST HAS EVER SEEN--- A MERE BOY MAKING FACES AT TYRANNOSAURUS REX, MOST FEARSOME OF DINOSAURS.
YAH! YAH! G'WAN, YOU OVERGROWN LIZARD!
STRONG AS STEEL CABLE, A NOOSED, SILKEN ROPE DROPS OVER THE SCALY NECK!
AFTER THIS, ROPING DOGIES SHOULD BE NOTHING AT ALL!
MAN AGAINST MONSTER! THE GREAT UNCHANGED STORY AS OLD AS TIME--- BUT WHO WILL WRITE THE FINAL CHAPTER NOW?
YANKING UP THIS TREE WILL BE A JOB, JUMBO--- IT'S AN OLD, TOUGH TREE WITH THICK, STRONG ROOTS!
THE VERY EARTH SEEMS TO TREMBLE IN AWE AS THE MOUNTAIN OF FLESH STRUGGLES TITANICALLY AGAINST THE EVER-TIGHTENING NOOSE!
LOTS OF BRAWN, BUT NOT MUCH SENSE! THE OLD ADAGE AGAIN-- "THE BIGGER THEY ARE---"
BUT A GIANT CAN BE STRANGLED AS QUICKLY AS A PYGMY-- AND AT LAST THE MASSIVE HULK CRASHES TO THE GROUND LIKE A FELLED TREE. ONCE AGAIN MAN HAS WON!
WOW! WHAT A LIZARD!
NOW WE'VE FOUGHT EVERYTHING! WONDER WHAT OTHER CUTE PETS MOLOFF AND HIS UGLY CREW HAVE AROUND HERE?
6

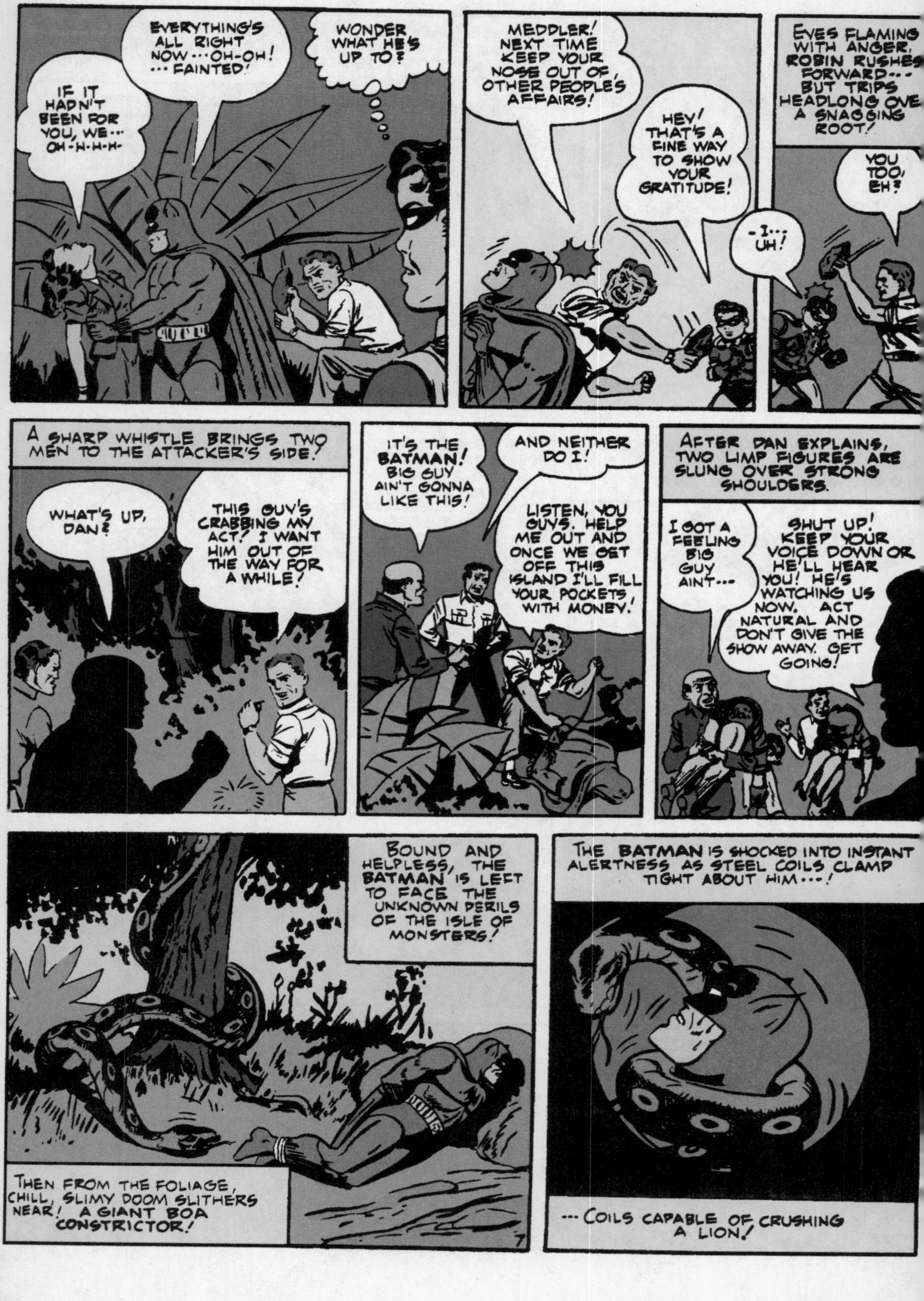
IF IT HADN'T BEEN FOR YOU, WE... OH-H-H-H-
EVERYTHING'S ALL RIGHT NOW...OH-OH! ...FAINTED!
WONDER WHAT HE'S UP TO?
MEDDLER! NEXT TIME KEEP YOUR NOSE OUT OF OTHER PEOPLE'S AFFAIRS!
HEY! THAT'S A FINE WAY TO SHOW YOUR GRATITUDE!
-I... UH!
EYES FLAMING WITH ANGER, ROBIN RUSHES FORWARD... BUT TRIPS HEADLONG OVE A SNAGGING ROOT!
YOU TOO, EH?
A SHARP WHISTLE BRINGS TWO MEN TO THE ATTACKER'S SIDE!
WHAT'S UP, DAN?
THIS GUY'S CRABBING MY ACT! I WANT HIM OUT OF THE WAY FOR A WHILE!
IT'S THE BATMAN! BIG GUY AIN'T GONNA LIKE THIS!
AND NEITHER DO I!
LISTEN, YOU GUYS. HELP ME OUT AND ONCE WE GET OFF THIS ISLAND I'LL FILL YOUR POCKETS WITH MONEY!
AFTER DAN EXPLAINS, TWO LIMP FIGURES ARE SLUNG OVER STRONG SHOULDERS.
I GOT A FEELING BIG GUY AINT...
SHUT UP! KEEP YOUR VOICE DOWN OR HE'LL HEAR YOU! HE'S WATCHING US NOW. ACT NATURAL AND DON'T GIVE THE SHOW AWAY. GET GOING!
BOUND AND HELPLESS, THE BATMAN IS LEFT TO FACE THE UNKNOWN PERILS OF THE ISLE OF MONSTERS!
THEN FROM THE FOLIAGE, CHILL, SLIMY DOOM SLITHERS NEAR! A GIANT BOA CONSTRICTOR!
THE BATMAN IS SHOCKED INTO INSTANT ALERTNESS AS STEEL COILS CLAMP TIGHT ABOUT HIM...!
...COILS CAPABLE OF CRUSHING A LION!

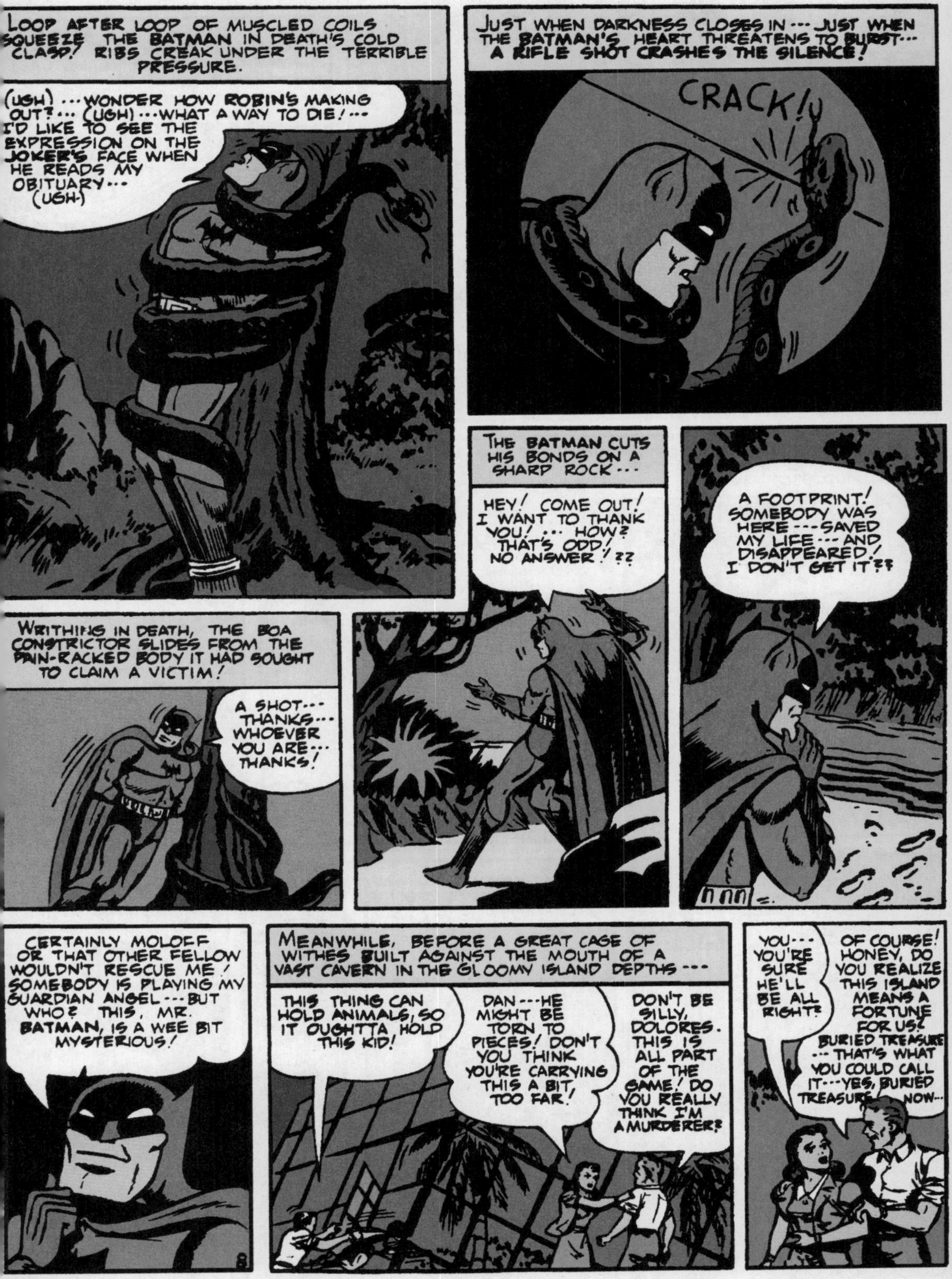
LOOP AFTER LOOP OF MUSCLED COILS SQUEEZE THE BATMAN IN DEATH'S COLD CLASP! RIBS CREAK UNDER THE TERRIBLE PRESSURE.
(UGH) ... WONDER HOW ROBIN'S MAKING OUT? ... (UGH) ... WHAT A WAY TO DIE! ... I'D LIKE TO SEE THE EXPRESSION ON THE JOKER'S FACE WHEN HE READS MY OBITUARY... (UGH)
JUST WHEN DARKNESS CLOSES IN --- JUST WHEN THE BATMAN'S HEART THREATENS TO BURST--- A RIFLE SHOT CRASHES THE SILENCE!
CRACK!
THE BATMAN CUTS HIS BONDS ON A SHARP ROCK ...
HEY! COME OUT! I WANT TO THANK YOU! ... HOW? THAT'S ODD! NO ANSWER! ??
A FOOTPRINT! SOMEBODY WAS HERE --- SAVED MY LIFE --- AND DISAPPEARED! I DON'T GET IT ??
WRITHING IN DEATH, THE BOA CONSTRICTOR SLIDES FROM THE PAIN-RACKED BODY IT HAD SOUGHT TO CLAIM A VICTIM!
A SHOT--- THANKS--- WHOEVER YOU ARE--- THANKS!
CERTAINLY MOLOFF OR THAT OTHER FELLOW WOULDN'T RESCUE ME! SOMEBODY IS PLAYING MY GUARDIAN ANGEL --- BUT WHO? THIS, MR. BATMAN, IS A WEE BIT MYSTERIOUS!
8
MEANWHILE, BEFORE A GREAT CAGE OF WITHES BUILT AGAINST THE MOUTH OF A VAST CAVERN IN THE GLOOMY ISLAND DEPTHS ---
THIS THING CAN HOLD ANIMALS, SO IT OUGHTTA HOLD THIS KID!
DAN---HE MIGHT BE TORN TO PIECES! DON'T YOU THINK YOU'RE CARRYING THIS A BIT TOO FAR!
DON'T BE SILLY, DOLORES. THIS IS ALL PART OF THE GAME! DO YOU REALLY THINK I'M A MURDERER?
YOU--- YOU'RE SURE HE'LL BE ALL RIGHT?
OF COURSE! HONEY, DO YOU REALIZE THIS ISLAND MEANS A FORTUNE FOR US? BURIED TREASURE --- THAT'S WHAT YOU COULD CALL IT--- YES, BURIED TREASURE! NOW...

AFTER THEY DEPART...

SOMETHING QUEER IS GOING ON HERE THAT NEEDS EXPLAINING---I WONDER WHAT HAPPENS NEXT?...

AS IF IN ANSWER, A TUSKED, SHAGGY BEAST PADS SILENTLY TOWARD THE UNSUSPECTING LAD!

FEEL LIKE STRETCHING MY---UH! A SABER-TOOTHED TIGER!

SUPERBLY-TRAINED MUSCLES RESPOND WITH LIGHTNING SPEED TO THE STIMULUS OF DANGER!

SABER-TOOTHED TIGERS WENT OUT OF STYLE IN THE STONE AGE---BUT AFTER THAT DINOSAUR I'LL BELIEVE ANYTHING NOW!

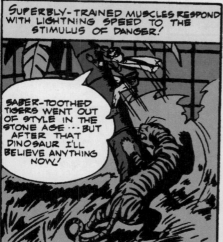

BUT THE ANGRY SABER-TOOTH IS NOT TO BE CHEATED!

OH, OH! MY BELT RADIO. IF THE BATMAN IS ALIVE, HE'LL COME! BATMAN, CAN YOU HEAR ME? A TIGER HAS ME TREED!!!

AND IN THE FOREST NOT TOO FAR AWAY...

SNAKE? NO...I DIDN'T! BIG GUY---...AH...BUT THE SECRET OF YOUR PROTECTION LIES WITH ME.

MOLOFF! YOU...YOU KILLED THE SNAKE!

...A TIGER HAS ME TREED!

NO, BATMAN..I DID NOT SAVE YOUR LIFE...I HAVE COME BACK TO TAKE IT! IT IS AS SIMPLE AS ALL THAT!

MY RADIO...ROBIN IN TROUBLE!

OUT OF MY WAY! ROBIN NEEDS ME! OUT OF MY WAY! COMING, ROBIN...

HEARTENED BY THE BATMAN'S CRY, ROBIN STRIKES BACK AT THE SNARLING MAN-KILLER!

COMING, ROBIN!

I'M WARNING YOU. YOU'D BETTER SCRAM BEFORE THE BATMAN GETS HERE!

LIKE A BLOODHOUND ON THE SCENT, THE BATMAN FOLLOWS THE BLIND TRAIL OF THE URGING VOICE EMANATING FROM HIS WIRELESS.
AFTER HIM! DON'T LET HIM GET AWAY!
HMM ... IN THAT CASE, I'LL GIVE HIM SOMETHING TO THINK ABOUT.
ARE YOU COMING, BATMAN?
SNAP!
LURCHING THROUGH BRAMBLE, STUMBLING OVER SNAGGING BRUSH AND ROOTS, SICK WITH APPREHENSION, THE BATMAN FOLLOWS THE INVISIBLE RADIO BEAM!
I'M GOING IN THE WRONG DIRECTION... ROBIN'S VOICE ...IT'S GETTING WEAKER ... I'LL TRY ANOTHER PATH
TIGER GETTING BOLDER..
VOICE IS STRONG NOW! I'VE GOT THE TRAIL ... OH-OH MOLOFF ON MY TRAIL NOW!
THIS WAY! HE CAN'T BE FAR!
CANT.. HOLD.. OUT.. MUCH.. LONGER!
AN INSTANT LATER, A HUMAN ANTHROPOID DARTS THROUGH THE TREETOPS, MUSCLES RIPPLING IN RHYTHM! ... SWING AND CLUTCH ... CLUTCH AND SWING ...
NOW LET MOLOFF AND HIS MEN FOLLOW MY TRAIL! COMING, ROBIN, ... KEEP PUNCHING!
BATMAN! WHERE ARE YOU?
SUDDENLY A FORMIDABLE FIGURE CRASHES THROUGH THE RUSTIC CAGE!
ROBIN!
BATMAN! AM I GLAD TO SEE YOU!
MAN AND BEAST FALL HEAVILY. STEELY LEGS LOCK ABOUT THE WRITHING TIGER.
FIRST SABER-TOOTH I'VE EVER WRESTLED --- BUT I GUESS THERE'S A FIRST TIME FOR EVERYTHING!
C'MON, BATMAN- SNAP HIS NECK!
STRONG HANDS CLAMP AROUND POINTED TUSKS AND ---
HEY! SOMETHING'S WRONG! TEETH AREN'T PULLED THAT EASY!
10

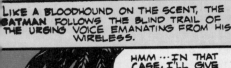

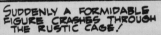

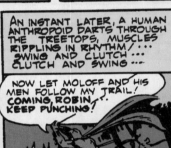

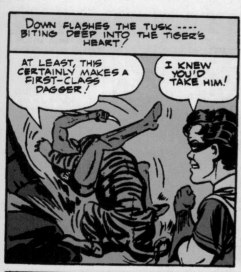

DOWN FLASHES THE TUSK ---- BITING DEEP INTO THE TIGER'S HEART!
AT LEAST, THIS CERTAINLY MAKES A FIRST-CLASS DAGGER!
I KNEW YOU'D TAKE HIM!
--AND THEY KEPT TALKING ABOUT THIS "BIG GUY" AS IF THEY WERE AFRAID OF HIM!
DINOSAURS-- A PHONEY SABER-TOOTHED TIGER--- A CRAZY PROFESSOR WITH AN ARMY OF CAVE-MEN--- A PRETTY GIRL--- A FELLOW WHO SLUGS US FOR SAVING HIS LIFE--- AND THIS "BIG GUY" WHO SAVED MY LIFE! IT'S A PUZZLE --- THE STRANGEST PUZZLE I'VE EVER ENCOUNTERED!
AND NOTICE --- THESE FERNS AND TREES ARE CERTAINLY NOT OF THE MESOZOIC PERIOD OF THE DINOSAUR! HMM!
THE DUO ESCAPES FROM THE MAKESHIFT CAGE...
I -- SAY I HEAR VOICES
FROM THE BROW OF A CLIFF, THE DYNAMIC DUO SEES A CURIOUS SCENE BELOW.
THE BATMAN WILL NEVER FIND YOU HERE! THIS TIME I HAVE YOU! HA! HA!
SO HE THINKS! ROBIN, YOU SLIP AROUND AND TACKLE THEM FROM THE FLANK!
IN SPECTACULAR AERIAL ASSAULT.
THE LAST ROUND-UP, FELLAS!
THE BATMAN--- SENSATIONAL AS USUAL! I'VE GOT TO KILL HIM--- NOW!
MEANWHILE, ROBIN, UPON CIRCLING THE GROUP, MAKES A STARTLING DISCOVERY!
A MACHINE GUN!
BE SURE YOU SHOOT THE BATMAN!
DON'T WORRY, BIG GUY-- I NEVER MISS!
YOU'RE NOT GOING TO KILL THE BATMAN THIS DAY- OR ANY OTHER DAY!
I'LL WRECK THIS THING BEFORE YOU HURT SOMEBODY--- HUH? A MOVIE CAMERA WITH A TELESCOPIC LENS!
ONE OF THE GREATEST PICTURES EVER FILMED!

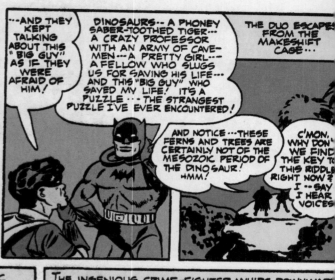

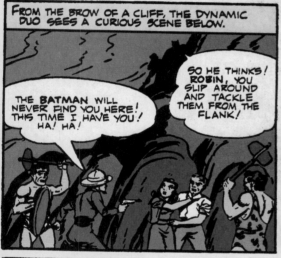

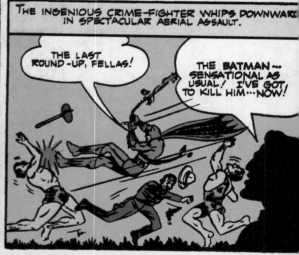

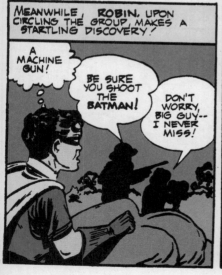

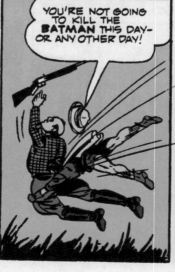

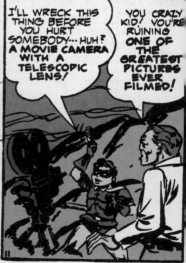

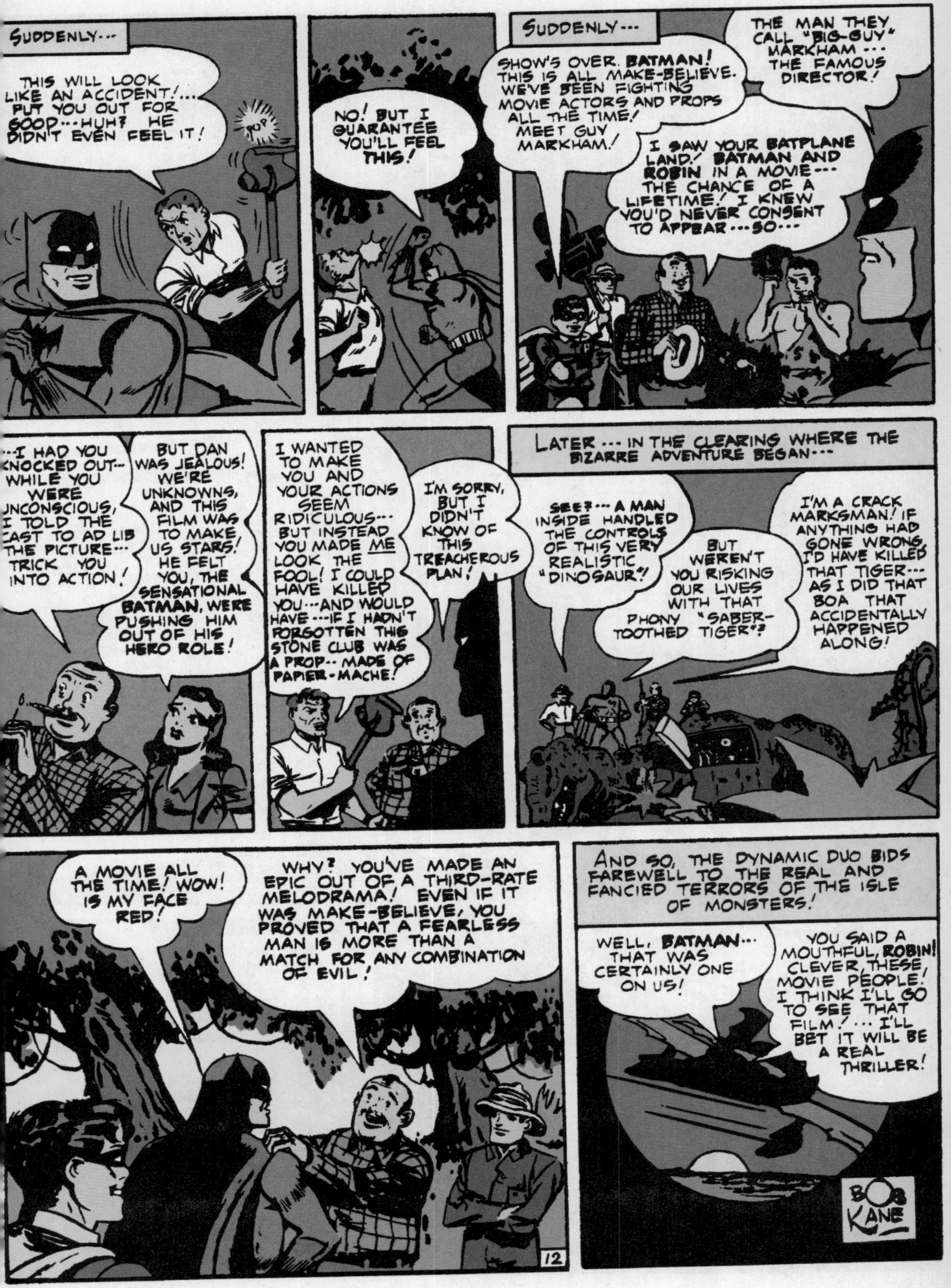
SUDDENLY...
THIS WILL LOOK LIKE AN ACCIDENT!... PUT YOU OUT FOR GOOD...HUH? HE DIDN'T EVEN FEEL IT!
POP
NO! BUT I GUARANTEE YOU'LL FEEL THIS!
SUDDENLY...
SHOW'S OVER, BATMAN! THIS IS ALL MAKE-BELIEVE. WE'VE BEEN FIGHTING MOVIE ACTORS AND PROPS ALL THE TIME! MEET GUY MARKHAM!
THE MAN THEY CALL "BIG-GUY" MARKHAM... THE FAMOUS DIRECTOR!
I SAW YOUR BATPLANE LAND! BATMAN AND ROBIN IN A MOVIE... THE CHANCE OF A LIFETIME! I KNEW YOU'D NEVER CONSENT TO APPEAR...SO...
...I HAD YOU KNOCKED OUT-- WHILE YOU WERE UNCONSCIOUS, I TOLD THE CAST TO AD LIB THE PICTURE... TRICK YOU INTO ACTION!
BUT DAN WAS JEALOUS! WE'RE UNKNOWNS, AND THIS FILM WAS TO MAKE US STARS! HE FELT YOU, THE SENSATIONAL BATMAN, WERE PUSHING HIM OUT OF HIS HERO ROLE!
I WANTED TO MAKE YOU AND YOUR ACTIONS SEEM RIDICULOUS... BUT INSTEAD YOU MADE ME LOOK THE FOOL! I COULD HAVE KILLED YOU...AND WOULD HAVE...IF I HADN'T FORGOTTEN THIS STONE CLUB WAS A PROP-- MADE OF PAPIER-MACHE!
I'M SORRY, BUT I DIDN'T KNOW OF THIS TREACHEROUS PLAN!
LATER... IN THE CLEARING WHERE THE BIZARRE ADVENTURE BEGAN...
SEE?...A MAN INSIDE HANDLED THE CONTROLS OF THIS VERY REALISTIC "DINOSAUR"!
BUT WEREN'T YOU RISKING OUR LIVES WITH THAT PHONY "SABER-TOOTHED TIGER"?
I'M A CRACK MARKSMAN! IF ANYTHING HAD GONE WRONG, I'D HAVE KILLED THAT TIGER... AS I DID THAT BOA THAT ACCIDENTALLY HAPPENED ALONG!
A MOVIE ALL THE TIME! WOW! IS MY FACE RED!
WHY? YOU'VE MADE AN EPIC OUT OF A THIRD-RATE MELODRAMA! EVEN IF IT WAS MAKE-BELIEVE, YOU PROVED THAT A FEARLESS MAN IS MORE THAN A MATCH FOR ANY COMBINATION OF EVIL!
12
AND SO, THE DYNAMIC DUO BIDS FAREWELL TO THE REAL AND FANCIED TERRORS OF THE ISLE OF MONSTERS!
WELL, BATMAN... THAT WAS CERTAINLY ONE ON US!
YOU SAID A MOUTHFUL, ROBIN! CLEVER, THESE, MOVIE PEOPLE! I THINK I'LL GO TO SEE THAT FILM!... I'LL BET IT WILL BE A REAL THRILLER!
BOB KANE

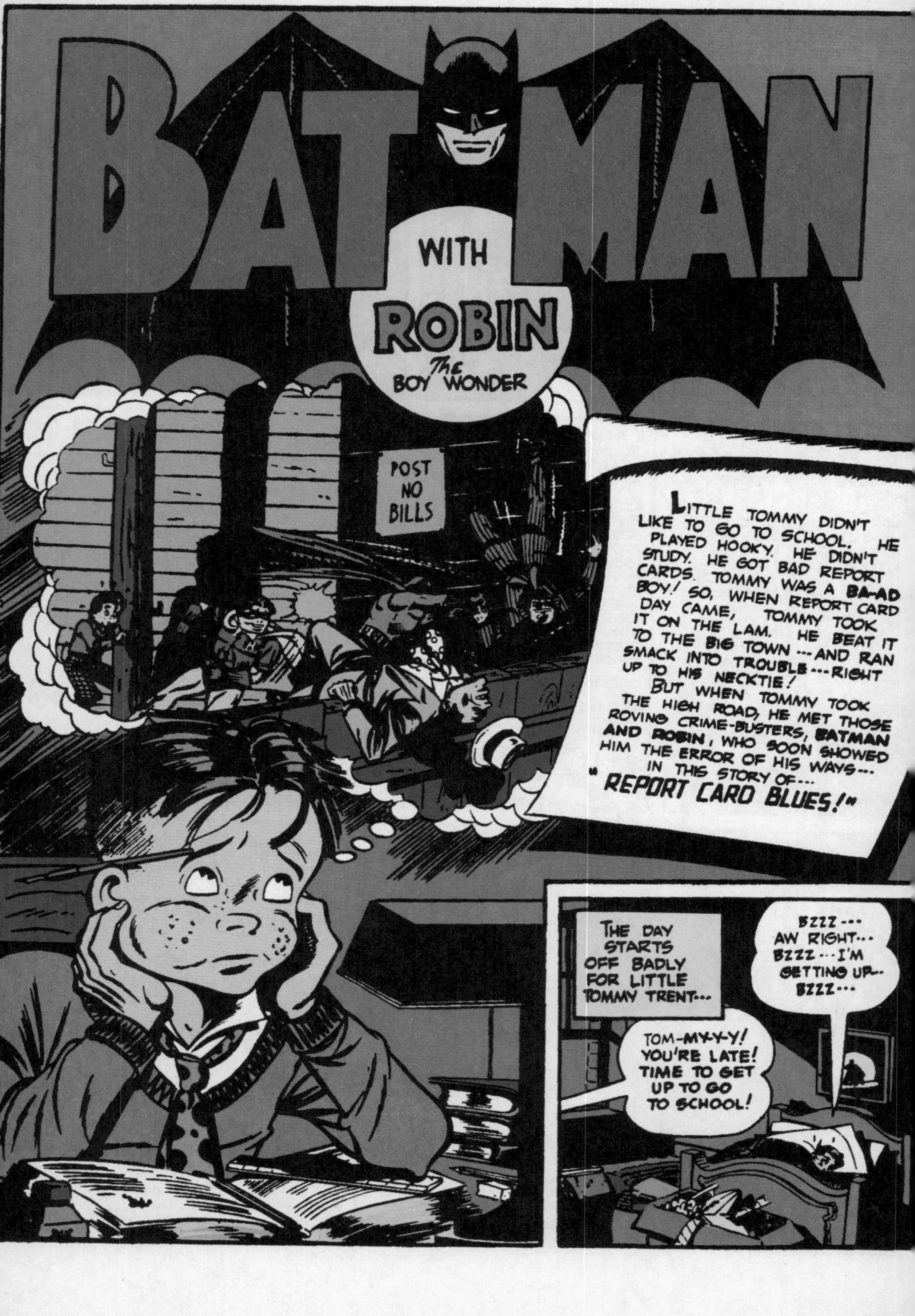
BATMAN
WITH
ROBIN
The BOY WONDER
POST NO BILLS
LITTLE TOMMY DIDN'T LIKE TO GO TO SCHOOL. HE PLAYED HOOKY. HE DIDN'T STUDY. HE GOT BAD REPORT CARDS. TOMMY WAS A BA-AD BOY! SO, WHEN REPORT CARD DAY CAME, TOMMY TOOK IT ON THE LAM. HE BEAT IT TO THE BIG TOWN --- AND RAN SMACK INTO TROUBLE --- RIGHT UP TO HIS NECKTIE! BUT WHEN TOMMY TOOK THE HIGH ROAD, HE MET THOSE ROVING CRIME-BUSTERS, BATMAN AND ROBIN, WHO SOON SHOWED HIM THE ERROR OF HIS WAYS--- IN THIS STORY OF--- "REPORT CARD BLUES!"
THE DAY STARTS OFF BADLY FOR LITTLE TOMMY TRENT...
TOM-MY-Y-Y! YOU'RE LATE! TIME TO GET UP TO GO TO SCHOOL!
BZZZ --- AW RIGHT... BZZZ --- I'M GETTING UP... BZZZ ---

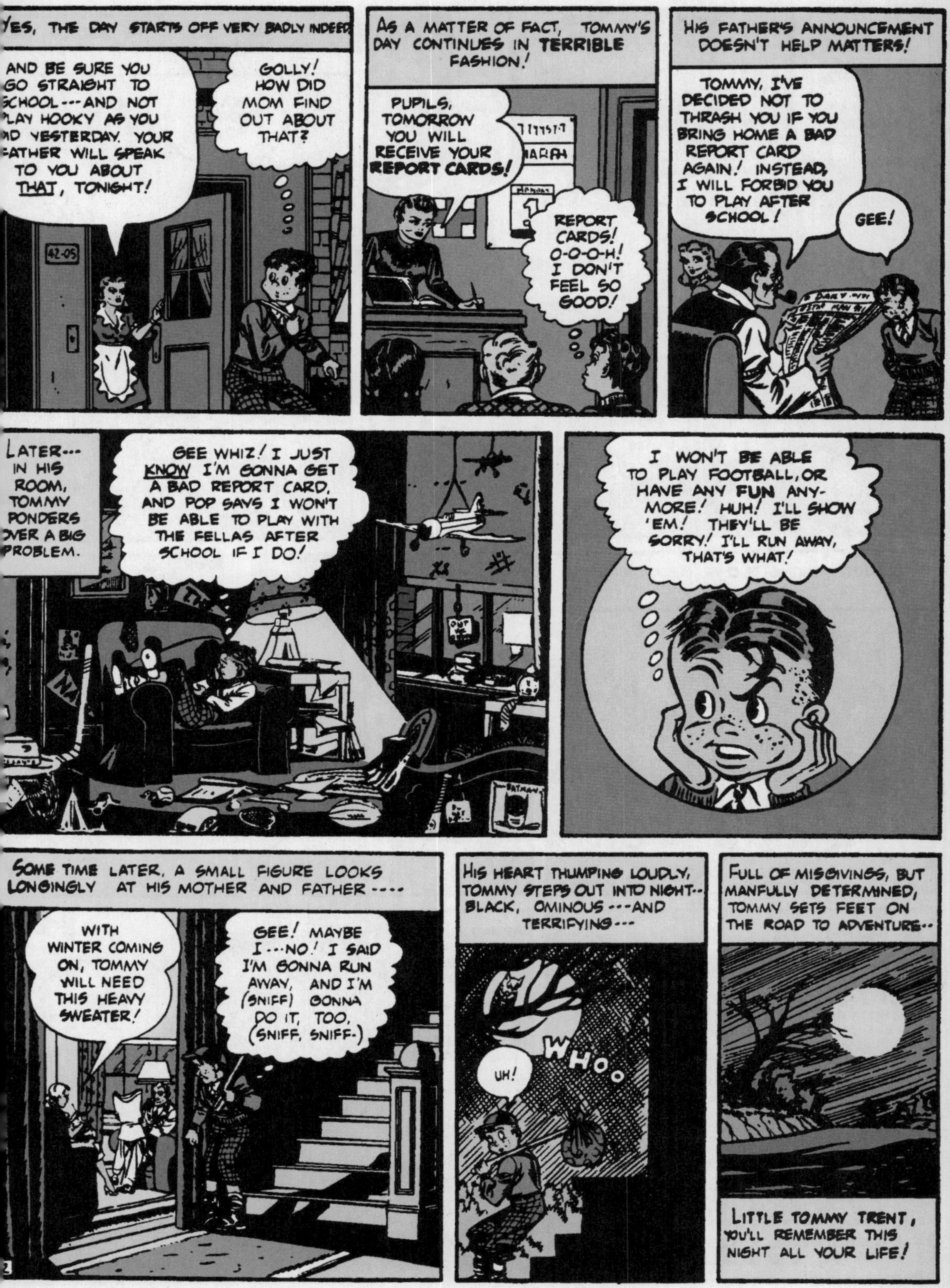
YES, THE DAY STARTS OFF VERY BADLY INDEED
AND BE SURE YOU GO STRAIGHT TO SCHOOL---AND NOT PLAY HOOKY AS YOU DID YESTERDAY. YOUR FATHER WILL SPEAK TO YOU ABOUT THAT, TONIGHT!
GOLLY! HOW DID MOM FIND OUT ABOUT THAT?
42-05
AS A MATTER OF FACT, TOMMY'S DAY CONTINUES IN TERRIBLE FASHION!
PUPILS, TOMORROW YOU WILL RECEIVE YOUR REPORT CARDS!
REPORT CARDS! O-O-O-H! I DON'T FEEL SO GOOD!
HIS FATHER'S ANNOUNCEMENT DOESN'T HELP MATTERS!
TOMMY, I'VE DECIDED NOT TO THRASH YOU IF YOU BRING HOME A BAD REPORT CARD AGAIN! INSTEAD, I WILL FORBID YOU TO PLAY AFTER SCHOOL!
GEE!
LATER--- IN HIS ROOM, TOMMY PONDERS OVER A BIG PROBLEM.
GEE WHIZ! I JUST KNOW I'M GONNA GET A BAD REPORT CARD, AND POP SAYS I WON'T BE ABLE TO PLAY WITH THE FELLAS AFTER SCHOOL IF I DO!
I WON'T BE ABLE TO PLAY FOOTBALL, OR HAVE ANY FUN ANYMORE! HUH! I'LL SHOW 'EM! THEY'LL BE SORRY! I'LL RUN AWAY, THAT'S WHAT!
SOME TIME LATER, A SMALL FIGURE LOOKS LONGINGLY AT HIS MOTHER AND FATHER ----
WITH WINTER COMING ON, TOMMY WILL NEED THIS HEAVY SWEATER!
GEE! MAYBE I---NO! I SAID I'M GONNA RUN AWAY, AND I'M (SNIFF) GONNA DO IT, TOO, (SNIFF, SNIFF-)
HIS HEART THUMPING LOUDLY, TOMMY STEPS OUT INTO NIGHT-- BLACK, OMINOUS ---AND TERRIFYING---
WHOO
UH!
FULL OF MISGIVINGS, BUT MANFULLY DETERMINED, TOMMY SETS FEET ON THE ROAD TO ADVENTURE--
LITTLE TOMMY TRENT, YOU'LL REMEMBER THIS NIGHT ALL YOUR LIFE!

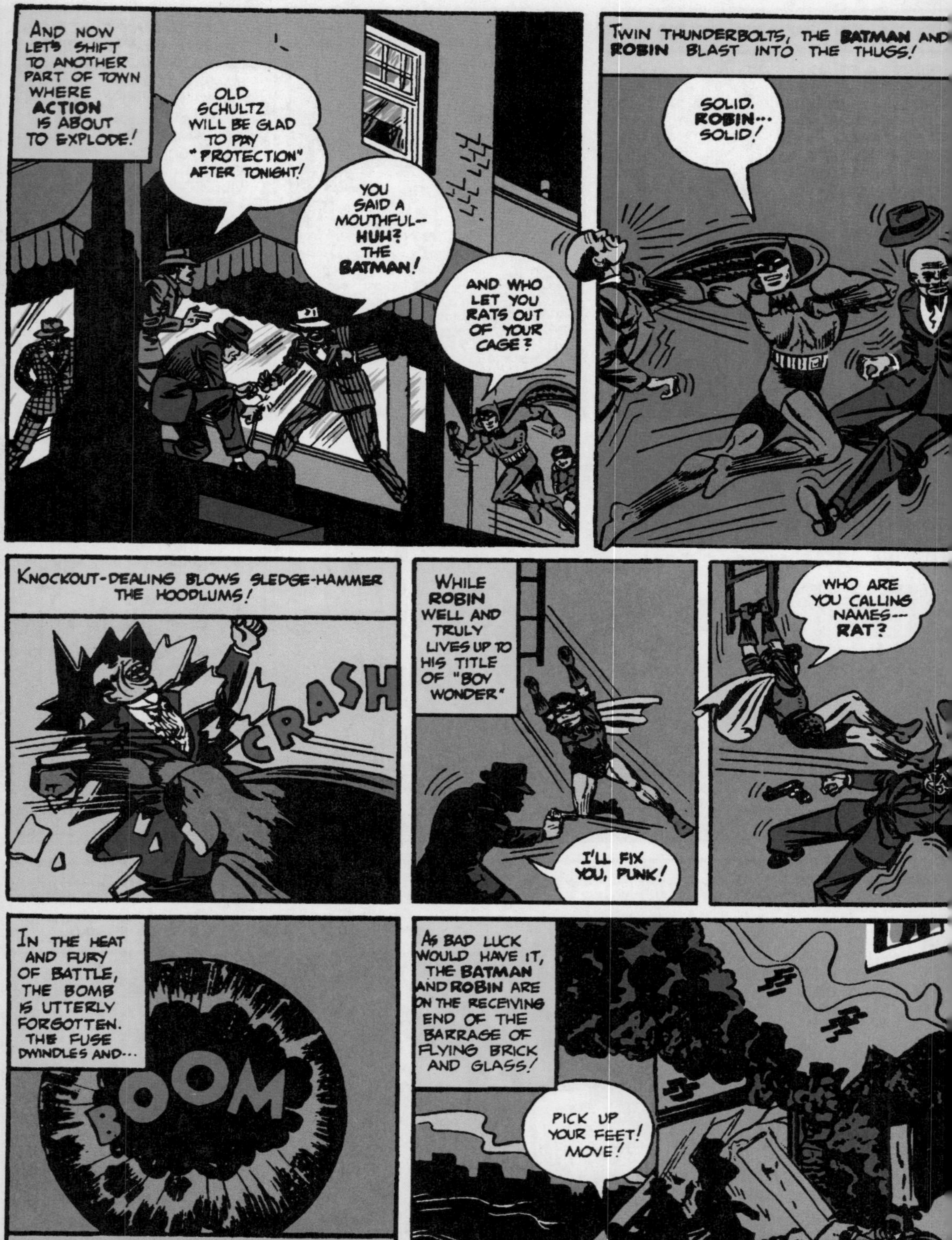
AND NOW LET'S SHIFT TO ANOTHER PART OF TOWN WHERE ACTION IS ABOUT TO EXPLODE!
OLD SCHULTZ WILL BE GLAD TO PAY "PROTECTION" AFTER TONIGHT!
YOU SAID A MOUTHFUL-- HUH? THE BATMAN!
AND WHO LET YOU RATS OUT OF YOUR CAGE?
TWIN THUNDERBOLTS, THE BATMAN AND ROBIN BLAST INTO THE THUGS!
SOLID, ROBIN... SOLID!
KNOCKOUT-DEALING BLOWS SLEDGE-HAMMER THE HOODLUMS!
CRASH
WHILE ROBIN WELL AND TRULY LIVES UP TO HIS TITLE OF "BOY WONDER"
I'LL FIX YOU, PUNK!
WHO ARE YOU CALLING NAMES--- RAT?
IN THE HEAT AND FURY OF BATTLE, THE BOMB IS UTTERLY FORGOTTEN. THE FUSE DWINDLES AND...
BOOM
...A WINDOW-SHATTERING, EAR-DEAFENING EXPLOSION!
3
AS BAD LUCK WOULD HAVE IT, THE BATMAN AND ROBIN ARE ON THE RECEIVING END OF THE BARRAGE OF FLYING BRICK AND GLASS!
PICK UP YOUR FEET! MOVE!

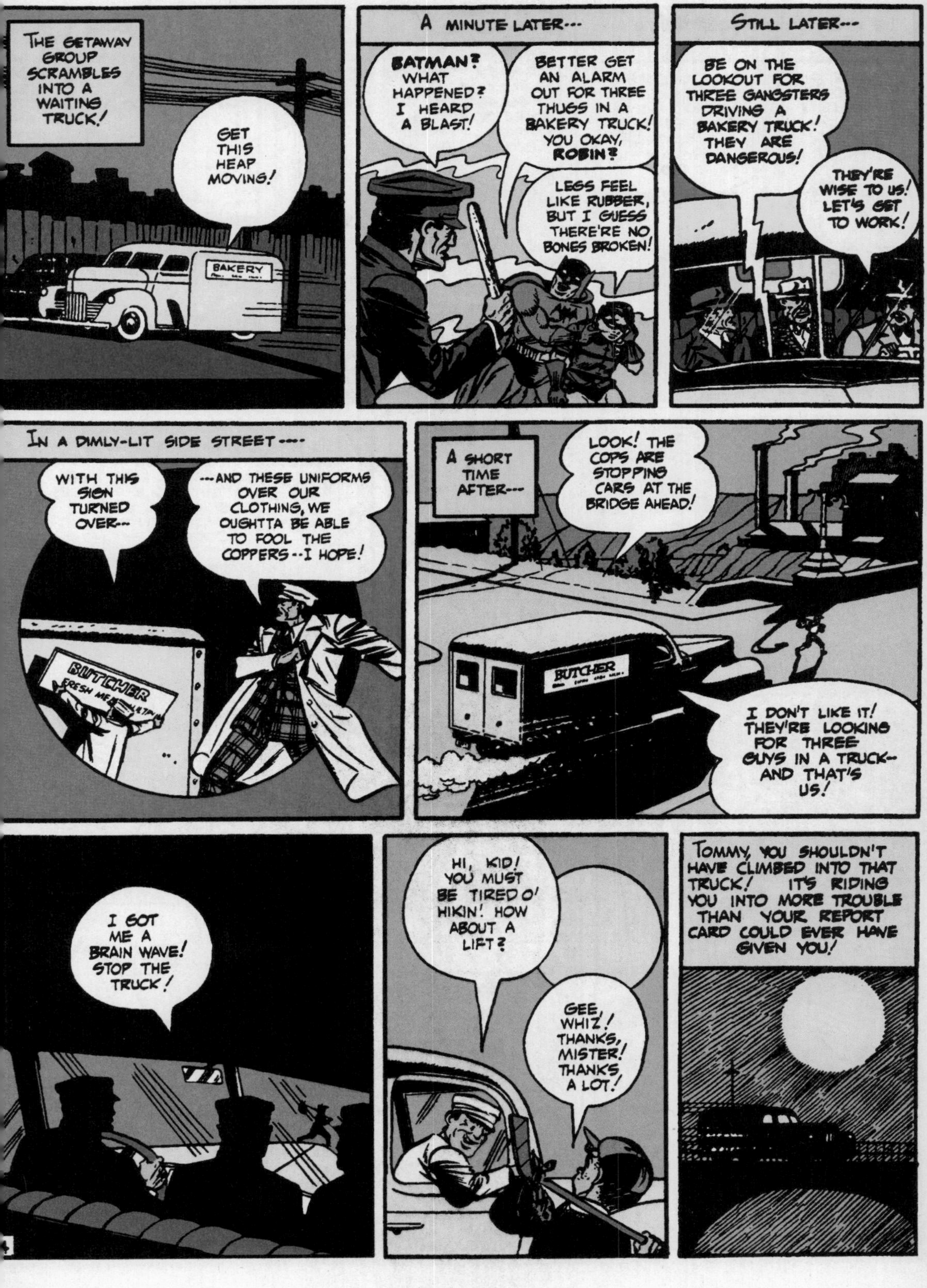
THE GETAWAY GROUP SCRAMBLES INTO A WAITING TRUCK!
GET THIS HEAP MOVING!
BAKERY
A MINUTE LATER---
BATMAN? WHAT HAPPENED? I HEARD A BLAST!
BETTER GET AN ALARM OUT FOR THREE THUGS IN A BAKERY TRUCK! YOU OKAY, ROBIN?
LEGS FEEL LIKE RUBBER, BUT I GUESS THERE'RE NO BONES BROKEN!
STILL LATER---
BE ON THE LOOKOUT FOR THREE GANGSTERS DRIVING A BAKERY TRUCK! THEY ARE DANGEROUS!
THEY'RE WISE TO US! LET'S GET TO WORK!
IN A DIMLY-LIT SIDE STREET----
WITH THIS SIGN TURNED OVER--
---AND THESE UNIFORMS OVER OUR CLOTHING, WE OUGHTTA BE ABLE TO FOOL THE COPPERS--I HOPE!
BUTCHER
A SHORT TIME AFTER---
LOOK! THE COPS ARE STOPPING CARS AT THE BRIDGE AHEAD!
BUTCHER
I DON'T LIKE IT! THEY'RE LOOKING FOR THREE GUYS IN A TRUCK-- AND THAT'S US!
I GOT ME A BRAIN WAVE! STOP THE TRUCK!
HI, KID! YOU MUST BE TIRED O' HIKIN'! HOW ABOUT A LIFT?
GEE, WHIZ! THANKS, MISTER! THANKS A LOT!
TOMMY, YOU SHOULDN'T HAVE CLIMBED INTO THAT TRUCK! IT'S RIDING YOU INTO MORE TROUBLE THAN YOUR REPORT CARD COULD EVER HAVE GIVEN YOU!

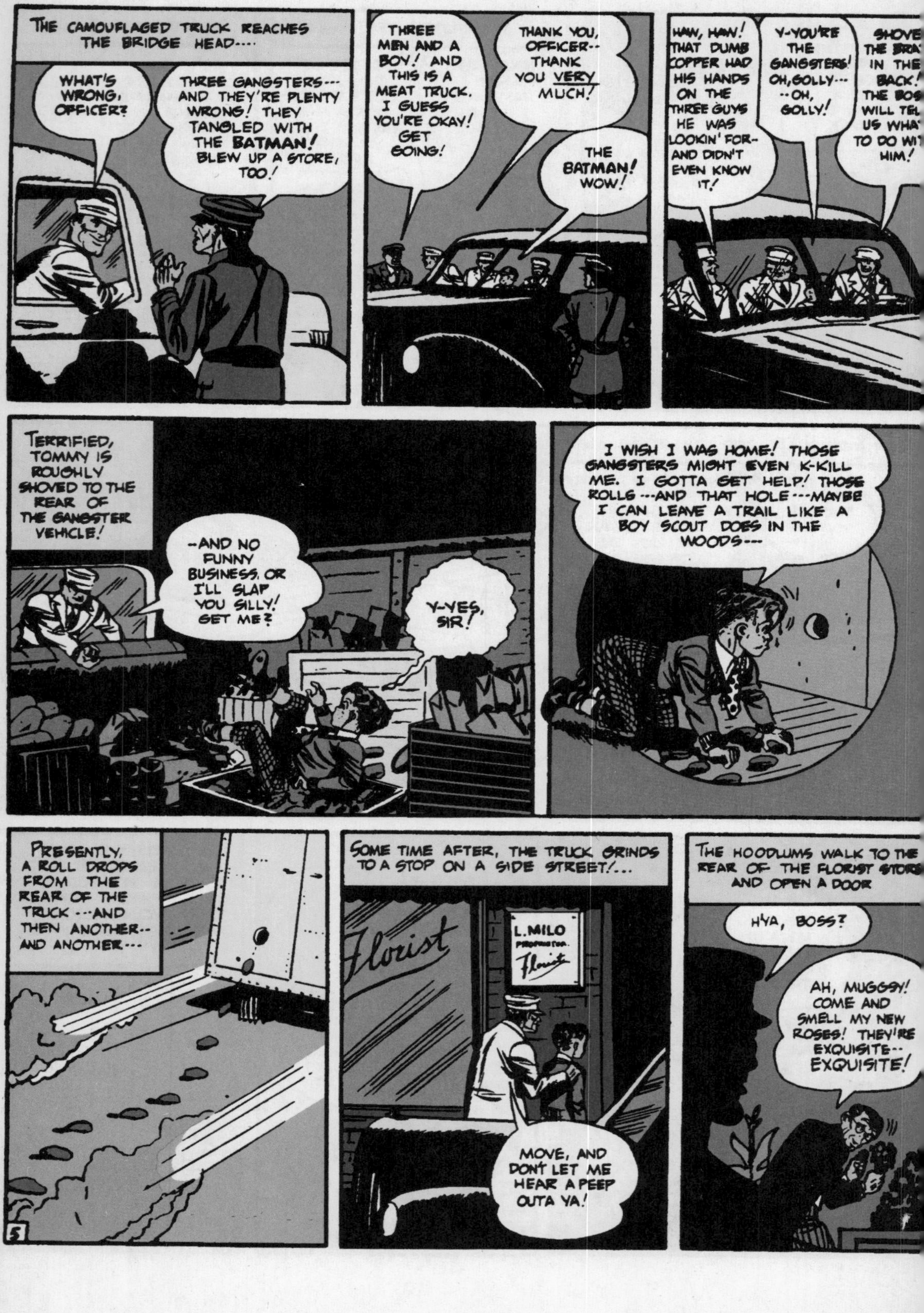
THE CAMOUFLAGED TRUCK REACHES THE BRIDGE HEAD....
WHAT'S WRONG, OFFICER?
THREE GANGSTERS--- AND THEY'RE PLENTY WRONG! THEY TANGLED WITH THE BATMAN! BLEW UP A STORE, TOO!
THREE MEN AND A BOY! AND THIS IS A MEAT TRUCK. I GUESS YOU'RE OKAY! GET GOING!
THANK YOU, OFFICER-- THANK YOU VERY MUCH!
THE BATMAN! WOW!
HAW, HAW! THAT DUMB COPPER HAD HIS HANDS ON THE THREE GUYS HE WAS LOOKIN' FOR-AND DIDN'T EVEN KNOW IT!
Y-YOU'RE THE GANGSTERS! OH, GOLLY--- --OH, GOLLY!
SHOVE THE BRA IN THE BACK! THE BOS WILL TEL US WHA TO DO WI HIM!
TERRIFIED, TOMMY IS ROUGHLY SHOVED TO THE REAR OF THE GANGSTER VEHICLE!
-AND NO FUNNY BUSINESS, OR I'LL SLAP YOU SILLY! GET ME?
Y-YES, SIR!
I WISH I WAS HOME! THOSE GANGSTERS MIGHT EVEN K-KILL ME. I GOTTA GET HELP! THOSE ROLLS ---AND THAT HOLE ---MAYBE I CAN LEAVE A TRAIL LIKE A BOY SCOUT DOES IN THE WOODS---
PRESENTLY, A ROLL DROPS FROM THE REAR OF THE TRUCK ---AND THEN ANOTHER-- AND ANOTHER---
5
SOME TIME AFTER, THE TRUCK GRINDS TO A STOP ON A SIDE STREET!...
Florist
L. MILO
PROPRIETOR
Florist
MOVE, AND DON'T LET ME HEAR A PEEP OUTA YA!
THE HOODLUMS WALK TO THE REAR OF THE FLORIST STOR AND OPEN A DOOR
H'YA, BOSS?
AH, MUGGSY! COME AND SMELL MY NEW ROSES! THEY'RE EXQUISITE-- EXQUISITE!

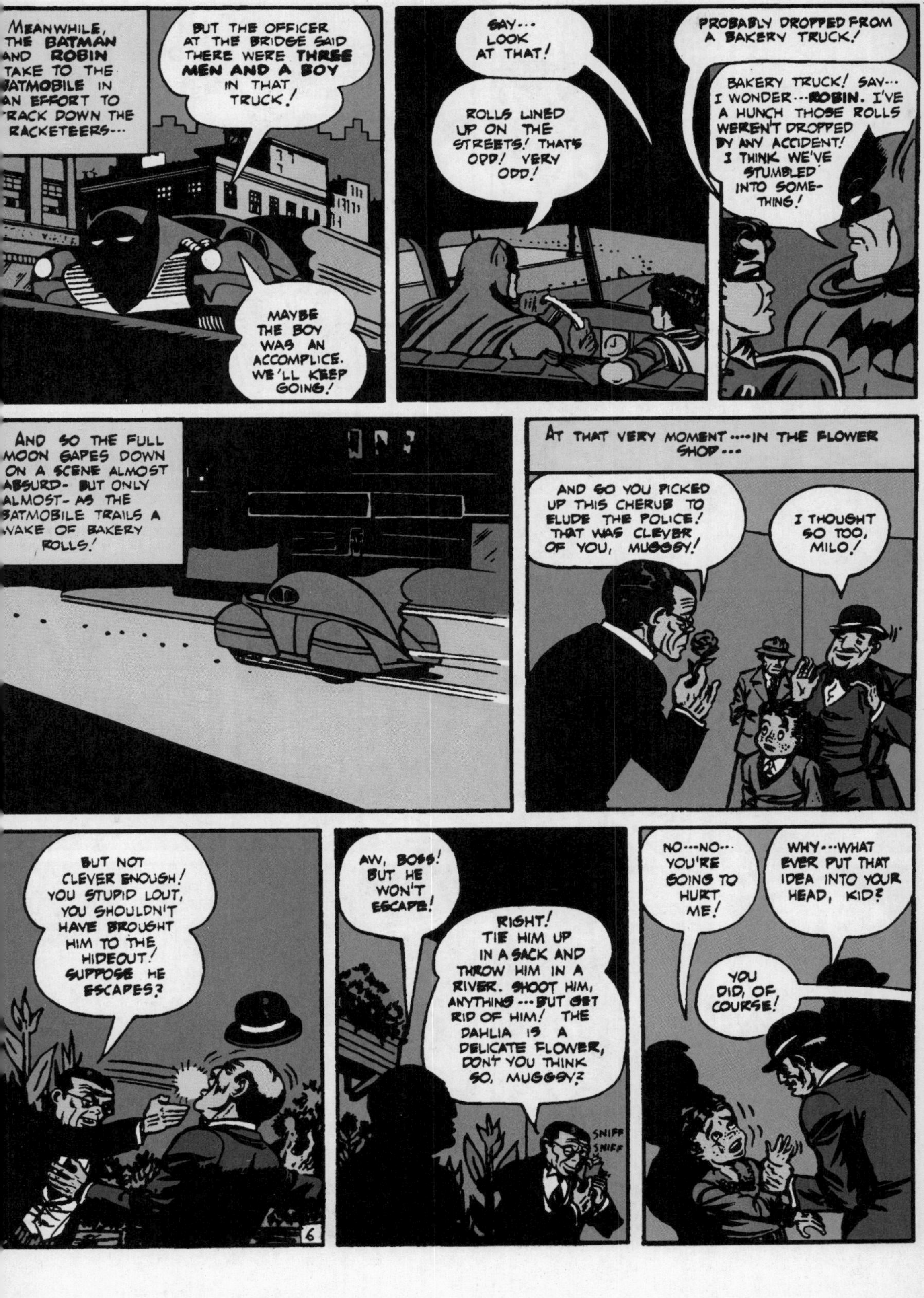
MEANWHILE, THE BATMAN AND ROBIN TAKE TO THE BATMOBILE IN AN EFFORT TO TRACK DOWN THE RACKETEERS...
BUT THE OFFICER AT THE BRIDGE SAID THERE WERE THREE MEN AND A BOY IN THAT TRUCK!
MAYBE THE BOY WAS AN ACCOMPLICE. WE'LL KEEP GOING!
SAY... LOOK AT THAT!
ROLLS LINED UP ON THE STREETS! THAT'S ODD! VERY ODD!
PROBABLY DROPPED FROM A BAKERY TRUCK!
BAKERY TRUCK! SAY... I WONDER... ROBIN. I'VE A HUNCH THOSE ROLLS WEREN'T DROPPED BY ANY ACCIDENT! I THINK WE'VE STUMBLED INTO SOME-THING!
AND SO THE FULL MOON GAPES DOWN ON A SCENE ALMOST ABSURD- BUT ONLY ALMOST- AS THE BATMOBILE TRAILS A WAKE OF BAKERY ROLLS!
AT THAT VERY MOMENT....IN THE FLOWER SHOP...
AND SO YOU PICKED UP THIS CHERUB TO ELUDE THE POLICE! THAT WAS CLEVER OF YOU, MUGGSY!
I THOUGHT SO TOO, MILO!
BUT NOT CLEVER ENOUGH! YOU STUPID LOUT, YOU SHOULDN'T HAVE BROUGHT HIM TO THE HIDEOUT! SUPPOSE HE ESCAPES?
6
AW, BOSS! BUT HE WON'T ESCAPE!
RIGHT! TIE HIM UP IN A SACK AND THROW HIM IN A RIVER. SHOOT HIM, ANYTHING ...BUT GET RID OF HIM! THE DAHLIA IS A DELICATE FLOWER, DON'T YOU THINK SO, MUGGSY?
SNIFF SNIFF
NO---NO--- YOU'RE GOING TO HURT ME!
WHY---WHAT EVER PUT THAT IDEA INTO YOUR HEAD, KID?
YOU DID, OF COURSE!

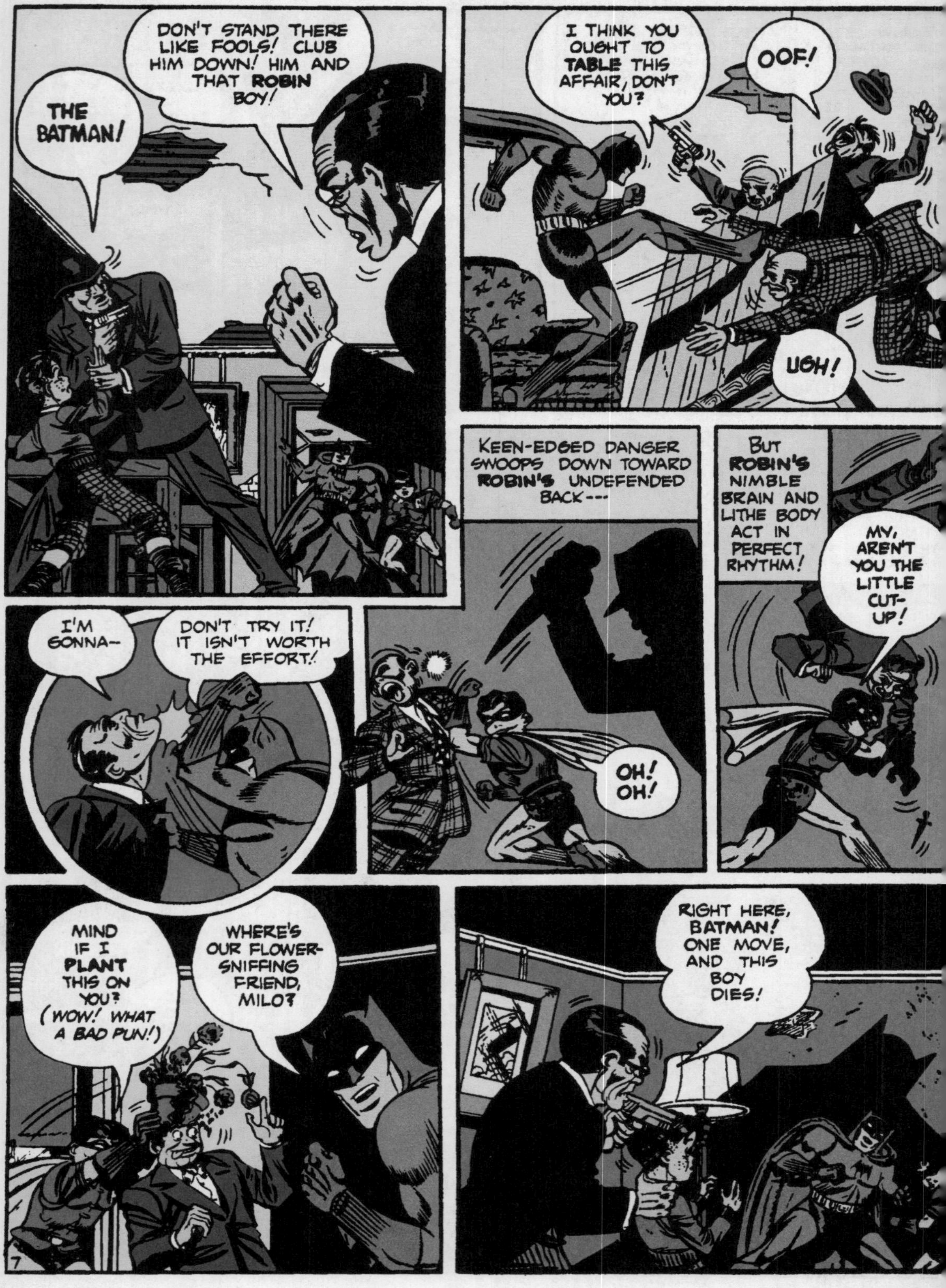
THE BATMAN!
DON'T STAND THERE LIKE FOOLS! CLUB HIM DOWN! HIM AND THAT ROBIN BOY!
I THINK YOU OUGHT TO TABLE THIS AFFAIR, DON'T YOU?
OOF!
UGH!
KEEN-EDGED DANGER SWOOPS DOWN TOWARD ROBIN'S UNDEFENDED BACK---
BUT ROBIN'S NIMBLE BRAIN AND LITHE BODY ACT IN PERFECT RHYTHM!
MY, AREN'T YOU THE LITTLE CUT-UP!
I'M GONNA--
DON'T TRY IT! IT ISN'T WORTH THE EFFORT!
OH! OH!
MIND IF I PLANT THIS ON YOU? (WOW! WHAT A BAD PUN!)
WHERE'S OUR FLOWER-SNIFFING FRIEND, MILO?
7
RIGHT HERE, BATMAN! ONE MOVE, AND THIS BOY DIES!

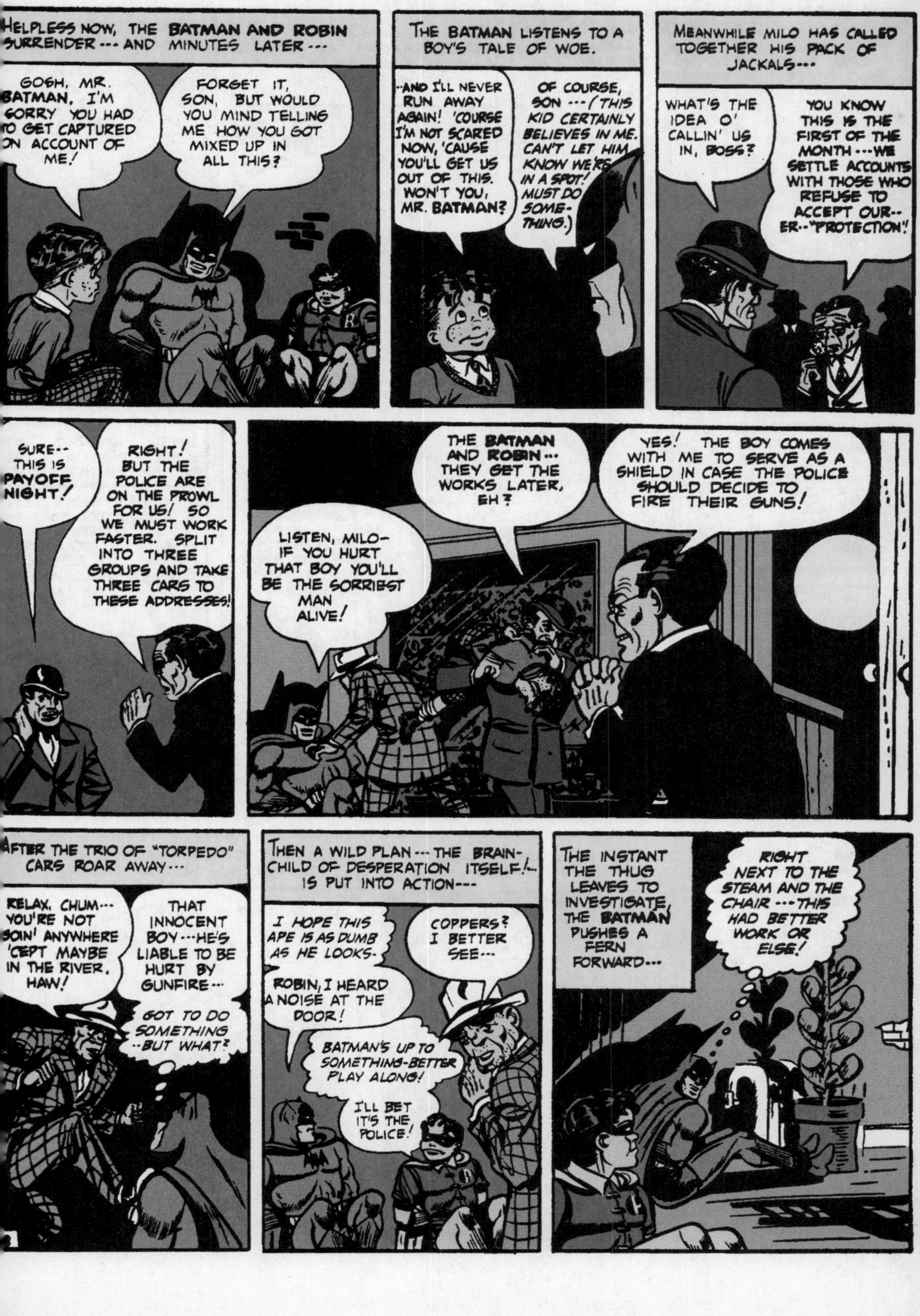
HELPLESS NOW, THE BATMAN AND ROBIN SURRENDER --- AND MINUTES LATER ---
GOSH, MR. BATMAN, I'M SORRY YOU HAD TO GET CAPTURED ON ACCOUNT OF ME!
FORGET IT, SON, BUT WOULD YOU MIND TELLING ME HOW YOU GOT MIXED UP IN ALL THIS?
THE BATMAN LISTENS TO A BOY'S TALE OF WOE.
--AND I'LL NEVER RUN AWAY AGAIN! 'COURSE I'M NOT SCARED NOW, 'CAUSE YOU'LL GET US OUT OF THIS. WON'T YOU, MR. BATMAN?
OF COURSE, SON --- (THIS KID CERTAINLY BELIEVES IN ME. CAN'T LET HIM KNOW WE'RE IN A SPOT! MUST DO SOME-THING.)
MEANWHILE MILO HAS CALLED TOGETHER HIS PACK OF JACKALS---
WHAT'S THE IDEA O' CALLIN' US IN, BOSS?
YOU KNOW THIS IS THE FIRST OF THE MONTH --- WE SETTLE ACCOUNTS WITH THOSE WHO REFUSE TO ACCEPT OUR-- ER--"PROTECTION"!
SURE-- THIS IS PAYOFF NIGHT!
RIGHT! BUT THE POLICE ARE ON THE PROWL FOR US! SO WE MUST WORK FASTER. SPLIT INTO THREE GROUPS AND TAKE THREE CARS TO THESE ADDRESSES!
LISTEN, MILO- IF YOU HURT THAT BOY YOU'LL BE THE SORRIEST MAN ALIVE!
THE BATMAN AND ROBIN... THEY GET THE WORKS LATER, EH?
YES! THE BOY COMES WITH ME TO SERVE AS A SHIELD IN CASE THE POLICE SHOULD DECIDE TO FIRE THEIR GUNS!
AFTER THE TRIO OF "TORPEDO" CARS ROAR AWAY---
RELAX, CHUM--- YOU'RE NOT GOIN' ANYWHERE 'CEPT MAYBE IN THE RIVER. HAW!
THAT INNOCENT BOY---HE'S LIABLE TO BE HURT BY GUNFIRE---
GOT TO DO SOMETHING --BUT WHAT?
THEN A WILD PLAN --- THE BRAIN-CHILD OF DESPERATION ITSELF!-- IS PUT INTO ACTION---
I HOPE THIS APE IS AS DUMB AS HE LOOKS-
COPPERS? I BETTER SEE---
ROBIN, I HEARD A NOISE AT THE DOOR!
BATMAN'S UP TO SOMETHING-BETTER PLAY ALONG!
I'LL BET IT'S THE POLICE!
THE INSTANT THE THUG LEAVES TO INVESTIGATE, THE BATMAN PUSHES A FERN FORWARD---
RIGHT NEXT TO THE STEAM AND THE CHAIR --- THIS HAD BETTER WORK OR ELSE!

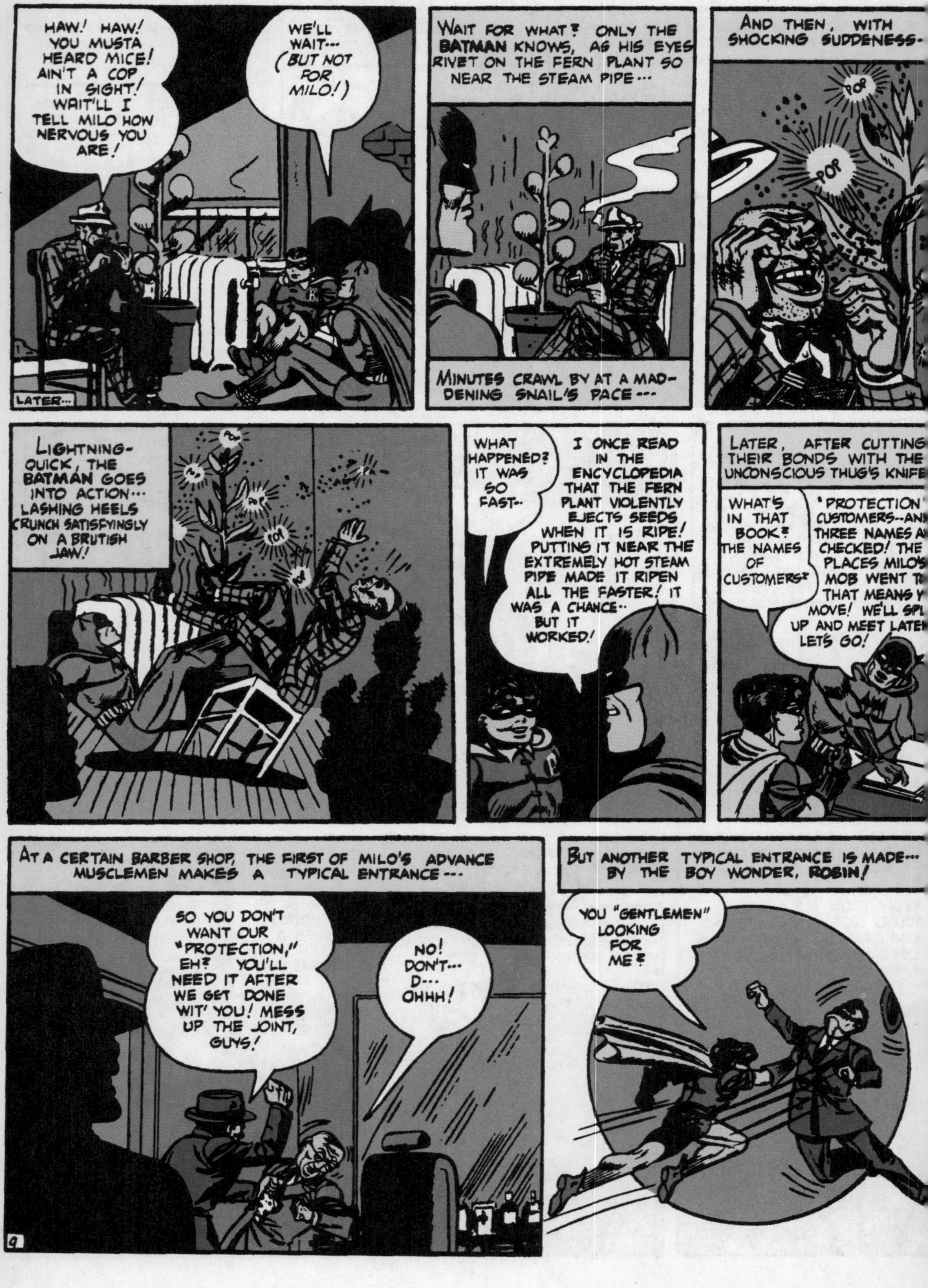
HAW! HAW! YOU MUSTA HEARD MICE! AIN'T A COP IN SIGHT! WAIT'LL I TELL MILO HOW NERVOUS YOU ARE!
WE'LL WAIT--- (BUT NOT FOR MILO!)
LATER---
WAIT FOR WHAT? ONLY THE BATMAN KNOWS, AS HIS EYES RIVET ON THE FERN PLANT SO NEAR THE STEAM PIPE---
MINUTES CRAWL BY AT A MADDENING SNAIL'S PACE---
AND THEN, WITH SHOCKING SUDDENESS-
POP
POP
LIGHTNING-QUICK, THE BATMAN GOES INTO ACTION--- LASHING HEELS CRUNCH SATISFYINGLY ON A BRUTISH JAW!
WHAT HAPPENED? IT WAS SO FAST--
I ONCE READ IN THE ENCYCLOPEDIA THAT THE FERN PLANT VIOLENTLY EJECTS SEEDS WHEN IT IS RIPE! PUTTING IT NEAR THE EXTREMELY HOT STEAM PIPE MADE IT RIPEN ALL THE FASTER! IT WAS A CHANCE-- BUT IT WORKED!
LATER, AFTER CUTTING THEIR BONDS WITH THE UNCONSCIOUS THUG'S KNIFE
WHAT'S IN THAT BOOK? THE NAMES OF CUSTOMERS?
'PROTECTION' CUSTOMERS--AN THREE NAMES A CHECKED! THE PLACES MILO'S MOB WENT T THAT MEANS Y MOVE! WE'LL SPL UP AND MEET LATE LET'S GO!
AT A CERTAIN BARBER SHOP, THE FIRST OF MILO'S ADVANCE MUSCLEMEN MAKES A TYPICAL ENTRANCE---
SO YOU DON'T WANT OUR "PROTECTION," EH? YOU'LL NEED IT AFTER WE GET DONE WIT' YOU! MESS UP THE JOINT, GUYS!
NO! DON'T--- D--- OHHH!
9
BUT ANOTHER TYPICAL ENTRANCE IS MADE--- BY THE BOY WONDER, ROBIN!
YOU "GENTLEMEN" LOOKING FOR ME?

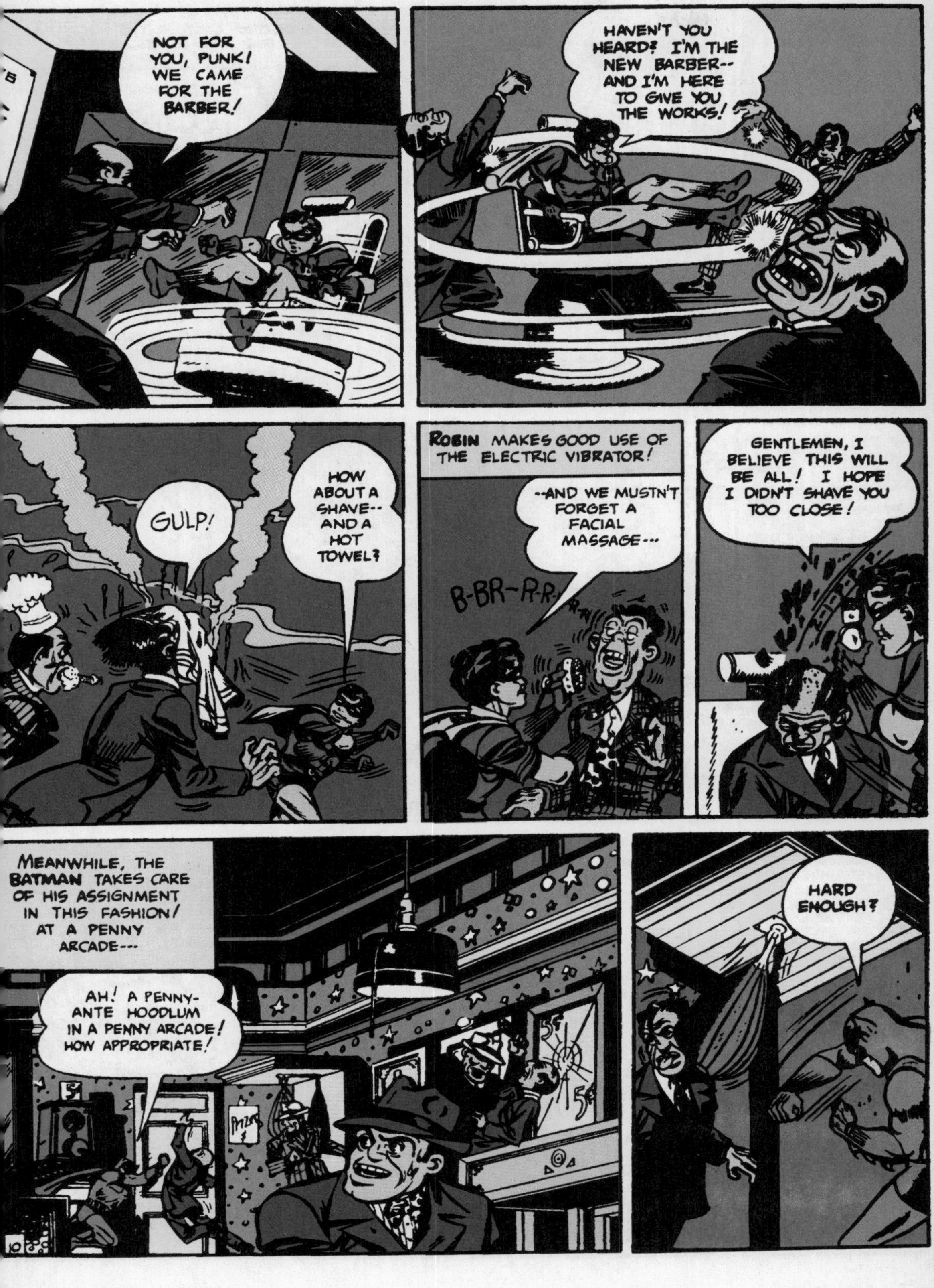
NOT FOR YOU, PUNK! WE CAME FOR THE BARBER!
HAVEN'T YOU HEARD? I'M THE NEW BARBER-- AND I'M HERE TO GIVE YOU THE WORKS!
GULP!
HOW ABOUT A SHAVE-- AND A HOT TOWEL?
ROBIN MAKES GOOD USE OF THE ELECTRIC VIBRATOR!
--AND WE MUSTN'T FORGET A FACIAL MASSAGE---
B-BR-R-R
GENTLEMEN, I BELIEVE THIS WILL BE ALL! I HOPE I DIDN'T SHAVE YOU TOO CLOSE!
MEANWHILE, THE BATMAN TAKES CARE OF HIS ASSIGNMENT IN THIS FASHION! AT A PENNY ARCADE---
AH! A PENNY-ANTE HOODLUM IN A PENNY ARCADE! HOW APPROPRIATE!
HARD ENOUGH?

NOW I'D LIKE TO TEST MY MARKSMANSHIP! YOU CAN HELP!

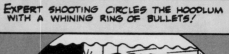

EXPERT SHOOTING CIRCLES THE HOODLUM WITH A WHINING RING OF BULLETS!

BANG BONG CRA

SENSES KEENLY TUNED TO DANGER, THE BATMAN PIVOTS QUICKLY AND SURPRISES A COWARDLY ATTACKER!

SO SORRY, BUT I'M ALLERGIC TO BEING SHOT IN THE BACK!

C-R-A-C-K

PLUNK

YOU'RE TELLING ME?

☆YOUR FORTUNE☆ A TALL DARK MAN WILL ENTER YOUR LIFE AND CAUSE YOU MUCH TROUBLE

BUT TROUBLE LOOMS AHEAD FOR THE BATMAN— AT THE THIRD "PAYOFF" STOP-- A DEPARTMENT STORE---

THE BATMAN— GOT LOOSE—MOPPED US UP AT THE ARCADE ---

SO---THAT MEANS HE KNOWS OUR PLANS---AND WILL COME HERE NEXT! WELL, HE'LL WALK RIGHT INTO A TRAP!

GOLLY--- THEY CAN'T KILL THE BATMAN... I'LL CALL A POLICEMAN--- I'LL WARN HIM--- I'LL—

TRY TO SNEAK OUT, WILL YOU? STAY THERE-- AND BE QUIET!

SLAP! OW!

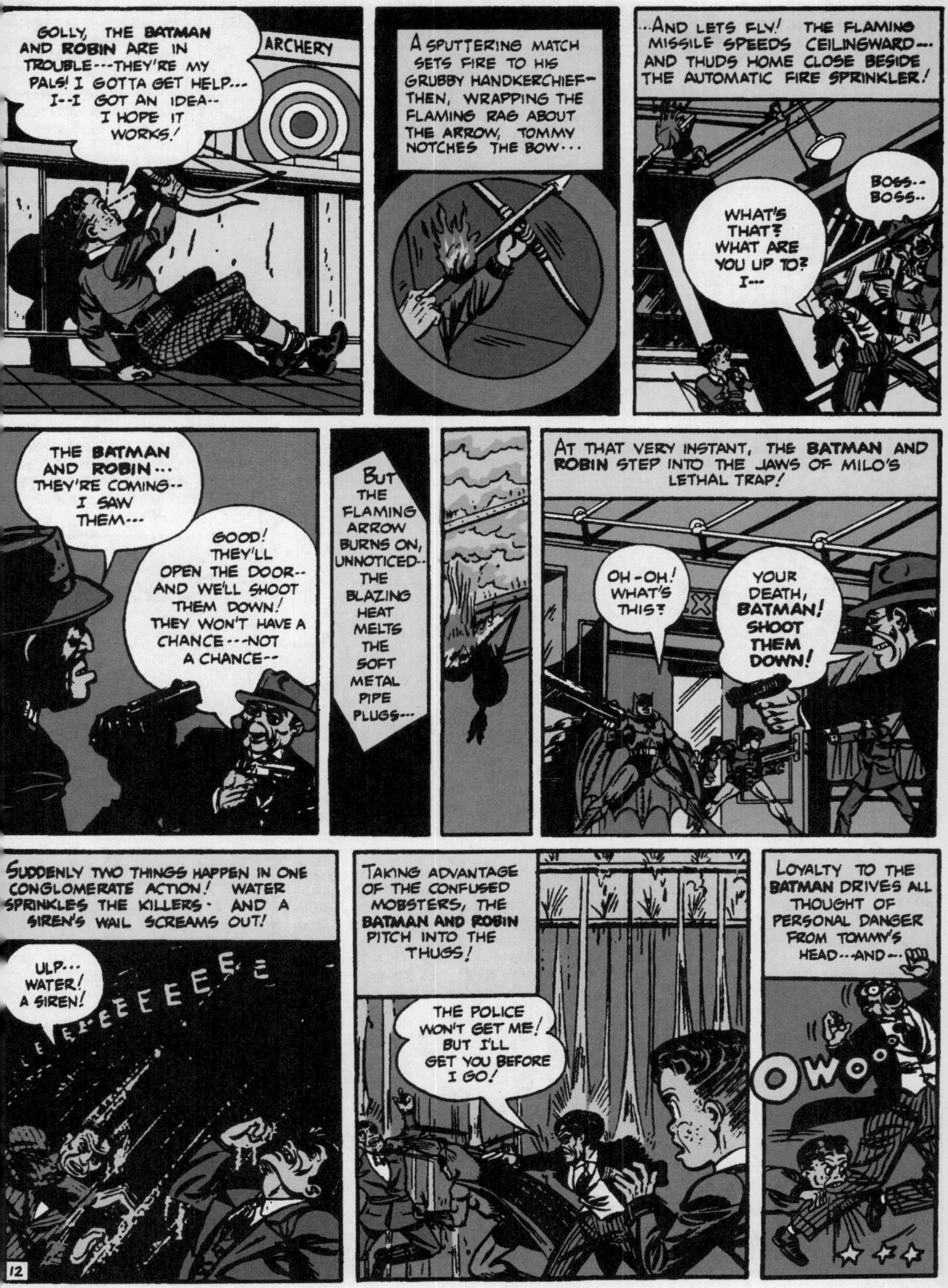
GOLLY, THE BATMAN AND ROBIN ARE IN TROUBLE---THEY'RE MY PALS! I GOTTA GET HELP--- I--I GOT AN IDEA-- I HOPE IT WORKS!
ARCHERY
A SPUTTERING MATCH SETS FIRE TO HIS GRUBBY HANDKERCHIEF-- THEN, WRAPPING THE FLAMING RAG ABOUT THE ARROW, TOMMY NOTCHES THE BOW...
...AND LETS FLY! THE FLAMING MISSILE SPEEDS CEILINGWARD--- AND THUDS HOME CLOSE BESIDE THE AUTOMATIC FIRE SPRINKLER!
WHAT'S THAT? WHAT ARE YOU UP TO? I---
BOSS-- BOSS--
THE BATMAN AND ROBIN... THEY'RE COMING-- I SAW THEM---
GOOD! THEY'LL OPEN THE DOOR-- AND WE'LL SHOOT THEM DOWN! THEY WON'T HAVE A CHANCE---NOT A CHANCE--
BUT THE FLAMING ARROW BURNS ON, UNNOTICED-- THE BLAZING HEAT MELTS THE SOFT METAL PIPE PLUGS---
AT THAT VERY INSTANT, THE BATMAN AND ROBIN STEP INTO THE JAWS OF MILO'S LETHAL TRAP!
OH-OH! WHAT'S THIS?
YOUR DEATH, BATMAN! SHOOT THEM DOWN!
SUDDENLY TWO THINGS HAPPEN IN ONE CONGLOMERATE ACTION! WATER SPRINKLES THE KILLERS - AND A SIREN'S WAIL SCREAMS OUT!
ULP... WATER! A SIREN!
EEEEEEEEEEE
12
TAKING ADVANTAGE OF THE CONFUSED MOBSTERS, THE BATMAN AND ROBIN PITCH INTO THE THUGS!
THE POLICE WON'T GET ME! BUT I'LL GET YOU BEFORE I GO!
LOYALTY TO THE BATMAN DRIVES ALL THOUGHT OF PERSONAL DANGER FROM TOMMY'S HEAD---AND---
OWOO

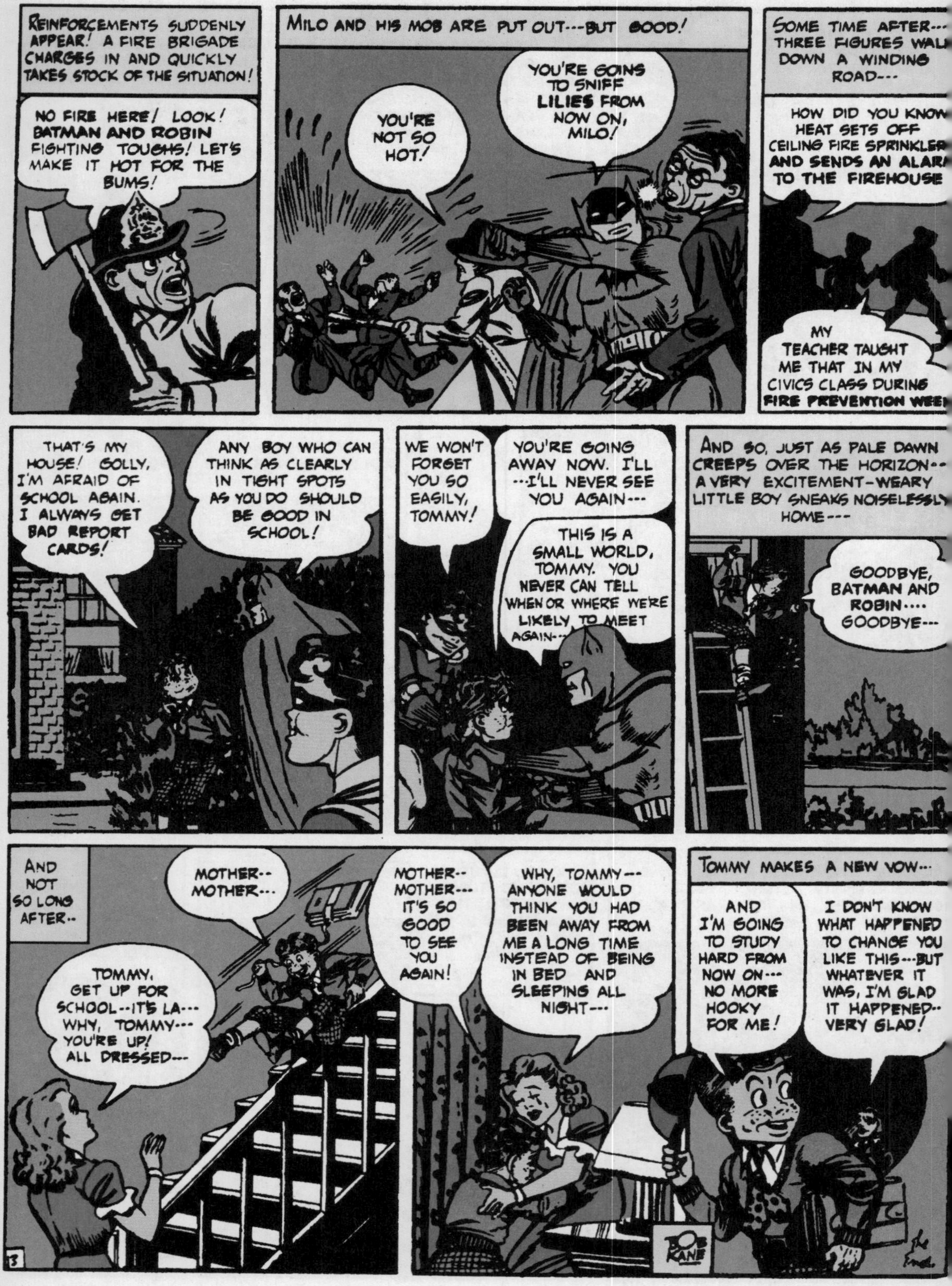
REINFORCEMENTS SUDDENLY APPEAR! A FIRE BRIGADE CHARGES IN AND QUICKLY TAKES STOCK OF THE SITUATION!
NO FIRE HERE! LOOK! BATMAN AND ROBIN FIGHTING TOUGHS! LET'S MAKE IT HOT FOR THE BUMS!
MILO AND HIS MOB ARE PUT OUT---BUT GOOD!
YOU'RE NOT SO HOT!
YOU'RE GOING TO SNIFF LILIES FROM NOW ON, MILO!
SOME TIME AFTER--- THREE FIGURES WAL DOWN A WINDING ROAD---
HOW DID YOU KNOW HEAT SETS OFF CEILING FIRE SPRINKLER AND SENDS AN ALAR TO THE FIREHOUSE
MY TEACHER TAUGHT ME THAT IN MY CIVICS CLASS DURING FIRE PREVENTION WEE
THAT'S MY HOUSE! GOLLY, I'M AFRAID OF SCHOOL AGAIN. I ALWAYS GET BAD REPORT CARDS!
ANY BOY WHO CAN THINK AS CLEARLY IN TIGHT SPOTS AS YOU DO SHOULD BE GOOD IN SCHOOL!
WE WON'T FORGET YOU SO EASILY, TOMMY!
YOU'RE GOING AWAY NOW. I'LL ---I'LL NEVER SEE YOU AGAIN---
THIS IS A SMALL WORLD, TOMMY. YOU NEVER CAN TELL WHEN OR WHERE WE'RE LIKELY TO MEET AGAIN---
AND SO, JUST AS PALE DAWN CREEPS OVER THE HORIZON-- A VERY EXCITEMENT-WEARY LITTLE BOY SNEAKS NOISELESSLY HOME---
GOODBYE, BATMAN AND ROBIN.... GOODBYE---
AND NOT SO LONG AFTER--
MOTHER-- MOTHER---
TOMMY, GET UP FOR SCHOOL--IT'S LA--- WHY, TOMMY--- YOU'RE UP! ALL DRESSED---
MOTHER-- MOTHER--- IT'S SO GOOD TO SEE YOU AGAIN!
WHY, TOMMY--- ANYONE WOULD THINK YOU HAD BEEN AWAY FROM ME A LONG TIME INSTEAD OF BEING IN BED AND SLEEPING ALL NIGHT---
TOMMY MAKES A NEW VOW---
AND I'M GOING TO STUDY HARD FROM NOW ON--- NO MORE HOOKY FOR ME!
I DON'T KNOW WHAT HAPPENED TO CHANGE YOU LIKE THIS---BUT WHATEVER IT WAS, I'M GLAD IT HAPPENED-- VERY GLAD!
13
BOB KANE
The End.

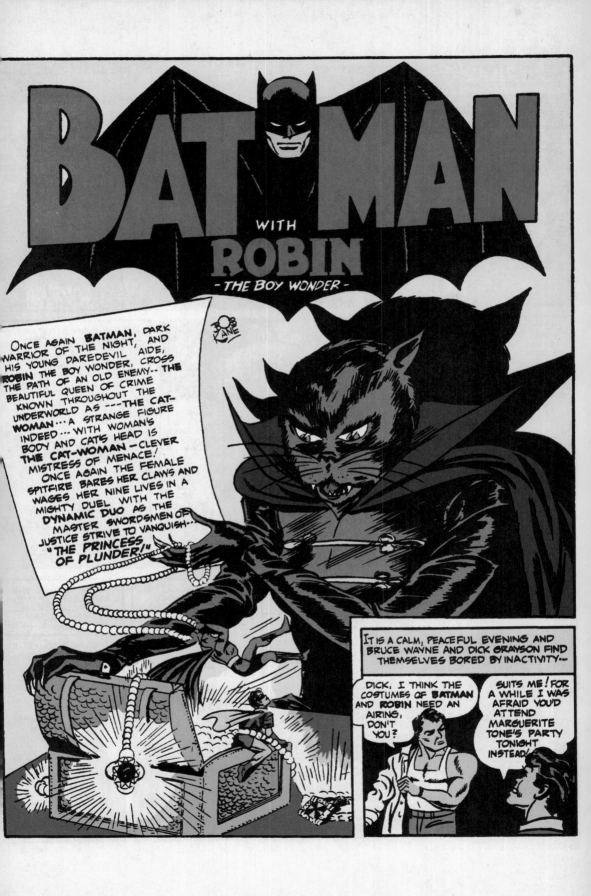

BAT MAN

WITH ROBIN
-THE BOY WONDER-

ONCE AGAIN **BATMAN**, DARK WARRIOR OF THE NIGHT, AND HIS YOUNG DAREDEVIL AIDE, **ROBIN** THE BOY WONDER, CROSS THE PATH OF AN OLD ENEMY-- THE BEAUTIFUL QUEEN OF CRIME KNOWN THROUGHOUT THE UNDERWORLD AS ---**THE CAT-WOMAN**...A STRANGE FIGURE INDEED...WITH WOMAN'S BODY AND CAT'S HEAD IS **THE CAT-WOMAN**--CLEVER MISTRESS OF MENACE!

ONCE AGAIN THE FEMALE SPITFIRE BARES HER CLAWS AND WAGES HER NINE LIVES IN A MIGHTY DUEL WITH THE DYNAMIC DUO AS THE MASTER SWORDSMEN OF JUSTICE STRIVE TO VANQUISH-- *"THE PRINCESS OF PLUNDER!"*

IT IS A CALM, PEACEFUL EVENING AND BRUCE WAYNE AND DICK GRAYSON FIND THEMSELVES BORED BY INACTIVITY--

DICK, I THINK THE COSTUMES OF **BATMAN** AND **ROBIN** NEED AN AIRING, DON'T YOU?

SUITS ME! FOR A WHILE I WAS AFRAID YOU'D ATTEND MARGUERITE TONE'S PARTY TONIGHT INSTEAD!

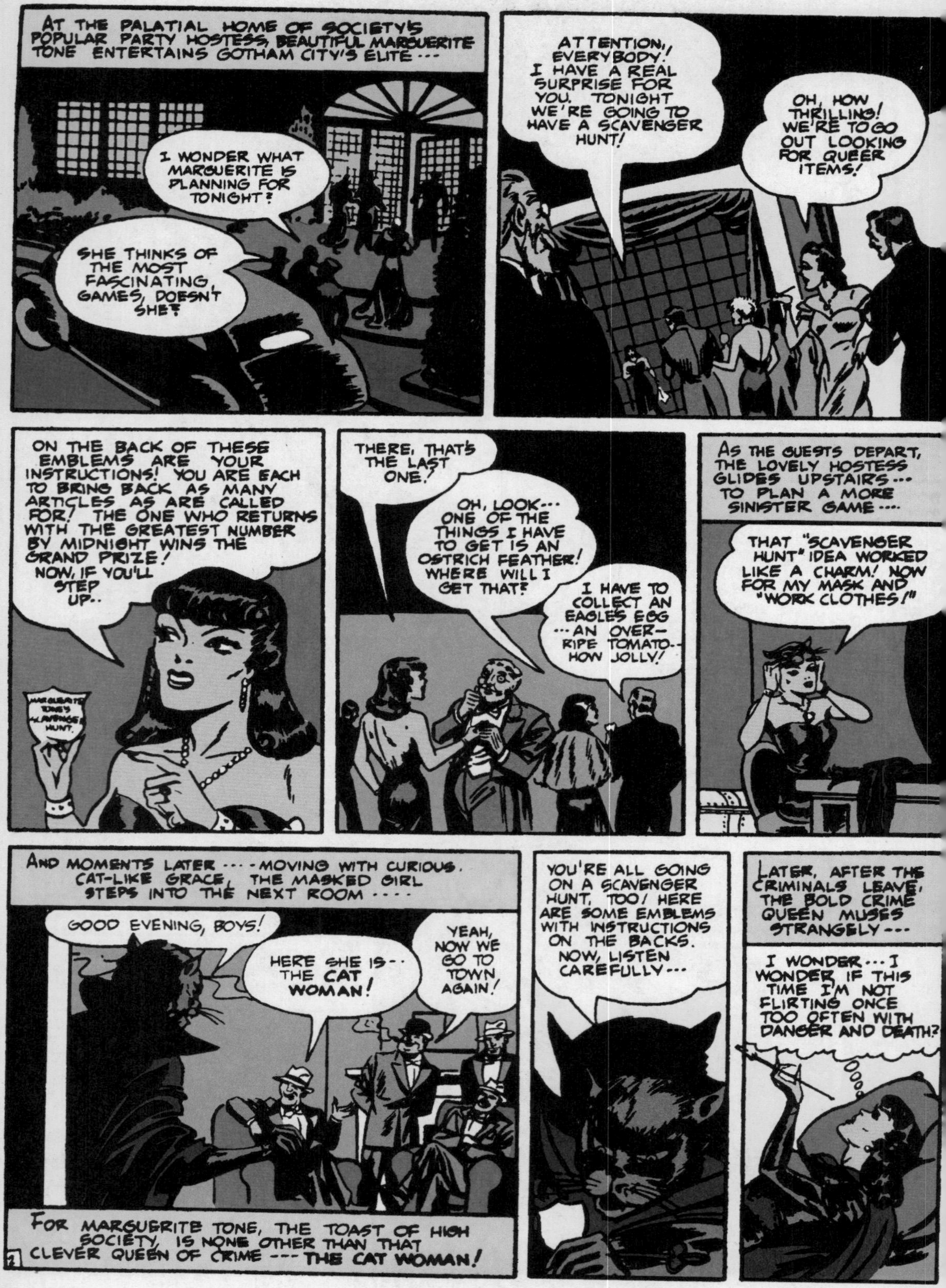
AT THE PALATIAL HOME OF SOCIETY'S POPULAR PARTY HOSTESS, BEAUTIFUL MARGUERITE TONE ENTERTAINS GOTHAM CITY'S ELITE ---
I WONDER WHAT MARGUERITE IS PLANNING FOR TONIGHT?
SHE THINKS OF THE MOST FASCINATING GAMES, DOESN'T SHE?
ATTENTION, EVERYBODY! I HAVE A REAL SURPRISE FOR YOU. TONIGHT WE'RE GOING TO HAVE A SCAVENGER HUNT!
OH, HOW THRILLING! WE'RE TO GO OUT LOOKING FOR QUEER ITEMS!
ON THE BACK OF THESE EMBLEMS ARE YOUR INSTRUCTIONS! YOU ARE EACH TO BRING BACK AS MANY ARTICLES AS ARE CALLED FOR! THE ONE WHO RETURNS WITH THE GREATEST NUMBER BY MIDNIGHT WINS THE GRAND PRIZE! NOW, IF YOU'LL STEP UP..
MARGUERITE TONE'S SCAVENGER HUNT
THERE, THAT'S THE LAST ONE.
OH, LOOK--- ONE OF THE THINGS I HAVE TO GET IS AN OSTRICH FEATHER! WHERE WILL I GET THAT?
I HAVE TO COLLECT AN EAGLE'S EGG ---AN OVER-RIPE TOMATO-- HOW JOLLY!
AS THE GUESTS DEPART, THE LOVELY HOSTESS GLIDES UPSTAIRS--- TO PLAN A MORE SINISTER GAME ----
THAT "SCAVENGER HUNT" IDEA WORKED LIKE A CHARM! NOW FOR MY MASK AND "WORK CLOTHES!"
AND MOMENTS LATER ----MOVING WITH CURIOUS CAT-LIKE GRACE, THE MASKED GIRL STEPS INTO THE NEXT ROOM ----
GOOD EVENING, BOYS!
HERE SHE IS-- THE CAT WOMAN!
YEAH, NOW WE GO TO TOWN AGAIN!
FOR MARGUERITE TONE, THE TOAST OF HIGH SOCIETY, IS NONE OTHER THAN THAT CLEVER QUEEN OF CRIME --- THE CAT WOMAN!
YOU'RE ALL GOING ON A SCAVENGER HUNT, TOO! HERE ARE SOME EMBLEMS WITH INSTRUCTIONS ON THE BACKS. NOW, LISTEN CAREFULLY---
LATER, AFTER THE CRIMINALS LEAVE, THE BOLD CRIME QUEEN MUSES STRANGELY ---
I WONDER--- I WONDER IF THIS TIME I'M NOT FLIRTING ONCE TOO OFTEN WITH DANGER AND DEATH?

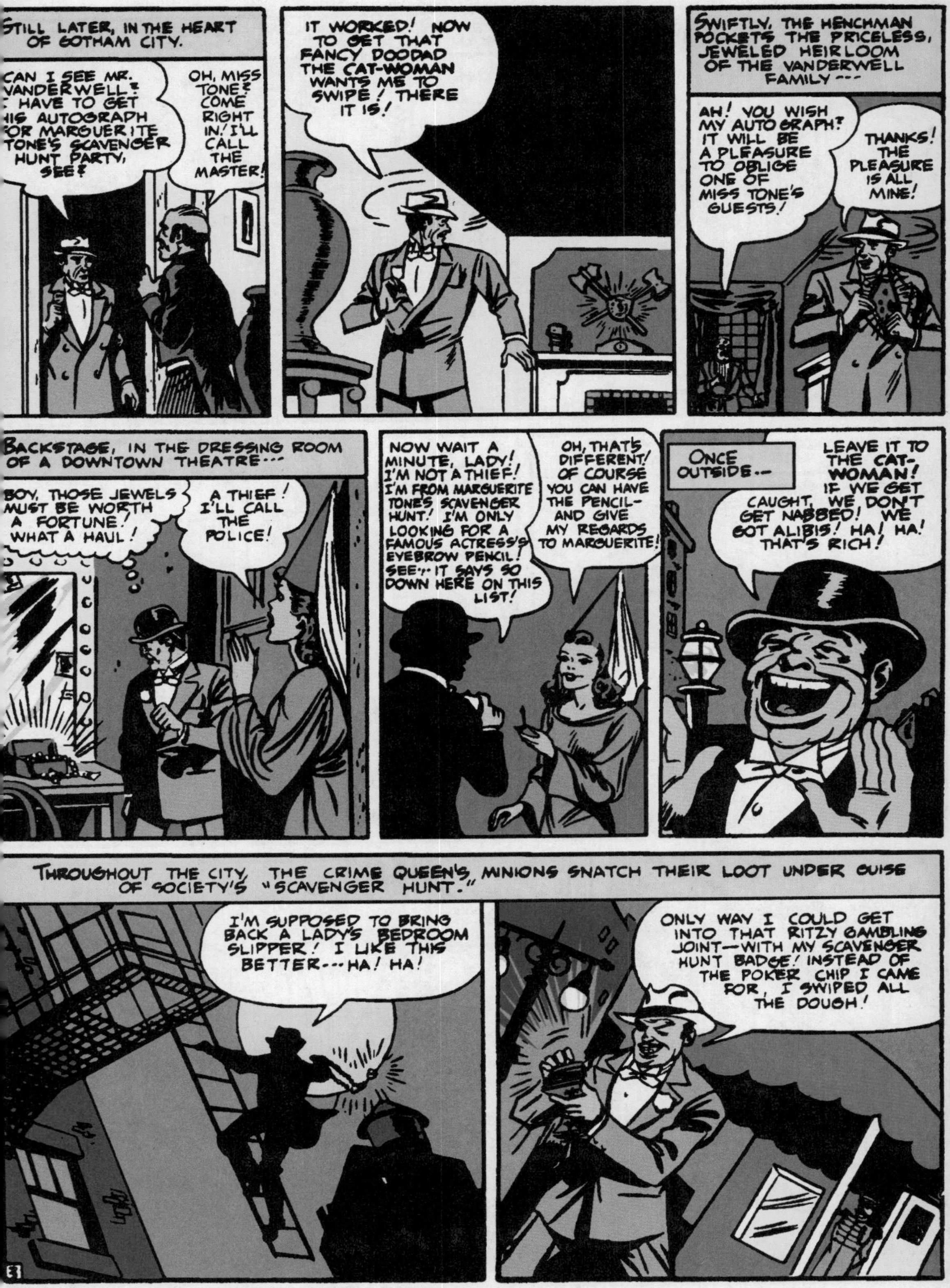
STILL LATER, IN THE HEART OF GOTHAM CITY.
CAN I SEE MR. VANDERWELL? I HAVE TO GET HIS AUTOGRAPH FOR MARGUERITE TONE'S SCAVENGER HUNT PARTY, SEE?
OH, MISS TONE? COME RIGHT IN! I'LL CALL THE MASTER!
IT WORKED! NOW TO GET THAT FANCY DOODAD THE CAT-WOMAN WANTS ME TO SWIPE! THERE IT IS!
SWIFTLY, THE HENCHMAN POCKETS THE PRICELESS, JEWELED HEIRLOOM OF THE VANDERWELL FAMILY---
AH! YOU WISH MY AUTOGRAPH? IT WILL BE A PLEASURE TO OBLIGE ONE OF MISS TONE'S GUESTS!
THANKS! THE PLEASURE IS ALL MINE!
BACKSTAGE, IN THE DRESSING ROOM OF A DOWNTOWN THEATRE---
BOY, THOSE JEWELS MUST BE WORTH A FORTUNE! WHAT A HAUL!
A THIEF! I'LL CALL THE POLICE!
NOW WAIT A MINUTE, LADY! I'M NOT A THIEF! I'M FROM MARGUERITE TONE'S SCAVENGER HUNT! I'M ONLY LOOKING FOR A FAMOUS ACTRESS'S EYEBROW PENCIL! SEE-- IT SAYS SO DOWN HERE ON THIS LIST!
OH, THAT'S DIFFERENT! OF COURSE YOU CAN HAVE THE PENCIL-- AND GIVE MY REGARDS TO MARGUERITE!
ONCE OUTSIDE--
LEAVE IT TO THE CAT-WOMAN! IF WE GET CAUGHT, WE DON'T GET NABBED! WE GOT ALIBIS! HA! HA! THAT'S RICH!
THROUGHOUT THE CITY, THE CRIME QUEEN'S MINIONS SNATCH THEIR LOOT UNDER GUISE OF SOCIETY'S "SCAVENGER HUNT."
I'M SUPPOSED TO BRING BACK A LADY'S BEDROOM SLIPPER! I LIKE THIS BETTER---HA! HA!
ONLY WAY I COULD GET INTO THAT RITZY GAMBLING JOINT—WITH MY SCAVENGER HUNT BADGE! INSTEAD OF THE POKER CHIP I CAME FOR, I SWIPED ALL THE DOUGH!

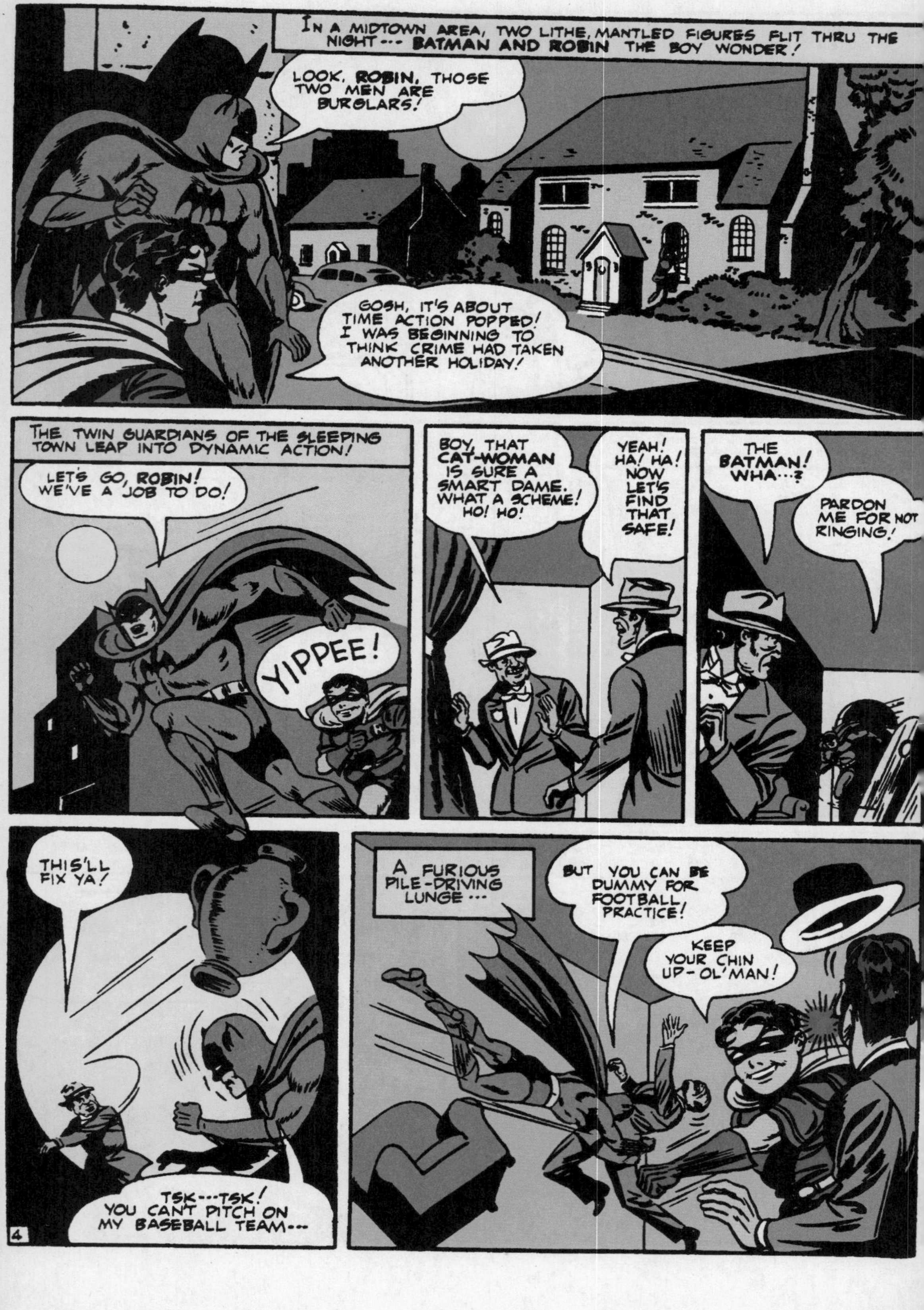
IN A MIDTOWN AREA, TWO LITHE, MANTLED FIGURES FLIT THRU THE NIGHT--- BATMAN AND ROBIN THE BOY WONDER!
LOOK, ROBIN, THOSE TWO MEN ARE BURGLARS!
GOSH, IT'S ABOUT TIME ACTION POPPED! I WAS BEGINNING TO THINK CRIME HAD TAKEN ANOTHER HOLIDAY!
THE TWIN GUARDIANS OF THE SLEEPING TOWN LEAP INTO DYNAMIC ACTION!
LET'S GO, ROBIN! WE'VE A JOB TO DO!
YIPPEE!
BOY, THAT CAT-WOMAN IS SURE A SMART DAME. WHAT A SCHEME! HO! HO!
YEAH! HA! HA! NOW LET'S FIND THAT SAFE!
THE BATMAN! WHA...?
PARDON ME FOR NOT RINGING!
THIS'LL FIX YA!
TSK---TSK! YOU CAN'T PITCH ON MY BASEBALL TEAM---
4
A FURIOUS PILE-DRIVING LUNGE ---
BUT YOU CAN BE DUMMY FOR FOOTBALL PRACTICE!
KEEP YOUR CHIN UP-OL'MAN!

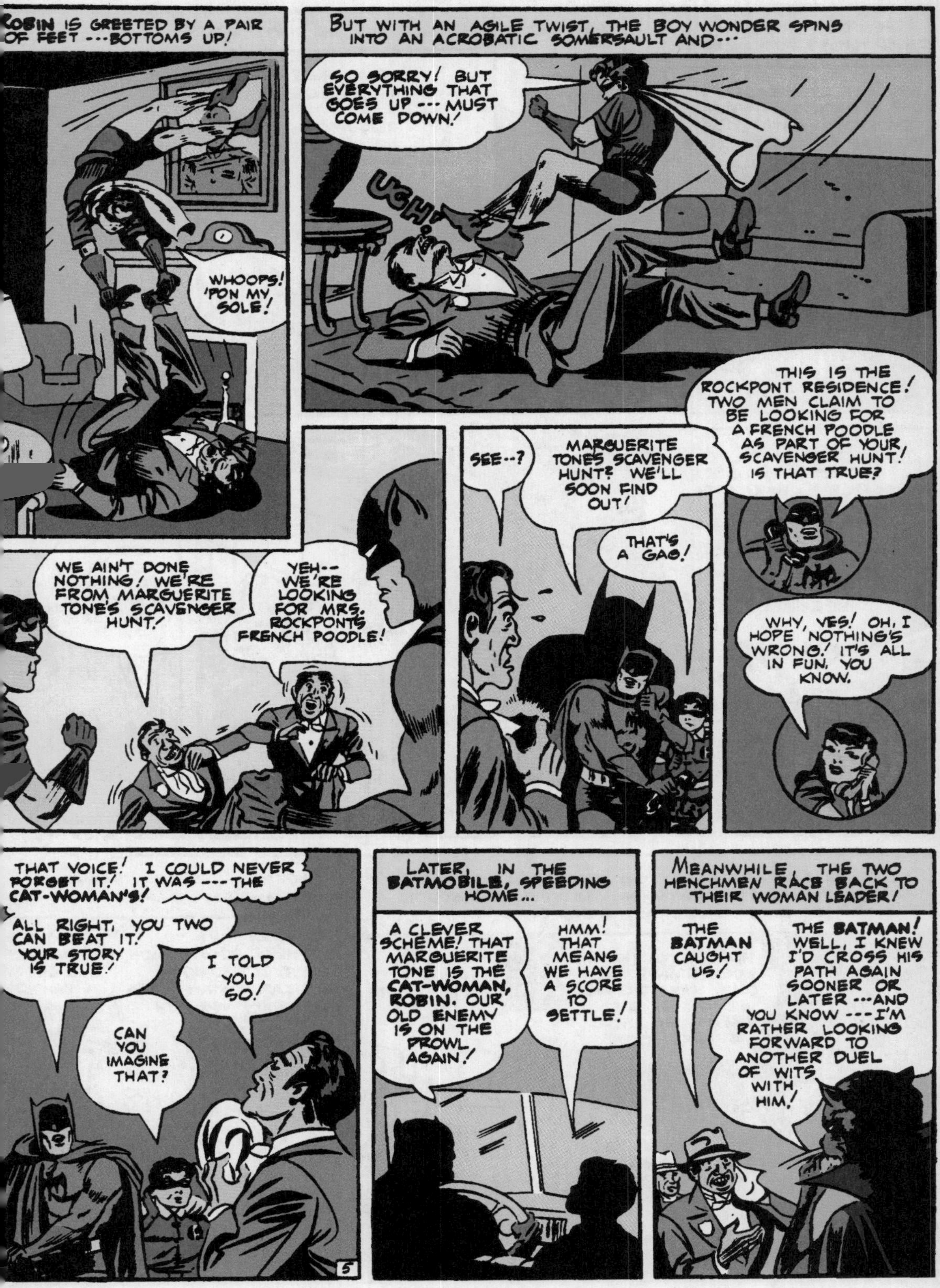
ROBIN IS GREETED BY A PAIR OF FEET ---BOTTOMS UP!
WHOOPS! 'PON MY SOLE!
BUT WITH AN AGILE TWIST, THE BOY WONDER SPINS INTO AN ACROBATIC SOMERSAULT AND---
SO SORRY! BUT EVERYTHING THAT GOES UP --- MUST COME DOWN!
UGH!
WE AIN'T DONE NOTHING! WE'RE FROM MARGUERITE TONE'S SCAVENGER HUNT!
YEH-- WE'RE LOOKING FOR MRS. ROCKPONT'S FRENCH POODLE!
SEE--?
MARGUERITE TONE'S SCAVENGER HUNT? WE'LL SOON FIND OUT!
THAT'S A GAG!
THIS IS THE ROCKPONT RESIDENCE! TWO MEN CLAIM TO BE LOOKING FOR A FRENCH POODLE AS PART OF YOUR SCAVENGER HUNT! IS THAT TRUE?
WHY, YES! OH, I HOPE NOTHING'S WRONG! IT'S ALL IN FUN, YOU KNOW.
THAT VOICE! I COULD NEVER FORGET IT! IT WAS --- THE CAT-WOMAN'S!
ALL RIGHT, YOU TWO CAN BEAT IT! YOUR STORY IS TRUE!
I TOLD YOU SO!
CAN YOU IMAGINE THAT?
5
LATER, IN THE BATMOBILE, SPEEDING HOME...
A CLEVER SCHEME! THAT MARGUERITE TONE IS THE CAT-WOMAN, ROBIN. OUR OLD ENEMY IS ON THE PROWL AGAIN!
HMM! THAT MEANS WE HAVE A SCORE TO SETTLE!
MEANWHILE, THE TWO HENCHMEN RACE BACK TO THEIR WOMAN LEADER!
THE BATMAN CAUGHT US!
THE BATMAN! WELL, I KNEW I'D CROSS HIS PATH AGAIN SOONER OR LATER ---AND YOU KNOW --- I'M RATHER LOOKING FORWARD TO ANOTHER DUEL OF WITS WITH HIM!

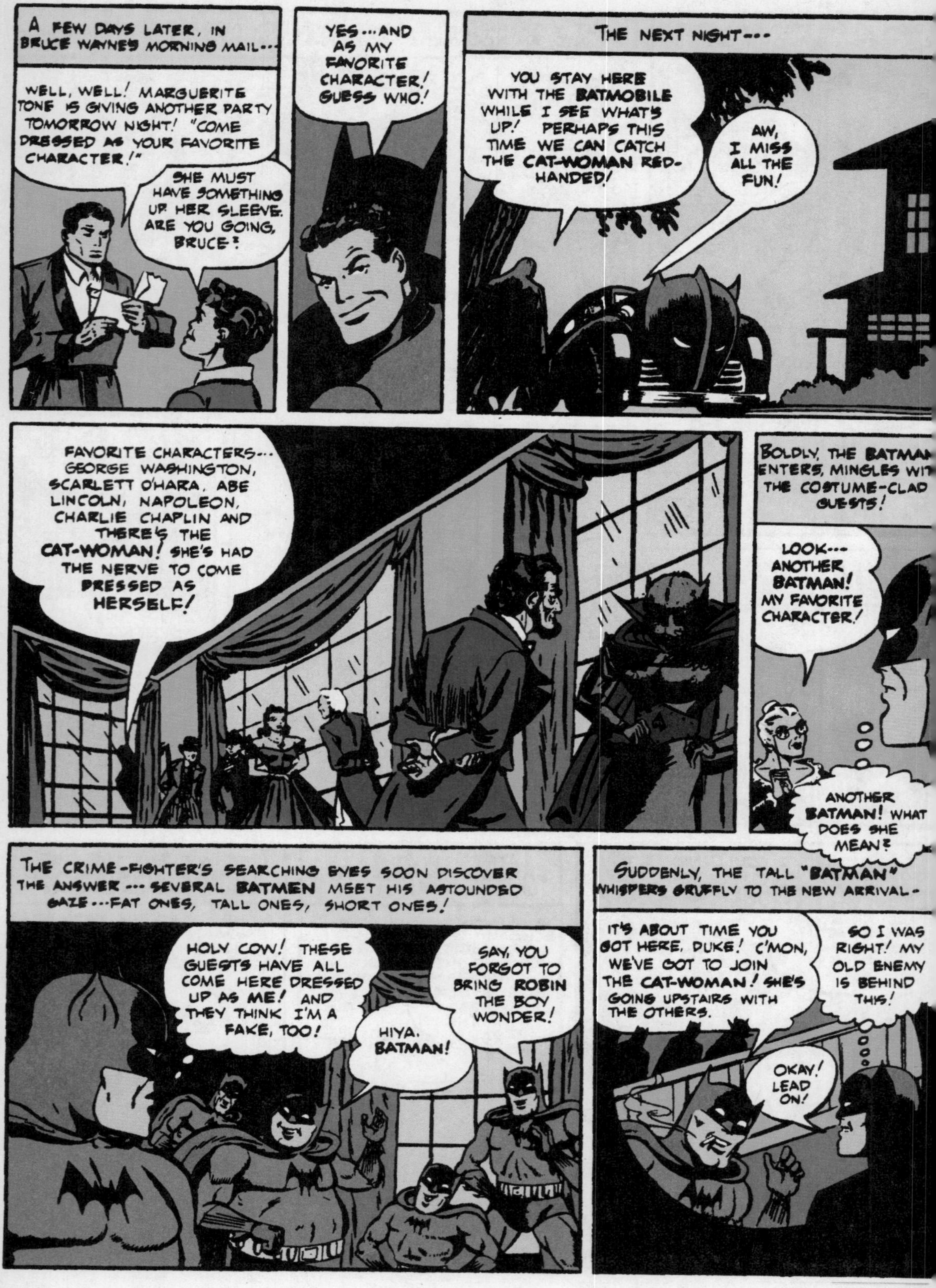
A FEW DAYS LATER, IN BRUCE WAYNE'S MORNING MAIL---
WELL, WELL! MARGUERITE TONE IS GIVING ANOTHER PARTY TOMORROW NIGHT! "COME DRESSED AS YOUR FAVORITE CHARACTER!"
SHE MUST HAVE SOMETHING UP HER SLEEVE. ARE YOU GOING, BRUCE?
YES...AND AS MY FAVORITE CHARACTER! GUESS WHO!
THE NEXT NIGHT---
YOU STAY HERE WITH THE BATMOBILE WHILE I SEE WHAT'S UP! PERHAPS THIS TIME WE CAN CATCH THE CAT-WOMAN RED-HANDED!
AW, I MISS ALL THE FUN!
FAVORITE CHARACTERS... GEORGE WASHINGTON, SCARLETT O'HARA, ABE LINCOLN, NAPOLEON, CHARLIE CHAPLIN AND THERE'S THE CAT-WOMAN! SHE'S HAD THE NERVE TO COME DRESSED AS HERSELF!
BOLDLY, THE BATMAN ENTERS, MINGLES WITH THE COSTUME-CLAD GUESTS!
LOOK--- ANOTHER BATMAN! MY FAVORITE CHARACTER!
ANOTHER BATMAN! WHAT DOES SHE MEAN?
THE CRIME-FIGHTER'S SEARCHING EYES SOON DISCOVER THE ANSWER --- SEVERAL BATMEN MEET HIS ASTOUNDED GAZE ...FAT ONES, TALL ONES, SHORT ONES!
HOLY COW! THESE GUESTS HAVE ALL COME HERE DRESSED UP AS ME! AND THEY THINK I'M A FAKE, TOO!
HIYA. BATMAN!
SAY, YOU FORGOT TO BRING ROBIN THE BOY WONDER!
SUDDENLY, THE TALL "BATMAN" WHISPERS GRUFFLY TO THE NEW ARRIVAL-
IT'S ABOUT TIME YOU GOT HERE, DUKE! C'MON, WE'VE GOT TO JOIN THE CAT-WOMAN! SHE'S GOING UPSTAIRS WITH THE OTHERS.
SO I WAS RIGHT! MY OLD ENEMY IS BEHIND THIS!
OKAY! LEAD ON!

UPSTAIRS, IN THE CAT-WOMAN'S SITTING ROOM, FOUR FIGURES ROBED IN THE BATMAN'S DARK DENIM DISCUSS —CRIME!

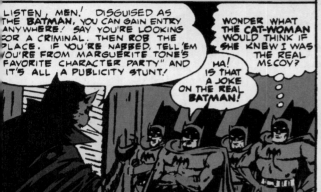

LISTEN, MEN! DISGUISED AS THE BATMAN, YOU CAN GAIN ENTRY ANYWHERE! SAY YOU'RE LOOKING FOR A CRIMINAL. THEN ROB THE PLACE. IF YOU'RE NABBED, TELL 'EM YOU'RE FROM MARGUERITE TONE'S "FAVORITE CHARACTER PARTY" AND IT'S ALL A PUBLICITY STUNT!

WONDER WHAT THE CAT-WOMAN WOULD THINK IF SHE KNEW I WAS THE REAL McCOY?

HA! IS THAT A JOKE ON THE REAL BATMAN!

ABRUPTLY, THE DOOR BURSTS OPEN AND ....

I'M LATE---I HAD A FLAT TIRE AND WAS DELAYED!

SOMETHING'S WRONG! THERE ARE ONLY SUPPOSED TO BE FOUR OF YOU HERE! ONE OF YOU IS AN IMPOSTOR---TAKE OFF YOUR MASKS!

THE BATMAN IS TRAPPED --- BUT UNDISMAYED!

I'LL KEEP MINE ON, IF YOU DON'T MIND! MY FACE IS MY FORTUNE!

AFTER HIM! HE'S THE REAL BATMAN!

BUT LIKE A STEEL SPRING SUDDENLY RELEASED, THE CRIME-FIGHTER UNCOILS INTO ACTION!

SO YOU WANT TO BE A BATMAN? I'LL SHOW YOU HOW!

THEY'RE ALL MIXED UP BY THE COSTUMES! HERE I AM, MUGOS!

SUDDENLY, SWIFT AS A STRIKING PUMA, THE CRIME QUEEN'S SLIM HANDS STREAK OUT---

I'LL GET YOU MYSELF!

BUT BATMAN HAS SPIED CAT-WOMAN'S REFLECTION IN THE MIRROR --- AND MOVES WITH THE BLURRING SPEED OF LIGHT---

IS THAT NICE? TAKE A LITTLE NAP---YOU'RE ALL EXCITED!

SLAP!

ABRUPTLY ··· A CONCERTED RUSH BY THE FALSE BATMEN BEARS THE VALIANT BATTLER TOWARDS AN OPEN WINDOW!

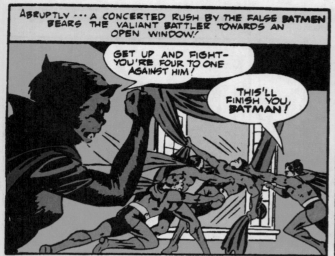

GET UP AND FIGHT— YOU'RE FOUR TO ONE AGAINST HIM!

THIS'LL FINISH YOU, BATMAN!

COME ON, YOU PHONIES! WE'RE JUST STARTING!

THIS IS TOO EASY! STAND UP AND FIGHT!

SUDDENLY, A MINIATURE WHIRLWIND SWEEPS IN FROM THE OPEN WINDOW ···· IT IS ROBIN THE BOY WONDER!

RIDE 'EM, COWBOY! I WAS GETTING BORED OUTSIDE!

HI-PAL!

AS THOUGH ANIMATED BY ONE GEAR, THE DYNAMIC DUO SHIFTS INTO HIGH!

I THOUGHT I SAW SOME SPECKS ON THIS RUG! I'LL CLEAN IT!

WE'LL CLEAN IT UP FOR THE CAT-WOMAN!

THE TIGRESS QUEEN QUICKLY REGAINS HER POISE!

YOUR ROUND, BATMAN! BUT YOU CAN'T PROVE I COMMITTED ANY CRIME! YOU SPOILED MY SCHEME, THOUGH— AND I WON'T FORGET THAT!

YOU'RE CLEVER, CAT! BUT YOU'LL MAKE A SLIP SOONER OR LATER.

MOMENTS LATER, AFTER TWO CAPED FIGURES MERGE INTO THE INKY NIGHT...

HOW BRAVE AND STRONG HE IS! IF ONLY HE WOULD TEAM UP WITH ME --- NOBODY WOULD BE ABLE TO STOP US ---NOBODY!

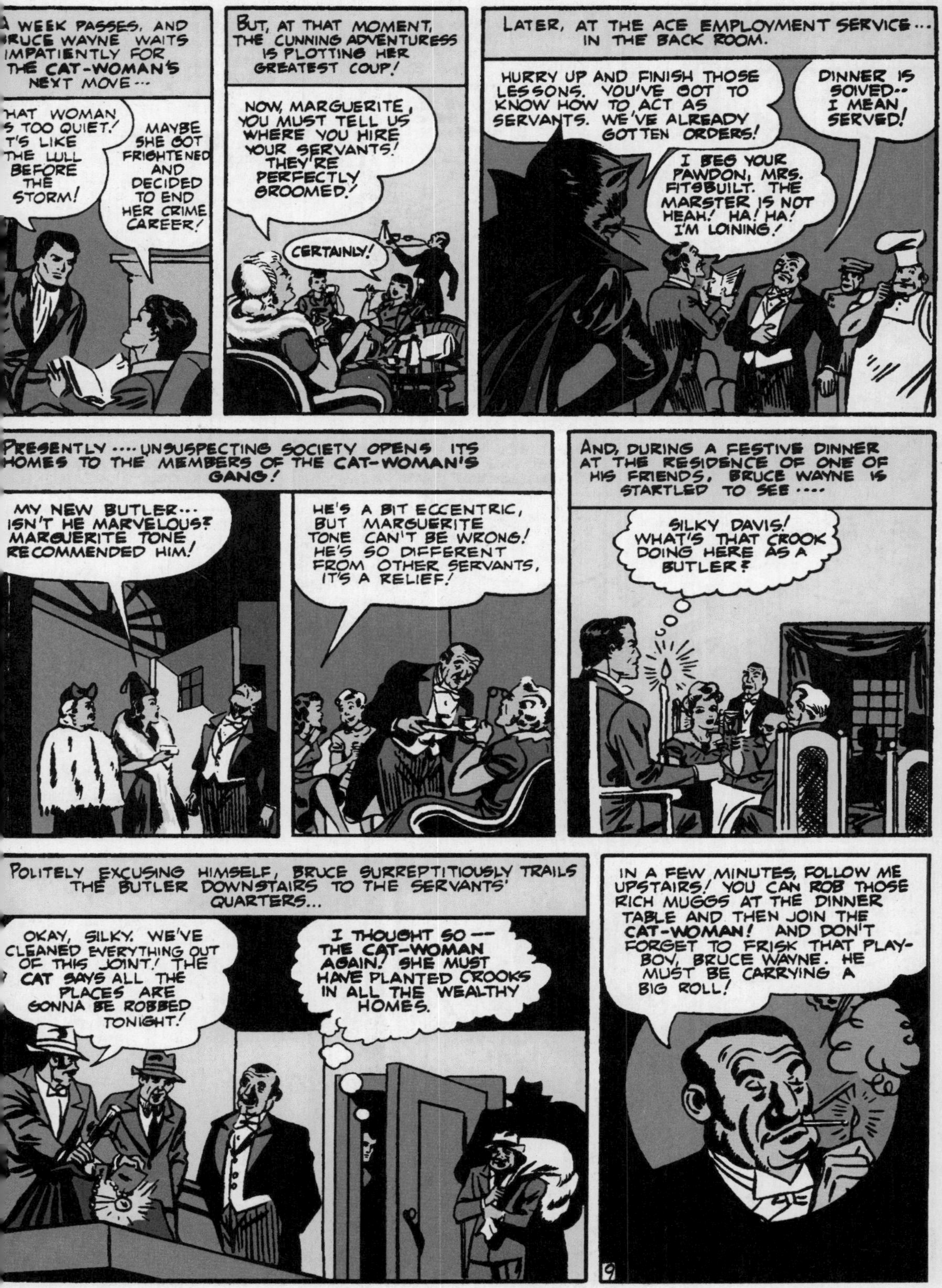
A WEEK PASSES, AND BRUCE WAYNE WAITS IMPATIENTLY FOR THE CAT-WOMAN'S NEXT MOVE...
THAT WOMAN IS TOO QUIET! IT'S LIKE THE LULL BEFORE THE STORM!
MAYBE SHE GOT FRIGHTENED AND DECIDED TO END HER CRIME CAREER!
BUT, AT THAT MOMENT, THE CUNNING ADVENTURESS IS PLOTTING HER GREATEST COUP!
NOW, MARGUERITE, YOU MUST TELL US WHERE YOU HIRE YOUR SERVANTS! THEY'RE PERFECTLY GROOMED!
CERTAINLY!
LATER, AT THE ACE EMPLOYMENT SERVICE... IN THE BACK ROOM.
HURRY UP AND FINISH THOSE LESSONS. YOU'VE GOT TO KNOW HOW TO ACT AS SERVANTS. WE'VE ALREADY GOTTEN ORDERS!
DINNER IS SOIVED-- I MEAN SERVED!
I BEG YOUR PAWDON, MRS. FITSBUILT. THE MARSTER IS NOT HEAH! HA! HA! I'M LOINING!
PRESENTLY.... UNSUSPECTING SOCIETY OPENS ITS HOMES TO THE MEMBERS OF THE CAT-WOMAN'S GANG!
MY NEW BUTLER... ISN'T HE MARVELOUS? MARGUERITE TONE RECOMMENDED HIM!
HE'S A BIT ECCENTRIC, BUT MARGUERITE TONE CAN'T BE WRONG! HE'S SO DIFFERENT FROM OTHER SERVANTS, IT'S A RELIEF!
AND, DURING A FESTIVE DINNER AT THE RESIDENCE OF ONE OF HIS FRIENDS, BRUCE WAYNE IS STARTLED TO SEE....
SILKY DAVIS! WHAT'S THAT CROOK DOING HERE AS A BUTLER?
POLITELY EXCUSING HIMSELF, BRUCE SURREPTITIOUSLY TRAILS THE BUTLER DOWNSTAIRS TO THE SERVANTS' QUARTERS...
OKAY, SILKY. WE'VE CLEANED EVERYTHING OUT OF THIS JOINT! THE CAT SAYS ALL THE PLACES ARE GONNA BE ROBBED TONIGHT!
I THOUGHT SO --- THE CAT-WOMAN AGAIN! SHE MUST HAVE PLANTED CROOKS IN ALL THE WEALTHY HOMES.
IN A FEW MINUTES, FOLLOW ME UPSTAIRS! YOU CAN ROB THOSE RICH MUGGS AT THE DINNER TABLE AND THEN JOIN THE CAT-WOMAN! AND DON'T FORGET TO FRISK THAT PLAY-BOY, BRUCE WAYNE. HE MUST BE CARRYING A BIG ROLL!
9

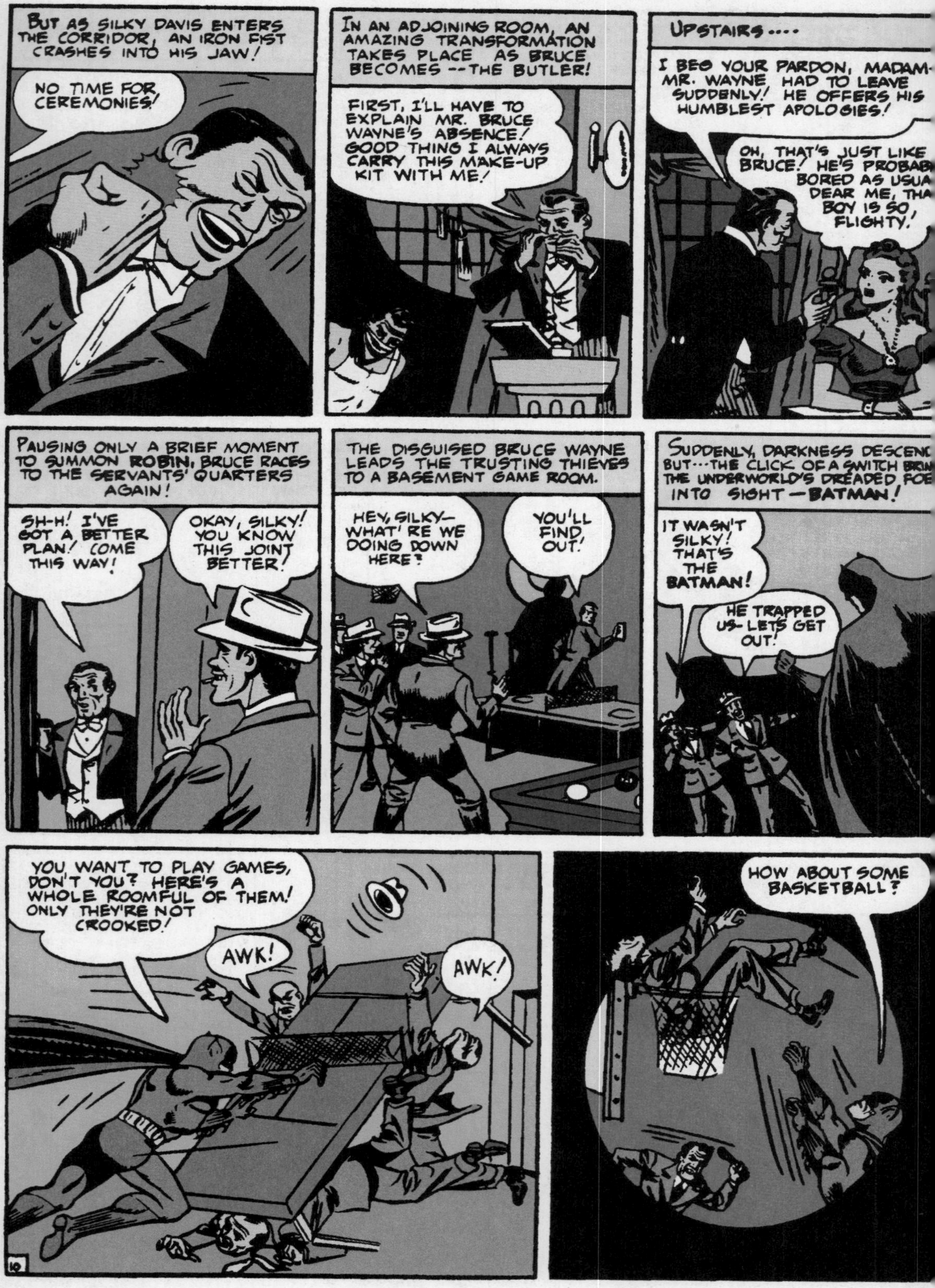
BUT AS SILKY DAVIS ENTERS THE CORRIDOR, AN IRON FIST CRASHES INTO HIS JAW!
NO TIME FOR CEREMONIES!
IN AN ADJOINING ROOM, AN AMAZING TRANSFORMATION TAKES PLACE AS BRUCE BECOMES --THE BUTLER!
FIRST, I'LL HAVE TO EXPLAIN MR. BRUCE WAYNE'S ABSENCE! GOOD THING I ALWAYS CARRY THIS MAKE-UP KIT WITH ME!
UPSTAIRS....
I BEG YOUR PARDON, MADAM- MR. WAYNE HAD TO LEAVE SUDDENLY! HE OFFERS HIS HUMBLEST APOLOGIES!
OH, THAT'S JUST LIKE BRUCE! HE'S PROBAB BORED AS USUA DEAR ME, THA BOY IS SO, FLIGHTY!
PAUSING ONLY A BRIEF MOMENT TO SUMMON **ROBIN**, BRUCE RACES TO THE SERVANTS' QUARTERS AGAIN!
SH-H! I'VE GOT A BETTER PLAN! COME THIS WAY!
OKAY, SILKY! YOU KNOW THIS JOINT BETTER!
THE DISGUISED BRUCE WAYNE LEADS THE TRUSTING THIEVES TO A BASEMENT GAME ROOM.
HEY, SILKY-WHAT'RE WE DOING DOWN HERE?
YOU'LL FIND OUT!
SUDDENLY, DARKNESS DESCEN BUT...THE CLICK OF A SWITCH BRI THE UNDERWORLD'S DREADED FOE INTO SIGHT—**BATMAN**!
IT WASN'T SILKY! THAT'S THE **BATMAN**!
HE TRAPPED US-LET'S GET OUT!
YOU WANT TO PLAY GAMES, DON'T YOU? HERE'S A WHOLE ROOMFUL OF THEM! ONLY THEY'RE NOT CROOKED!
AWK!
AWK!
10
HOW ABOUT SOME BASKETBALL?

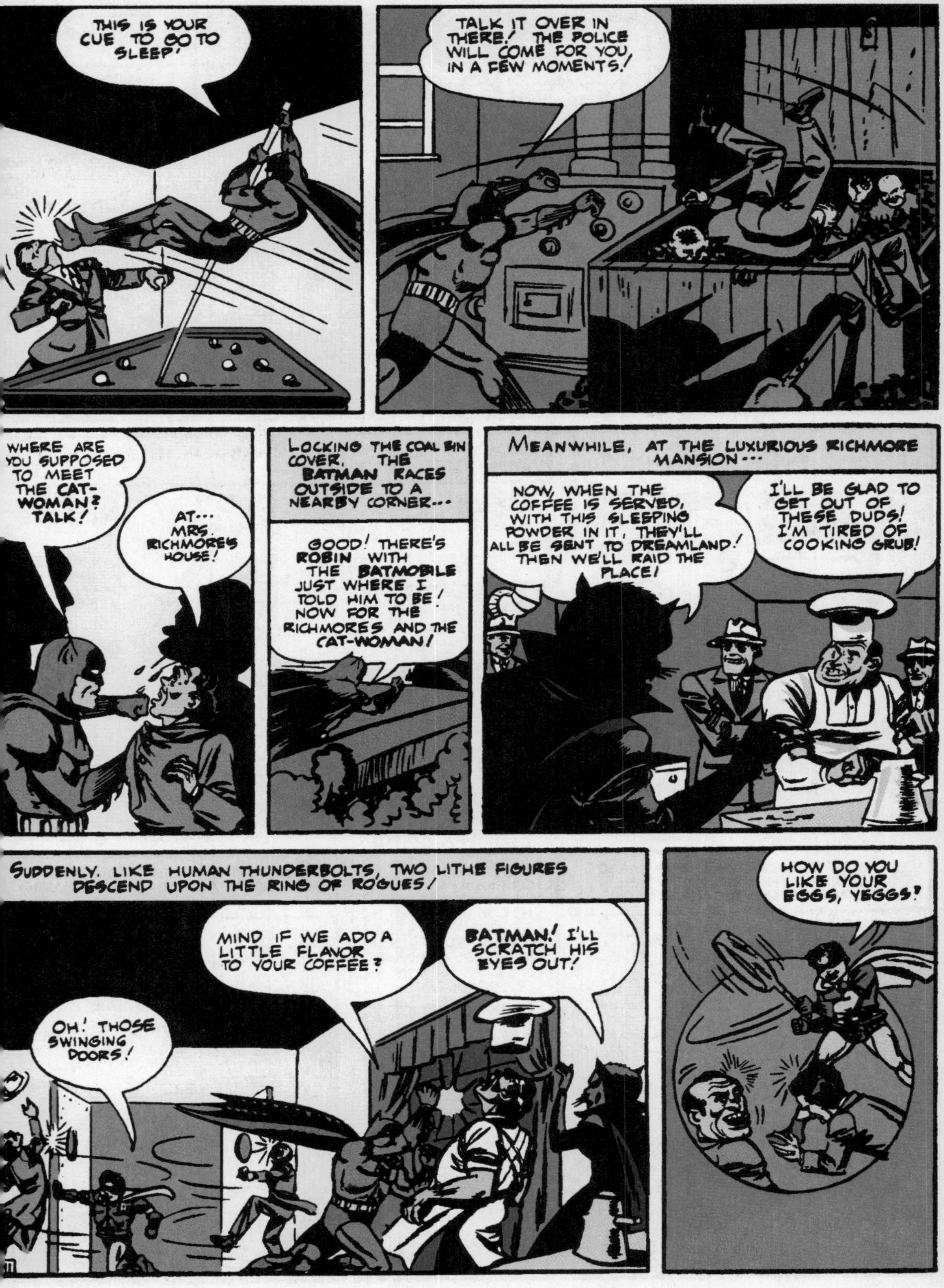
THIS IS YOUR CUE TO GO TO SLEEP!
TALK IT OVER IN THERE! THE POLICE WILL COME FOR YOU IN A FEW MOMENTS!
WHERE ARE YOU SUPPOSED TO MEET THE CAT-WOMAN? TALK!
AT... MRS. RICHMORE'S HOUSE!
LOCKING THE COAL BIN COVER, THE BATMAN RACES OUTSIDE TO A NEARBY CORNER...
GOOD! THERE'S ROBIN WITH THE BATMOBILE JUST WHERE I TOLD HIM TO BE! NOW FOR THE RICHMORES AND THE CAT-WOMAN!
MEANWHILE, AT THE LUXURIOUS RICHMORE MANSION...
NOW, WHEN THE COFFEE IS SERVED, WITH THIS SLEEPING POWDER IN IT, THEY'LL ALL BE SENT TO DREAMLAND! THEN WE'LL RAID THE PLACE!
I'LL BE GLAD TO GET OUT OF THESE DUDS! I'M TIRED OF COOKING GRUB!
SUDDENLY, LIKE HUMAN THUNDERBOLTS, TWO LITHE FIGURES DESCEND UPON THE RING OF ROGUES!
OH! THOSE SWINGING DOORS!
MIND IF WE ADD A LITTLE FLAVOR TO YOUR COFFEE?
BATMAN! I'LL SCRATCH HIS EYES OUT!
HOW DO YOU LIKE YOUR EGGS, YEGGS?

GO BAKE YOURSELF A CAKE!

I'LL FLATTEN YOU INTO A PRETTY SHAPE WITH THIS, COOKIE!

SUDDENLY---- THE VICIOUS GLEAM OF FLASHING STEEL ---

ULP!

LOW BRIDGE, BATMAN!

A LIGHTNING LUNGE TO THE LEFT, AND THE BLADE THUDS HOME HARMLESSLY ABOVE ---

FLOUR
FLOUR
FLOUR
FLOUR

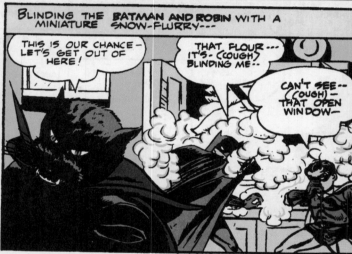

BLINDING THE BATMAN AND ROBIN WITH A MINIATURE SNOW-FLURRY---

THIS IS OUR CHANCE-- LET'S GET OUT OF HERE!

THAT FLOUR--- IT'S-(COUGH) BLINDING ME--

CAN'T SEE-- (COUGH)-- THAT OPEN WINDOW--

UNDER COVER OF THE MAN-MADE DUST CLOUD, THE BANDIT QUEEN AND HER HENCHMEN ESCAPE.

THAT WIND--- IT'S BLOWING THE FLOUR ALL OVER THE ROOM--- AND THE CAT-WOMAN IS GETTING AWAY!

TOO LATE TO FOLLOW THEM! WE'LL HAVE TO---WHAT'S THIS ON THE FLOOR?

"LOST AND FOUND-- CONFIDENTIAL AGENCY. VALUABLES RETRIEVED FOR A SUITABLE REWARD!" HMM! A NEAT LITTLE RACKET! THE CAT-WOMAN OPERATES A LOST AND FOUND BUREAU-

--AND HOLDS UP THE PEOPLE SHE ROBBED FOR A SUM OF MONEY TO GET THEIR JEWELS AND THINGS BACK! WE'VE GOT TO BREAK IT UP, BATMAN!

DOWN AT THE CONFIDENTIAL AGENCY, A BLAZE OF EXCITEMENT IS IGNITED---

YES, MR. VANDERWELL, FOR THE SLIGHT SUM OF $5000 WE WILL RECOVER YOUR HEIRLOOM!

EVERYBODY CLEAR OUT OF HERE! WE'RE LEAVING TOWN! THE BATMAN AND ROBIN ARE TOO CLOSE TO US!

12

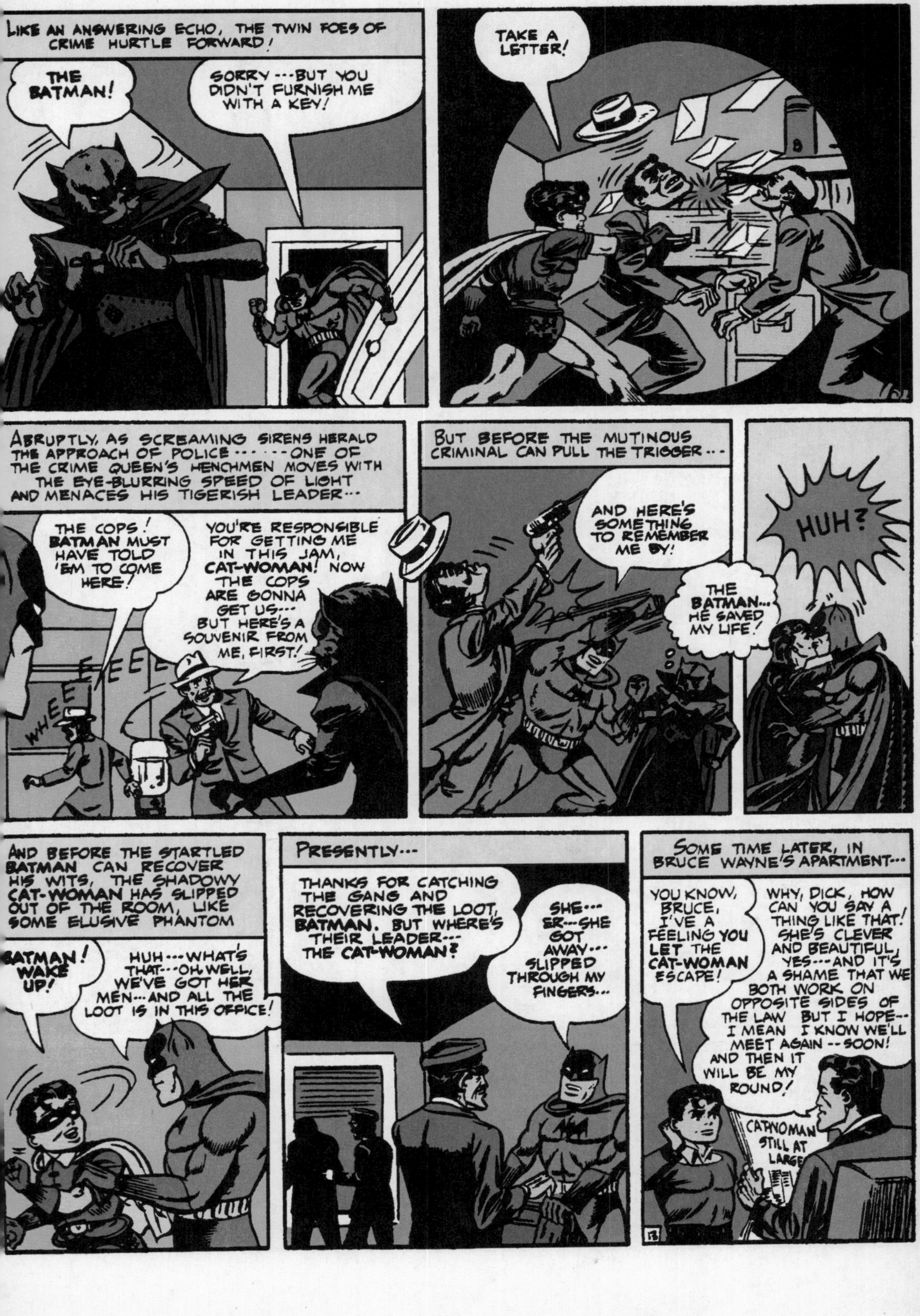
LIKE AN ANSWERING ECHO, THE TWIN FOES OF CRIME HURTLE FORWARD!
THE BATMAN!
SORRY ---BUT YOU DIDN'T FURNISH ME WITH A KEY!
TAKE A LETTER!
ABRUPTLY, AS SCREAMING SIRENS HERALD THE APPROACH OF POLICE ------ONE OF THE CRIME QUEEN'S HENCHMEN MOVES WITH THE EYE-BLURRING SPEED OF LIGHT AND MENACES HIS TIGERISH LEADER...
THE COPS! BATMAN MUST HAVE TOLD 'EM TO COME HERE!
YOU'RE RESPONSIBLE FOR GETTING ME IN THIS JAM, CAT-WOMAN! NOW THE COPS ARE GONNA GET US--- BUT HERE'S A SOUVENIR FROM ME, FIRST!
WHEEEEEE
BUT BEFORE THE MUTINOUS CRIMINAL CAN PULL THE TRIGGER...
AND HERE'S SOMETHING TO REMEMBER ME BY!
THE BATMAN... HE SAVED MY LIFE!
HUH?
AND BEFORE THE STARTLED BATMAN CAN RECOVER HIS WITS, THE SHADOWY CAT-WOMAN HAS SLIPPED OUT OF THE ROOM, LIKE SOME ELUSIVE PHANTOM
BATMAN! WAKE UP!
HUH---WHAT'S THAT---OH, WELL, WE'VE GOT HER MEN...AND ALL THE LOOT IS IN THIS OFFICE!
PRESENTLY...
THANKS FOR CATCHING THE GANG AND RECOVERING THE LOOT, BATMAN. BUT WHERE'S THEIR LEADER--- THE CAT-WOMAN?
SHE--- ER---SHE GOT AWAY--- SLIPPED THROUGH MY FINGERS...
SOME TIME LATER, IN BRUCE WAYNE'S APARTMENT...
YOU KNOW, BRUCE, I'VE A FEELING YOU LET THE CAT-WOMAN ESCAPE!
WHY, DICK, HOW CAN YOU SAY A THING LIKE THAT! SHE'S CLEVER AND BEAUTIFUL, YES---AND IT'S A SHAME THAT WE BOTH WORK ON OPPOSITE SIDES OF THE LAW BUT I HOPE-- I MEAN I KNOW WE'LL MEET AGAIN --SOON! AND THEN IT WILL BE MY ROUND!
CATWOMAN STILL AT LARGE
13

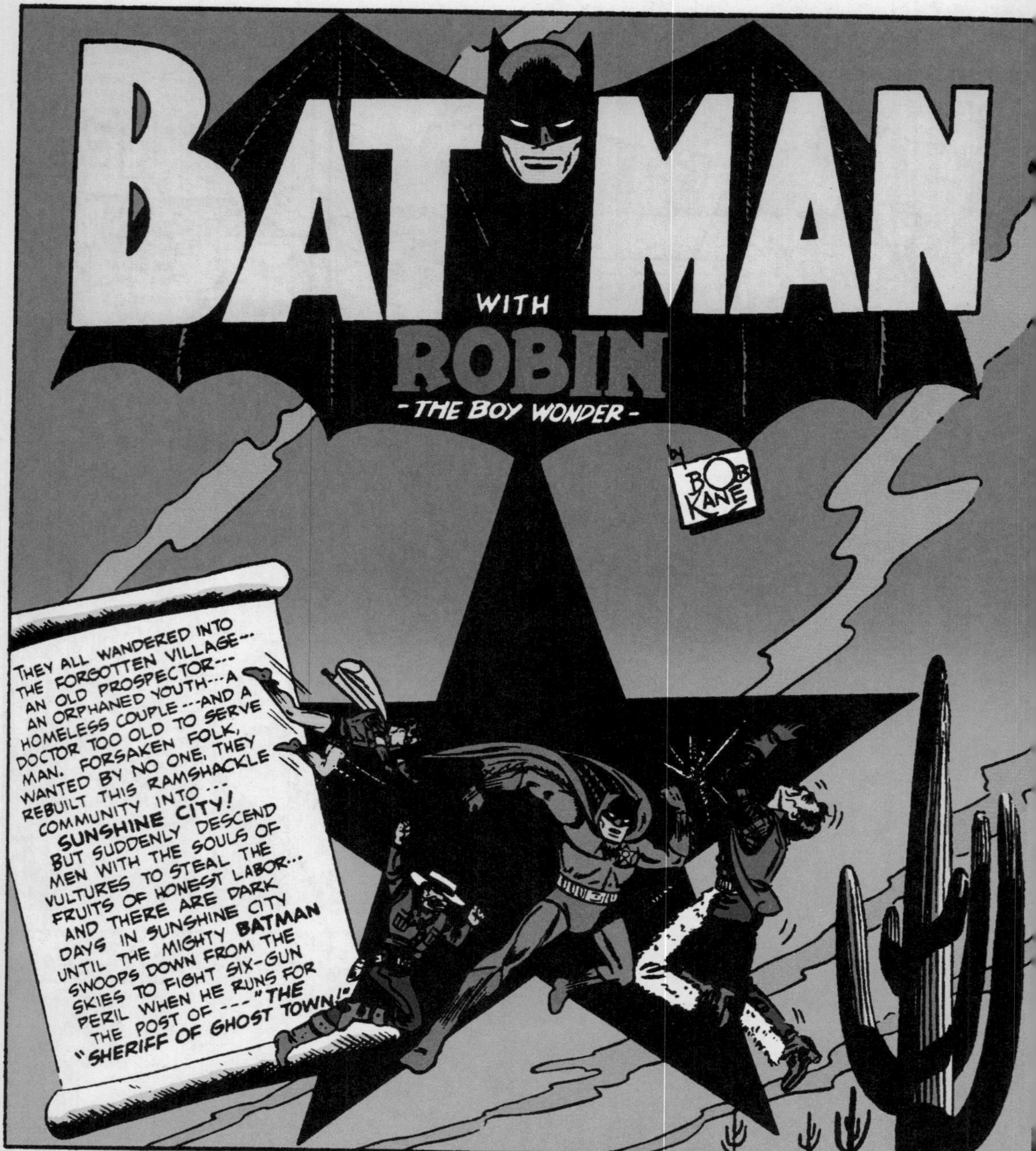
BATMAN
WITH
ROBIN
-THE BOY WONDER-
by BOB KANE
THEY ALL WANDERED INTO THE FORGOTTEN VILLAGE-- AN OLD PROSPECTOR--- AN ORPHANED YOUTH---A HOMELESS COUPLE---AND A DOCTOR TOO OLD TO SERVE MAN. FORSAKEN FOLK, WANTED BY NO ONE, THEY REBUILT THIS RAMSHACKLE COMMUNITY INTO--- SUNSHINE CITY! BUT SUDDENLY DESCEND MEN WITH THE SOULS OF VULTURES TO STEAL THE FRUITS OF HONEST LABOR... AND THERE ARE DARK DAYS IN SUNSHINE CITY UNTIL THE MIGHTY BATMAN SWOOPS DOWN FROM THE SKIES TO FIGHT SIX-GUN PERIL WHEN HE RUNS FOR THE POST OF ---"THE SHERIFF OF GHOST TOWN!"

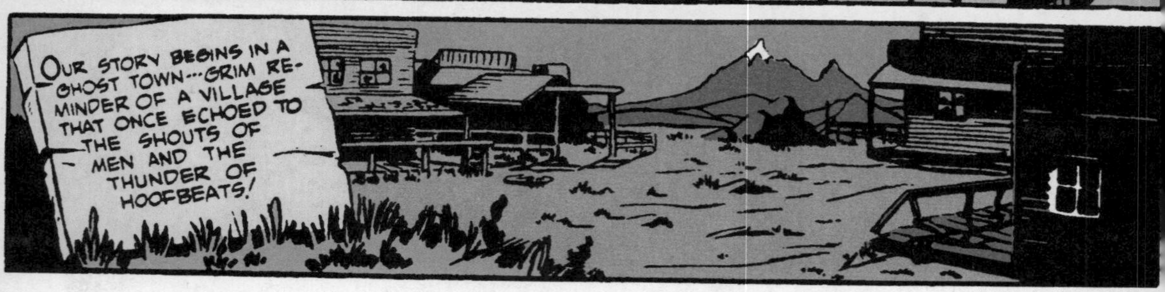
OUR STORY BEGINS IN A GHOST TOWN---GRIM RE-MINDER OF A VILLAGE THAT ONCE ECHOED TO THE SHOUTS OF MEN AND THE THUNDER OF HOOFBEATS!

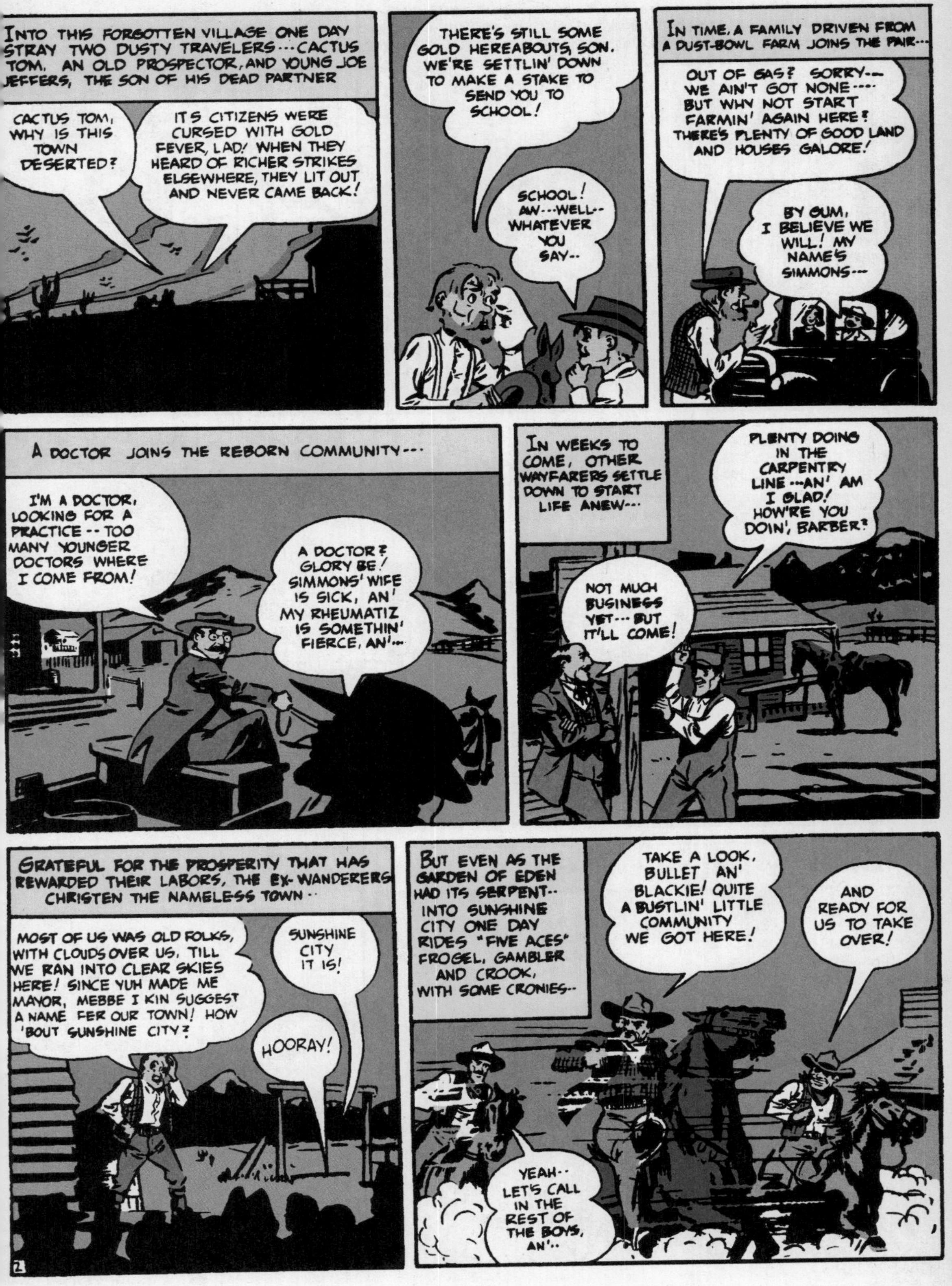

INTO THIS FORGOTTEN VILLAGE ONE DAY STRAY TWO DUSTY TRAVELERS --- CACTUS TOM, AN OLD PROSPECTOR, AND YOUNG JOE JEFFERS, THE SON OF HIS DEAD PARTNER
CACTUS TOM, WHY IS THIS TOWN DESERTED?
ITS CITIZENS WERE CURSED WITH GOLD FEVER, LAD! WHEN THEY HEARD OF RICHER STRIKES ELSEWHERE, THEY LIT OUT AND NEVER CAME BACK!
THERE'S STILL SOME GOLD HEREABOUTS, SON. WE'RE SETTLIN' DOWN TO MAKE A STAKE TO SEND YOU TO SCHOOL!
SCHOOL! AW---WELL-- WHATEVER YOU SAY--
IN TIME, A FAMILY DRIVEN FROM A DUST-BOWL FARM JOINS THE PAIR---
OUT OF GAS? SORRY--- WE AIN'T GOT NONE---- BUT WHY NOT START FARMIN' AGAIN HERE? THERE'S PLENTY OF GOOD LAND AND HOUSES GALORE!
BY GUM, I BELIEVE WE WILL! MY NAME'S SIMMONS---
A DOCTOR JOINS THE REBORN COMMUNITY---
I'M A DOCTOR, LOOKING FOR A PRACTICE -- TOO MANY YOUNGER DOCTORS WHERE I COME FROM!
A DOCTOR? GLORY BE! SIMMONS' WIFE IS SICK, AN' MY RHEUMATIZ IS SOMETHIN' FIERCE, AN'...
IN WEEKS TO COME, OTHER WAYFARERS SETTLE DOWN TO START LIFE ANEW---
PLENTY DOING IN THE CARPENTRY LINE ---AN' AM I GLAD! HOW'RE YOU DOIN', BARBER?
NOT MUCH BUSINESS YET--- BUT IT'LL COME!
GRATEFUL FOR THE PROSPERITY THAT HAS REWARDED THEIR LABORS, THE EX-WANDERERS CHRISTEN THE NAMELESS TOWN ..
MOST OF US WAS OLD FOLKS, WITH CLOUDS OVER US, TILL WE RAN INTO CLEAR SKIES HERE! SINCE YUH MADE ME MAYOR, MEBBE I KIN SUGGEST A NAME FER OUR TOWN! HOW 'BOUT SUNSHINE CITY?
SUNSHINE CITY IT IS!
HOORAY!
2
BUT EVEN AS THE GARDEN OF EDEN HAD ITS SERPENT-- INTO SUNSHINE CITY ONE DAY RIDES "FIVE ACES" FROGEL, GAMBLER AND CROOK, WITH SOME CRONIES--
TAKE A LOOK, BULLET AN' BLACKIE! QUITE A BUSTLIN' LITTLE COMMUNITY WE GOT HERE!
AND READY FOR US TO TAKE OVER!
YEAH-- LET'S CALL IN THE REST OF THE BOYS, AN'..

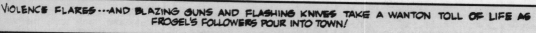
VIOLENCE FLARES...AND BLAZING GUNS AND FLASHING KNIVES TAKE A WANTON TOLL OF LIFE AS FROGEL'S FOLLOWERS POUR INTO TOWN!

THAT WHEEL'S CROOKED! I WANT--- OHHH...

THIS'LL TEACH YUH T' SQUAWK!

TAKE A CHANCE!

PLENTY GOLD DUST IN THESE SADDLE-BAGS!

OUGHTTA BE--- IT'S THE MONTH'S OUTPUT OF THE WHOLE TOWN!

HURRY! MY HUSBAND! THEY'VE STABBED HIM!

HE SHOULDA MINDED HIS OWN BUSINESS, LADY!

Hoping to preserve their new-found happiness, the founders of Sunshine City meet in the little red schoolhouse...

FELLER CITIZENS, WE WAS DOIN' FINE TILL THEM CROOKS CAME! WE GOT TO GET RID O' THE VARMINTS!

THAT'S RIGHT, MAYOR!

But the wily Frogel shows his defiance of law and order!

THAT'S RIGHT, BLACKIE- BURN HER DOWN TO THE GROUND!

BOSS, YOU'RE HOT STUFF! HAW, HAW!

SUNSH SCHOOL

Presently-----inside the schoolhouse----

WE GOTTA GIT TO-GETHER, AN'...WHAT'S THIS?

FIRE!

RUN FOR YOUR LIVES!

Later, in the tiny shack Cactus Tom shares with Joe ...

DON'T FEEL SO BAD, CACTUS TOM!

IT AIN'T ME I'M FRETTED 'BOUT---IT'S ALL THE OLD FOLKS THAT COME HERE FER A NEW LIFE! AN OLD COOT LIKE ME CAN'T HELP 'EM! WHAT WE NEED IS THE BRAVEST MAN IN THE COUNTRY TO CLEAR OUT THEM BUZZARDS!

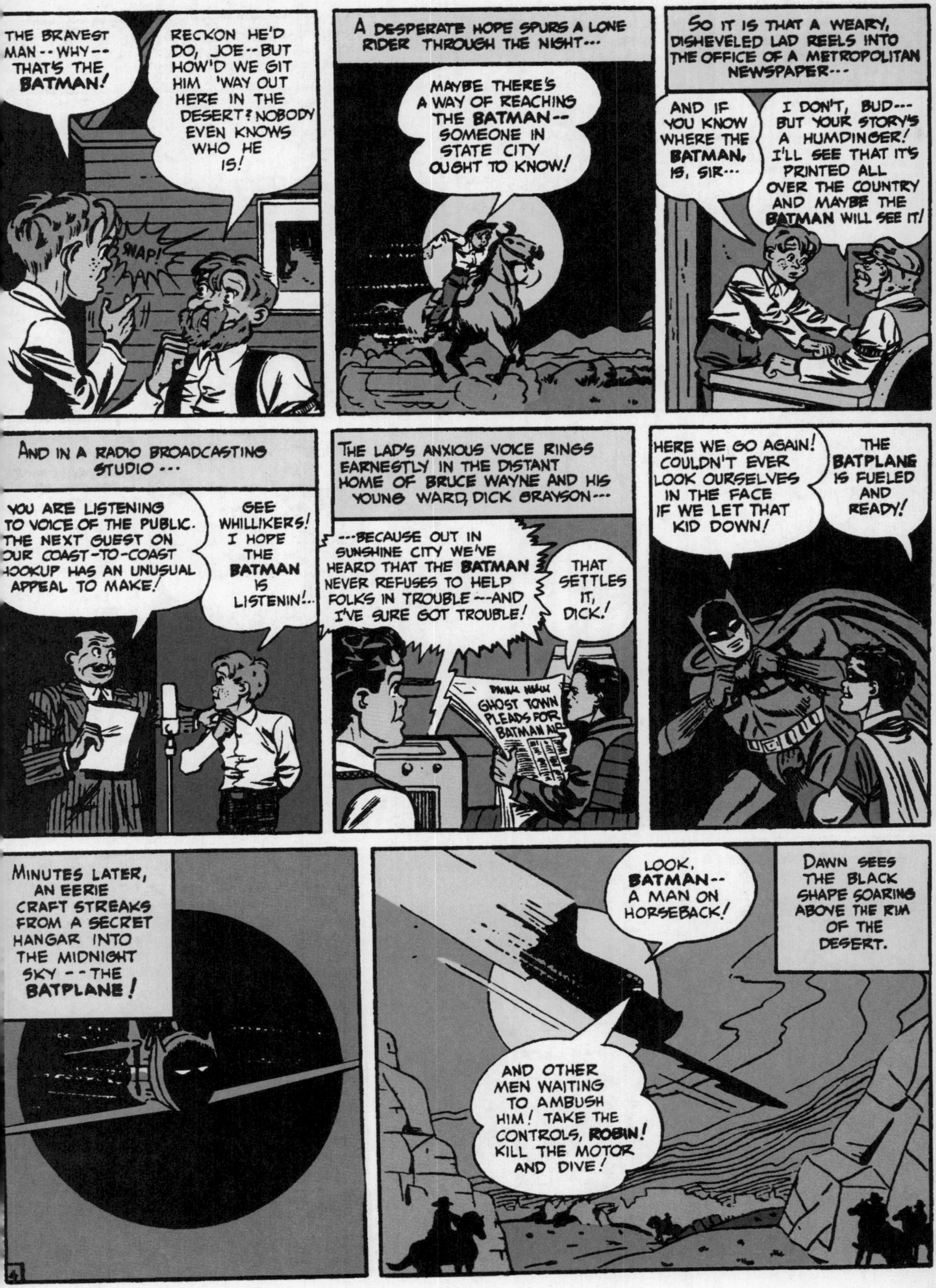
THE BRAVEST MAN -- WHY -- THAT'S THE BATMAN!
RECKON HE'D DO, JOE -- BUT HOW'D WE GIT HIM 'WAY OUT HERE IN THE DESERT? NOBODY EVEN KNOWS WHO HE IS!
SNAP!
A DESPERATE HOPE SPURS A LONE RIDER THROUGH THE NIGHT---
MAYBE THERE'S A WAY OF REACHING THE BATMAN -- SOMEONE IN STATE CITY OUGHT TO KNOW!
SO IT IS THAT A WEARY, DISHEVELED LAD REELS INTO THE OFFICE OF A METROPOLITAN NEWSPAPER---
AND IF YOU KNOW WHERE THE BATMAN IS, SIR---
I DON'T, BUD--- BUT YOUR STORY'S A HUMDINGER! I'LL SEE THAT IT'S PRINTED ALL OVER THE COUNTRY AND MAYBE THE BATMAN WILL SEE IT!
AND IN A RADIO BROADCASTING STUDIO ---
YOU ARE LISTENING TO VOICE OF THE PUBLIC. THE NEXT GUEST ON OUR COAST-TO-COAST HOOKUP HAS AN UNUSUAL APPEAL TO MAKE!
GEE WHILLIKERS! I HOPE THE BATMAN IS LISTENIN'!...
THE LAD'S ANXIOUS VOICE RINGS EARNESTLY IN THE DISTANT HOME OF BRUCE WAYNE AND HIS YOUNG WARD, DICK GRAYSON---
---BECAUSE OUT IN SUNSHINE CITY WE'VE HEARD THAT THE BATMAN NEVER REFUSES TO HELP FOLKS IN TROUBLE ---AND I'VE SURE GOT TROUBLE!
THAT SETTLES IT, DICK!
GHOST TOWN PLEADS FOR BATMAN
HERE WE GO AGAIN! COULDN'T EVER LOOK OURSELVES IN THE FACE IF WE LET THAT KID DOWN!
THE BATPLANE IS FUELED AND READY!
MINUTES LATER, AN EERIE CRAFT STREAKS FROM A SECRET HANGAR INTO THE MIDNIGHT SKY -- THE BATPLANE!
DAWN SEES THE BLACK SHAPE SOARING ABOVE THE RIM OF THE DESERT.
LOOK, BATMAN -- A MAN ON HORSEBACK!
AND OTHER MEN WAITING TO AMBUSH HIM! TAKE THE CONTROLS, ROBIN! KILL THE MOTOR AND DIVE!

RETURNING HOME, YOUNG JOE IS UNPREPARED FOR THE SUDDEN CRACKLE OF OUTLAW SIX-SHOOTERS THAT BLAZE AT HIM FROM BEHIND...

GEE--WHILLIKERS... THEY'RE AFTER ME!

YOU WON'T MAKE US NO MORE TROUBLE, KID!

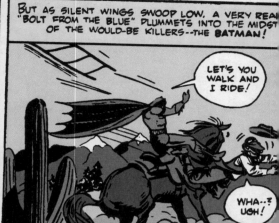

BUT AS SILENT WINGS SWOOP LOW, A VERY REAL "BOLT FROM THE BLUE" PLUMMETS INTO THE MIDST OF THE WOULD-BE KILLERS--THE BATMAN!

LET'S YOU WALK AND I RIDE!

WHA--? UGH!

I'M JUST A ROPIN' COWBOY, YIPPEE!

I'M SLIPPIN'! ON!

AMID GRAY CLOUDS OF DUST, THE OUTLAWS HEAD FOR DISTANT PARTS---

BE SEEING YOU LADS LATER!

LET'S BEAT IT! THAT GUY'S THE BATMAN!

GOLLY, MR. BATMAN....YOU SAVED MY LIFE!

THINK NOTHING OF IT, JOE --- FROM WHAT I HEAR, YOU'RE TRYING TO SAVE A TOWN!

HEART-WARMING CHEERS RING THRU THE AIR AS THE WORLD-FAMOUS DUO RIDES INTO SUNSHINE CITY!

THIS IS THE BIGGEST DAY OF MY LIFE!

HOORAY FOR THE BATMAN!

FOLKS, I NOMINATE THE BATMAN FOR SHERIFF!

AS SHERIFF, I'D HAVE THE LAW ON MY SIDE...

THANKS, CACTUS TOM!

THE BATMAN FOR SHERIFF!

HALL

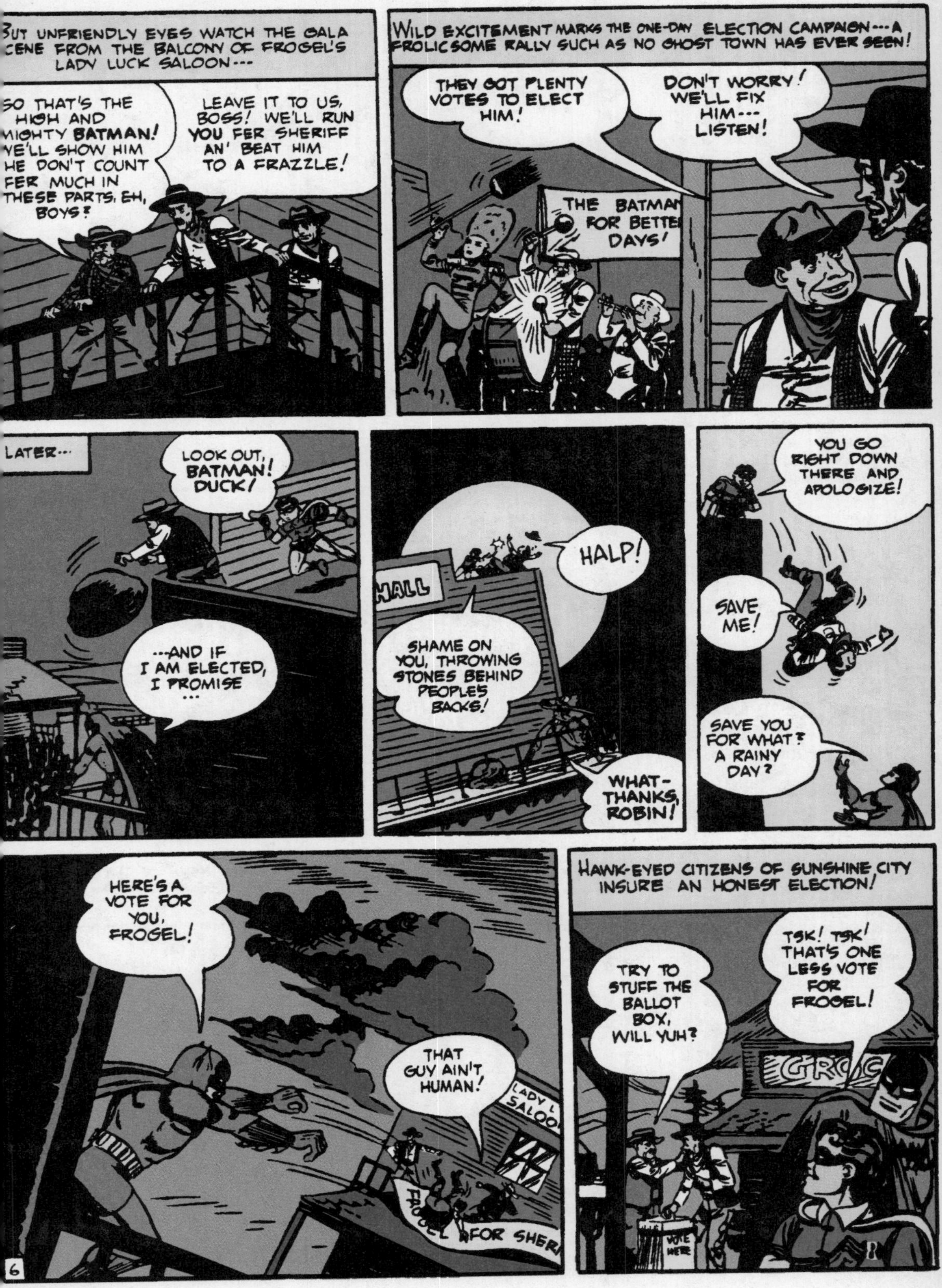

BUT UNFRIENDLY EYES WATCH THE GALA CENE FROM THE BALCONY OF FROGEL'S LADY LUCK SALOON---
SO THAT'S THE HIGH AND MIGHTY BATMAN! WE'LL SHOW HIM HE DON'T COUNT FER MUCH IN THESE PARTS, EH, BOYS?
LEAVE IT TO US, BOSS! WE'LL RUN YOU FER SHERIFF AN' BEAT HIM TO A FRAZZLE!
WILD EXCITEMENT MARKS THE ONE-DAY ELECTION CAMPAIGN---A FROLICSOME RALLY SUCH AS NO GHOST TOWN HAS EVER SEEN!
THEY GOT PLENTY VOTES TO ELECT HIM!
DON'T WORRY! WE'LL FIX HIM--- LISTEN!
THE BATMAN FOR BETTE DAYS!
LATER---
LOOK OUT, BATMAN! DUCK!
---AND IF I AM ELECTED, I PROMISE ---
HALL
HALP!
SHAME ON YOU, THROWING STONES BEHIND PEOPLE'S BACKS!
WHAT- THANKS, ROBIN!
YOU GO RIGHT DOWN THERE AND APOLOGIZE!
SAVE ME!
SAVE YOU FOR WHAT? A RAINY DAY?
HERE'S A VOTE FOR YOU, FROGEL!
THAT GUY AIN'T HUMAN!
LADY L SALOO
FOR SHER
6
HAWK-EYED CITIZENS OF SUNSHINE CITY INSURE AN HONEST ELECTION!
TRY TO STUFF THE BALLOT BOX, WILL YUH?
TSK! TSK! THAT'S ONE LESS VOTE FOR FROGEL!
GROC
VOTE HERE

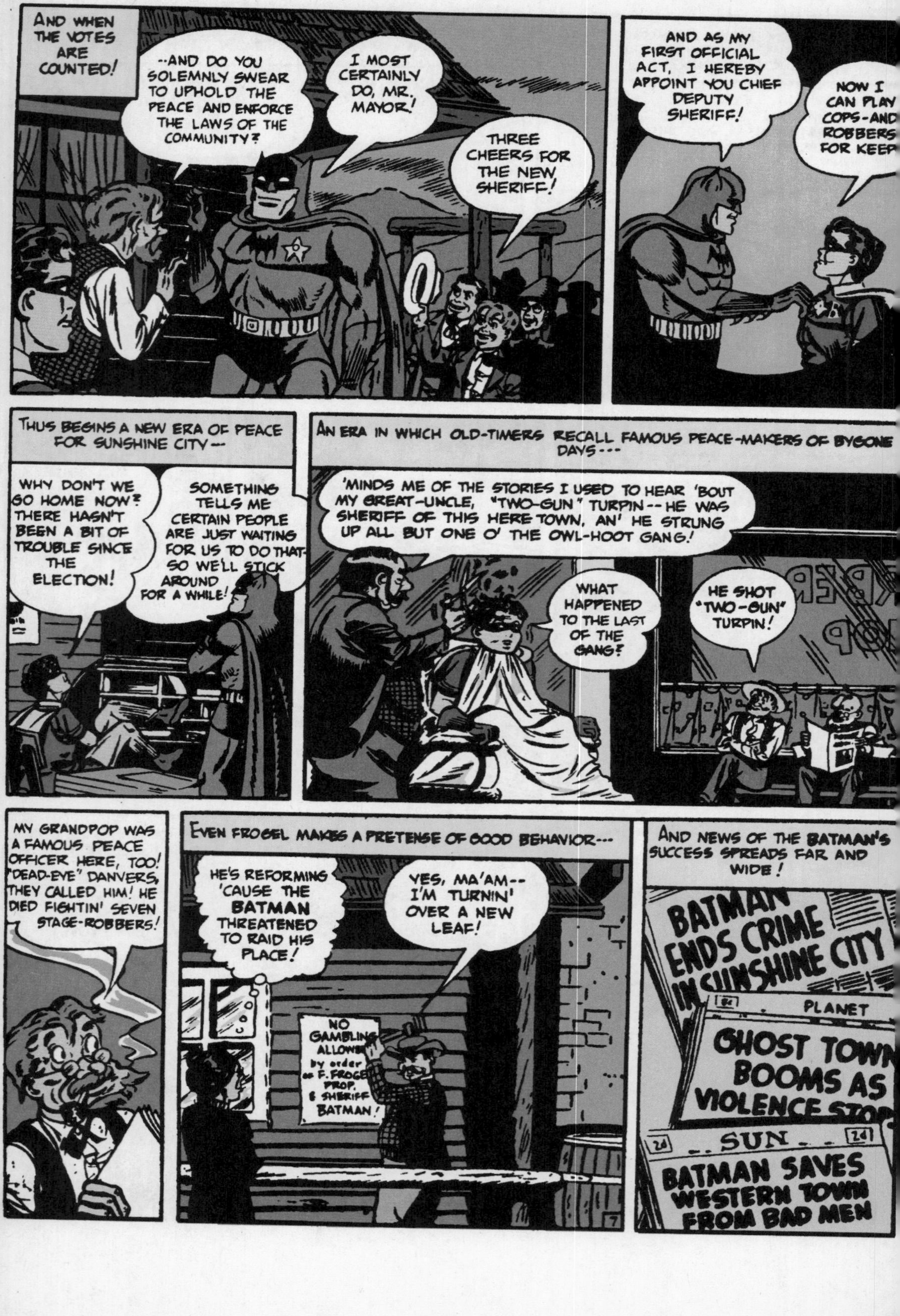
AND WHEN THE VOTES ARE COUNTED!
--AND DO YOU SOLEMNLY SWEAR TO UPHOLD THE PEACE AND ENFORCE THE LAWS OF THE COMMUNITY?
I MOST CERTAINLY DO, MR. MAYOR!
THREE CHEERS FOR THE NEW SHERIFF!
AND AS MY FIRST OFFICIAL ACT, I HEREBY APPOINT YOU CHIEF DEPUTY SHERIFF!
NOW I CAN PLAY COPS-AND ROBBERS FOR KEEP
THUS BEGINS A NEW ERA OF PEACE FOR SUNSHINE CITY--
WHY DON'T WE GO HOME NOW? THERE HASN'T BEEN A BIT OF TROUBLE SINCE THE ELECTION!
SOMETHING TELLS ME CERTAIN PEOPLE ARE JUST WAITING FOR US TO DO THAT-SO WE'LL STICK AROUND FOR A WHILE!
AN ERA IN WHICH OLD-TIMERS RECALL FAMOUS PEACE-MAKERS OF BYGONE DAYS---
'MINDS ME OF THE STORIES I USED TO HEAR 'BOUT MY GREAT-UNCLE, "TWO-GUN" TURPIN-- HE WAS SHERIFF OF THIS HERE TOWN, AN' HE STRUNG UP ALL BUT ONE O' THE OWL-HOOT GANG!
WHAT HAPPENED TO THE LAST OF THE GANG?
HE SHOT "TWO-GUN" TURPIN!
MY GRANDPOP WAS A FAMOUS PEACE OFFICER HERE, TOO! "DEAD-EYE" DANVERS, THEY CALLED HIM! HE DIED FIGHTIN' SEVEN STAGE-ROBBERS!
EVEN FROGEL MAKES A PRETENSE OF GOOD BEHAVIOR---
HE'S REFORMING 'CAUSE THE BATMAN THREATENED TO RAID HIS PLACE!
YES, MA'AM-- I'M TURNIN' OVER A NEW LEAF!
NO GAMBLING ALLOWED by order of F. FROGEL PROP. & SHERIFF BATMAN!
AND NEWS OF THE BATMAN'S SUCCESS SPREADS FAR AND WIDE!
BATMAN ENDS CRIME IN SUNSHINE CITY
PLANET
GHOST TOWN BOOMS AS VIOLENCE STOPS
SUN
BATMAN SAVES WESTERN TOWN FROM BAD MEN

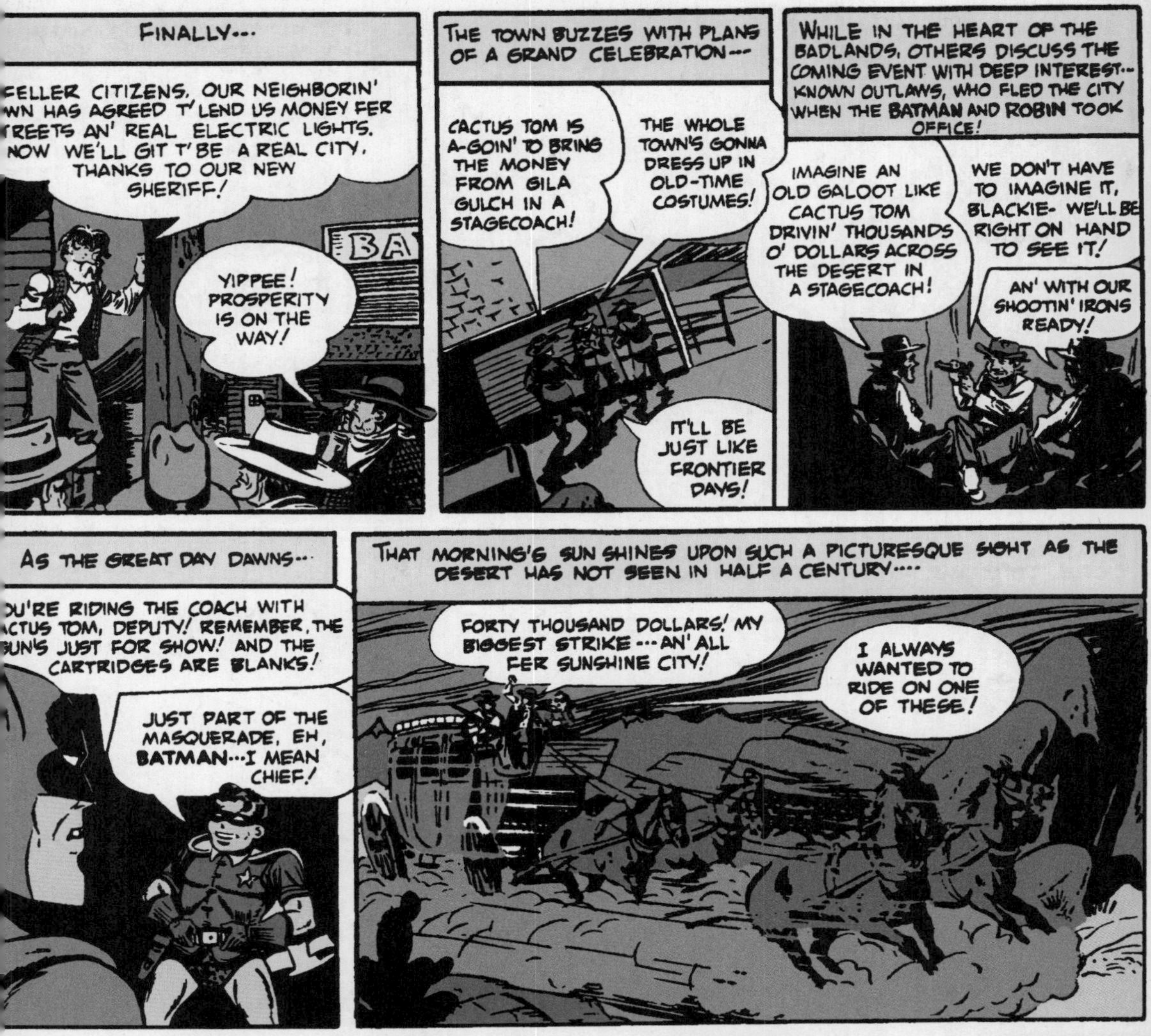
FINALLY...
FELLER CITIZENS, OUR NEIGHBORIN' WN HAS AGREED T' LEND US MONEY FER TREETS AN' REAL ELECTRIC LIGHTS. NOW WE'LL GIT T' BE A REAL CITY, THANKS TO OUR NEW SHERIFF!
YIPPEE! PROSPERITY IS ON THE WAY!
BA
THE TOWN BUZZES WITH PLANS OF A GRAND CELEBRATION---
CACTUS TOM IS A-GOIN' TO BRING THE MONEY FROM GILA GULCH IN A STAGECOACH!
THE WHOLE TOWN'S GONNA DRESS UP IN OLD-TIME COSTUMES!
IT'LL BE JUST LIKE FRONTIER DAYS!
WHILE IN THE HEART OF THE BADLANDS, OTHERS DISCUSS THE COMING EVENT WITH DEEP INTEREST-- KNOWN OUTLAWS, WHO FLED THE CITY WHEN THE BATMAN AND ROBIN TOOK OFFICE!
IMAGINE AN OLD GALOOT LIKE CACTUS TOM DRIVIN' THOUSANDS O' DOLLARS ACROSS THE DESERT IN A STAGECOACH!
WE DON'T HAVE TO IMAGINE IT, BLACKIE- WE'LL BE RIGHT ON HAND TO SEE IT!
AN' WITH OUR SHOOTIN' IRONS READY!
AS THE GREAT DAY DAWNS...
OU'RE RIDING THE COACH WITH ACTUS TOM, DEPUTY! REMEMBER, THE UN'S JUST FOR SHOW! AND THE CARTRIDGES ARE BLANKS!
JUST PART OF THE MASQUERADE, EH, BATMAN...I MEAN CHIEF!
THAT MORNING'S SUN SHINES UPON SUCH A PICTURESQUE SIGHT AS THE DESERT HAS NOT SEEN IN HALF A CENTURY....
FORTY THOUSAND DOLLARS! MY BIGGEST STRIKE --- AN' ALL FER SUNSHINE CITY!
I ALWAYS WANTED TO RIDE ON ONE OF THESE!
'FORE THE BATMAN CAME, WE WOULDN'T DARE CART MONEY AROUND LIKE THIS!
IT'S SAFE ENOUGH NOW, SINCE FROGEL'S PALS LIT OUT FER OTHER PARTS!
8
SAFE? LET'S LOOK AHEAD- TO WHERE THE ANCIENT COACH'S PATH TWISTS BETWEEN STEEP WALLS OF ROCK!
WE'RE REALLY HELPIN' 'EM WITH THEIR SHOW- THIS IS LIKE THE OLD DAYS, TOO!
GIT READY, BOYS! I KIN HEAR 'EM!

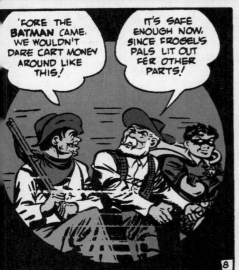

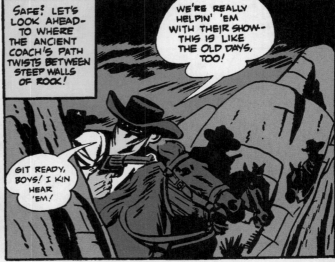

A SUDDEN THUNDER OF GUNS--A CHORUS OF WILD YELLS--AND THE TRIO IS INESCAPABLY TRAPPED!

HALT! STAND AN' DELIVER!

I'LL STOP 'EM-- OUCH!

I'LL BE HANGED IF I WILL!

THEY'VE KILLED TOM!

AAAH!

THIS GUN'S NO GOOD TO ME WITHOUT BULLETS SO YOU CAN HAVE IT!

YOU WON'T LIVE T' HANG, YUH OLD FOOL-- OH-H-H--!

SNATCHING THE BLACKSNAKE WHIP FROM CACTUS TOM'S LIMP FINGERS, THE BOY WONDER LASHES OUT FURIOUSLY

YOU DIRTY KILLERS!

OW! GET THAT WHIP AWAY FROM HIM!

I'VE GOT THE LITTLE BRAT!

YOU'LL NEVER GET AWAY WITH THIS-- NEVER!

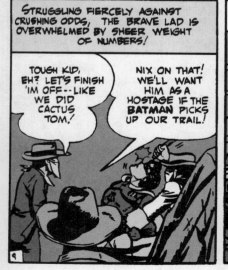

STRUGGLING FIERCELY AGAINST CRUSHING ODDS, THE BRAVE LAD IS OVERWHELMED BY SHEER WEIGHT OF NUMBERS!

TOUGH KID, EH? LET'S FINISH 'IM OFF--LIKE WE DID CACTUS TOM!

NIX ON THAT! WE'LL WANT HIM AS A HOSTAGE IF THE BATMAN PICKS UP OUR TRAIL!

YOU KILLERS WILL PAY FOR THIS!

HERE'S THE FORTY GRAND! LET'S GIT BACK TO THE HIDEOUT!

AS THE ROBBERS HEAD INTO THE MAZE OF ROCK

THE BATMAN WILL NEVER FIND US OUT HERE UNLESS I CAN LEAVE A TRAIL ---CAN'T GET AT THE RADIO IN MY BELT BUCKLE! I'VE GOT IT--THESE BLANK CARTRIDGES!

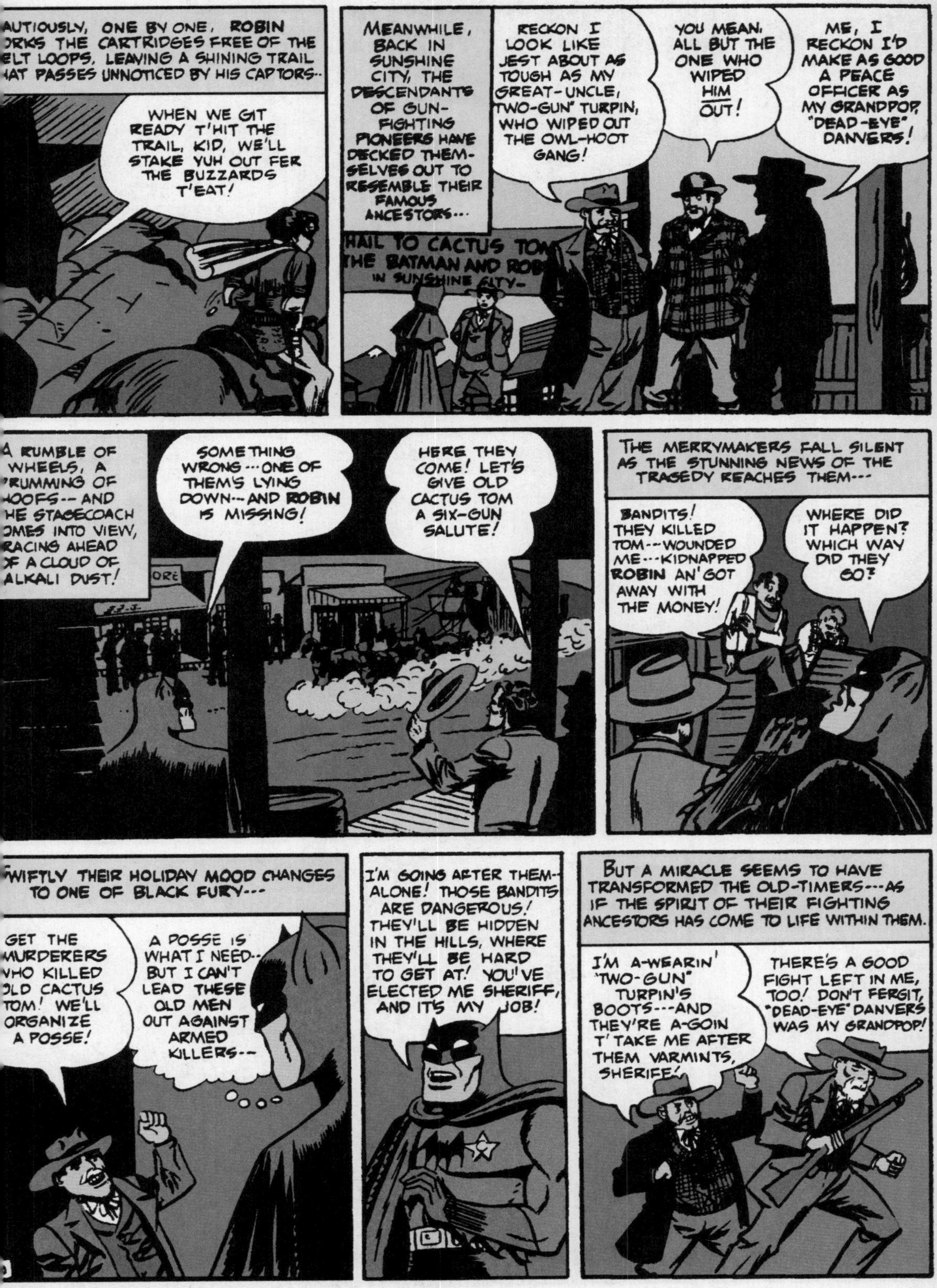
AUTIOUSLY, ONE BY ONE, ROBIN ORKS THE CARTRIDGES FREE OF THE ELT LOOPS, LEAVING A SHINING TRAIL HAT PASSES UNNOTICED BY HIS CAPTORS..
WHEN WE GIT READY T'HIT THE TRAIL, KID, WE'LL STAKE YUH OUT FER THE BUZZARDS T'EAT!
MEANWHILE, BACK IN SUNSHINE CITY, THE DESCENDANTS OF GUN-FIGHTING PIONEERS HAVE DECKED THEM-SELVES OUT TO RESEMBLE THEIR FAMOUS ANCESTORS...
RECKON I LOOK LIKE JEST ABOUT AS TOUGH AS MY GREAT-UNCLE, "TWO-GUN" TURPIN, WHO WIPED OUT THE OWL-HOOT GANG!
YOU MEAN, ALL BUT THE ONE WHO WIPED HIM OUT!
ME, I RECKON I'D MAKE AS GOOD A PEACE OFFICER AS MY GRANDPOP, "DEAD-EYE" DANVERS!
HAIL TO CACTUS TOM THE BATMAN AND ROB IN SUNSHINE CITY-
A RUMBLE OF WHEELS, A RUMMING OF HOOFS-- AND HE STAGECOACH OMES INTO VIEW, RACING AHEAD OF A CLOUD OF ALKALI DUST!
SOMETHING WRONG---ONE OF THEM'S LYING DOWN--AND ROBIN IS MISSING!
HERE THEY COME! LET'S GIVE OLD CACTUS TOM A SIX-GUN SALUTE!
THE MERRYMAKERS FALL SILENT AS THE STUNNING NEWS OF THE TRAGEDY REACHES THEM---
BANDITS! THEY KILLED TOM--WOUNDED ME---KIDNAPPED ROBIN AN' GOT AWAY WITH THE MONEY!
WHERE DID IT HAPPEN? WHICH WAY DID THEY GO?
SWIFTLY THEIR HOLIDAY MOOD CHANGES TO ONE OF BLACK FURY---
GET THE MURDERERS WHO KILLED OLD CACTUS TOM! WE'LL ORGANIZE A POSSE!
A POSSE IS WHAT I NEED-- BUT I CAN'T LEAD THESE OLD MEN OUT AGAINST ARMED KILLERS--
I'M GOING AFTER THEM-- ALONE! THOSE BANDITS ARE DANGEROUS! THEY'LL BE HIDDEN IN THE HILLS, WHERE THEY'LL BE HARD TO GET AT! YOU'VE ELECTED ME SHERIFF, AND IT'S MY JOB!
BUT A MIRACLE SEEMS TO HAVE TRANSFORMED THE OLD-TIMERS---AS IF THE SPIRIT OF THEIR FIGHTING ANCESTORS HAS COME TO LIFE WITHIN THEM.
I'M A-WEARIN' "TWO-GUN" TURPIN'S BOOTS---AND THEY'RE A-GOIN T' TAKE ME AFTER THEM VARMINTS, SHERIFF!
THERE'S A GOOD FIGHT LEFT IN ME, TOO! DON'T FERGIT, "DEAD-EYE" DANVERS WAS MY GRANDPOP!

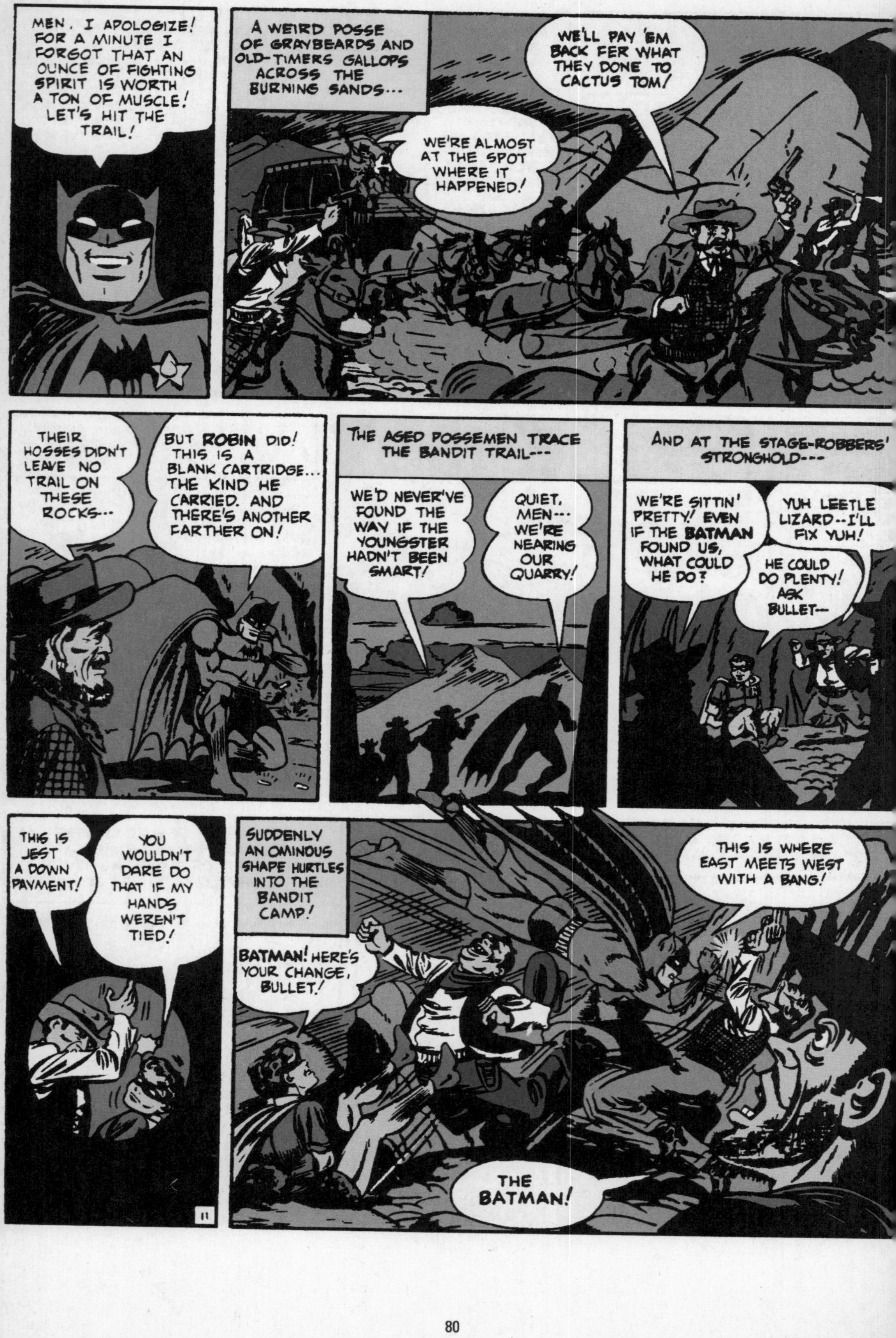
MEN, I APOLOGIZE! FOR A MINUTE I FORGOT THAT AN OUNCE OF FIGHTING SPIRIT IS WORTH A TON OF MUSCLE! LET'S HIT THE TRAIL!
A WEIRD POSSE OF GRAYBEARDS AND OLD-TIMERS GALLOPS ACROSS THE BURNING SANDS...
WE'RE ALMOST AT THE SPOT WHERE IT HAPPENED!
WE'LL PAY 'EM BACK FER WHAT THEY DONE TO CACTUS TOM!
THEIR HOSSES DIDN'T LEAVE NO TRAIL ON THESE ROCKS...
BUT ROBIN DID! THIS IS A BLANK CARTRIDGE... THE KIND HE CARRIED. AND THERE'S ANOTHER FARTHER ON!
THE AGED POSSEMEN TRACE THE BANDIT TRAIL---
WE'D NEVER'VE FOUND THE WAY IF THE YOUNGSTER HADN'T BEEN SMART!
QUIET, MEN--- WE'RE NEARING OUR QUARRY!
AND AT THE STAGE-ROBBERS' STRONGHOLD---
WE'RE SITTIN' PRETTY! EVEN IF THE BATMAN FOUND US, WHAT COULD HE DO?
YUH LEETLE LIZARD--I'LL FIX YUH!
HE COULD DO PLENTY! ASK BULLET---
THIS IS JEST A DOWN PAYMENT!
YOU WOULDN'T DARE DO THAT IF MY HANDS WEREN'T TIED!
11
SUDDENLY AN OMINOUS SHAPE HURTLES INTO THE BANDIT CAMP!
BATMAN! HERE'S YOUR CHANGE, BULLET!
THIS IS WHERE EAST MEETS WEST WITH A BANG!
THE BATMAN!

SPLIT SECONDS LATER, THE BAND OF SPIRITED OLD-TIMERS HURLS DEFIANCE AT THE FOE, FIGHTING WITH THE BRAVADO OF PLAINSMEN OF THE WEST.

I'M TOO OLD FER MY FISTS BUT MY CRUTCH WILL DO!

YIPPEE!

WAHOO! I'M "TWO-GUN" TURPIN!

ARE THINGS BLACK ENOUGH FOR YOU, BLACKIE?

OWOOOO!

YES, SIR—MY GRANDPOP, "DEAD-EYE" DANVERS, COULDN'T HAVE DONE BETTER! NOW ONE O' YOU RATTLE-SNAKES CUT THAT BOY LOOSE!

D-DON'T SHOOT! W-WE SURRENDER!

THANKS, "DEAD-EYE"!

THERE'S A CREEK BELOW! IT WILL COOL OFF YOUR BLISTERS—OR WOULD YOU RATHER TALK?

I-I'LL TALK! FROGEL ORDERED US TO STICK UP THE COACH AN' KILL CACTUS TOM!

LEAVING THE BANDITS SAFELY BOUND AND GUARDED, THE DYNAMIC DUO RACES BACK TO SUNSHINE CITY FOR A FINAL ACCOUNTING WITH FIVE ACES FROGEL!

GOT TO FIND FROGEL BEFORE SOMEONE WARNS HIM THE GAME IS UP!

HEY—WATCH OUT FOR SPEED COPS!

BUT A WARNING IS ALREADY ON ITS WAY TO THE GAMBLER, CUTTING SHORT HIS BARROOM BRAGGING···

THE BOYS'LL MAKE SHORT WORK O' THEM OLD DUFFERS, AN' THE BATMAN, TOO!···HUH? WHAT'S THIS?

BOSS! THE BATMAN (GASP) ROUNDED 'EM UP···HE'S COMIN' HERE AFTER YOU!

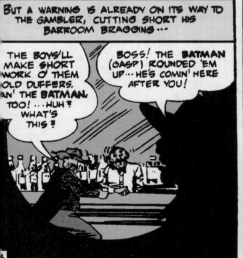

ALL RIGHT···I'LL FINISH HIM MYSELF! HE DON'T BELIEVE IN USIN' SHOOTIN' IRONS···THE FOOL···SO HE WON'T HAVE A CHANCE!

IT AIN'T GUNS I'M AFRAID OF SO MUCH AS THE BATMAN!

I DON'T WANNA GET MIXED UP IN NO GUN—FIGHTIN'!

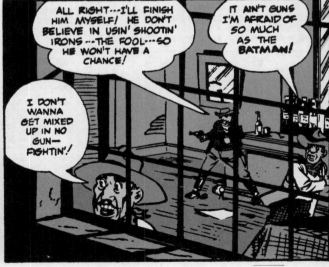

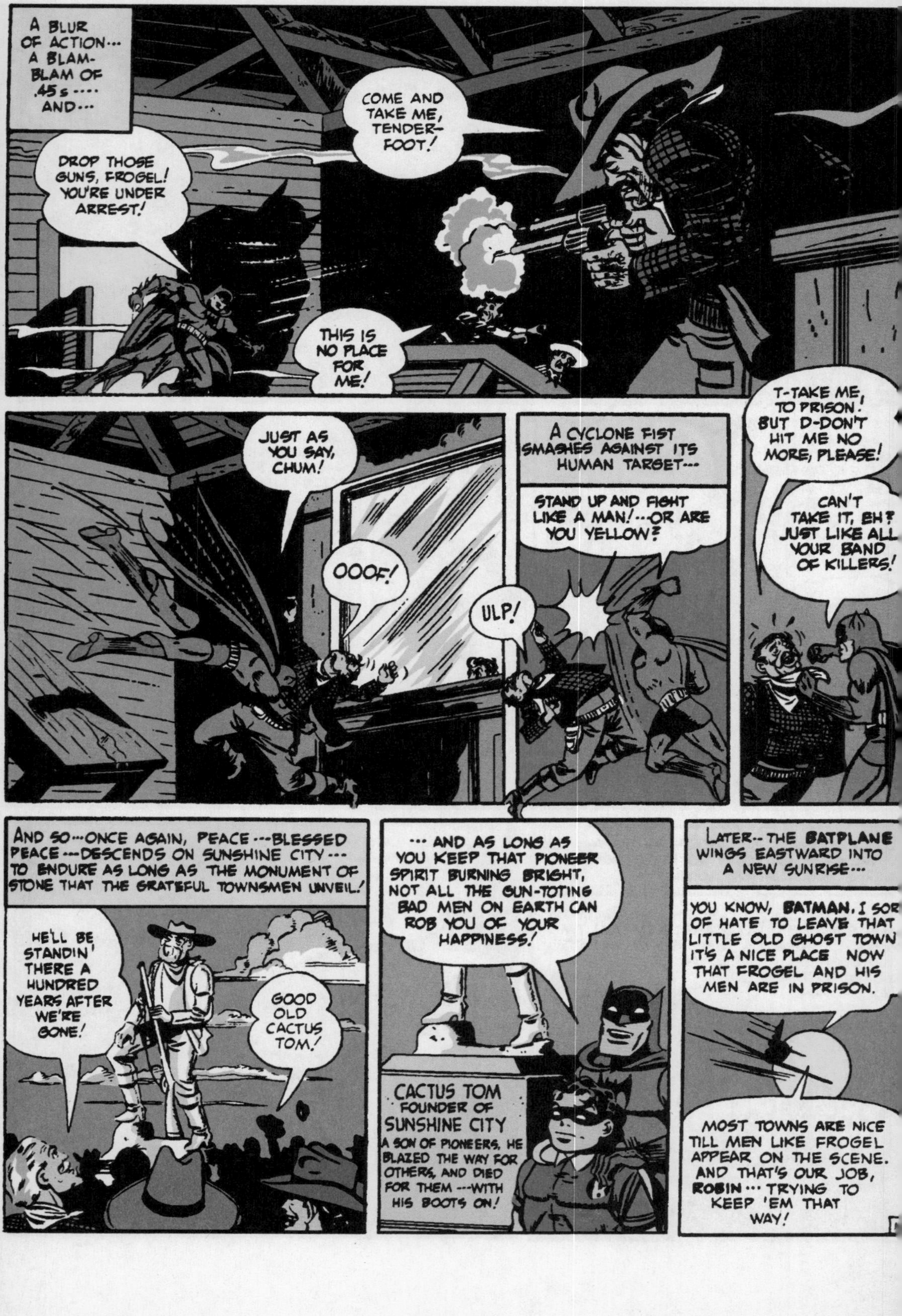

A BLUR OF ACTION... A BLAM-BLAM OF .45s.... AND...
DROP THOSE GUNS, FROGEL! YOU'RE UNDER ARREST!
COME AND TAKE ME, TENDER-FOOT!
THIS IS NO PLACE FOR ME!
JUST AS YOU SAY, CHUM!
OOOF!
A CYCLONE FIST SMASHES AGAINST ITS HUMAN TARGET---
STAND UP AND FIGHT LIKE A MAN!---OR ARE YOU YELLOW?
ULP!
T-TAKE ME TO PRISON! BUT D-DON'T HIT ME NO MORE, PLEASE!
CAN'T TAKE IT, EH? JUST LIKE ALL YOUR BAND OF KILLERS!
AND SO---ONCE AGAIN, PEACE---BLESSED PEACE---DESCENDS ON SUNSHINE CITY---TO ENDURE AS LONG AS THE MONUMENT OF STONE THAT THE GRATEFUL TOWNSMEN UNVEIL!
HE'LL BE STANDIN' THERE A HUNDRED YEARS AFTER WE'RE GONE!
GOOD OLD CACTUS TOM!
--- AND AS LONG AS YOU KEEP THAT PIONEER SPIRIT BURNING BRIGHT, NOT ALL THE GUN-TOTING BAD MEN ON EARTH CAN ROB YOU OF YOUR HAPPINESS!
CACTUS TOM FOUNDER OF SUNSHINE CITY
A SON OF PIONEERS, HE BLAZED THE WAY FOR OTHERS, AND DIED FOR THEM ---WITH HIS BOOTS ON!
LATER-- THE BATPLANE WINGS EASTWARD INTO A NEW SUNRISE---
YOU KNOW, BATMAN, I SOR OF HATE TO LEAVE THAT LITTLE OLD GHOST TOWN IT'S A NICE PLACE NOW THAT FROGEL AND HIS MEN ARE IN PRISON.
MOST TOWNS ARE NICE TILL MEN LIKE FROGEL APPEAR ON THE SCENE. AND THAT'S OUR JOB, ROBIN--- TRYING TO KEEP 'EM THAT WAY!

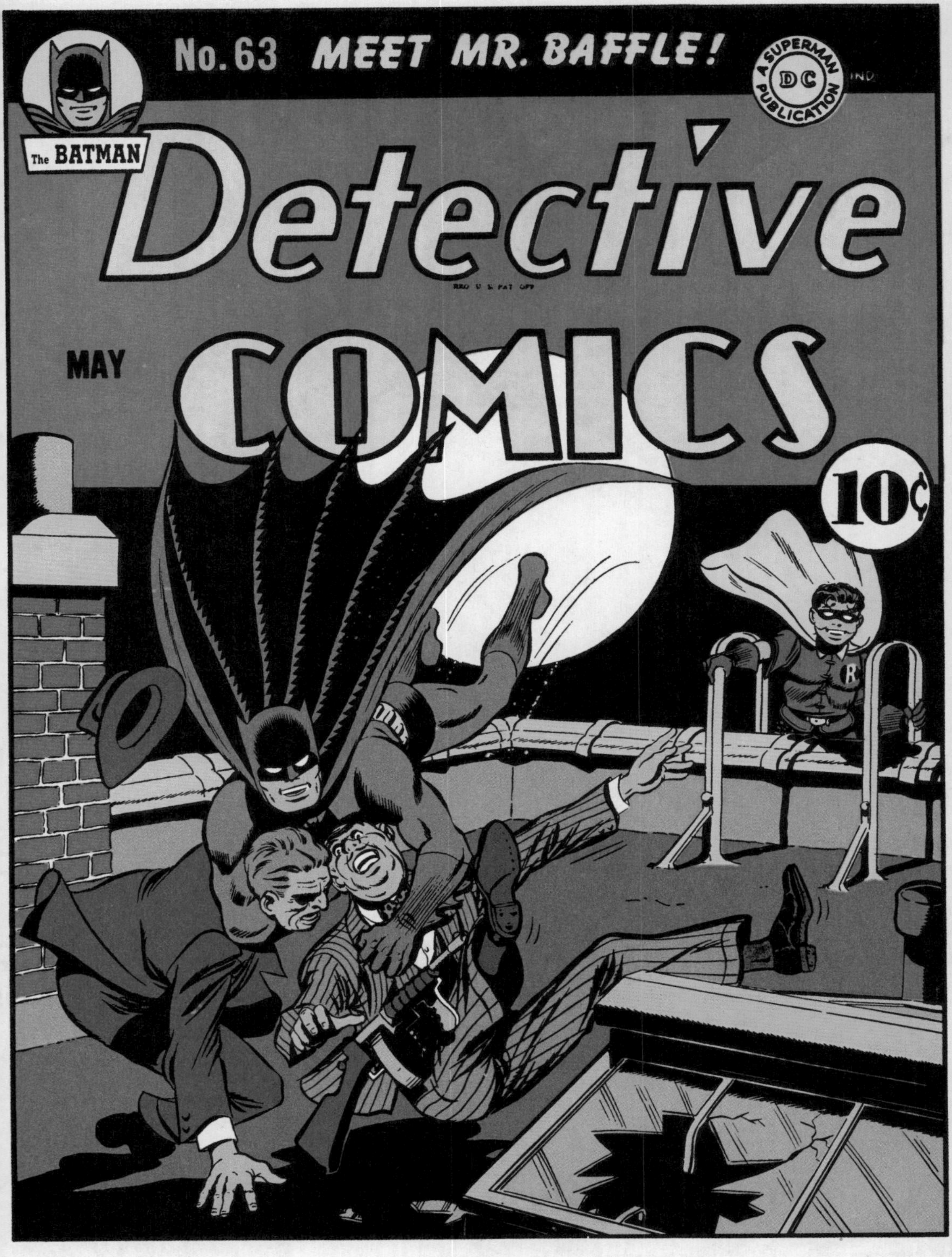
No. 63
MEET MR. BAFFLE!
A SUPERMAN DC PUBLICATION
INC.
The BATMAN
Detective
MAY
COMICS
10¢

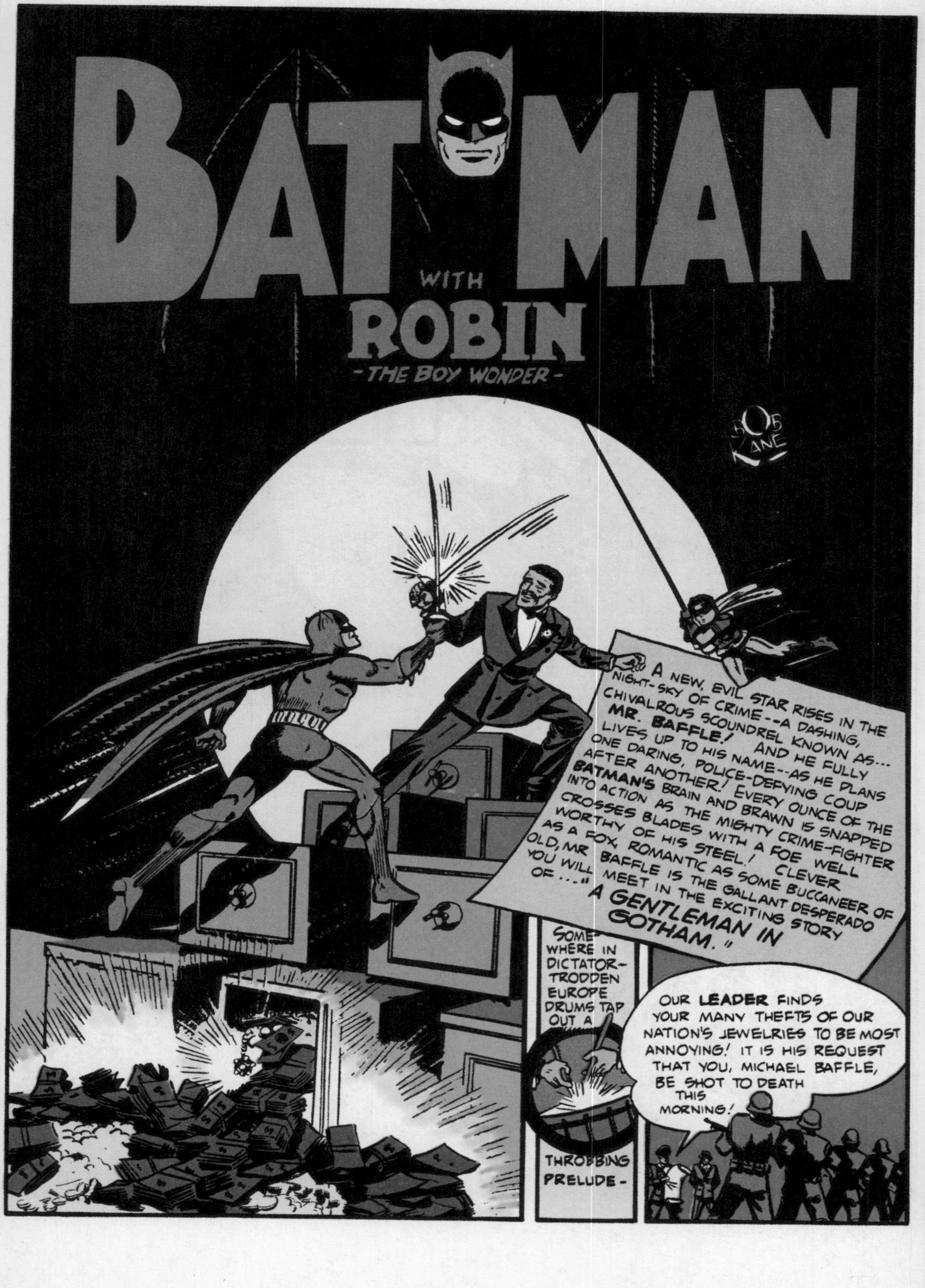
BATMAN
WITH
ROBIN
-THE BOY WONDER-
BOB KANE
A NEW, EVIL STAR RISES IN THE NIGHT-SKY OF CRIME--A DASHING, CHIVALROUS SCOUNDREL KNOWN AS... MR. BAFFLE! AND HE FULLY LIVES UP TO HIS NAME--AS HE PLANS ONE DARING, POLICE-DEFYING COUP AFTER ANOTHER! EVERY OUNCE OF THE BATMAN'S BRAIN AND BRAWN IS SNAPPED INTO ACTION AS THE MIGHTY CRIME-FIGHTER CROSSES BLADES WITH A FOE WELL WORTHY OF HIS STEEL! CLEVER AS A FOX, ROMANTIC AS SOME BUCCANEER OF OLD, MR BAFFLE IS THE GALLANT DESPERADO YOU WILL MEET IN THE EXCITING STORY OF..." A GENTLEMAN IN GOTHAM."
SOME-WHERE IN DICTATOR-TRODDEN EUROPE DRUMS TAP OUT A
THROBBING PRELUDE-
OUR LEADER FINDS YOUR MANY THEFTS OF OUR NATION'S JEWELRIES TO BE MOST ANNOYING! IT IS HIS REQUEST THAT YOU, MICHAEL BAFFLE, BE SHOT TO DEATH THIS MORNING!

THE BLINDFOLD FOR THE EYES!

BLINDFOLD? YOU WOULDN'T WANT TO DEPRIVE ME OF SEEING THE SUNRISE FOR THE LAST TIME!

COOL, COMPOSED, THE PRISONER LOOKS SERENELY AT DOOM PEERING FROM FIVE METAL-COLD EYES!

READY... TAKE AIM!...

THE COMMANDER SNAPS DOWN HIS SWORD. THE MEN FIRE--- THE PRISONER CLUTCHES HIS BREAST AND BEGINS TO CRUMPLE.

FIRE!

SILENCE NOW···AND ON THE COLD GROUND IS SPRAWLED A STILL FIGURE SEEMINGLY SMOTHERED IN ETERNAL SLEEP!

MARCH!

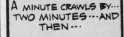

A MINUTE CRAWLS BY··· TWO MINUTES···AND THEN···

ALL THIS IS SUCH A BEASTLY NUISANCE! WASN'T WORTH IT, REALLY! GOT MY CLOTHES FILTHY WITH DUST!

OH, WELL··· MUST TAKE THE GOOD WITH THE BAD. THAT'S LIFE, I GUESS!

AND IN THE BARRACKS···

AH, IT WAS WELL WORTH PUTTING **BLANKS** IN OUR GUNS IN EXCHANGE FOR THESE STOLEN JEWELS BAFFLE GAVE US!

LET US HOPE THE COMMANDER NEVER FINDS OUT!

AND THE COMMANDER···

I HOPE MY MEN NEVER FIND OUT I RECEIVED THESE JEWELS FROM BAFFLE FOR NOT INSPECTING THE RIFLES!

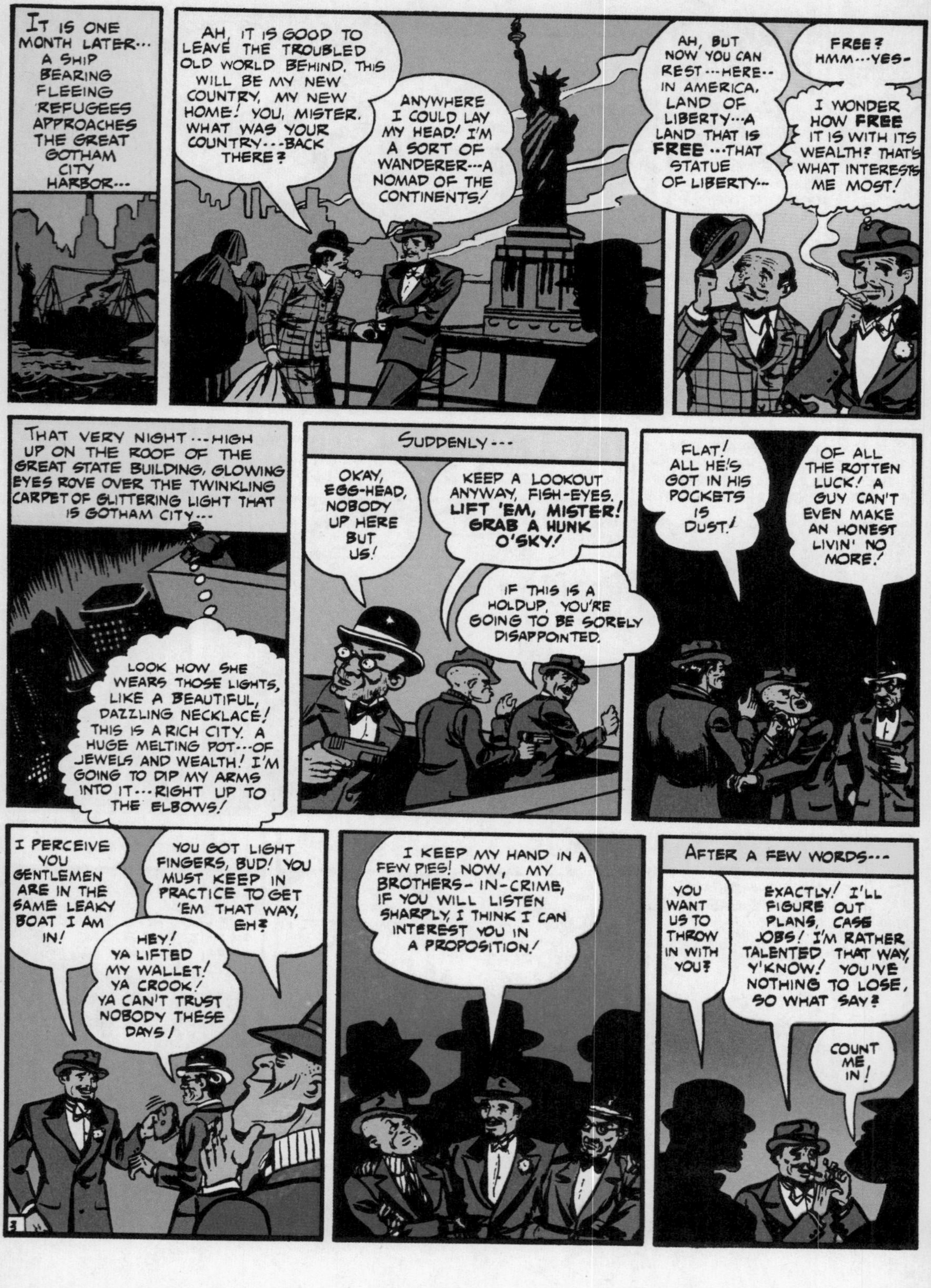
IT IS ONE MONTH LATER... A SHIP BEARING FLEEING REFUGEES APPROACHES THE GREAT GOTHAM CITY HARBOR...
AH, IT IS GOOD TO LEAVE THE TROUBLED OLD WORLD BEHIND. THIS WILL BE MY NEW COUNTRY, MY NEW HOME! YOU, MISTER. WHAT WAS YOUR COUNTRY---BACK THERE?
ANYWHERE I COULD LAY MY HEAD! I'M A SORT OF WANDERER---A NOMAD OF THE CONTINENTS!
AH, BUT NOW YOU CAN REST---HERE-- IN AMERICA, LAND OF LIBERTY---A LAND THAT IS FREE---THAT STATUE OF LIBERTY--
FREE? HMM---YES-
I WONDER HOW FREE IT IS WITH ITS WEALTH? THAT'S WHAT INTERESTS ME MOST!
THAT VERY NIGHT---HIGH UP ON THE ROOF OF THE GREAT STATE BUILDING, GLOWING EYES ROVE OVER THE TWINKLING CARPET OF GLITTERING LIGHT THAT IS GOTHAM CITY---
LOOK HOW SHE WEARS THOSE LIGHTS, LIKE A BEAUTIFUL, DAZZLING NECKLACE! THIS IS A RICH CITY. A HUGE MELTING POT---OF JEWELS AND WEALTH! I'M GOING TO DIP MY ARMS INTO IT---RIGHT UP TO THE ELBOWS!
SUDDENLY---
OKAY, EGG-HEAD, NOBODY UP HERE BUT US!
KEEP A LOOKOUT ANYWAY, FISH-EYES. LIFT 'EM, MISTER! GRAB A HUNK O'SKY!
IF THIS IS A HOLDUP, YOU'RE GOING TO BE SORELY DISAPPOINTED.
FLAT! ALL HE'S GOT IN HIS POCKETS IS DUST!
OF ALL THE ROTTEN LUCK! A GUY CAN'T EVEN MAKE AN HONEST LIVIN' NO MORE!
I PERCEIVE YOU GENTLEMEN ARE IN THE SAME LEAKY BOAT I AM IN!
YOU GOT LIGHT FINGERS, BUD! YOU MUST KEEP IN PRACTICE TO GET 'EM THAT WAY, EH?
HEY! YA LIFTED MY WALLET! YA CROOK! YA CAN'T TRUST NOBODY THESE DAYS!
I KEEP MY HAND IN A FEW PIES! NOW, MY BROTHERS-IN-CRIME, IF YOU WILL LISTEN SHARPLY, I THINK I CAN INTEREST YOU IN A PROPOSITION!
AFTER A FEW WORDS---
YOU WANT US TO THROW IN WITH YOU?
EXACTLY! I'LL FIGURE OUT PLANS, CASE JOBS! I'M RATHER TALENTED THAT WAY, Y'KNOW! YOU'VE NOTHING TO LOSE, SO WHAT SAY?
COUNT ME IN!

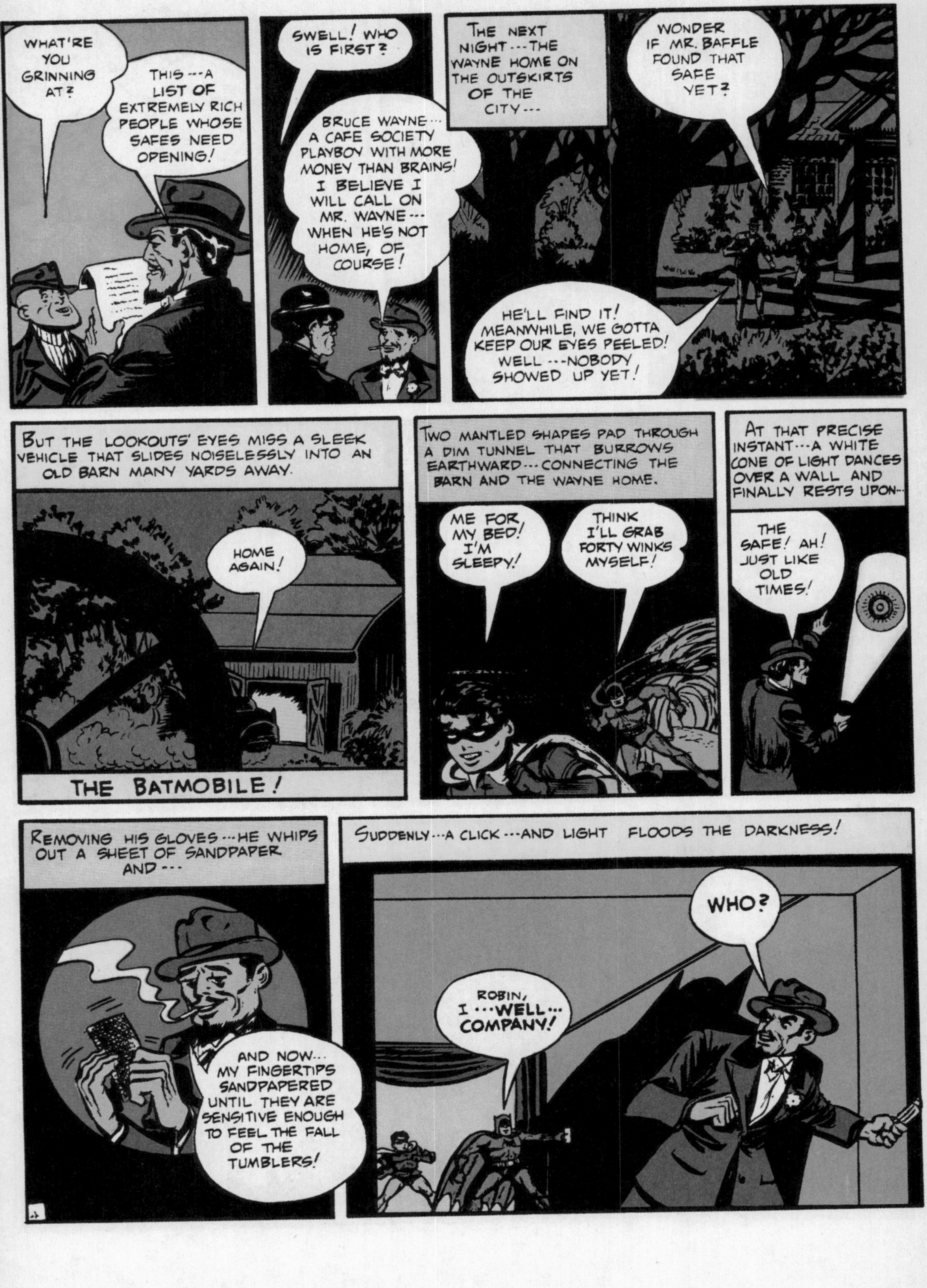
WHAT'RE YOU GRINNING AT?
THIS---A LIST OF EXTREMELY RICH PEOPLE WHOSE SAFES NEED OPENING!
SWELL! WHO IS FIRST?
BRUCE WAYNE... A CAFE SOCIETY PLAYBOY WITH MORE MONEY THAN BRAINS! I BELIEVE I WILL CALL ON MR. WAYNE--- WHEN HE'S NOT HOME, OF COURSE!
THE NEXT NIGHT---THE WAYNE HOME ON THE OUTSKIRTS OF THE CITY---
WONDER IF MR. BAFFLE FOUND THAT SAFE YET?
HE'LL FIND IT! MEANWHILE, WE GOTTA KEEP OUR EYES PEELED! WELL ---NOBODY SHOWED UP YET!
BUT THE LOOKOUTS' EYES MISS A SLEEK VEHICLE THAT SLIDES NOISELESSLY INTO AN OLD BARN MANY YARDS AWAY.
HOME AGAIN!
THE BATMOBILE!
TWO MANTLED SHAPES PAD THROUGH A DIM TUNNEL THAT BURROWS EARTHWARD--- CONNECTING THE BARN AND THE WAYNE HOME.
ME FOR MY BED! I'M SLEEPY!
THINK I'LL GRAB FORTY WINKS MYSELF!
AT THAT PRECISE INSTANT---A WHITE CONE OF LIGHT DANCES OVER A WALL AND FINALLY RESTS UPON...
THE SAFE! AH! JUST LIKE OLD TIMES!
REMOVING HIS GLOVES---HE WHIPS OUT A SHEET OF SANDPAPER AND---
AND NOW... MY FINGERTIPS SANDPAPERED UNTIL THEY ARE SENSITIVE ENOUGH TO FEEL THE FALL OF THE TUMBLERS!
SUDDENLY---A CLICK---AND LIGHT FLOODS THE DARKNESS!
WHO?
ROBIN, I---WELL... COMPANY!

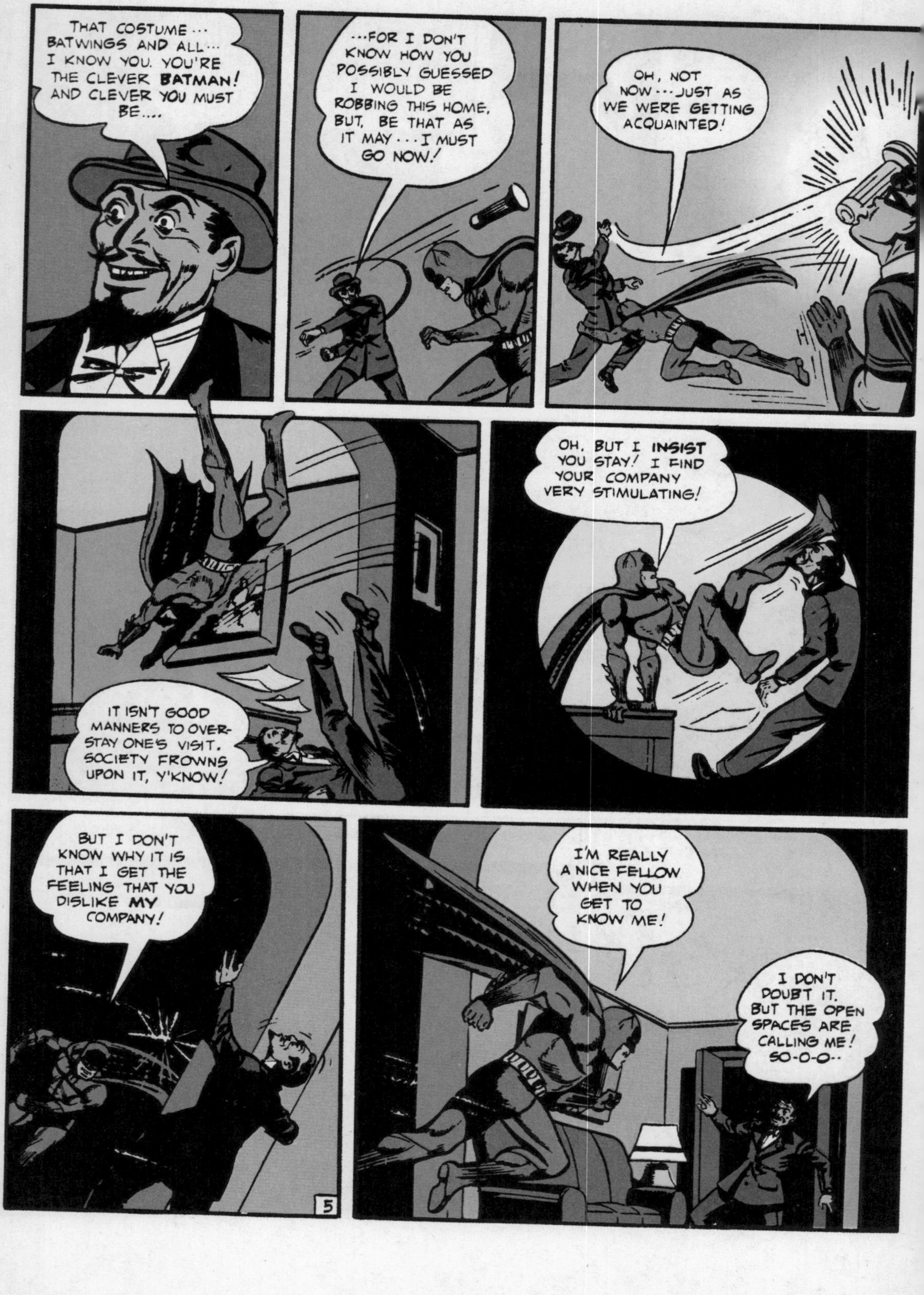
THAT COSTUME... BATWINGS AND ALL... I KNOW YOU. YOU'RE THE CLEVER BATMAN! AND CLEVER YOU MUST BE....
...FOR I DON'T KNOW HOW YOU POSSIBLY GUESSED I WOULD BE ROBBING THIS HOME, BUT, BE THAT AS IT MAY... I MUST GO NOW!
OH, NOT NOW... JUST AS WE WERE GETTING ACQUAINTED!
IT ISN'T GOOD MANNERS TO OVER-STAY ONE'S VISIT. SOCIETY FROWNS UPON IT, Y'KNOW!
OH, BUT I INSIST YOU STAY! I FIND YOUR COMPANY VERY STIMULATING!
BUT I DON'T KNOW WHY IT IS THAT I GET THE FEELING THAT YOU DISLIKE MY COMPANY!
5
I'M REALLY A NICE FELLOW WHEN YOU GET TO KNOW ME!
I DON'T DOUBT IT. BUT THE OPEN SPACES ARE CALLING ME! SO-O-O--

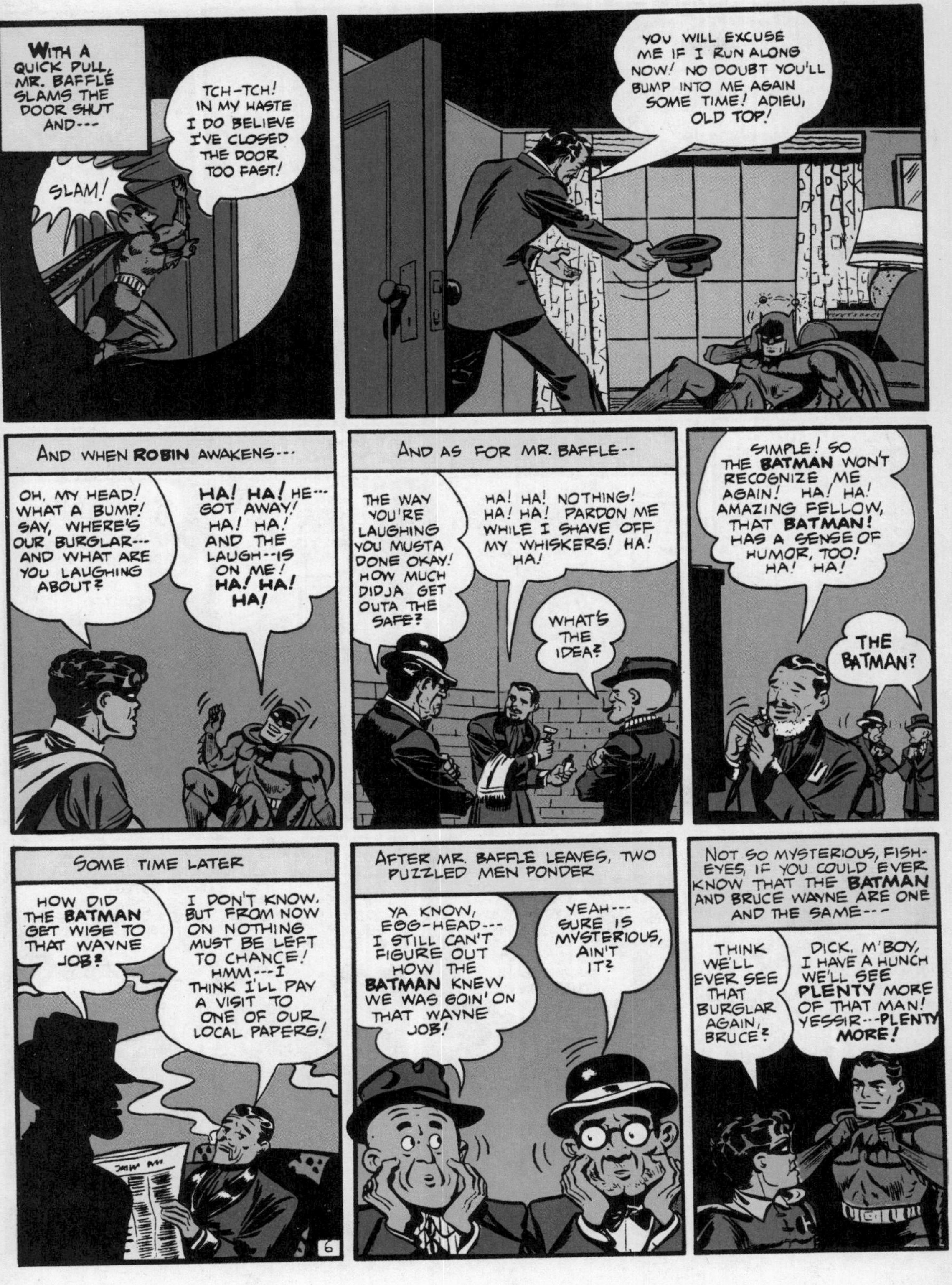
WITH A QUICK PULL, MR. BAFFLE SLAMS THE DOOR SHUT AND---
TCH-TCH! IN MY HASTE I DO BELIEVE I'VE CLOSED THE DOOR TOO FAST!
SLAM!
YOU WILL EXCUSE ME IF I RUN ALONG NOW! NO DOUBT YOU'LL BUMP INTO ME AGAIN SOME TIME! ADIEU, OLD TOP!
AND WHEN ROBIN AWAKENS---
OH, MY HEAD! WHAT A BUMP! SAY, WHERE'S OUR BURGLAR--- AND WHAT ARE YOU LAUGHING ABOUT?
HA! HA! HE--- GOT AWAY! HA! HA! AND THE LAUGH--IS ON ME! HA! HA! HA!
AND AS FOR MR. BAFFLE--
THE WAY YOU'RE LAUGHING YOU MUSTA DONE OKAY! HOW MUCH DIDJA GET OUTA THE SAFE?
HA! HA! NOTHING! HA! HA! PARDON ME WHILE I SHAVE OFF MY WHISKERS! HA! HA!
WHAT'S THE IDEA?
SIMPLE! SO THE BATMAN WON'T RECOGNIZE ME AGAIN! HA! HA! AMAZING FELLOW, THAT BATMAN! HAS A SENSE OF HUMOR, TOO! HA! HA!
THE BATMAN?
SOME TIME LATER
HOW DID THE BATMAN GET WISE TO THAT WAYNE JOB?
I DON'T KNOW. BUT FROM NOW ON NOTHING MUST BE LEFT TO CHANCE! HMM---I THINK I'LL PAY A VISIT TO ONE OF OUR LOCAL PAPERS!
6
AFTER MR. BAFFLE LEAVES, TWO PUZZLED MEN PONDER
YA KNOW, EGG-HEAD--- I STILL CAN'T FIGURE OUT HOW THE BATMAN KNEW WE WAS GOIN' ON THAT WAYNE JOB!
YEAH--- SURE IS MYSTERIOUS, AIN'T IT?
NOT SO MYSTERIOUS, FISH-EYES, IF YOU COULD EVER KNOW THAT THE BATMAN AND BRUCE WAYNE ARE ONE AND THE SAME---
THINK WE'LL EVER SEE THAT BURGLAR AGAIN, BRUCE?
DICK, M'BOY, I HAVE A HUNCH WE'LL SEE PLENTY MORE OF THAT MAN! YESSIR---PLENTY MORE!

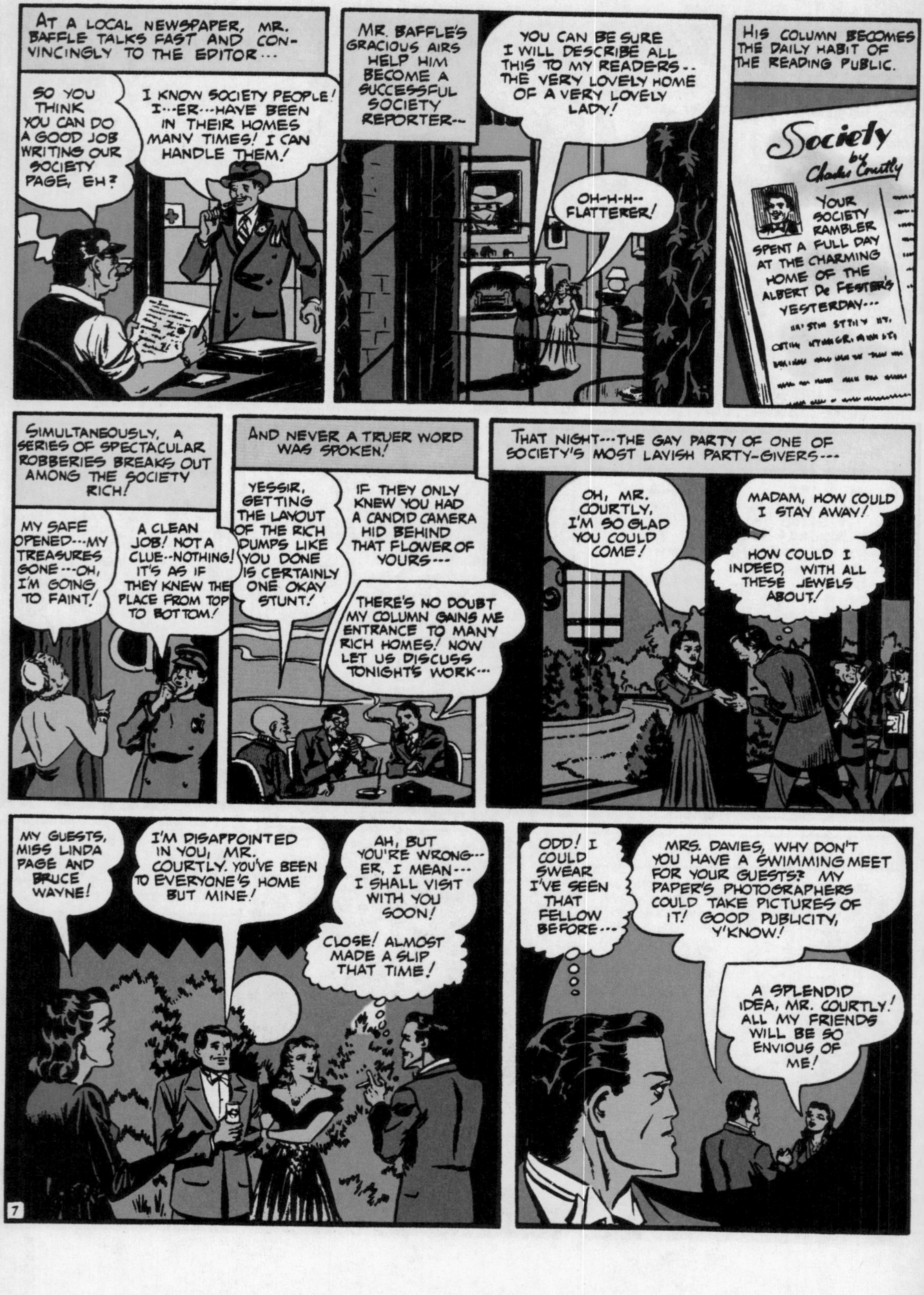

AT A LOCAL NEWSPAPER, MR. BAFFLE TALKS FAST AND CONVINCINGLY TO THE EDITOR...
SO YOU THINK YOU CAN DO A GOOD JOB WRITING OUR SOCIETY PAGE, EH?
I KNOW SOCIETY PEOPLE! I...ER...HAVE BEEN IN THEIR HOMES MANY TIMES! I CAN HANDLE THEM!
MR. BAFFLE'S GRACIOUS AIRS HELP HIM BECOME A SUCCESSFUL SOCIETY REPORTER--
YOU CAN BE SURE I WILL DESCRIBE ALL THIS TO MY READERS.. THE VERY LOVELY HOME OF A VERY LOVELY LADY!
OH-H-H-- FLATTERER!
HIS COLUMN BECOMES THE DAILY HABIT OF THE READING PUBLIC.
Society by Charles Courtly
YOUR SOCIETY RAMBLER SPENT A FULL DAY AT THE CHARMING HOME OF THE ALBERT De FESTER'S YESTERDAY...
SIMULTANEOUSLY, A SERIES OF SPECTACULAR ROBBERIES BREAKS OUT AMONG THE SOCIETY RICH!
MY SAFE OPENED...MY TREASURES GONE...OH, I'M GOING TO FAINT!
A CLEAN JOB! NOT A CLUE--NOTHING! IT'S AS IF THEY KNEW THE PLACE FROM TOP TO BOTTOM!
AND NEVER A TRUER WORD WAS SPOKEN!
YESSIR, GETTING THE LAYOUT OF THE RICH DUMPS LIKE YOU DONE IS CERTAINLY ONE OKAY STUNT!
IF THEY ONLY KNEW YOU HAD A CANDID CAMERA HID BEHIND THAT FLOWER OF YOURS---
THERE'S NO DOUBT MY COLUMN GAINS ME ENTRANCE TO MANY RICH HOMES! NOW LET US DISCUSS TONIGHT'S WORK...
THAT NIGHT---THE GAY PARTY OF ONE OF SOCIETY'S MOST LAVISH PARTY-GIVERS---
OH, MR. COURTLY, I'M SO GLAD YOU COULD COME!
MADAM, HOW COULD I STAY AWAY!
HOW COULD I INDEED, WITH ALL THESE JEWELS ABOUT!
MY GUESTS, MISS LINDA PAGE AND BRUCE WAYNE!
I'M DISAPPOINTED IN YOU, MR. COURTLY. YOU'VE BEEN TO EVERYONE'S HOME BUT MINE!
AH, BUT YOU'RE WRONG-- ER, I MEAN--- I SHALL VISIT WITH YOU SOON!
CLOSE! ALMOST MADE A SLIP THAT TIME!
7
ODD! I COULD SWEAR I'VE SEEN THAT FELLOW BEFORE...
MRS. DAVIES, WHY DON'T YOU HAVE A SWIMMING MEET FOR YOUR GUESTS? MY PAPER'S PHOTOGRAPHERS COULD TAKE PICTURES OF IT! GOOD PUBLICITY, Y'KNOW!
A SPLENDID IDEA, MR. COURTLY! ALL MY FRIENDS WILL BE SO ENVIOUS OF ME!

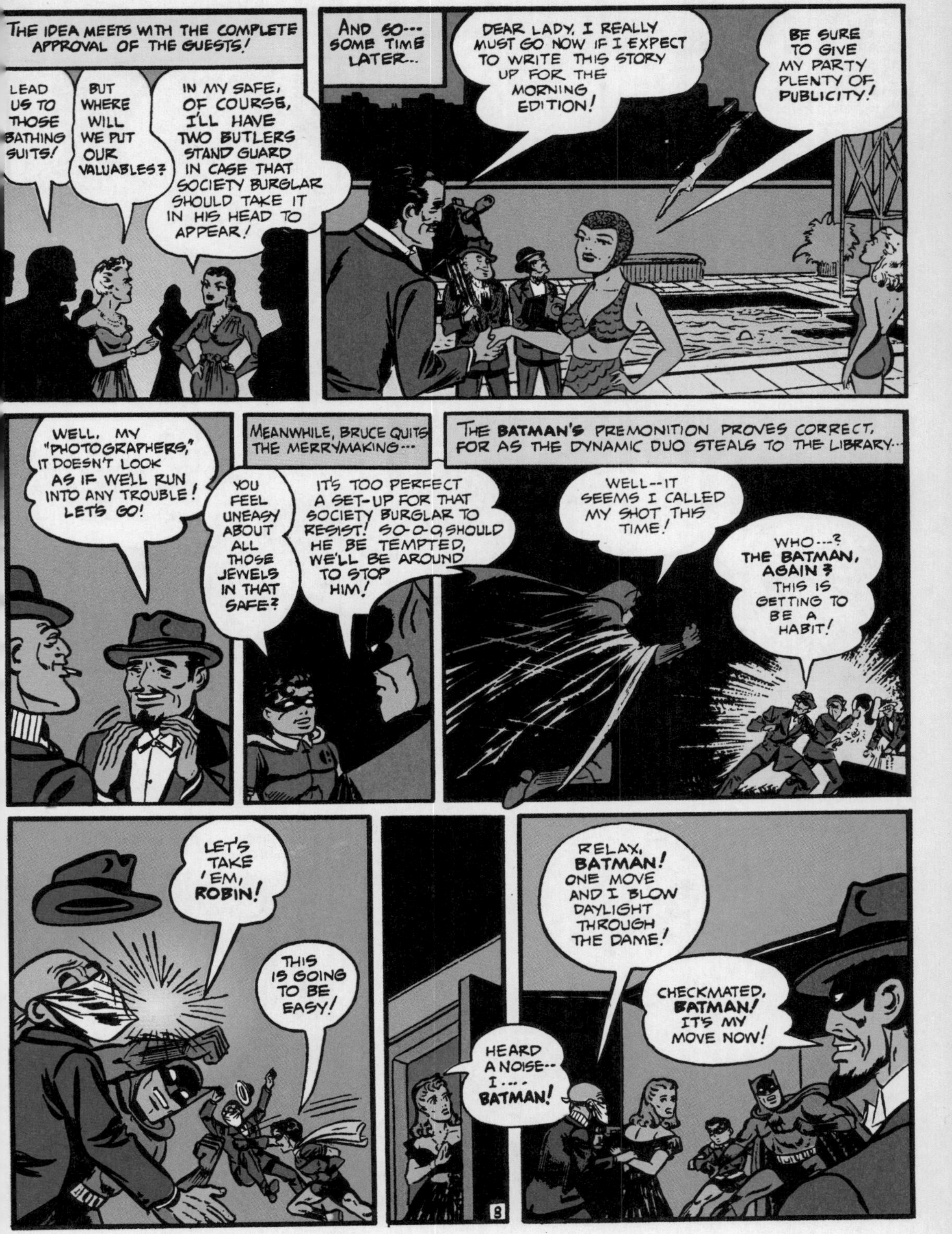
THE IDEA MEETS WITH THE COMPLETE APPROVAL OF THE GUESTS!
LEAD US TO THOSE BATHING SUITS!
BUT WHERE WILL WE PUT OUR VALUABLES?
IN MY SAFE, OF COURSE, I'LL HAVE TWO BUTLERS STAND GUARD IN CASE THAT SOCIETY BURGLAR SHOULD TAKE IT IN HIS HEAD TO APPEAR!
AND SO--- SOME TIME LATER..
DEAR LADY, I REALLY MUST GO NOW IF I EXPECT TO WRITE THIS STORY UP FOR THE MORNING EDITION!
BE SURE TO GIVE MY PARTY PLENTY OF PUBLICITY!
WELL, MY "PHOTOGRAPHERS," IT DOESN'T LOOK AS IF WE'LL RUN INTO ANY TROUBLE! LET'S GO!
MEANWHILE, BRUCE QUITS THE MERRYMAKING---
YOU FEEL UNEASY ABOUT ALL THOSE JEWELS IN THAT SAFE?
IT'S TOO PERFECT A SET-UP FOR THAT SOCIETY BURGLAR TO RESIST! SO-O-O, SHOULD HE BE TEMPTED, WE'LL BE AROUND TO STOP HIM!
THE BATMAN'S PREMONITION PROVES CORRECT, FOR AS THE DYNAMIC DUO STEALS TO THE LIBRARY---
WELL--IT SEEMS I CALLED MY SHOT THIS TIME!
WHO---? THE BATMAN, AGAIN? THIS IS GETTING TO BE A HABIT!
LET'S TAKE 'EM, ROBIN!
THIS IS GOING TO BE EASY!
HEARD A NOISE-- I.... BATMAN!
RELAX, BATMAN! ONE MOVE AND I BLOW DAYLIGHT THROUGH THE DAME!
CHECKMATED, BATMAN! IT'S MY MOVE NOW!
8

AH, MY DEAR---I AM INDEED GRATEFUL FOR YOUR VERY TIMELY ENTRANCE. YOU APPEARED AS IF ON CUE!

HOW QUEER! HIS FINGERTIPS ARE ALL RAW--- AS IF RUBBED BY AN ABRASIVE!

ADIEU, BATMAN! BY THE WAY, I WOULDN'T HAVE REALLY LET MY MAN HURT THAT GIRL! I'M TOO MUCH A GENTLEMAN TO PERMIT THAT!

SLAM!

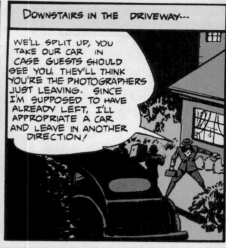

DOWNSTAIRS IN THE DRIVEWAY---

WE'LL SPLIT UP, YOU TAKE OUR CAR IN CASE GUESTS SHOULD SEE YOU, THEY'LL THINK YOU'RE THE PHOTOGRAPHERS JUST LEAVING. SINCE I'M SUPPOSED TO HAVE ALREADY LEFT, I'LL APPROPRIATE A CAR AND LEAVE IN ANOTHER DIRECTION!

WHILE UPSTAIRS ---

NO USE! THIS DOOR IS AS SOLID AS STEEL! HEY, WHERE ARE YOU GOING?

I THINK I CAN MAKE MUCH BETTER TIME THIS WAY!

OUT INTO EMPTY SPACE LEAPS THE ACROBATMAN. HIS LITHE BODY LOOPS INTO A PERFECT SOMERSAULT!

HIS SUPERB BODY UNCOILS--- HITS THE SPRING BOARD- BOUNCES UP LIKE A RUBBER BALL ---

THE BATMAN!

...AND BOUNDS OVER THE HIGH HEDGE TO THE DRIVEWAY!

BULL'S-EYE!

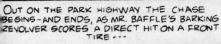

OUT ON THE PARK HIGHWAY THE CHASE BEGINS-AND ENDS, AS MR. BAFFLE'S BARKING REVOLVER SCORES A DIRECT HIT ON A FRONT TIRE---

AND THAT, MY DEAR BATMAN, BLOWS YOU RIGHT OUT OF THIS FOX HUNT!

CAN'T USE THAT CAR! I---WAIT! THIS RACE ISN'T OVER YET!

INTO A HANSOM CAB SPRINGS THE BATMAN. THE CRACK OF A WHIP, AND THE HORSE BOLTS FORWARD IN SHOCKED SURPRISE!

C'MON, PEGASUS! STRETCH THOSE LEGS!

THE MOON'S CYCLOPEAN EYE STARES AT AN UNFAMILIAR SIGHT--- A HORSE-DRAWN CARRIAGE CHASING A SPEEDING AUTOMOBILE!

THE BATMAN!

YIPPEE! LOOK AT THIS NAG TRAVEL! DOBBIN, YOUR MAMMY MUST HAVE BEEN A RACE HORSE! YIPPEE!

A LITHE LEAP!

HELLO AGAIN!

I SEE YOU CAN'T KEEP A GOOD MAN DOWN!

IN THE ROCKETING, CAREENING CAR, CRIMINAL AND RACKET-WRECKER COME TO GRIPS!

SOMEHOW I HAVE THE FEELING THAT WE'VE FOUGHT BEFORE SOME PLACE!

YOU'D BE SURPRISED IF YOU REALLY KNEW! UGH!

SUDDENLY TWISTING FREE, MR BAFFLE HURLS THE BAG OF LOOT FROM HIM!

THERE GO THE JEWELS! BETTER MAKE A QUICK CHOICE! EITHER YOU TAKE ME OR RECOVER THEM!

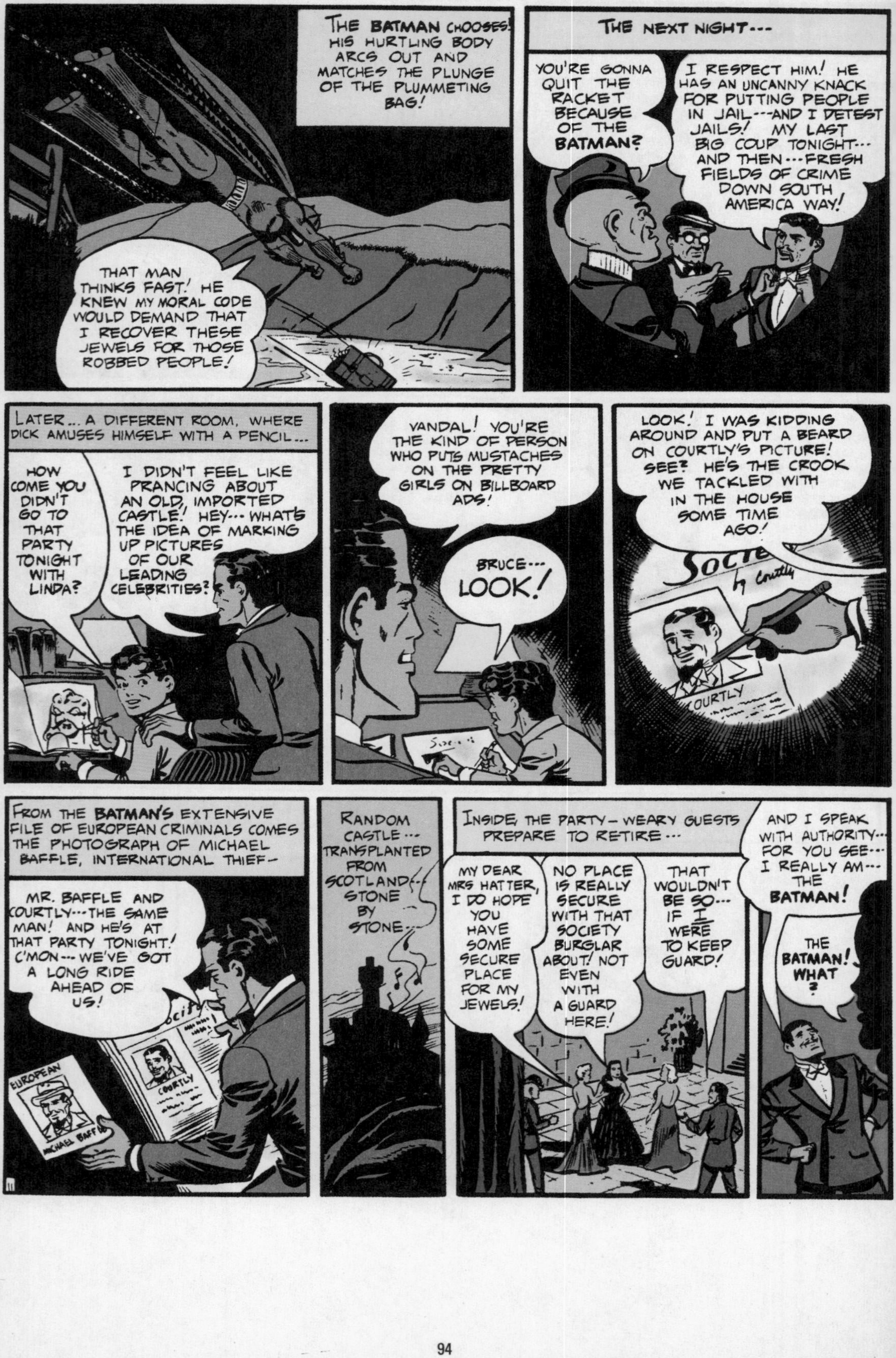
THE BATMAN CHOOSES! HIS HURTLING BODY ARCS OUT AND MATCHES THE PLUNGE OF THE PLUMMETING BAG!
THAT MAN THINKS FAST! HE KNEW MY MORAL CODE WOULD DEMAND THAT I RECOVER THESE JEWELS FOR THOSE ROBBED PEOPLE!
THE NEXT NIGHT---
YOU'RE GONNA QUIT THE RACKET BECAUSE OF THE BATMAN?
I RESPECT HIM! HE HAS AN UNCANNY KNACK FOR PUTTING PEOPLE IN JAIL---AND I DETEST JAILS! MY LAST BIG COUP TONIGHT--- AND THEN---FRESH FIELDS OF CRIME DOWN SOUTH AMERICA WAY!
LATER... A DIFFERENT ROOM, WHERE DICK AMUSES HIMSELF WITH A PENCIL...
HOW COME YOU DIDN'T GO TO THAT PARTY TONIGHT WITH LINDA?
I DIDN'T FEEL LIKE PRANCING ABOUT AN OLD, IMPORTED CASTLE! HEY--- WHAT'S THE IDEA OF MARKING UP PICTURES OF OUR LEADING CELEBRITIES?
VANDAL! YOU'RE THE KIND OF PERSON WHO PUTS MUSTACHES ON THE PRETTY GIRLS ON BILLBOARD ADS!
BRUCE--- LOOK!
LOOK! I WAS KIDDING AROUND AND PUT A BEARD ON COURTLY'S PICTURE! SEE? HE'S THE CROOK WE TACKLED WITH IN THE HOUSE SOME TIME AGO!
SOCIETY
by Courtly
COURTLY
FROM THE BATMAN'S EXTENSIVE FILE OF EUROPEAN CRIMINALS COMES THE PHOTOGRAPH OF MICHAEL BAFFLE, INTERNATIONAL THIEF-
MR. BAFFLE AND COURTLY---THE SAME MAN! AND HE'S AT THAT PARTY TONIGHT! C'MON--- WE'VE GOT A LONG RIDE AHEAD OF US!
EUROPEAN
MICHAEL BAFFLE
COURTLY
RANDOM CASTLE--- TRANSPLANTED FROM SCOTLAND--- STONE BY STONE--
INSIDE, THE PARTY - WEARY GUESTS PREPARE TO RETIRE---
MY DEAR MRS HATTER, I DO HOPE YOU HAVE SOME SECURE PLACE FOR MY JEWELS!
NO PLACE IS REALLY SECURE WITH THAT SOCIETY BURGLAR ABOUT! NOT EVEN WITH A GUARD HERE!
THAT WOULDN'T BE SO--- IF I WERE TO KEEP GUARD!
AND I SPEAK WITH AUTHORITY--- FOR YOU SEE--- I REALLY AM--- THE BATMAN!
THE BATMAN! WHAT?

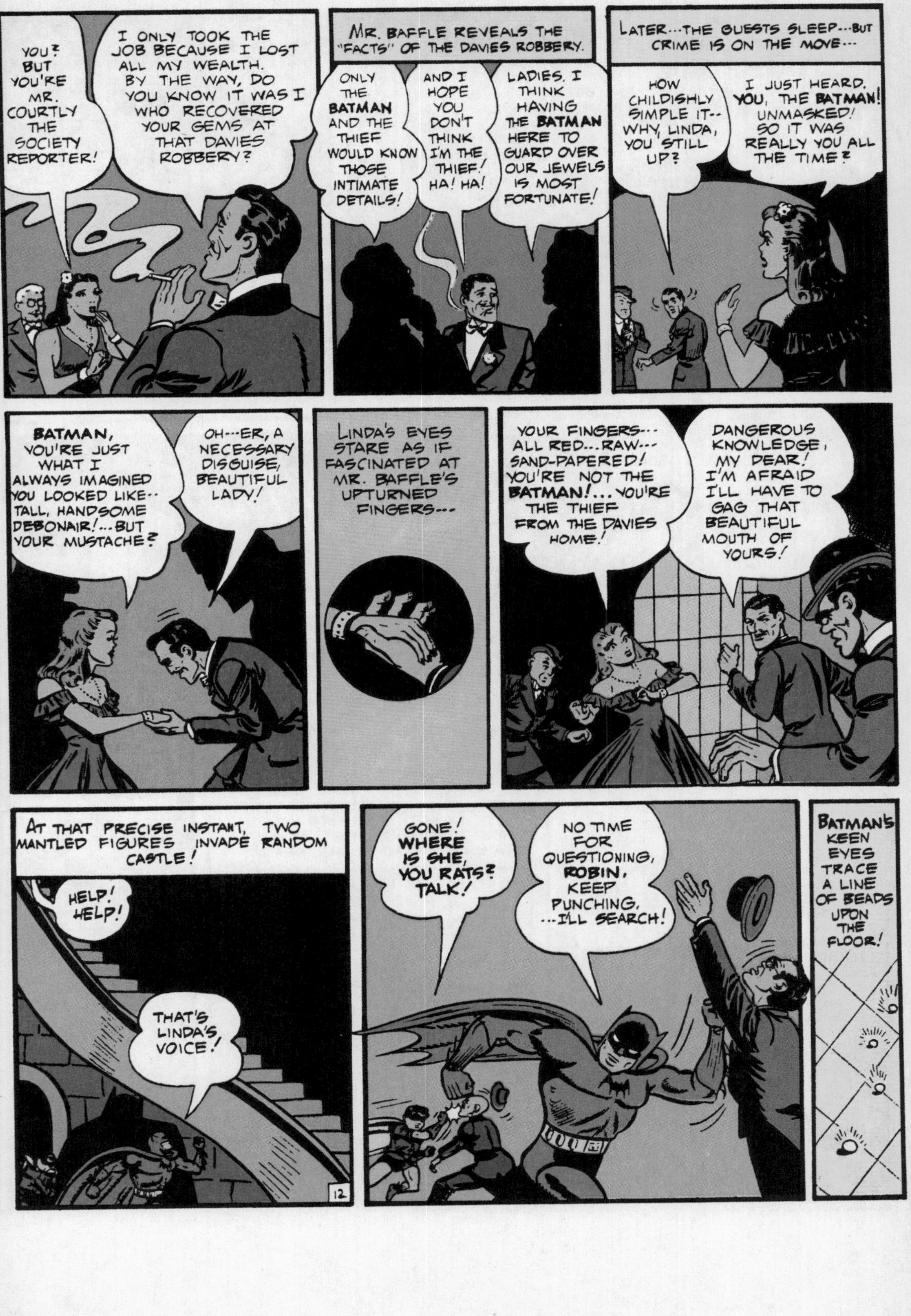

YOU? BUT YOU'RE MR. COURTLY THE SOCIETY REPORTER!
I ONLY TOOK THE JOB BECAUSE I LOST ALL MY WEALTH. BY THE WAY, DO YOU KNOW IT WAS I WHO RECOVERED YOUR GEMS AT THAT DAVIES ROBBERY?
MR. BAFFLE REVEALS THE "FACTS" OF THE DAVIES ROBBERY.
ONLY THE BATMAN AND THE THIEF WOULD KNOW THOSE INTIMATE DETAILS!
AND I HOPE YOU DON'T THINK I'M THE THIEF! HA! HA!
LADIES, I THINK HAVING THE BATMAN HERE TO GUARD OVER OUR JEWELS IS MOST FORTUNATE!
LATER...THE GUESTS SLEEP...BUT CRIME IS ON THE MOVE...
HOW CHILDISHLY SIMPLE IT-- WHY, LINDA, YOU STILL UP?
I JUST HEARD. YOU, THE BATMAN! UNMASKED! SO IT WAS REALLY YOU ALL THE TIME?
BATMAN, YOU'RE JUST WHAT I ALWAYS IMAGINED YOU LOOKED LIKE.. TALL, HANDSOME DEBONAIR!...BUT YOUR MUSTACHE?
OH---ER, A NECESSARY DISGUISE, BEAUTIFUL LADY!
LINDA'S EYES STARE AS IF FASCINATED AT MR. BAFFLE'S UPTURNED FINGERS...
YOUR FINGERS... ALL RED...RAW... SAND-PAPERED! YOU'RE NOT THE BATMAN!... YOU'RE THE THIEF FROM THE DAVIES HOME!
DANGEROUS KNOWLEDGE, MY DEAR! I'M AFRAID I'LL HAVE TO GAG THAT BEAUTIFUL MOUTH OF YOURS!
AT THAT PRECISE INSTANT, TWO MANTLED FIGURES INVADE RANDOM CASTLE!
HELP! HELP!
THAT'S LINDA'S VOICE!
12
GONE! WHERE IS SHE, YOU RATS? TALK!
NO TIME FOR QUESTIONING, ROBIN, KEEP PUNCHING. ...I'LL SEARCH!
BATMAN'S KEEN EYES TRACE A LINE OF BEADS UPON THE FLOOR!

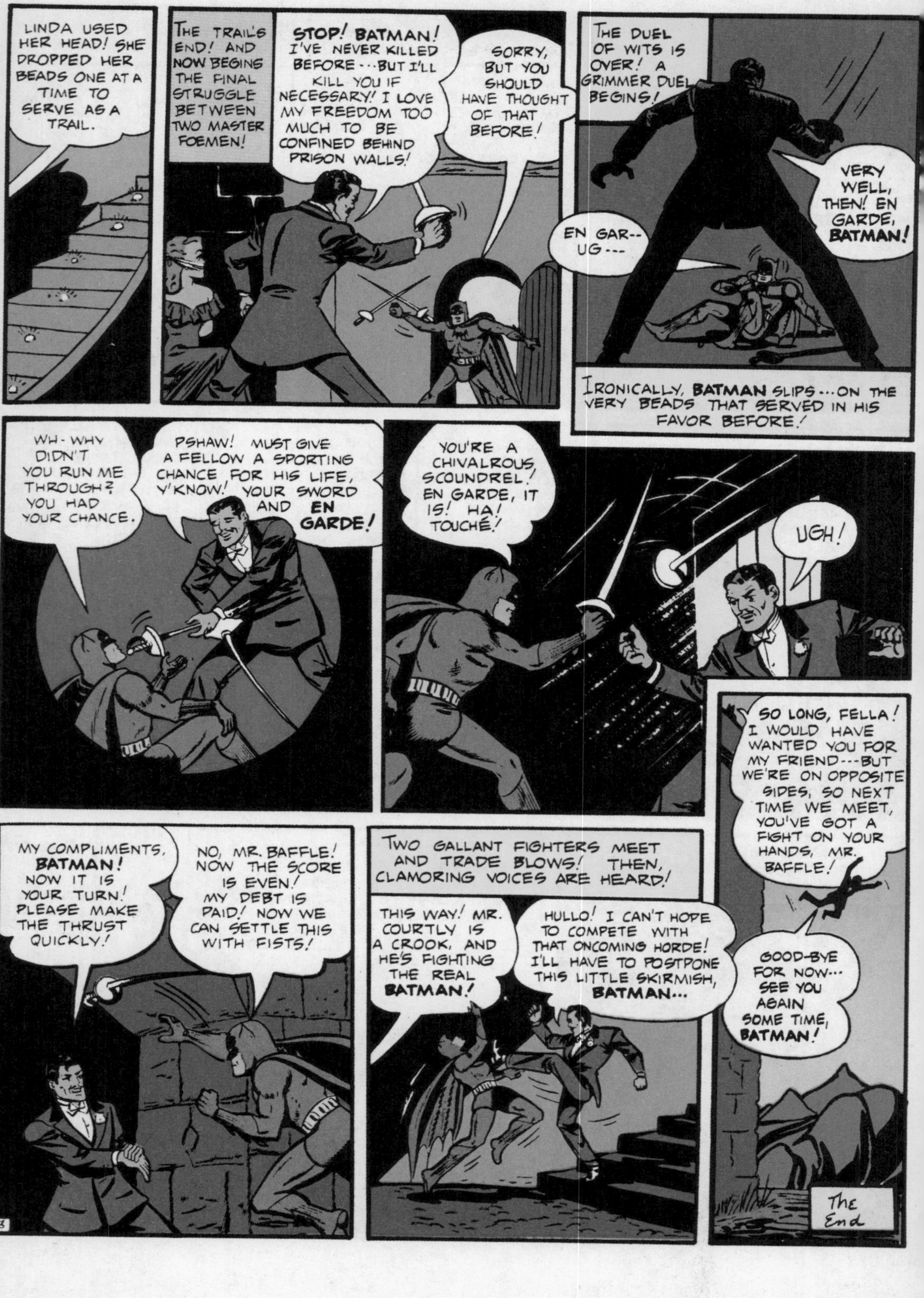
LINDA USED HER HEAD! SHE DROPPED HER BEADS ONE AT A TIME TO SERVE AS A TRAIL.
THE TRAIL'S END! AND NOW BEGINS THE FINAL STRUGGLE BETWEEN TWO MASTER FOEMEN!
STOP! BATMAN! I'VE NEVER KILLED BEFORE---BUT I'LL KILL YOU IF NECESSARY! I LOVE MY FREEDOM TOO MUCH TO BE CONFINED BEHIND PRISON WALLS!
SORRY, BUT YOU SHOULD HAVE THOUGHT OF THAT BEFORE!
THE DUEL OF WITS IS OVER! A GRIMMER DUEL BEGINS!
VERY WELL, THEN! EN GARDE, BATMAN!
EN GAR-- UG---
IRONICALLY, BATMAN SLIPS...ON THE VERY BEADS THAT SERVED IN HIS FAVOR BEFORE!
WH-WHY DIDN'T YOU RUN ME THROUGH? YOU HAD YOUR CHANCE.
PSHAW! MUST GIVE A FELLOW A SPORTING CHANCE FOR HIS LIFE, Y'KNOW! YOUR SWORD AND EN GARDE!
YOU'RE A CHIVALROUS SCOUNDREL! EN GARDE, IT IS! HA! TOUCHÉ!
UGH!
MY COMPLIMENTS, BATMAN! NOW IT IS YOUR TURN! PLEASE MAKE THE THRUST QUICKLY!
NO, MR. BAFFLE! NOW THE SCORE IS EVEN! MY DEBT IS PAID! NOW WE CAN SETTLE THIS WITH FISTS!
13
TWO GALLANT FIGHTERS MEET AND TRADE BLOWS! THEN, CLAMORING VOICES ARE HEARD!
THIS WAY! MR. COURTLY IS A CROOK, AND HE'S FIGHTING THE REAL BATMAN!
HULLO! I CAN'T HOPE TO COMPETE WITH THAT ONCOMING HORDE! I'LL HAVE TO POSTPONE THIS LITTLE SKIRMISH, BATMAN...
SO LONG, FELLA! I WOULD HAVE WANTED YOU FOR MY FRIEND---BUT WE'RE ON OPPOSITE SIDES, SO NEXT TIME WE MEET, YOU'VE GOT A FIGHT ON YOUR HANDS, MR. BAFFLE!
GOOD-BYE FOR NOW... SEE YOU AGAIN SOME TIME, BATMAN!
The End

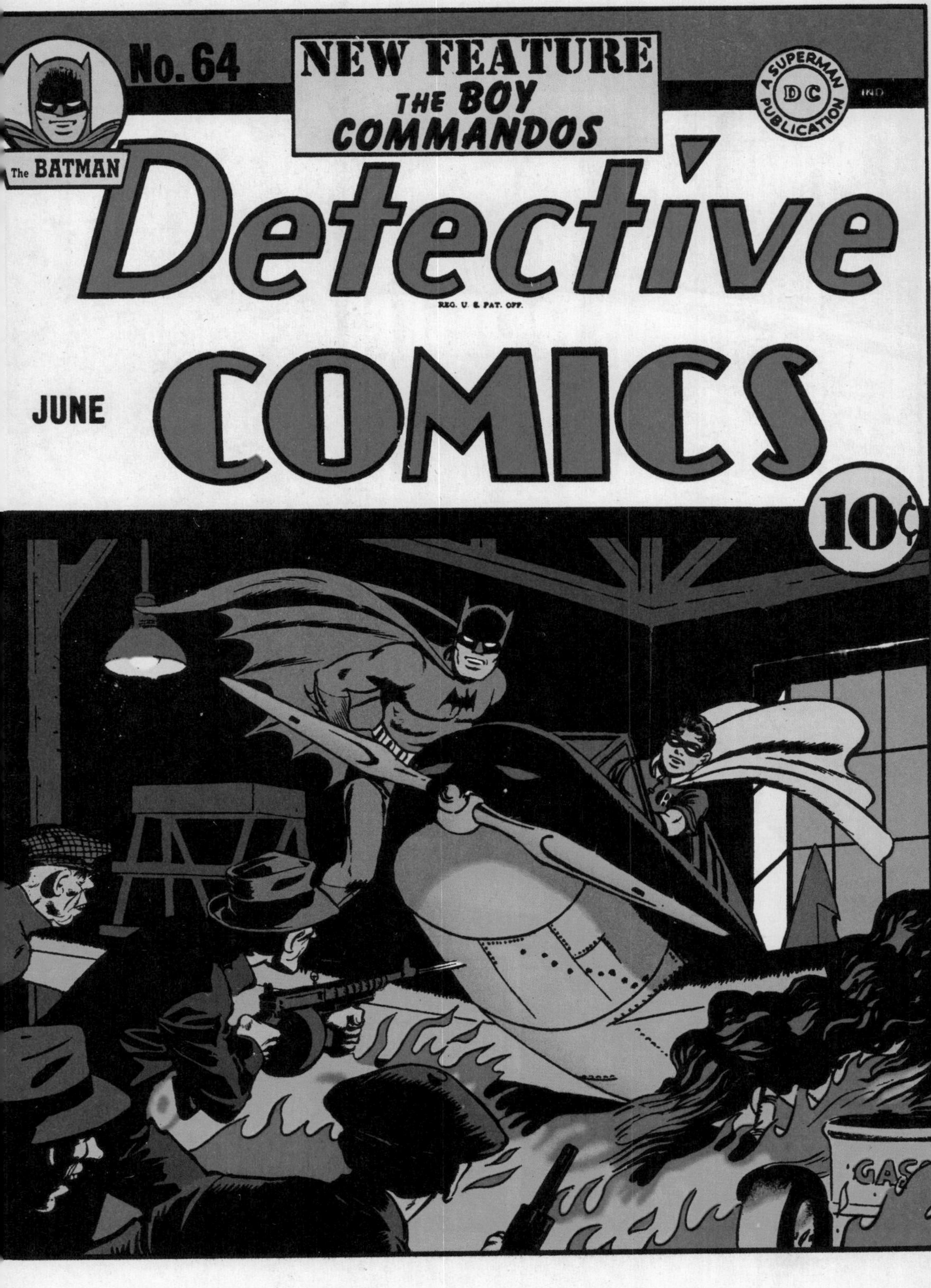
No. 64
NEW FEATURE
THE BOY COMMANDOS
A SUPERMAN DC PUBLICATION
IND
The BATMAN
Detective
REG. U. S. PAT. OFF.
JUNE
COMICS
10¢
GAS

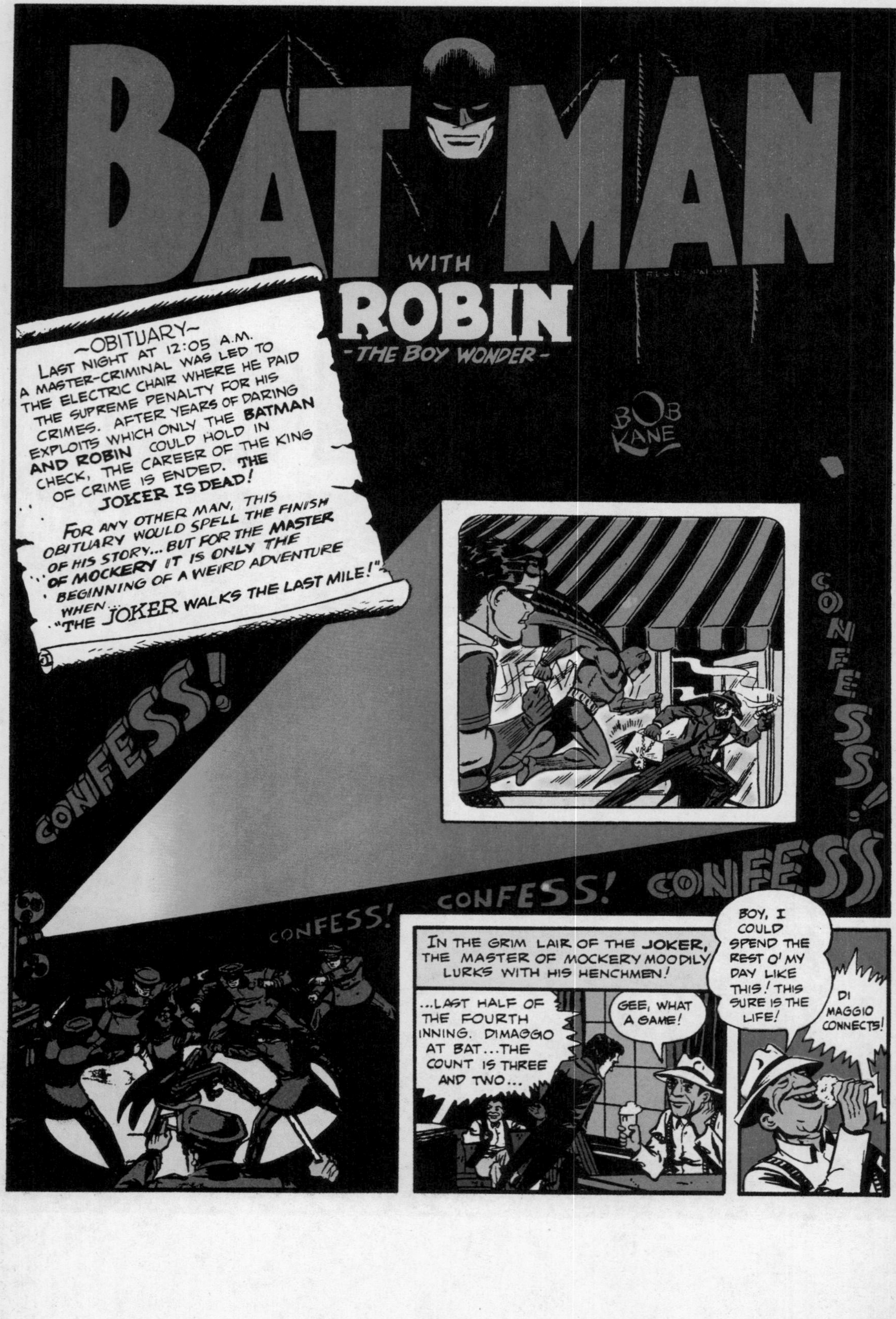
BATMAN
WITH
ROBIN
-THE BOY WONDER-
BOB KANE
~OBITUARY~
~OBITUARY~ LAST NIGHT AT 12:05 A.M. A MASTER-CRIMINAL WAS LED TO THE ELECTRIC CHAIR WHERE HE PAID THE SUPREME PENALTY FOR HIS CRIMES. AFTER YEARS OF DARING EXPLOITS WHICH ONLY THE BATMAN AND ROBIN COULD HOLD IN CHECK, THE CAREER OF THE KING OF CRIME IS ENDED. THE JOKER IS DEAD!
FOR ANY OTHER MAN, THIS OBITUARY WOULD SPELL THE FINISH OF HIS STORY... BUT FOR THE MASTER OF MOCKERY IT IS ONLY THE BEGINNING OF A WEIRD ADVENTURE WHEN... "THE JOKER WALKS THE LAST MILE!"
CONFESS!
CONFESS!
CONFESS!
CONFESS!
CONFESS!
CONFESS!
IN THE GRIM LAIR OF THE JOKER, THE MASTER OF MOCKERY MOODILY LURKS WITH HIS HENCHMEN!
...LAST HALF OF THE FOURTH INNING. DIMAGGIO AT BAT...THE COUNT IS THREE AND TWO...
GEE, WHAT A GAME!
BOY, I COULD SPEND THE REST O' MY DAY LIKE THIS! THIS SURE IS THE LIFE!
DI MAGGIO CONNECTS!

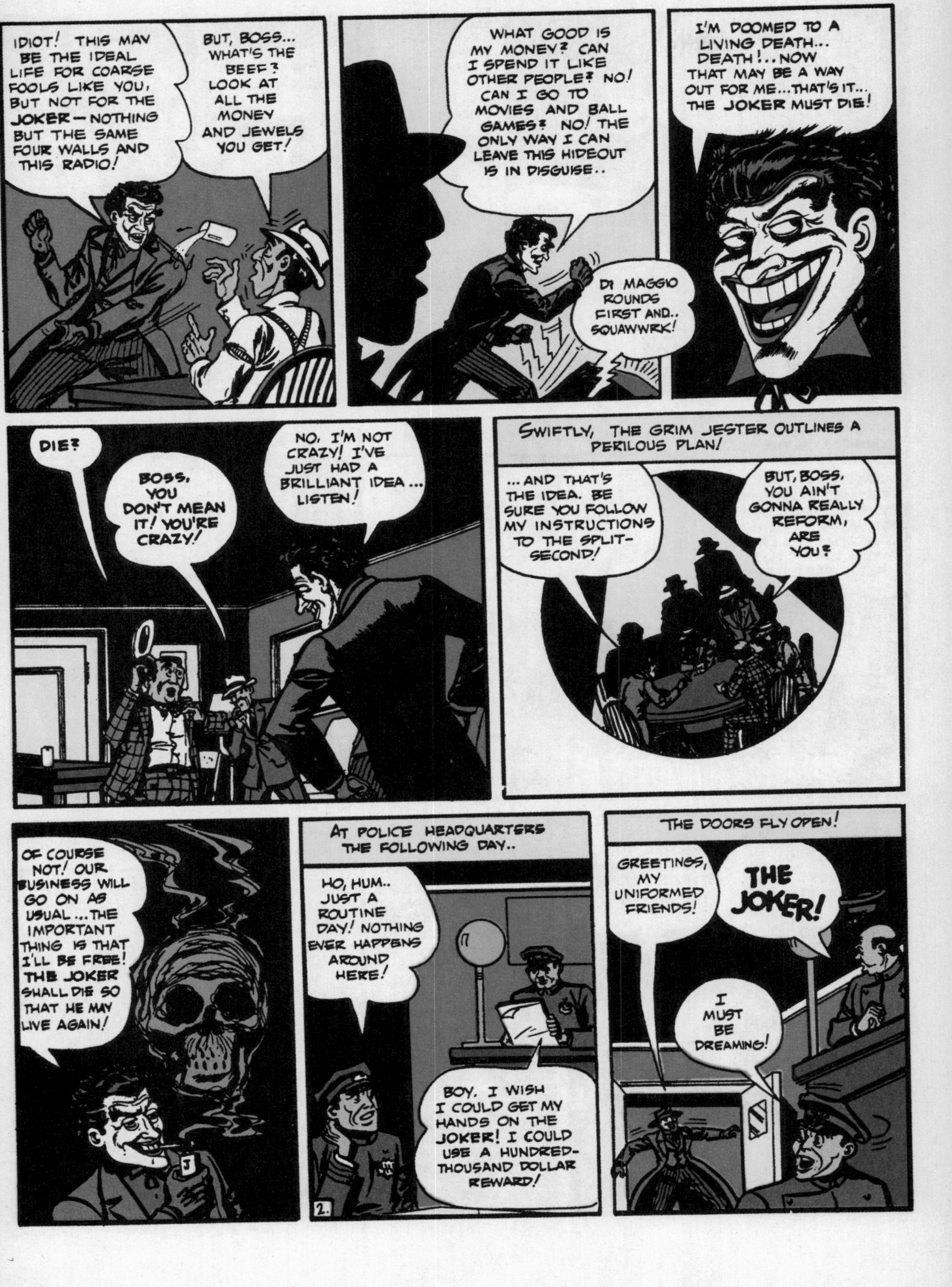
IDIOT! THIS MAY BE THE IDEAL LIFE FOR COARSE FOOLS LIKE YOU, BUT NOT FOR THE JOKER — NOTHING BUT THE SAME FOUR WALLS AND THIS RADIO!
BUT, BOSS... WHAT'S THE BEEF? LOOK AT ALL THE MONEY AND JEWELS YOU GET!
WHAT GOOD IS MY MONEY? CAN I SPEND IT LIKE OTHER PEOPLE? NO! CAN I GO TO MOVIES AND BALL GAMES? NO! THE ONLY WAY I CAN LEAVE THIS HIDEOUT IS IN DISGUISE..
DI MAGGIO ROUNDS FIRST AND.. SQUAWWRK!
I'M DOOMED TO A LIVING DEATH... DEATH!... NOW THAT MAY BE A WAY OUT FOR ME... THAT'S IT... THE JOKER MUST DIE!
DIE?
BOSS, YOU DON'T MEAN IT! YOU'RE CRAZY!
NO, I'M NOT CRAZY! I'VE JUST HAD A BRILLIANT IDEA ... LISTEN!
SWIFTLY, THE GRIM JESTER OUTLINES A PERILOUS PLAN!
... AND THAT'S THE IDEA. BE SURE YOU FOLLOW MY INSTRUCTIONS TO THE SPLIT-SECOND!
BUT, BOSS, YOU AIN'T GONNA REALLY REFORM, ARE YOU?
OF COURSE NOT! OUR BUSINESS WILL GO ON AS USUAL ... THE IMPORTANT THING IS THAT I'LL BE FREE! THE JOKER SHALL DIE SO THAT HE MAY LIVE AGAIN!
J
AT POLICE HEADQUARTERS THE FOLLOWING DAY..
HO, HUM.. JUST A ROUTINE DAY! NOTHING EVER HAPPENS AROUND HERE!
BOY, I WISH I COULD GET MY HANDS ON THE JOKER! I COULD USE A HUNDRED-THOUSAND DOLLAR REWARD!
2.
THE DOORS FLY OPEN!
GREETINGS, MY UNIFORMED FRIENDS!
THE JOKER!
I MUST BE DREAMING!

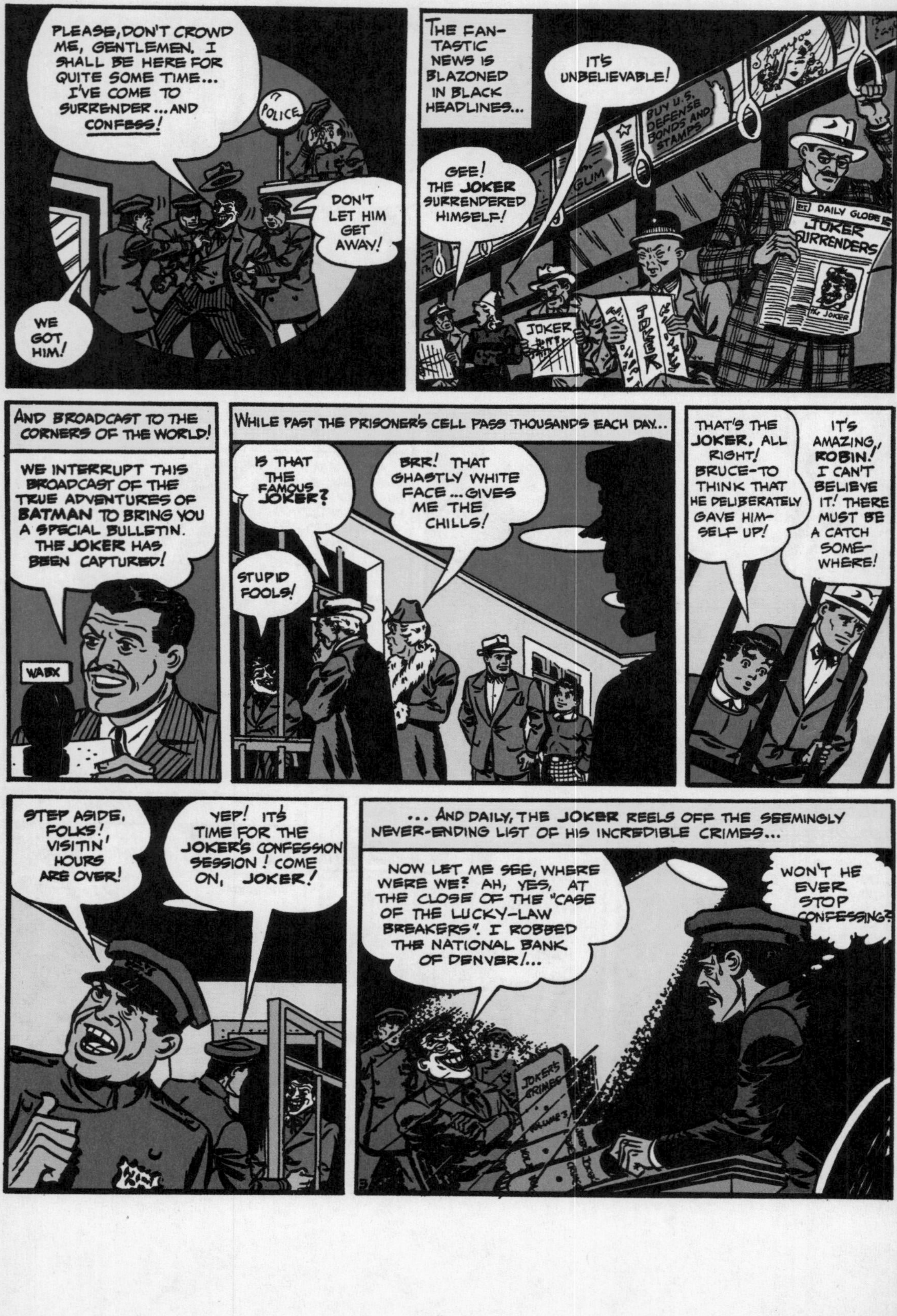
PLEASE, DON'T CROWD ME, GENTLEMEN. I SHALL BE HERE FOR QUITE SOME TIME... I'VE COME TO SURRENDER...AND CONFESS!
POLICE
DON'T LET HIM GET AWAY!
WE GOT HIM!
THE FANTASTIC NEWS IS BLAZONED IN BLACK HEADLINES...
IT'S UNBELIEVABLE!
BUY U.S. DEFENSE BONDS AND STAMPS
GUM
GEE! THE JOKER SURRENDERED HIMSELF!
DAILY GLOBE
JOKER SURRENDERS
THE JOKER
JOKER
JOKER
AND BROADCAST TO THE CORNERS OF THE WORLD!
WE INTERRUPT THIS BROADCAST OF THE TRUE ADVENTURES OF BATMAN TO BRING YOU A SPECIAL BULLETIN. THE JOKER HAS BEEN CAPTURED!
WABX
WHILE PAST THE PRISONER'S CELL PASS THOUSANDS EACH DAY...
IS THAT THE FAMOUS JOKER?
BRR! THAT GHASTLY WHITE FACE...GIVES ME THE CHILLS!
STUPID FOOLS!
THAT'S THE JOKER, ALL RIGHT! BRUCE-TO THINK THAT HE DELIBERATELY GAVE HIMSELF UP!
IT'S AMAZING, ROBIN! I CAN'T BELIEVE IT! THERE MUST BE A CATCH SOMEWHERE!
STEP ASIDE, FOLKS! VISITIN' HOURS ARE OVER!
YEP! IT'S TIME FOR THE JOKER'S CONFESSION SESSION! COME ON, JOKER!
...AND DAILY, THE JOKER REELS OFF THE SEEMINGLY NEVER-ENDING LIST OF HIS INCREDIBLE CRIMES...
NOW LET ME SEE, WHERE WERE WE? AH, YES, AT THE CLOSE OF THE "CASE OF THE LUCKY-LAW BREAKERS". I ROBBED THE NATIONAL BANK OF DENVER!...
WON'T HE EVER STOP CONFESSING?
JOKER'S CRIMES

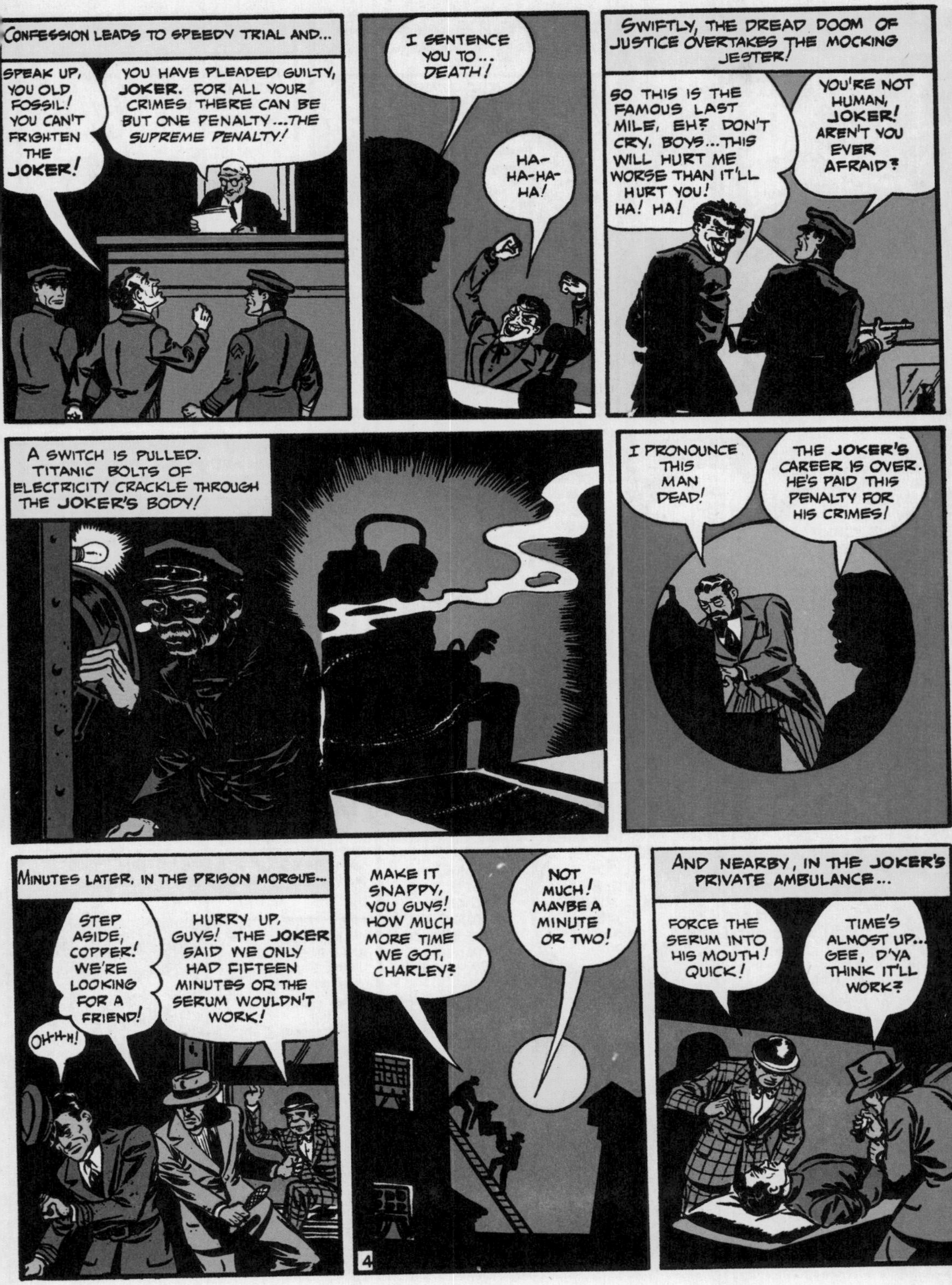

CONFESSION LEADS TO SPEEDY TRIAL AND...
SPEAK UP, YOU OLD FOSSIL! YOU CAN'T FRIGHTEN THE JOKER!
YOU HAVE PLEADED GUILTY, JOKER. FOR ALL YOUR CRIMES THERE CAN BE BUT ONE PENALTY...THE SUPREME PENALTY!
I SENTENCE YOU TO... DEATH!
HA-HA-HA-HA!
SWIFTLY, THE DREAD DOOM OF JUSTICE OVERTAKES THE MOCKING JESTER!
SO THIS IS THE FAMOUS LAST MILE, EH? DON'T CRY, BOYS...THIS WILL HURT ME WORSE THAN IT'LL HURT YOU! HA! HA!
YOU'RE NOT HUMAN, JOKER! AREN'T YOU EVER AFRAID?
A SWITCH IS PULLED. TITANIC BOLTS OF ELECTRICITY CRACKLE THROUGH THE JOKER'S BODY!
I PRONOUNCE THIS MAN DEAD!
THE JOKER'S CAREER IS OVER. HE'S PAID THIS PENALTY FOR HIS CRIMES!
MINUTES LATER, IN THE PRISON MORGUE...
STEP ASIDE, COPPER! WE'RE LOOKING FOR A FRIEND!
HURRY UP, GUYS! THE JOKER SAID WE ONLY HAD FIFTEEN MINUTES OR THE SERUM WOULDN'T WORK!
OH-H-H!
MAKE IT SNAPPY, YOU GUYS! HOW MUCH MORE TIME WE GOT, CHARLEY?
NOT MUCH! MAYBE A MINUTE OR TWO!
4
AND NEARBY, IN THE JOKER'S PRIVATE AMBULANCE...
FORCE THE SERUM INTO HIS MOUTH! QUICK!
TIME'S ALMOST UP... GEE, D'YA THINK IT'LL WORK?

SEE, CHARLEY...

SHUT UP! IT'S WORKING!

I...

THE SECRET DRUG COURSES THRU THE JOKER'S BODY, SHOCKING HIM BACK TO LIFE!

YOU'RE ALIVE!

RECLAIMED FROM THE DEAD! ALL CRIMES PAID FOR! THE SLATE WIPED CLEAN! THE JOKER IS FREE! HA! HA!

THE NEXT DAY...

THE PLANS ARE SET. YOU KNOW HOW TO GET MY MESSAGES. NOW GO! I WANT TO WINDOW-SHOP!

RIGHT, BOSS!

WHAT BEAUTIFUL WATCHES! I MUST GET A NEW ONE. THE OLD TURNIP I CARRY ISN'T VERY SMART!

TH-THE J-JOKER!

A FRANTIC CALL FOR HELP...AND INSTANTLY A POLICE CALL FLASHES THRU THE CITY.

POLICE! SEND HELP! TH-THE JOKER'S GETTING READY TO ROB MY STORE!

THE JOKER? THAT'S IMPOSSIBLE! MUST BE SOME THUG IMITATING HIM! I'LL SEND OUT A WARNING.

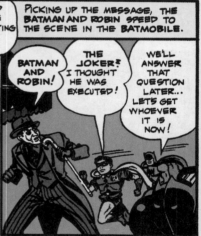

PICKING UP THE MESSAGE, THE BATMAN AND ROBIN SPEED TO THE SCENE IN THE BATMOBILE.

BATMAN AND ROBIN!

THE JOKER? I THOUGHT HE WAS EXECUTED!

WE'LL ANSWER THAT QUESTION LATER... LET'S GET WHOEVER IT IS NOW!

EVEN TRICKED YOUR WAY OUT OF AN EXECUTION, EH?

LOOK OUT, BRAT! YOU MISSED ME AGAIN!

OOPS! THAT'S THE JOKER, ALL RIGHT! I'D RECOGNIZE HIS TECHNIQUE ANYWHERE!

5

SNATCHING UP A REFUSE BIN, THE BATMAN STRIKES WITH LIGHTNING PRECISION...

ROBIN! WE'VE GOT TO TAKE THIS GARBAGE TO THE POLICE!

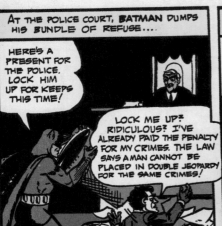

AT THE POLICE COURT, BATMAN DUMPS HIS BUNDLE OF REFUSE....

HERE'S A PRESENT FOR THE POLICE. LOCK HIM UP FOR KEEPS THIS TIME!

LOCK ME UP? RIDICULOUS? I'VE ALREADY PAID THE PENALTY FOR MY CRIMES. THE LAW SAYS A MAN CANNOT BE PLACED IN DOUBLE JEOPARDY FOR THE SAME CRIMES!

THROUGH A CUNNING LEGAL TRICK, THE JOKER IS FREE!

UNFORTUNATELY, THE JOKER IS RIGHT. SINCE HE WAS EXECUTED HE IS FREE NOW!

BATMAN, I COULD CHARGE YOU WITH ASSAULT, BUT NOW THAT I'M FREE, I'VE DECIDED TO BECOME GENEROUS! GOOD DAY. SIR!

YES, THE JOKER IS FREE, BUT STILL THE BATMAN AND ROBIN MAINTAIN A CEASELESS WATCH BY DAY...

SO FAR HE HASN'T LEFT HIS APARTMENT ALL DAY!

ANYTHING SO FAR, BRUCE?

NOTHING, DICK! HE HASN'T MADE A MOVE!

AND BY NIGHT

SHINE, KID. ANYTHING YET, DICK?

OKAY, MISTER... NOTHING, BRUCE!

WHILE INSIDE THE JOKER'S ROOM...

HA! THOSE STUPID DETECTIVES WATCH THE JOKER. THEY NEVER DREAM THAT I'M SENDING MESSAGES TO MY MEN WITH THIS HOTEL SIGN BEFORE THEIR VERY EYES!

I KNOW THE POLICE ARE TAPPING MY PHONE .. BUT THEY CAN'T SUSPECT THIS TRICK.. A CORD CONNECTED TO A SWITCH I'VE SPLICED ONTO THE CURRENT WIRES... HA! HA! HA! HA!

AND AS THE SIGN BLINKS OFF A DOT AND DASH CODE. FAR ACROSS THE CITY...

THE JOKER SAYS FOR US TO PULL THE ARENA JOB TONIGHT.. AND TO ROB HIM, TOO, SO'S HE'LL LOOK INNOCENT!

LATER... THE WAYNE HOME...

WE KNOW THE JOKER WON'T GO STRAIGHT! FREE, HE'S A GREATER MENACE THAN BEFORE! WE'VE GOT TO TRAP HIM!

BUT HOW?

WE'LL DOPE OUT SOMETHING, RIGHT NOW, LET'S GET SOME ENTERTAINMENT. YOU'VE WORKED HARD ENOUGH!

SWELL, BRUCE! LET'S SEE THE ICE SHOW!

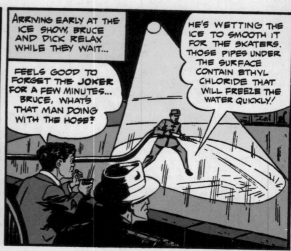

ARRIVING EARLY AT THE ICE SHOW, BRUCE AND DICK RELAX WHILE THEY WAIT...

FEELS GOOD TO FORGET THE JOKER FOR A FEW MINUTES... BRUCE, WHAT'S THAT MAN DOING WITH THE HOSE?

HE'S WETTING THE ICE TO SMOOTH IT FOR THE SKATERS. THOSE PIPES UNDER THE SURFACE CONTAIN ETHYL CHLORIDE THAT WILL FREEZE THE WATER QUICKLY!

BUT A MOMENT BEFORE THE PERFORMANCE BEGINS, ANOTHER PATRON ENTERS THE BOX!

AH, JUST IN TIME! PARDON ME, GENTLEMEN, I BELIEVE I HAVE A TICKET FOR THIS BOX, TOO!

OH... ER... NOT AT ALL!

G-GLUG!

THE SHOW IS ON! BUT AS GAY SKATERS GLIDE OVER THE GLASSY SURFACE...

BRUCE, LOOK! THE FREEZING PIPES UNDER THE ICE...

THEY'RE GLOWING WHITE HOT!

THE PIPES BLAST OPEN AT ONE END OF THE ARENA, RELEASING FUMES OF CHOKING ETHYL CHLORIDE GAS!

SOMEONE HEATED THE FREEZING SOLUTION AND RAN IT THROUGH THE FREEZING SYSTEM.

G-GAS! IT'S GETTING IN M-MY EYES!

AND WHILE THE BLINDED AUDIENCE REELS...

WE'RE BEING ROBBED!

SHUT UP, POP! HAND OVER YOUR WALLET!

ATTA BOY, CHARLEY! GEE, I WISH I HAD ME SKATES!

TH-THIS IS AN OUTRAGE. THE P-POLICE SHALL HEAR ABOUT THIS!

HAND OVER THAT GOLD WATCH AND WALLET! HEY, GUYS, GET A LOAD O' ME ROBBING THE JOKER! HA-HA!

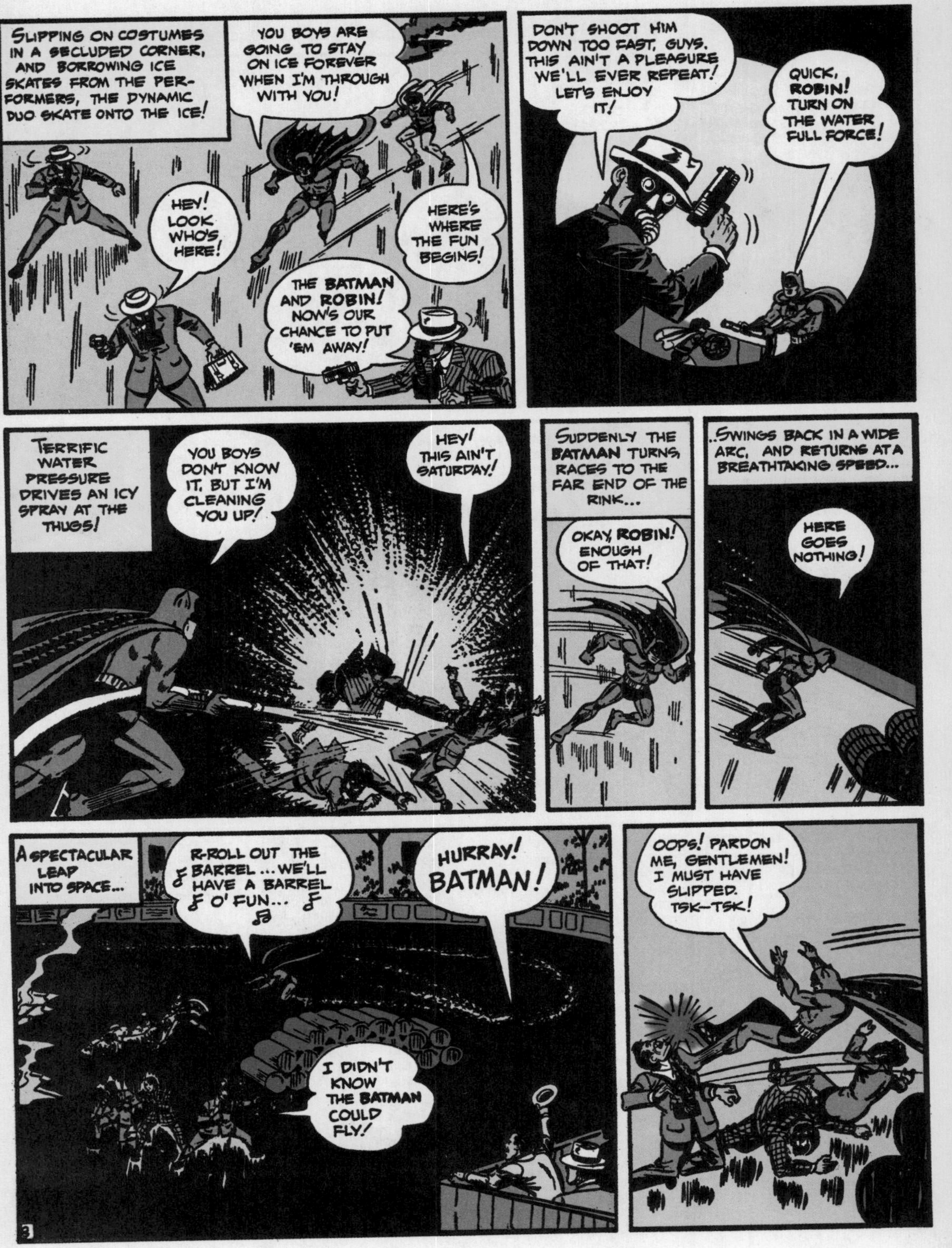
SLIPPING ON COSTUMES IN A SECLUDED CORNER, AND BORROWING ICE SKATES FROM THE PERFORMERS, THE DYNAMIC DUO SKATE ONTO THE ICE!
YOU BOYS ARE GOING TO STAY ON ICE FOREVER WHEN I'M THROUGH WITH YOU!
HEY! LOOK WHO'S HERE!
HERE'S WHERE THE FUN BEGINS!
THE BATMAN AND ROBIN! NOW'S OUR CHANCE TO PUT 'EM AWAY!
DON'T SHOOT HIM DOWN TOO FAST, GUYS. THIS AIN'T A PLEASURE WE'LL EVER REPEAT! LET'S ENJOY IT!
QUICK, ROBIN! TURN ON THE WATER FULL FORCE!
TERRIFIC WATER PRESSURE DRIVES AN ICY SPRAY AT THE THUGS!
YOU BOYS DON'T KNOW IT, BUT I'M CLEANING YOU UP!
HEY! THIS AIN'T SATURDAY!
SUDDENLY THE BATMAN TURNS, RACES TO THE FAR END OF THE RINK...
OKAY, ROBIN! ENOUGH OF THAT!
..SWINGS BACK IN A WIDE ARC, AND RETURNS AT A BREATHTAKING SPEED...
HERE GOES NOTHING!
A SPECTACULAR LEAP INTO SPACE...
R-ROLL OUT THE BARREL ... WE'LL HAVE A BARREL O' FUN...
HURRAY! BATMAN!
I DIDN'T KNOW THE BATMAN COULD FLY!
3
OOPS! PARDON ME, GENTLEMEN! I MUST HAVE SLIPPED. TSK-TSK!

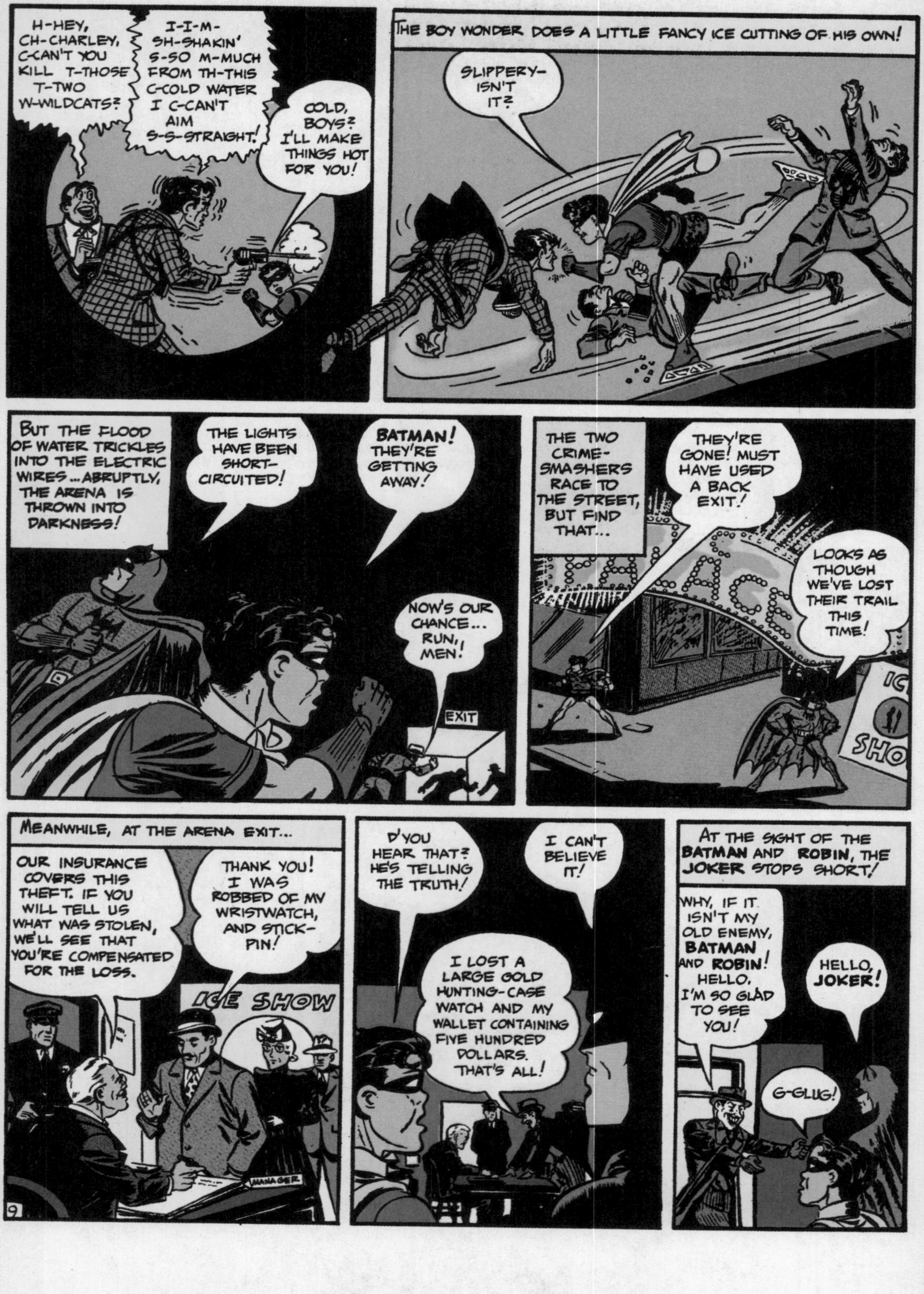
H-HEY, CH-CHARLEY, C-CAN'T YOU KILL T-THOSE T-TWO W-WILDCATS?
I-I-M-SH-SHAKIN' S-SO M-MUCH FROM TH-THIS C-COLD WATER I C-CAN'T AIM S-S-STRAIGHT!
COLD, BOYS? I'LL MAKE THINGS HOT FOR YOU!
THE BOY WONDER DOES A LITTLE FANCY ICE CUTTING OF HIS OWN!
SLIPPERY-ISN'T IT?
BUT THE FLOOD OF WATER TRICKLES INTO THE ELECTRIC WIRES...ABRUPTLY, THE ARENA IS THROWN INTO DARKNESS!
THE LIGHTS HAVE BEEN SHORT-CIRCUITED!
BATMAN! THEY'RE GETTING AWAY!
NOW'S OUR CHANCE... RUN, MEN!
EXIT
THE TWO CRIME-SMASHERS RACE TO THE STREET, BUT FIND THAT...
THEY'RE GONE! MUST HAVE USED A BACK EXIT!
LOOKS AS THOUGH WE'VE LOST THEIR TRAIL THIS TIME!
MEANWHILE, AT THE ARENA EXIT...
OUR INSURANCE COVERS THIS THEFT. IF YOU WILL TELL US WHAT WAS STOLEN, WE'LL SEE THAT YOU'RE COMPENSATED FOR THE LOSS.
THANK YOU! I WAS ROBBED OF MY WRISTWATCH, AND STICK-PIN!
ICE SHOW
MANAGER
9
D'YOU HEAR THAT? HE'S TELLING THE TRUTH!
I CAN'T BELIEVE IT!
I LOST A LARGE GOLD HUNTING-CASE WATCH AND MY WALLET CONTAINING FIVE HUNDRED DOLLARS. THAT'S ALL!
AT THE SIGHT OF THE BATMAN AND ROBIN, THE JOKER STOPS SHORT!
WHY, IF IT ISN'T MY OLD ENEMY, BATMAN AND ROBIN! HELLO, HELLO, I'M SO GLAD TO SEE YOU!
HELLO, JOKER!
G-GLUG!

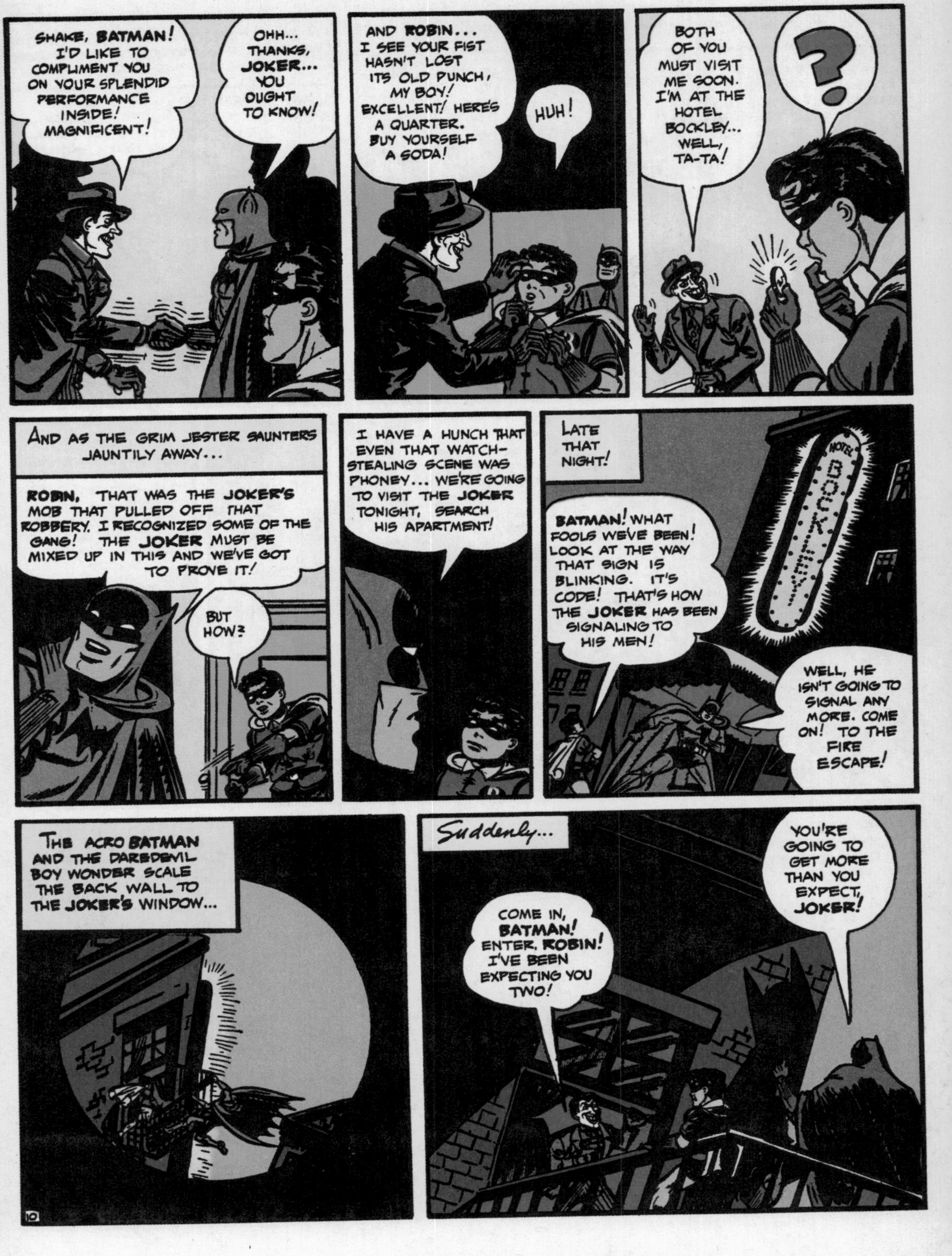
SHAKE, BATMAN! I'D LIKE TO COMPLIMENT YOU ON YOUR SPLENDID PERFORMANCE INSIDE! MAGNIFICENT!
OHH... THANKS, JOKER... YOU OUGHT TO KNOW!
AND ROBIN... I SEE YOUR FIST HASN'T LOST ITS OLD PUNCH, MY BOY! EXCELLENT! HERE'S A QUARTER. BUY YOURSELF A SODA!
HUH!
BOTH OF YOU MUST VISIT ME SOON. I'M AT THE HOTEL BOCKLEY... WELL, TA-TA!
?
AND AS THE GRIM JESTER SAUNTERS JAUNTILY AWAY...
ROBIN, THAT WAS THE JOKER'S MOB THAT PULLED OFF THAT ROBBERY. I RECOGNIZED SOME OF THE GANG! THE JOKER MUST BE MIXED UP IN THIS AND WE'VE GOT TO PROVE IT!
BUT HOW?
I HAVE A HUNCH THAT EVEN THAT WATCH-STEALING SCENE WAS PHONEY... WE'RE GOING TO VISIT THE JOKER TONIGHT, SEARCH HIS APARTMENT!
LATE THAT NIGHT!
HOTEL BOCKLEY
BATMAN! WHAT FOOLS WE'VE BEEN! LOOK AT THE WAY THAT SIGN IS BLINKING. IT'S CODE! THAT'S HOW THE JOKER HAS BEEN SIGNALING TO HIS MEN!
WELL, HE ISN'T GOING TO SIGNAL ANY MORE. COME ON! TO THE FIRE ESCAPE!
THE ACRO BATMAN AND THE DAREDEVIL BOY WONDER SCALE THE BACK WALL TO THE JOKER'S WINDOW...
10
Suddenly...
COME IN, BATMAN! ENTER, ROBIN! I'VE BEEN EXPECTING YOU TWO!
YOU'RE GOING TO GET MORE THAN YOU EXPECT, JOKER!

BUT WHEN THE LIGHTS FLASH ON...

THERE'LL BE NO ROUGH STUFF THIS TIME, MY FRIENDS. THESE POLICE WILL TESTIFY THAT YOU BROKE INTO MY ROOM. I'M CHARGING YOU WITH BURGLARY!

WH-WHY... THIS IS RIDICULOUS!

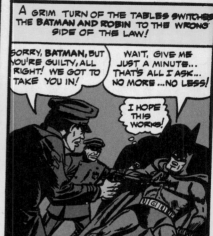

A GRIM TURN OF THE TABLES SWITCHES THE BATMAN AND ROBIN TO THE WRONG SIDE OF THE LAW!

SORRY, BATMAN, BUT YOU'RE GUILTY, ALL RIGHT! WE GOT TO TAKE YOU IN!

WAIT, GIVE ME JUST A MINUTE... THAT'S ALL I ASK... NO MORE ...NO LESS!

I HOPE THIS WORKS!

UNAWARE OF THE BATMAN'S RUSE, THE JOKER TAKES OUT HIS GOLD WATCH TO TIME HIS ENEMY. THEN...

ONE MINUTE! I...ER...

TOO LATE TO HIDE IT, JOKER! THAT'S THE GOLD WATCH THAT WAS STOLEN FROM THE JOKER THIS EVENING AT THE ICE SHOW!

WHAT ABOUT IT?

THE JOKER COULD ONLY HAVE RECEIVED HIS WATCH FROM THE CROOKS! THAT MAKES HIM AN ACCESSORY TO THE CRIME AND GUILTY OF RECEIVING STOLEN GOODS!

THE BATMAN IS RIGHT, JOKER, WE'LL HAVE TO TAKE YOU IN!

SO YOU TRICKED ME INTO TAKING OUT MY WATCH? AH, WELL, THE JOKER'S STILL TOO CLEVER FOR YOU!

WITH A LIGHTNING LEAP, THE HARLEQUIN OF HATE PLUNGES THROUGH THE GAPING WINDOW...

BYE-BYE, BLACKBIRD! IT'S BEEN NICE SEEING YOU!

COME ON, ROBIN- AFTER THE MANIAC!

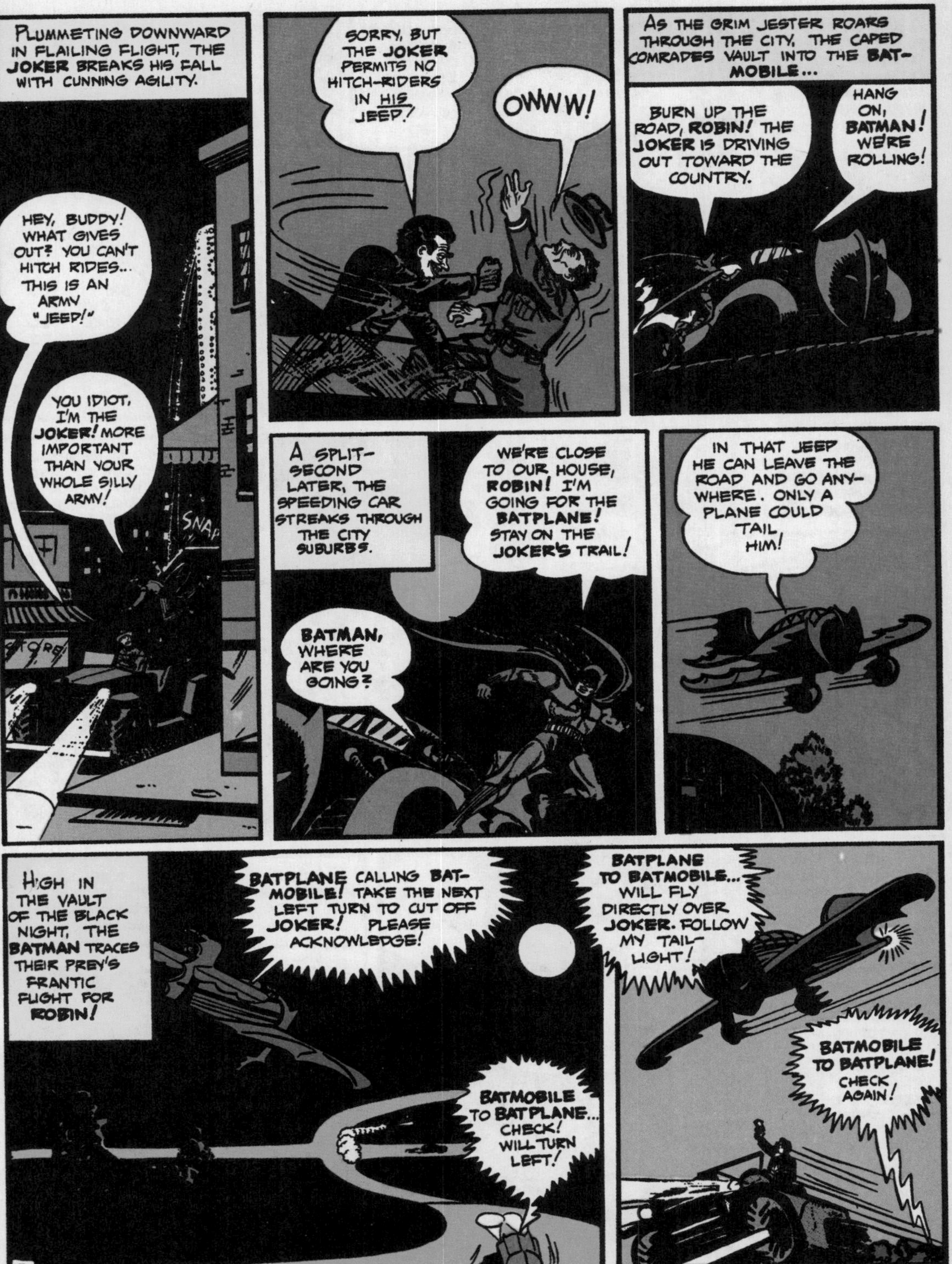
PLUMMETING DOWNWARD IN FLAILING FLIGHT, THE JOKER BREAKS HIS FALL WITH CUNNING AGILITY.
HEY, BUDDY! WHAT GIVES OUT? YOU CAN'T HITCH RIDES.. THIS IS AN ARMY "JEEP!"
YOU IDIOT, I'M THE JOKER! MORE IMPORTANT THAN YOUR WHOLE SILLY ARMY!
SNAP
STORE
SORRY, BUT THE JOKER PERMITS NO HITCH-RIDERS IN HIS JEEP!
OWWW!
AS THE GRIM JESTER ROARS THROUGH THE CITY, THE CAPED COMRADES VAULT INTO THE BAT-MOBILE...
BURN UP THE ROAD, ROBIN! THE JOKER IS DRIVING OUT TOWARD THE COUNTRY.
HANG ON, BATMAN! WE'RE ROLLING!
A SPLIT-SECOND LATER, THE SPEEDING CAR STREAKS THROUGH THE CITY SUBURBS.
WE'RE CLOSE TO OUR HOUSE, ROBIN! I'M GOING FOR THE BATPLANE! STAY ON THE JOKER'S TRAIL!
BATMAN, WHERE ARE YOU GOING?
IN THAT JEEP HE CAN LEAVE THE ROAD AND GO ANY-WHERE. ONLY A PLANE COULD TAIL HIM!
HIGH IN THE VAULT OF THE BLACK NIGHT, THE BATMAN TRACES THEIR PREY'S FRANTIC FLIGHT FOR ROBIN!
BATPLANE CALLING BAT-MOBILE! TAKE THE NEXT LEFT TURN TO CUT OFF JOKER! PLEASE ACKNOWLEDGE!
BATMOBILE TO BATPLANE... CHECK! WILL TURN LEFT!
12
BATPLANE TO BATMOBILE... WILL FLY DIRECTLY OVER JOKER. FOLLOW MY TAIL-LIGHT!
BATMOBILE TO BATPLANE! CHECK AGAIN!

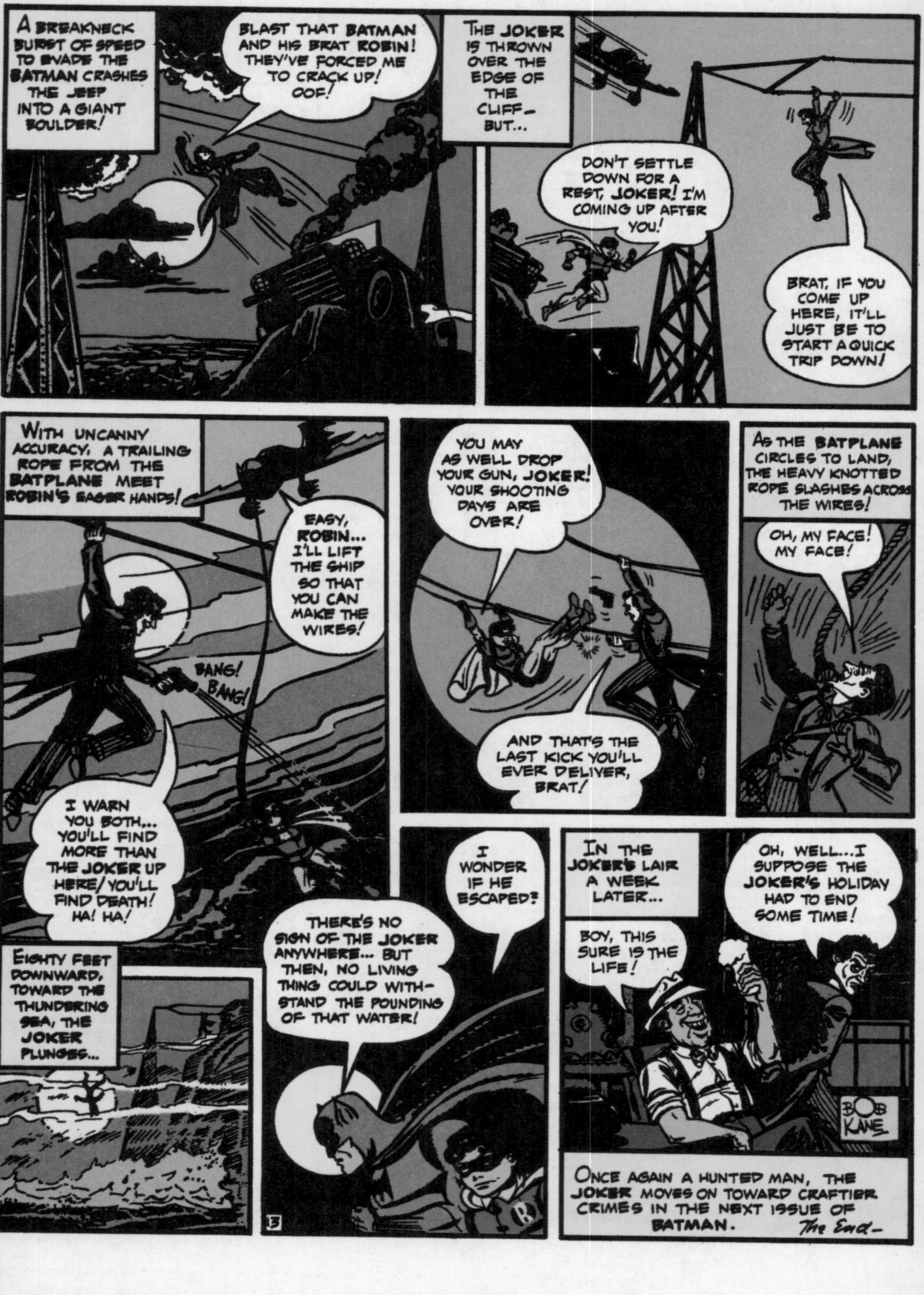
A BREAKNECK BURST OF SPEED TO EVADE THE BATMAN CRASHES THE JEEP INTO A GIANT BOULDER!
BLAST THAT BATMAN AND HIS BRAT ROBIN! THEY'VE FORCED ME TO CRACK UP! OOF!
THE JOKER IS THROWN OVER THE EDGE OF THE CLIFF– BUT...
DON'T SETTLE DOWN FOR A REST, JOKER! I'M COMING UP AFTER YOU!
BRAT, IF YOU COME UP HERE, IT'LL JUST BE TO START A QUICK TRIP DOWN!
WITH UNCANNY ACCURACY, A TRAILING ROPE FROM THE BATPLANE MEET ROBIN'S EAGER HANDS!
EASY, ROBIN... I'LL LIFT THE SHIP SO THAT YOU CAN MAKE THE WIRES!
BANG! BANG!
I WARN YOU BOTH... YOU'LL FIND MORE THAN THE JOKER UP HERE! YOU'LL FIND DEATH! HA! HA!
YOU MAY AS WELL DROP YOUR GUN, JOKER! YOUR SHOOTING DAYS ARE OVER!
AND THAT'S THE LAST KICK YOU'LL EVER DELIVER, BRAT!
AS THE BATPLANE CIRCLES TO LAND, THE HEAVY KNOTTED ROPE SLASHES ACROSS THE WIRES!
OH, MY FACE! MY FACE!
EIGHTY FEET DOWNWARD, TOWARD THE THUNDERING SEA, THE JOKER PLUNGES...
I WONDER IF HE ESCAPED?
THERE'S NO SIGN OF THE JOKER ANYWHERE... BUT THEN, NO LIVING THING COULD WITHSTAND THE POUNDING OF THAT WATER!
13
IN THE JOKER'S LAIR A WEEK LATER...
BOY, THIS SURE IS THE LIFE!
OH, WELL...I SUPPOSE THE JOKER'S HOLIDAY HAD TO END SOME TIME!
BOB KANE
ONCE AGAIN A HUNTED MAN, THE JOKER MOVES ON TOWARD CRAFTIER CRIMES IN THE NEXT ISSUE OF BATMAN.
The End–

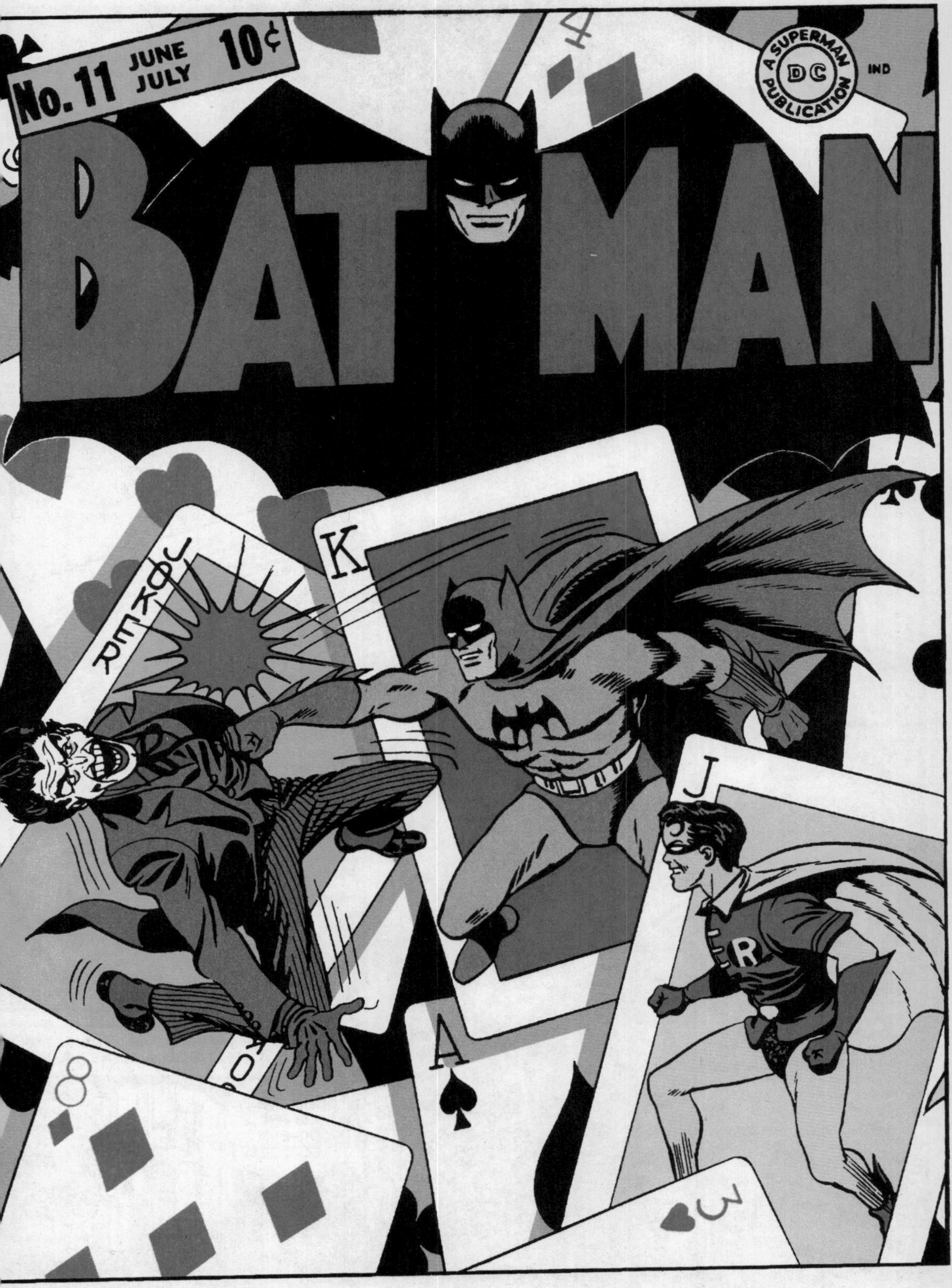
No. 11
JUNE
JULY
10¢
A SUPERMAN
DC
PUBLICATION
IND
BATMAN
JOKER
K
J
R
A
8
3

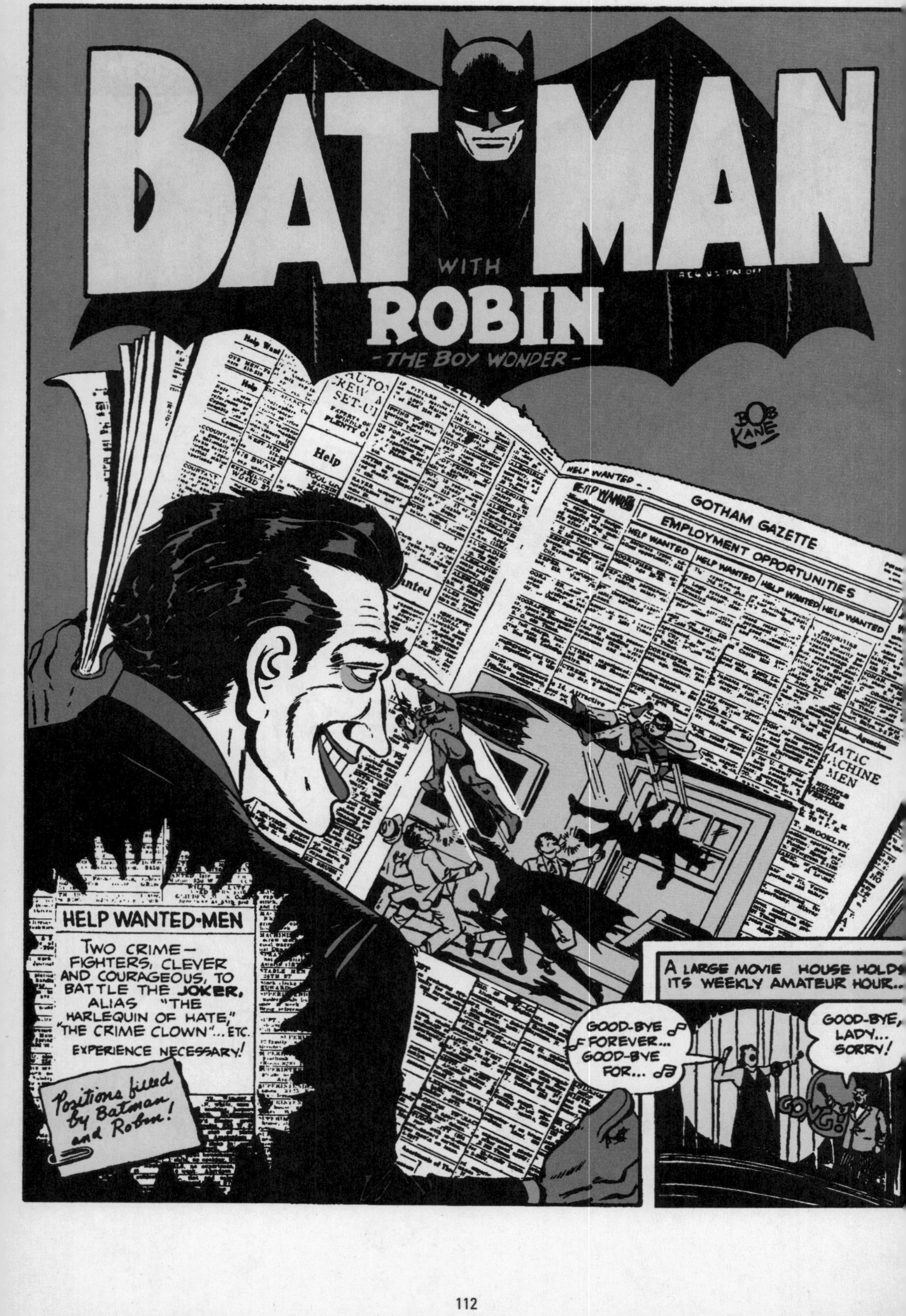
BATMAN
WITH
ROBIN
-THE BOY WONDER-
BOB KANE
GOTHAM GAZETTE
EMPLOYMENT OPPORTUNITIES
HELP WANTED-MEN
TWO CRIME-FIGHTERS, CLEVER AND COURAGEOUS, TO BATTLE THE JOKER, ALIAS "THE HARLEQUIN OF HATE," "THE CRIME CLOWN"... ETC. EXPERIENCE NECESSARY!
Positions filled by Batman and Robin!
A LARGE MOVIE HOUSE HOLDS ITS WEEKLY AMATEUR HOUR...
GOOD-BYE FOREVER... GOOD-BYE FOR...
GOOD-BYE, LADY... SORRY!
GONG!

THE SECOND CONTESTANT GIVES HIS IMPRESSION OF A FAMOUS COMEDIAN!

HA-CHA-CHA-CHA!

ANOTHER CANDIDATE!

AND NOW YOU, SIR... WHAT'S YOUR SPECIALTY?

I DO AN IMITATION OF...THE JOKER!

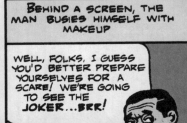

BEHIND A SCREEN, THE MAN BUSIES HIMSELF WITH MAKEUP

WELL, FOLKS, I GUESS YOU'D BETTER PREPARE YOURSELVES FOR A SCARE! WE'RE GOING TO SEE THE JOKER...BRR!

A MOMENT LATER, OUT STEPS A PERFECT DOUBLE FOR THAT GRINNING CRIME CLOWN—THE JOKER!

HA! HA! I'LL BEAT THE BATMAN YET! HA! HA!

HERE'S YOUR PRIZE ...FOR A GREAT IMPERSONATION! I ALMOST BELIEVED YOU WERE THE JOKER! WELL, NOW YOU CAN REMOVE THAT MAKEUP!

...BUT I CAN'T...

CLAP! CLAP!

CLAP! CLAP!

CLAP! CLAP!

CLAP! CLAP!

...THE OTHER WAS MAKEUP— THIS IS MY REAL FACE.. FOR I ACTUALLY AM THE JOKER! HA! HA! HA!

THE SCENE SHIFTS TO THE BUSY GYMNASIUM OF BRUCE WAYNE AND HIS WARD DICK GRAYSON!

GET IT, NOW? LEFT UPPERCUT FIRST...AND THEN FOLLOW WITH A RIGHT CROSS!

GOLLY... I COULDN'T EVEN SEE THAT ONE!

SUDDENLY, A STARTLING ANNOUNCEMENT PULLS BRUCE OFF GUARD... BUT DICK IS TOO INTENT AND EAGER...AND—

WE INTERRUPT TO BRING YOU A SPECIAL ANNOUNCEMENT! THE JOKER HAS ESCAPED FROM JAIL!

HUH?

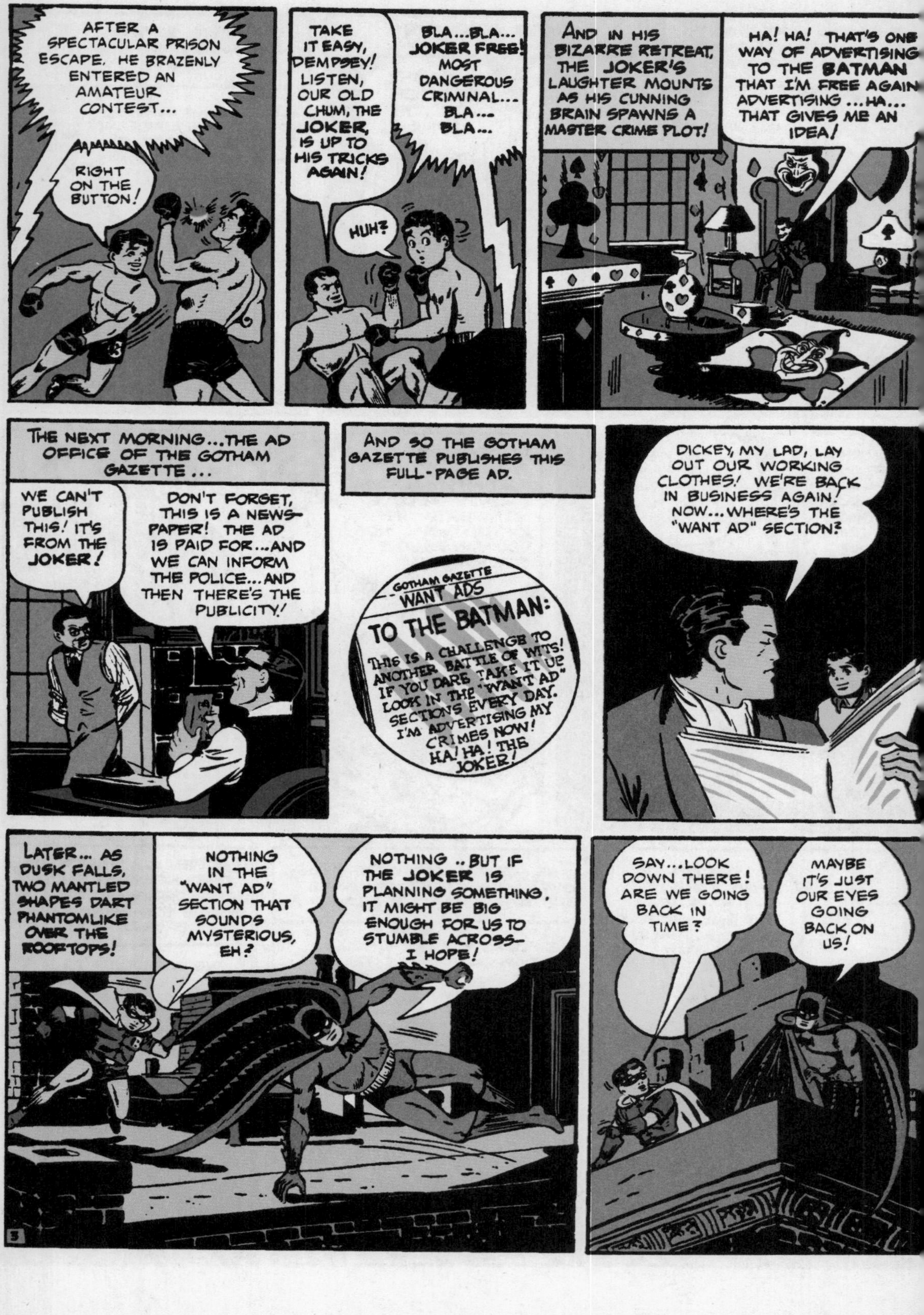
AFTER A SPECTACULAR PRISON ESCAPE, HE BRAZENLY ENTERED AN AMATEUR CONTEST...
RIGHT ON THE BUTTON!
TAKE IT EASY, DEMPSEY! LISTEN, OUR OLD CHUM, THE JOKER, IS UP TO HIS TRICKS AGAIN!
BLA...BLA... JOKER FREE! MOST DANGEROUS CRIMINAL... BLA... BLA...
HUH?
AND IN HIS BIZARRE RETREAT, THE JOKER'S LAUGHTER MOUNTS AS HIS CUNNING BRAIN SPAWNS A MASTER CRIME PLOT!
HA! HA! THAT'S ONE WAY OF ADVERTISING TO THE BATMAN THAT I'M FREE AGAIN ADVERTISING ...HA... THAT GIVES ME AN IDEA!
THE NEXT MORNING...THE AD OFFICE OF THE GOTHAM GAZETTE...
WE CAN'T PUBLISH THIS! IT'S FROM THE JOKER!
DON'T FORGET, THIS IS A NEWSPAPER! THE AD IS PAID FOR...AND WE CAN INFORM THE POLICE...AND THEN THERE'S THE PUBLICITY!
AND SO THE GOTHAM GAZETTE PUBLISHES THIS FULL-PAGE AD.
GOTHAM GAZETTE
WANT ADS
TO THE BATMAN:
THIS IS A CHALLENGE TO ANOTHER BATTLE OF WITS! IF YOU DARE TAKE IT UP LOOK IN THE "WANT AD" SECTIONS EVERY DAY. I'M ADVERTISING MY CRIMES NOW! HA! HA! THE JOKER!
DICKEY, MY LAD, LAY OUT OUR WORKING CLOTHES! WE'RE BACK IN BUSINESS AGAIN! NOW...WHERE'S THE "WANT AD" SECTION?
LATER... AS DUSK FALLS, TWO MANTLED SHAPES DART PHANTOMLIKE OVER THE ROOFTOPS!
NOTHING IN THE "WANT AD" SECTION THAT SOUNDS MYSTERIOUS, EH?
NOTHING .. BUT IF THE JOKER IS PLANNING SOMETHING, IT MIGHT BE BIG ENOUGH FOR US TO STUMBLE ACROSS- I HOPE!
3
SAY...LOOK DOWN THERE! ARE WE GOING BACK IN TIME?
MAYBE IT'S JUST OUR EYES GOING BACK ON US!

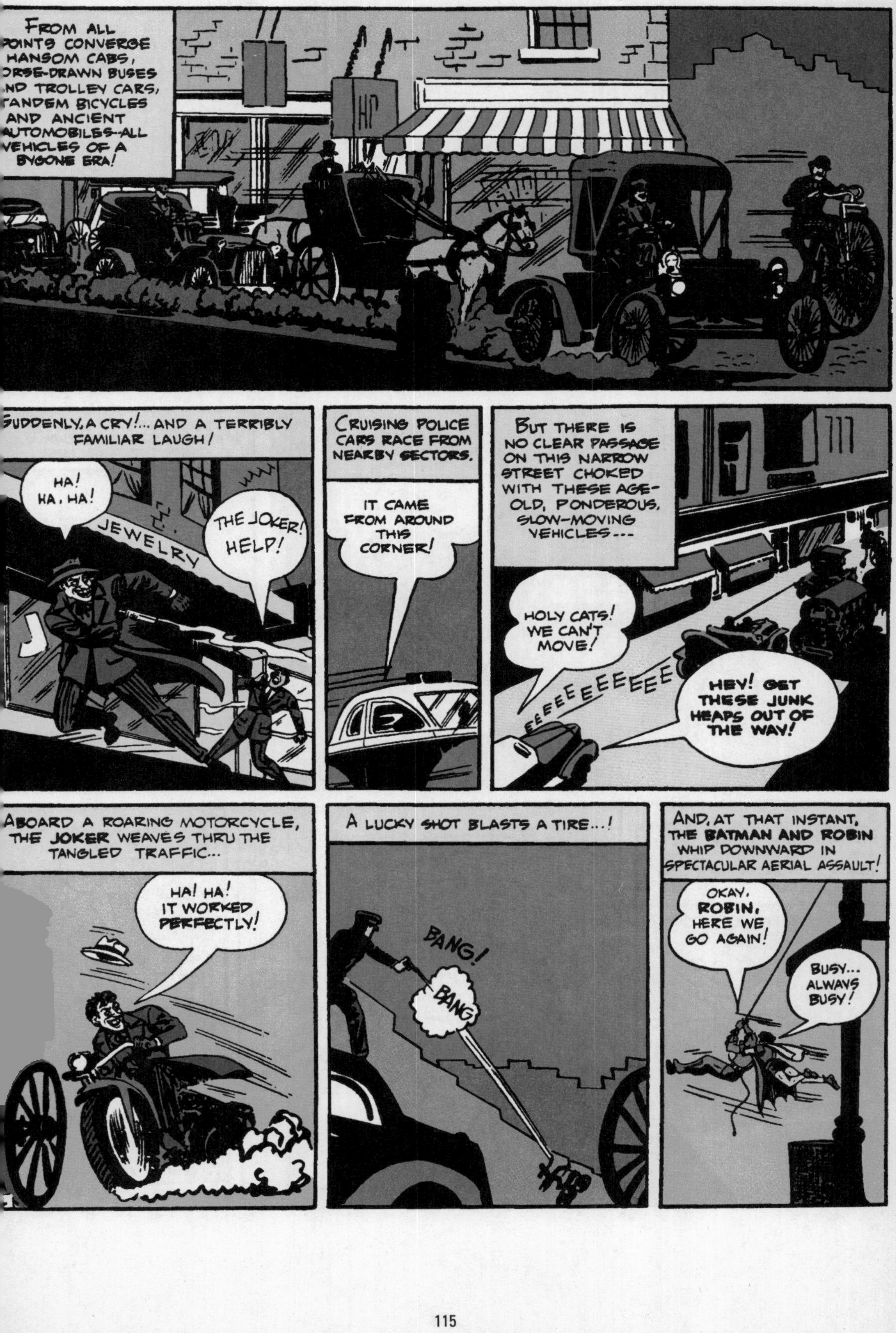
FROM ALL POINTS CONVERGE HANSOM CABS, ORSE-DRAWN BUSES ND TROLLEY CARS, TANDEM BICYCLES AND ANCIENT AUTOMOBILES--ALL VEHICLES OF A BYGONE ERA!
SUDDENLY, A CRY!... AND A TERRIBLY FAMILIAR LAUGH!
HA! HA, HA!
JEWELRY
THE JOKER! HELP!
CRUISING POLICE CARS RACE FROM NEARBY SECTORS.
IT CAME FROM AROUND THIS CORNER!
BUT THERE IS NO CLEAR PASSAGE ON THIS NARROW STREET CHOKED WITH THESE AGE-OLD, PONDEROUS, SLOW-MOVING VEHICLES---
HOLY CATS! WE CAN'T MOVE!
EEEEEEEEEEE
HEY! GET THESE JUNK HEAPS OUT OF THE WAY!
ABOARD A ROARING MOTORCYCLE, THE JOKER WEAVES THRU THE TANGLED TRAFFIC...
HA! HA! IT WORKED PERFECTLY!
A LUCKY SHOT BLASTS A TIRE...!
BANG!
BANG
AND, AT THAT INSTANT, THE BATMAN AND ROBIN WHIP DOWNWARD IN SPECTACULAR AERIAL ASSAULT!
OKAY, ROBIN, HERE WE GO AGAIN!
BUSY... ALWAYS BUSY!

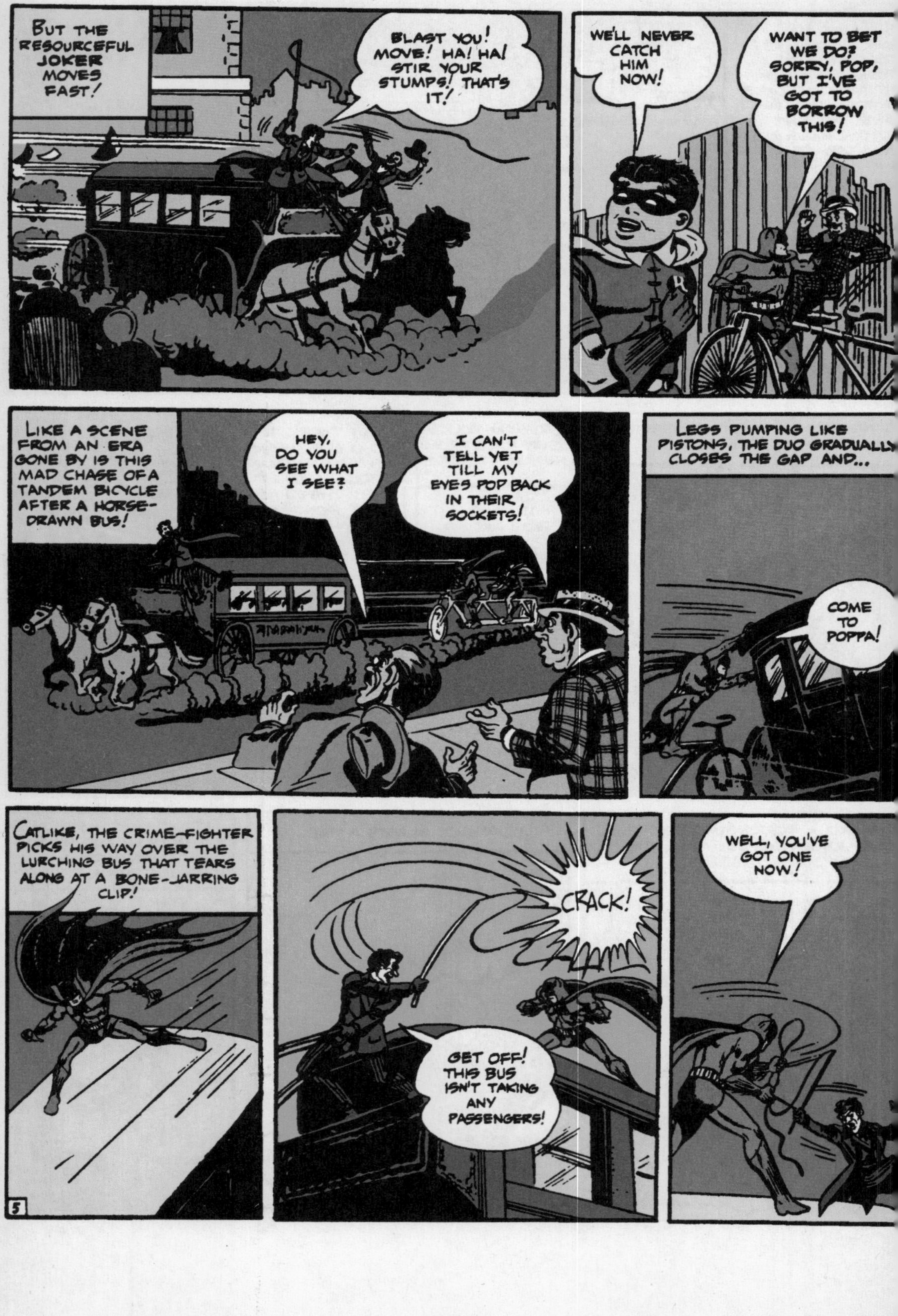

BUT THE RESOURCEFUL JOKER MOVES FAST!
BLAST YOU! MOVE! HA! HA! STIR YOUR STUMPS! THAT'S IT!
WE'LL NEVER CATCH HIM NOW!
WANT TO BET WE DO? SORRY, POP, BUT I'VE GOT TO BORROW THIS!
LIKE A SCENE FROM AN ERA GONE BY IS THIS MAD CHASE OF A TANDEM BICYCLE AFTER A HORSE-DRAWN BUS!
HEY, DO YOU SEE WHAT I SEE?
I CAN'T TELL YET TILL MY EYES POP BACK IN THEIR SOCKETS!
LEGS PUMPING LIKE PISTONS, THE DUO GRADUALLY CLOSES THE GAP AND...
COME TO POPPA!
CATLIKE, THE CRIME-FIGHTER PICKS HIS WAY OVER THE LURCHING BUS THAT TEARS ALONG AT A BONE-JARRING CLIP!
5
CRACK!
GET OFF! THIS BUS ISN'T TAKING ANY PASSENGERS!
WELL, YOU'VE GOT ONE NOW!

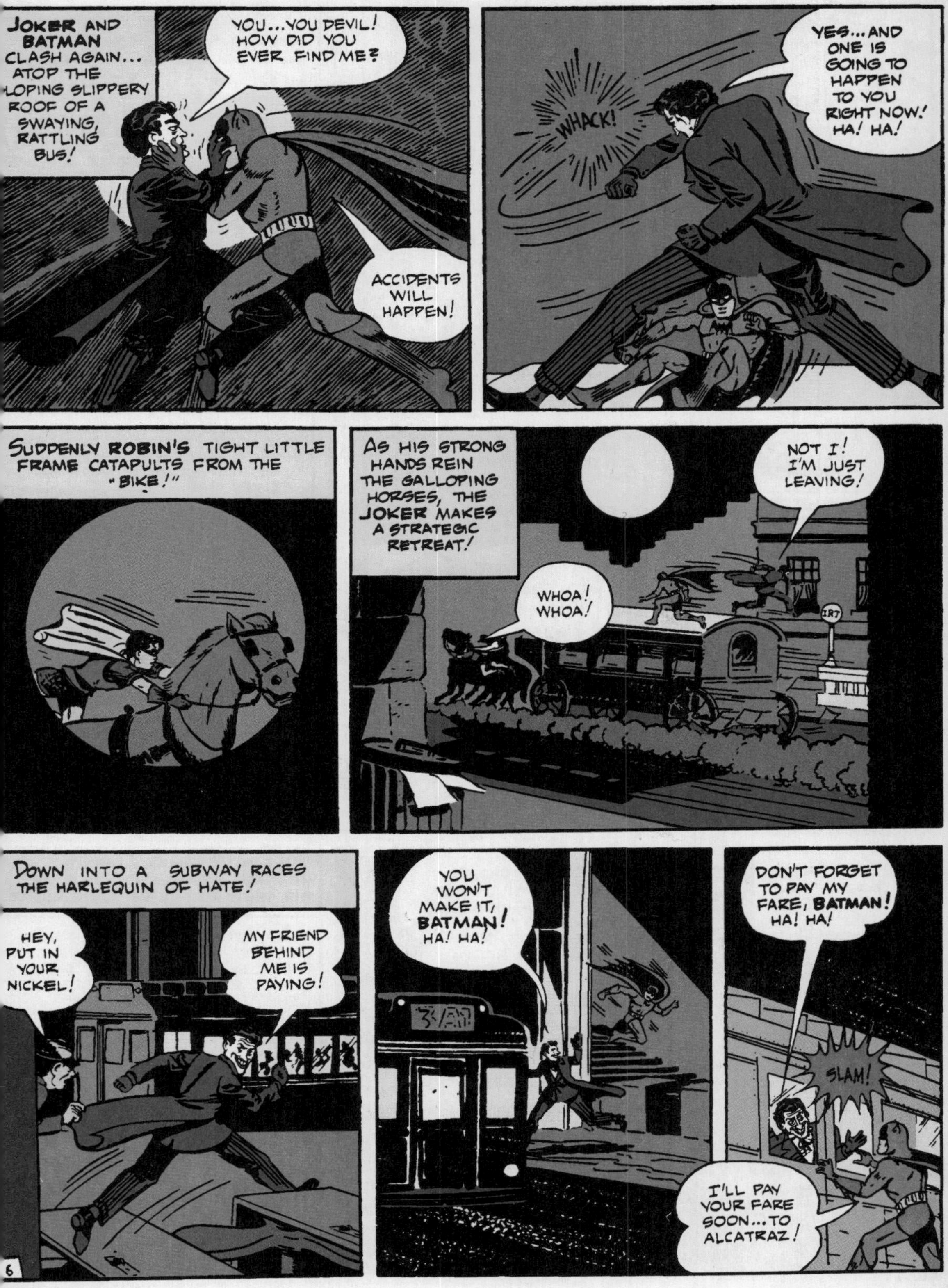
JOKER AND BATMAN CLASH AGAIN... ATOP THE LOPING SLIPPERY ROOF OF A SWAYING, RATTLING BUS!
YOU... YOU DEVIL! HOW DID YOU EVER FIND ME?
ACCIDENTS WILL HAPPEN!
WHACK!
YES... AND ONE IS GOING TO HAPPEN TO YOU RIGHT NOW! HA! HA!
SUDDENLY ROBIN'S TIGHT LITTLE FRAME CATAPULTS FROM THE "BIKE!"
AS HIS STRONG HANDS REIN THE GALLOPING HORSES, THE JOKER MAKES A STRATEGIC RETREAT!
NOT I! I'M JUST LEAVING!
WHOA! WHOA!
IRT
DOWN INTO A SUBWAY RACES THE HARLEQUIN OF HATE!
HEY, PUT IN YOUR NICKEL!
MY FRIEND BEHIND ME IS PAYING!
6
YOU WON'T MAKE IT, BATMAN! HA! HA!
DON'T FORGET TO PAY MY FARE, BATMAN! HA! HA!
SLAM!
I'LL PAY YOUR FARE SOON... TO ALCATRAZ!

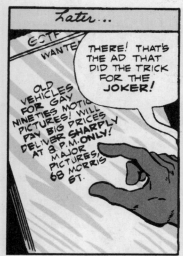

Later...
GOTH
WANTE
THERE! THAT'S THE AD THAT DID THE TRICK FOR THE JOKER!
OLD VEHICLES FOR GAY NINETIES MOTIO PICTURES! WILL PAY BIG PRICES DELIVER SHARPLY AT 8 P.M. ONLY! MAJOR PICTURES, 68 MORRIS ST.
BY MAKING ALL THOSE OLD BUGGIES APPEAR AT THE SAME TIME, AND BY PURPOSELY PICKING A NARROW STREET, THE JOKER BLOCKED OFF ALL PURSUIT BY THE POLICE! 68 MORRIS STREET HAPPENS TO BE A STORE NEXT DOOR TO THE JEWELER'S. CLEVER, EH?
AND HOW! I WONDER WHAT TRICK HE'S GOING TO PULL OUT OF HIS HAT NEXT?
THE NEXT DAY, THE TWO EAGERLY SCAN THE WANT ADS.
NO, NOT A THING HERE THAT SOUNDS SUSPICIOUS!
AND DON'T FORGET, ANYTHING HERE MIGHT BE USED FOR CRIME IN SOME WAY... BUT HOW CAN WE PICK THE RIGHT ONE?
WANTED
POLICE TO KEEP AWAY CROWDS THAT WILL MOB THE PREMIERE PERFORMANCE OF PRESTO THE MAGICIAN AT THE GOTHAM THEATER!
HA! HA! HERE'S A WANT AD! SWELL PUBLICITY STUNT FOR PRESTO, EH?
SAY ALMOST FORGOT! I'M GOING TO THAT SHOW. LINDA MAY PHONE IF SHE CAN MEET ME LATER, SO RELAY HER MESSAGE!
LOVE! AH, LOVE!
THE SAME AD IS READ BY THE HARLEQUIN OF HATE...
EVERYONE THINKS IT'S JUST PUBLICITY. EVEN THE BATMAN WON'T SUSPECT IT AS MY QUAINT WAY OF ADVERTISING ANOTHER CRIME! HA! HA!
WEALTHY "FIRST-NIGHTERS" ATTEND THE PREMIERE OF PRESTO, THE INTERNATIONALLY FAMOUS MAGICIAN!
FOR MY FIRST TRICK, I WILL NEED SOME ASSISTANCE, AND SO I WILL CHOOSE THREE LADIES FROM AMONG YOU...
AT THAT INSTANT, LINDA'S MESSAGE BRINGS DICK BEFORE THE THEATRE IN TIME TO OVERHEAR...
YOU MEAN, THAT YOU, THE PUBLICITY AGENT, DIDN'T PLACE THAT AD IN THE PAPER?
I WISH I HAD THOUGHT OF IT, BUT I DIDN'T! THE PAPER GOT THE MONEY AND INSTRUCTIONS ANONYMOUSLY THROUGH THE MAIL. I CAN'T UNDER-STAND IT!
BUT I CAN- THE JOKER!
7

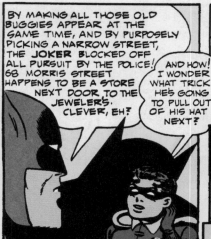

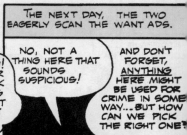

AND ONSTAGE...

I PLACE THE THREE LADIES INSIDE THE CABINET—SO!

I CLOSE THE DOOR... WAVE MY WAND...

AND PRESTO!... EMPTY! THEY HAVE DISAPPEARED!

AND NOW I MAKE MYSELF DISAPPEAR... LIKE THIS! HA! HA! HA!

THAT LAUGH! IT'S THE JOKER!

A SCANT INSTANT DISCARD OF OUTER GARB IN THE GLOOMY HALL... AND THE BATMAN LEAPS TO THE STAGE.

THE BATMAN!

IS HE PART OF THE SHOW?

WHAT?... THE BATMAN! I MUST HAVE MY GLASSES FIXED! M'EYES ARE GOIN' BAD!

OF COURSE! THE OLD TRAPDOOR STUNT!

BUT AS HE DROPS BELOW, A BLUDGEON CRASHES DOWN IN A CRUEL BLOW!

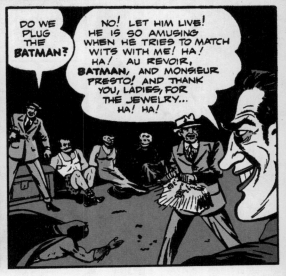

DO WE PLUG THE BATMAN?

NO! LET HIM LIVE! HE IS SO AMUSING WHEN HE TRIES TO MATCH WITS WITH ME! HA! HA! AU REVOIR, BATMAN, AND MONSIEUR PRESTO! AND THANK YOU, LADIES, FOR THE JEWELRY... HA! HA!

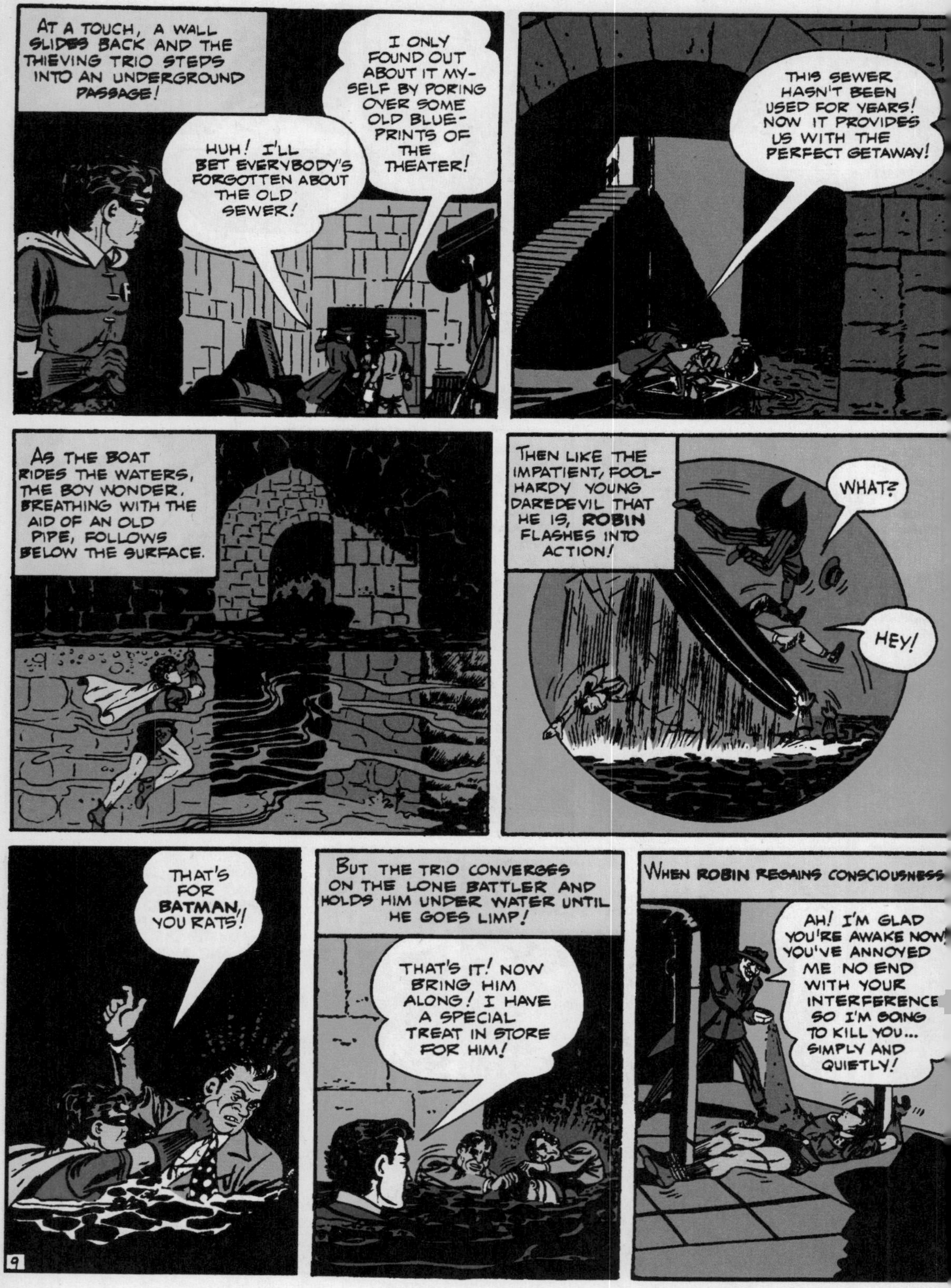

AT A TOUCH, A WALL SLIDES BACK AND THE THIEVING TRIO STEPS INTO AN UNDERGROUND PASSAGE!
HUH! I'LL BET EVERYBODY'S FORGOTTEN ABOUT THE OLD SEWER!
I ONLY FOUND OUT ABOUT IT MYSELF BY PORING OVER SOME OLD BLUE-PRINTS OF THE THEATER!
THIS SEWER HASN'T BEEN USED FOR YEARS! NOW IT PROVIDES US WITH THE PERFECT GETAWAY!
AS THE BOAT RIDES THE WATERS, THE BOY WONDER, BREATHING WITH THE AID OF AN OLD PIPE, FOLLOWS BELOW THE SURFACE.
THEN LIKE THE IMPATIENT, FOOL-HARDY YOUNG DAREDEVIL THAT HE IS, ROBIN FLASHES INTO ACTION!
WHAT?
HEY!
THAT'S FOR BATMAN, YOU RATS!
9
BUT THE TRIO CONVERGES ON THE LONE BATTLER AND HOLDS HIM UNDER WATER UNTIL HE GOES LIMP!
THAT'S IT! NOW BRING HIM ALONG! I HAVE A SPECIAL TREAT IN STORE FOR HIM!
WHEN ROBIN REGAINS CONSCIOUSNESS
AH! I'M GLAD YOU'RE AWAKE NOW! YOU'VE ANNOYED ME NO END WITH YOUR INTERFERENCE SO I'M GOING TO KILL YOU... SIMPLY AND QUIETLY!

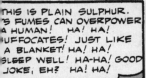
...THIS IS PLAIN SULPHUR. ITS FUMES CAN OVERPOWER A HUMAN! HA! HA! IT SUFFOCATES! JUST LIKE A BLANKET! HA! HA! SLEEP WELL! HA-HA! GOOD JOKE, EH? HA! HA!

THE DOOR CLOSES...AND HELPLESS **ROBIN** IS LEFT ALONE TO FACE A HORRIBLE, CHOKING DOOM!

I CAN'T GET LOOSE! I CAN'T GET LOOSE... COUGH!

MINUTES PASS AND THE SULPHUROUS FUMES RISE THICKLY ABOUT THE BOY LIKE A MALIGNANT CLOUD!

(COUGH) I'M GOING TO DIE... NO... MUSTN'T LOSE MY HEAD... MUST THINK... THINK... (COUGH)

SUDDENLY ROBIN'S PROBING FINGERS ENCOUNTER A WIRE...

A TELEPHONE WIRE... PROBABLY DISCONNECTED A LONG TIME AGO! IT'S SPLICED AT THIS POINT! MAYBE... MAYBE...

FUMBLING IN THEIR HASTE, HIS FINGERS SLOWLY, LABORIOUSLY UNWIND THE TAPE FROM THE SPLICED WIRES.

IT MIGHT WORK...THERE'S A CHANCE...I'VE GOT A CHANCE!

THEN, WHEN THE SPLICED WIRES ARE UNWOUND, **ROBIN** TAPS ONE WIRE AGAINST THE OTHER...

OUT INTO SPACE GOES A CALL FOR HELP! WILL IT BE HEARD... BEFORE IT IS TOO LATE?

LISTEN, MISS HENLEY, THIS S.O.S. HAS BEEN COMING OVER FOR THE LAST FEW MINUTES!

CALL THE POLICE! THEY'LL TRACE IT WITH THEIR SIGNAL-FINDER! HURRY!

AND SO A DESPERATE MESSAGE IS TRANSMITTED OVER THE WIRES...

S.O.S. ROBIN CALLING BATMAN

WILL IT BE PICKED UP BY THE BATMAN... IN TIME?

MINUTES LATER... A POWERFUL FRAME RIPS A DOOR FROM ITS HINGES...

WHAM

(COUGH) ROBIN, ROBIN! HE'S LYING SO STILL! MAYBE...NO... IT CAN'T BE!..

10

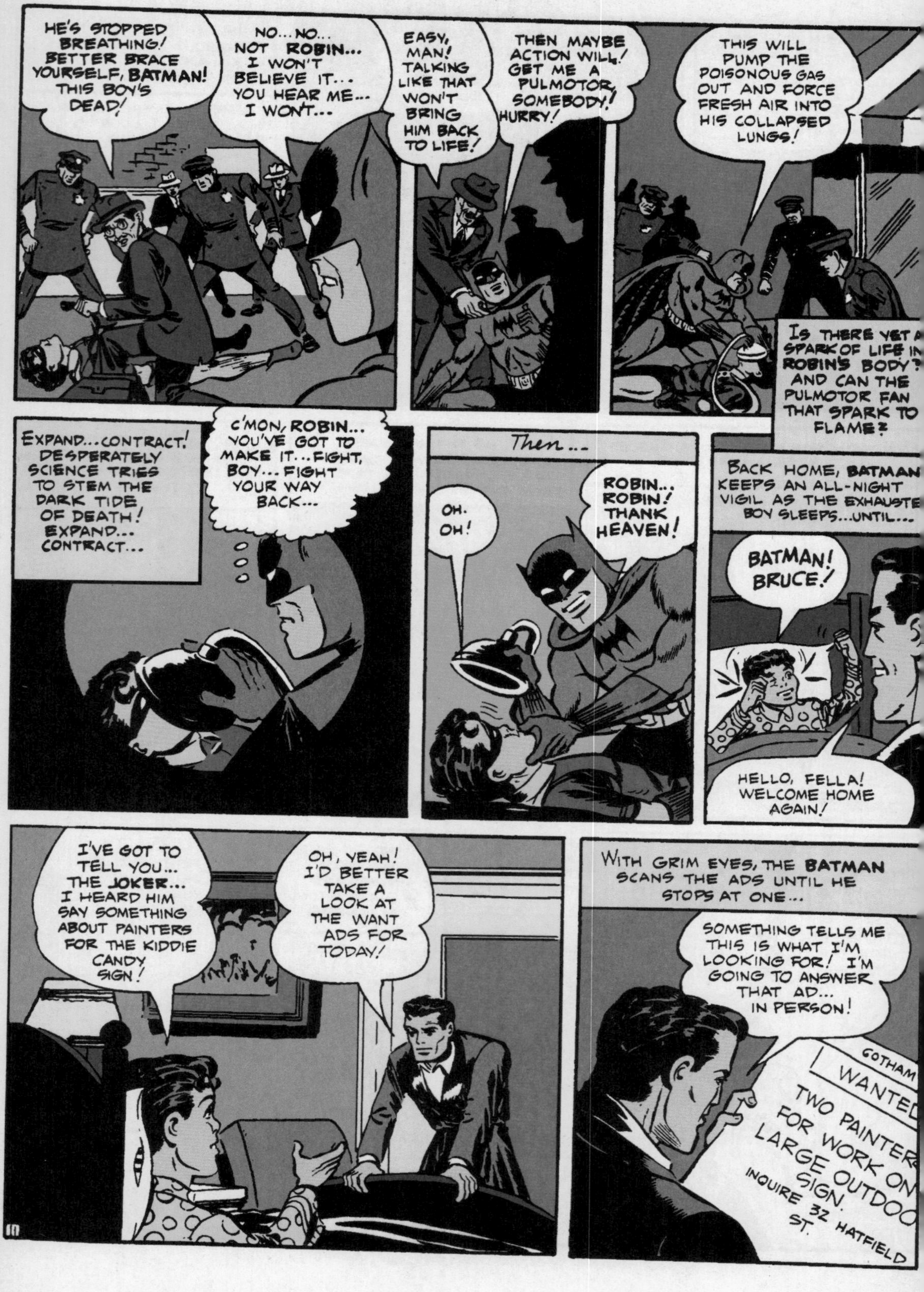

HE'S STOPPED BREATHING! BETTER BRACE YOURSELF, BATMAN! THIS BOY'S DEAD!
NO... NO... NOT ROBIN... I WON'T BELIEVE IT... YOU HEAR ME... I WON'T...
EASY, MAN! TALKING LIKE THAT WON'T BRING HIM BACK TO LIFE!
THEN MAYBE ACTION WILL! GET ME A PULMOTOR, SOMEBODY! HURRY!
THIS WILL PUMP THE POISONOUS GAS OUT AND FORCE FRESH AIR INTO HIS COLLAPSED LUNGS!
IS THERE YET A SPARK OF LIFE IN ROBIN'S BODY? AND CAN THE PULMOTOR FAN THAT SPARK TO FLAME?
EXPAND... CONTRACT! DESPERATELY SCIENCE TRIES TO STEM THE DARK TIDE OF DEATH! EXPAND... CONTRACT...
C'MON, ROBIN... YOU'VE GOT TO MAKE IT... FIGHT, BOY... FIGHT YOUR WAY BACK...
Then...
OH. OH!
ROBIN... ROBIN! THANK HEAVEN!
BACK HOME, BATMAN KEEPS AN ALL-NIGHT VIGIL AS THE EXHAUSTE BOY SLEEPS... UNTIL...
BATMAN! BRUCE!
HELLO, FELLA! WELCOME HOME AGAIN!
I'VE GOT TO TELL YOU... THE JOKER... I HEARD HIM SAY SOMETHING ABOUT PAINTERS FOR THE KIDDIE CANDY SIGN!
OH, YEAH! I'D BETTER TAKE A LOOK AT THE WANT ADS FOR TODAY!
WITH GRIM EYES, THE BATMAN SCANS THE ADS UNTIL HE STOPS AT ONE...
SOMETHING TELLS ME THIS IS WHAT I'M LOOKING FOR! I'M GOING TO ANSWER THAT AD... IN PERSON!
GOTHAM
WANTED
TWO PAINTER FOR WORK ON LARGE OUTDOO SIGN. INQUIRE 32 HATFIELD ST.
10

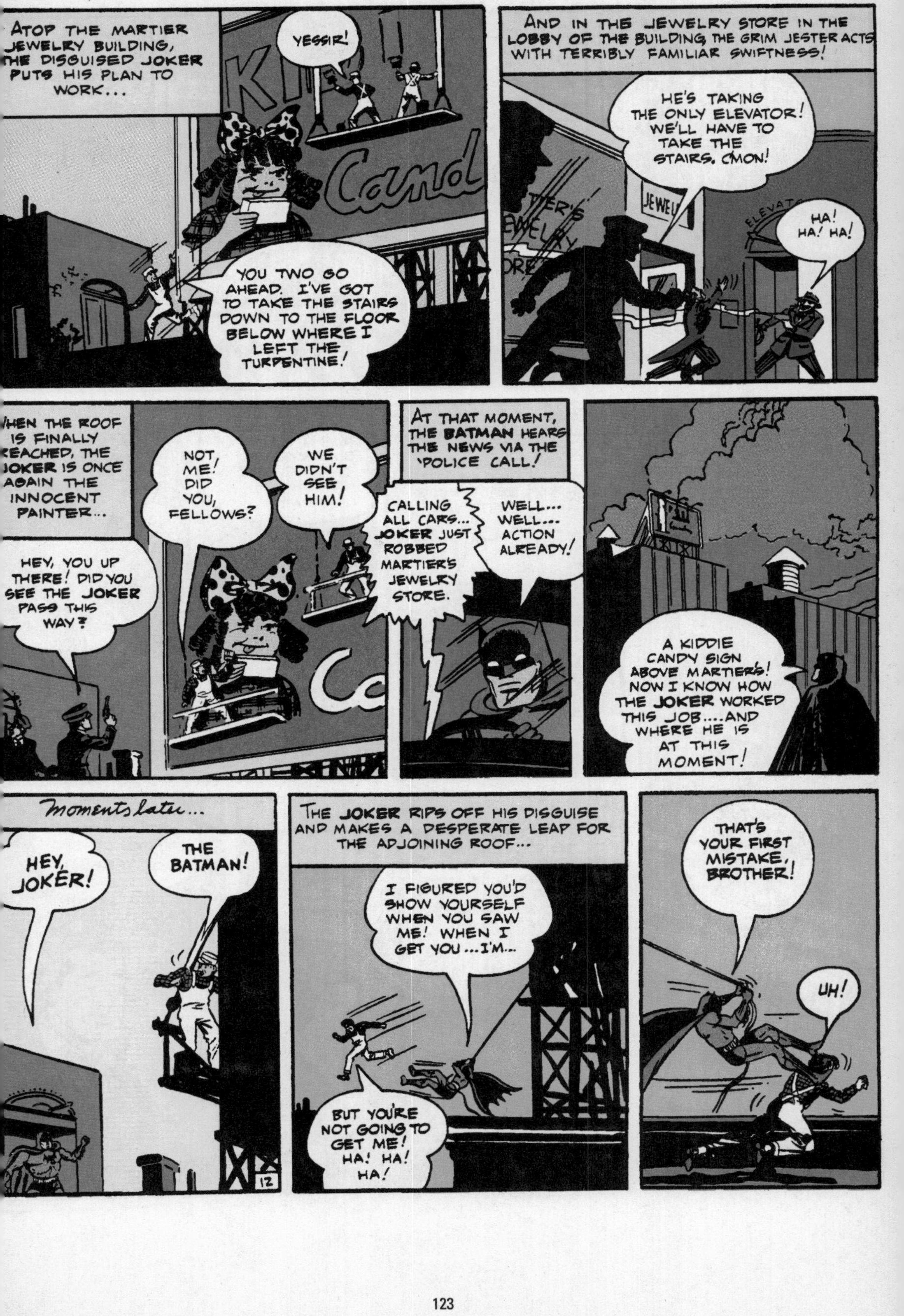
ATOP THE MARTIER JEWELRY BUILDING, THE DISGUISED JOKER PUTS HIS PLAN TO WORK...
YESSIR!
YOU TWO GO AHEAD. I'VE GOT TO TAKE THE STAIRS DOWN TO THE FLOOR BELOW WHERE I LEFT THE TURPENTINE!
AND IN THE JEWELRY STORE IN THE LOBBY OF THE BUILDING THE GRIM JESTER ACTS WITH TERRIBLY FAMILIAR SWIFTNESS!
HE'S TAKING THE ONLY ELEVATOR! WE'LL HAVE TO TAKE THE STAIRS. C'MON!
HA! HA! HA!
HEN THE ROOF IS FINALLY EACHED, THE JOKER IS ONCE AGAIN THE INNOCENT PAINTER...
HEY, YOU UP THERE! DID YOU SEE THE JOKER PASS THIS WAY?
NOT ME! DID YOU, FELLOWS?
WE DIDN'T SEE HIM!
AT THAT MOMENT, THE BATMAN HEARS THE NEWS VIA THE 'POLICE CALL'!
CALLING ALL CARS... JOKER JUST ROBBED MARTIER'S JEWELRY STORE.
WELL... WELL... ACTION ALREADY!
A KIDDIE CANDY SIGN ABOVE MARTIER'S! NOW I KNOW HOW THE JOKER WORKED THIS JOB.... AND WHERE HE IS AT THIS MOMENT!
Moments later...
HEY, JOKER!
THE BATMAN!
12
THE JOKER RIPS OFF HIS DISGUISE AND MAKES A DESPERATE LEAP FOR THE ADJOINING ROOF...
I FIGURED YOU'D SHOW YOURSELF WHEN YOU SAW ME! WHEN I GET YOU... I'M...
BUT YOU'RE NOT GOING TO GET ME! HA! HA! HA!
THAT'S YOUR FIRST MISTAKE, BROTHER!
UH!

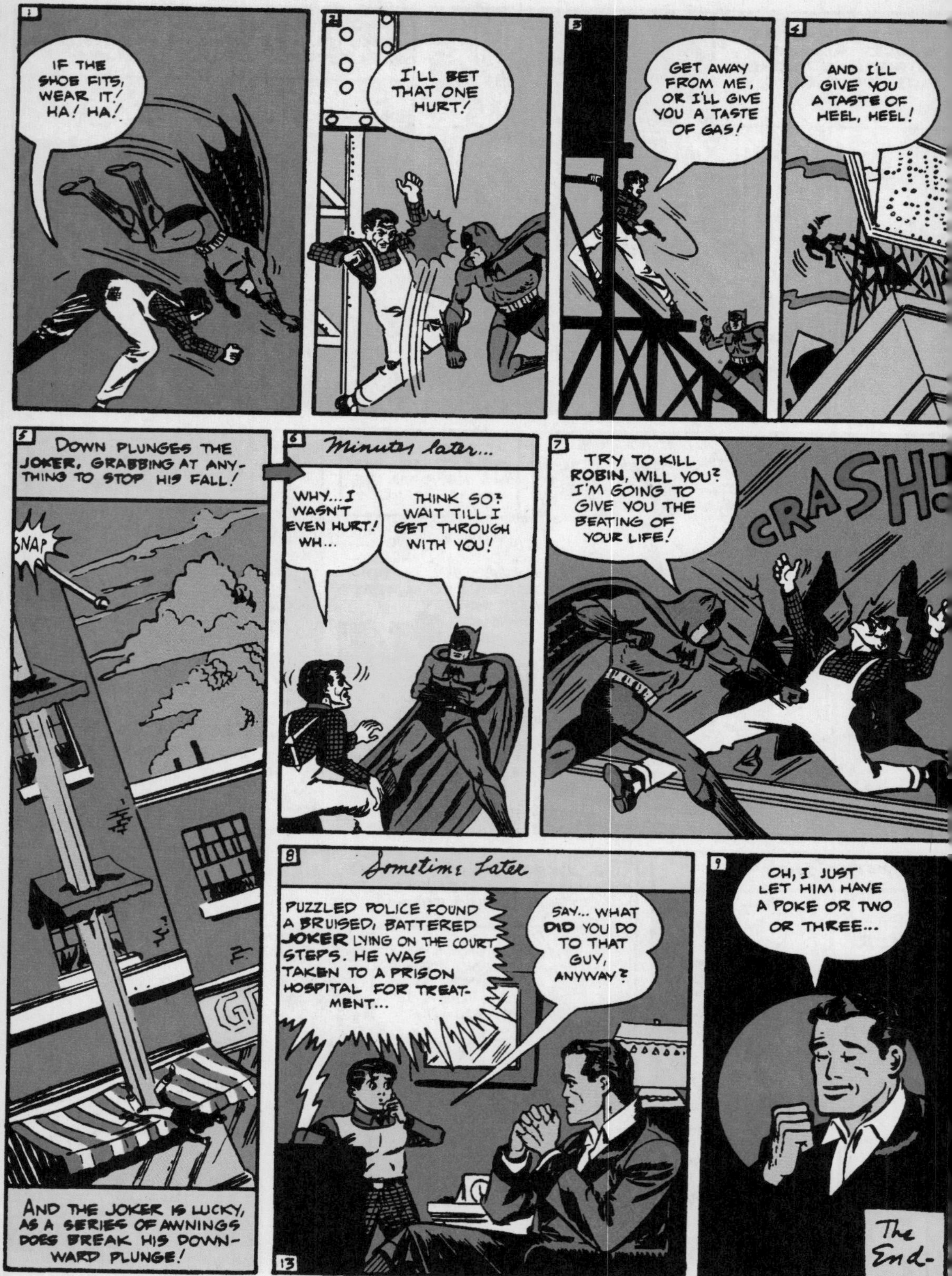

IF THE SHOE FITS, WEAR IT! HA! HA!
I'LL BET THAT ONE HURT!
GET AWAY FROM ME, OR I'LL GIVE YOU A TASTE OF GAS!
AND I'LL GIVE YOU A TASTE OF HEEL, HEEL!
DOWN PLUNGES THE JOKER, GRABBING AT ANYTHING TO STOP HIS FALL!
SNAP
AND THE JOKER IS LUCKY, AS A SERIES OF AWNINGS DOES BREAK HIS DOWNWARD PLUNGE!
Minutes later...
WHY... I WASN'T EVEN HURT! WH...
THINK SO? WAIT TILL I GET THROUGH WITH YOU!
TRY TO KILL ROBIN, WILL YOU? I'M GOING TO GIVE YOU THE BEATING OF YOUR LIFE!
CRASH!
Sometime Later
PUZZLED POLICE FOUND A BRUISED, BATTERED JOKER LYING ON THE COURT STEPS. HE WAS TAKEN TO A PRISON HOSPITAL FOR TREATMENT...
SAY... WHAT DID YOU DO TO THAT GUY, ANYWAY?
OH, I JUST LET HIM HAVE A POKE OR TWO OR THREE...
The End-

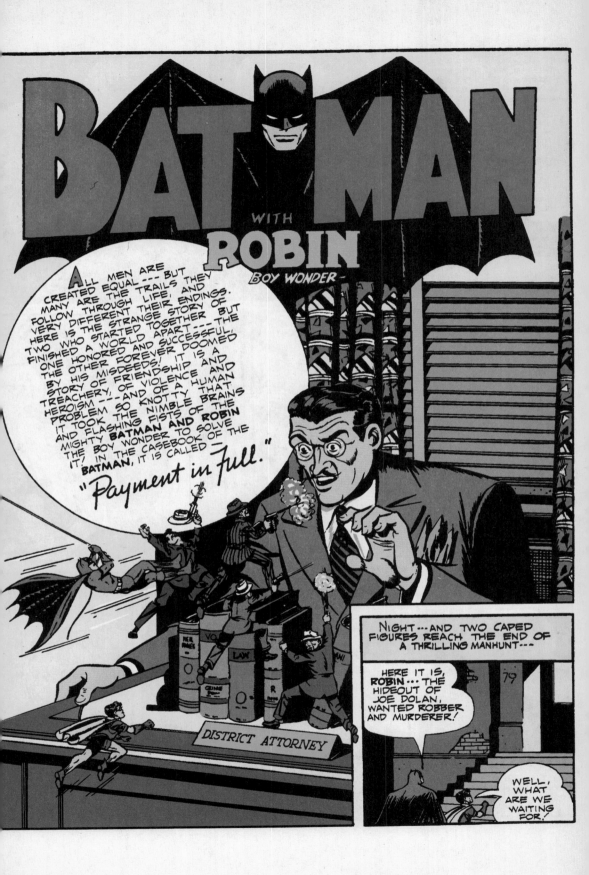

BAT MAN

WITH ROBIN

BOY WONDER —

A ALL MEN ARE CREATED EQUAL --- BUT MANY ARE THE TRAILS THEY FOLLOW THROUGH LIFE, AND VERY DIFFERENT THEIR ENDINGS. HERE IS THE STRANGE STORY OF TWO WHO STARTED TOGETHER BUT FINISHED A WORLD APART --- THE ONE HONORED AND SUCCESSFUL, THE OTHER FOREVER DOOMED BY HIS MISDEEDS! IT IS A STORY OF FRIENDSHIP AND TREACHERY, OF VIOLENCE AND HEROISM --- AND OF A HUMAN PROBLEM SO KNOTTY THAT IT TOOK THE NIMBLE BRAINS AND FLASHING FISTS OF THE MIGHTY **BATMAN AND ROBIN** THE BOY WONDER TO SOLVE IT! IN THE CASEBOOK OF THE **BATMAN**, IT IS CALLED —

"Payment in full."

DISTRICT ATTORNEY

NIGHT --- AND TWO CAPED FIGURES REACH THE END OF A THRILLING MANHUNT ---

HERE IT IS, ROBIN --- THE HIDEOUT OF JOE DOLAN, WANTED ROBBER AND MURDERER!

WELL, WHAT ARE WE WAITING FOR!

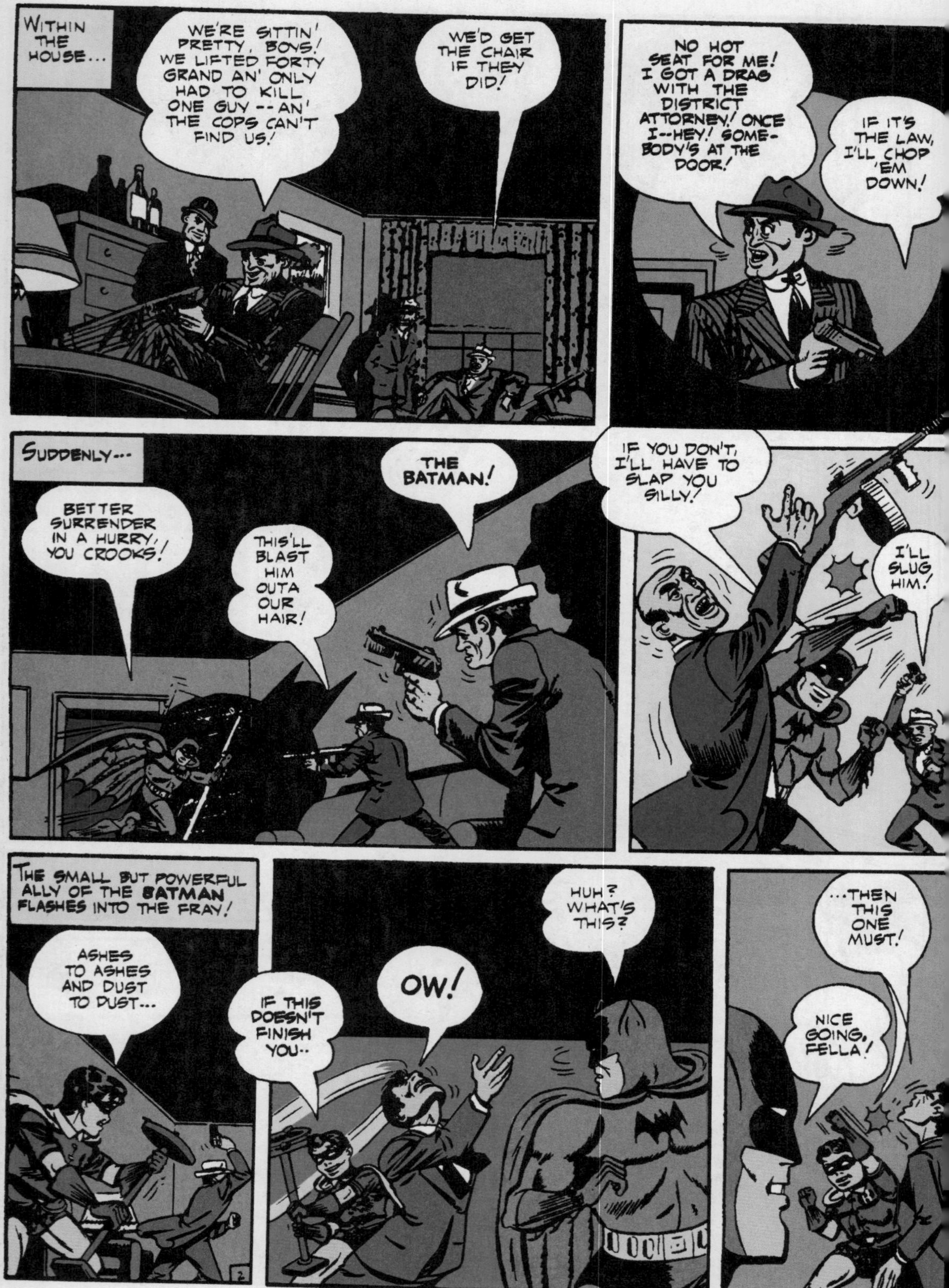
WITHIN THE HOUSE...
WE'RE SITTIN' PRETTY, BOYS! WE LIFTED FORTY GRAND AN' ONLY HAD TO KILL ONE GUY -- AN' THE COPS CAN'T FIND US!
WE'D GET THE CHAIR IF THEY DID!
NO HOT SEAT FOR ME! I GOT A DRAG WITH THE DISTRICT ATTORNEY! ONCE I--HEY! SOMEBODY'S AT THE DOOR!
IF IT'S THE LAW, I'LL CHOP 'EM DOWN!
SUDDENLY...
BETTER SURRENDER IN A HURRY, YOU CROOKS!
THIS'LL BLAST HIM OUTA OUR HAIR!
THE BATMAN!
IF YOU DON'T, I'LL HAVE TO SLAP YOU SILLY!
I'LL SLUG HIM!
THE SMALL BUT POWERFUL ALLY OF THE BATMAN FLASHES INTO THE FRAY!
ASHES TO ASHES AND DUST TO DUST...
2
IF THIS DOESN'T FINISH YOU..
OW!
HUH? WHAT'S THIS?
...THEN THIS ONE MUST!
NICE GOING, FELLA!

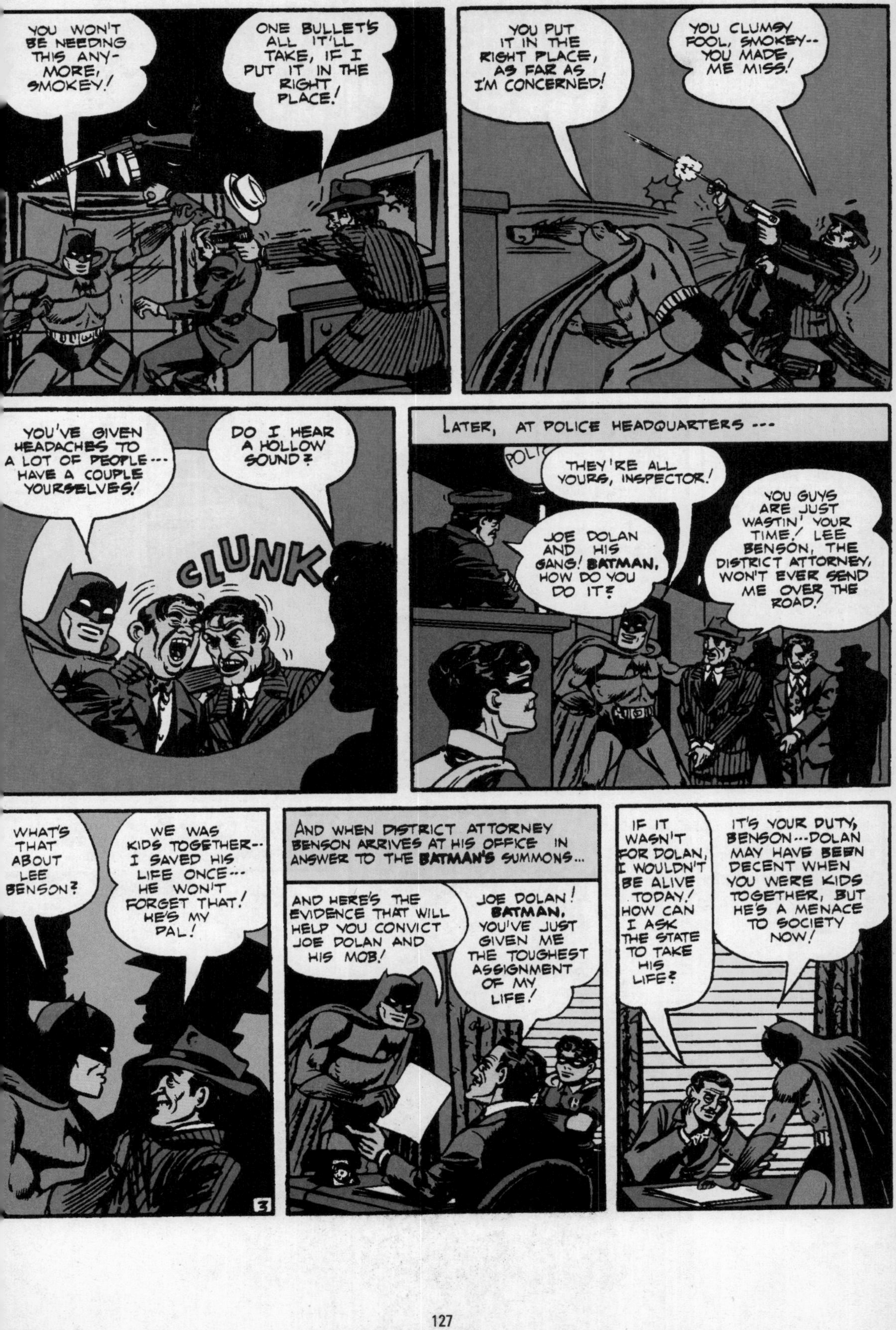
YOU WON'T BE NEEDING THIS ANY-MORE, SMOKEY!
ONE BULLET'S ALL IT'LL TAKE, IF I PUT IT IN THE RIGHT PLACE!
YOU PUT IT IN THE RIGHT PLACE, AS FAR AS I'M CONCERNED!
YOU CLUMSY FOOL, SMOKEY-- YOU MADE ME MISS!
YOU'VE GIVEN HEADACHES TO A LOT OF PEOPLE--- HAVE A COUPLE YOURSELVES!
DO I HEAR A HOLLOW SOUND?
CLUNK
LATER, AT POLICE HEADQUARTERS ---
THEY'RE ALL YOURS, INSPECTOR!
JOE DOLAN AND HIS GANG! BATMAN, HOW DO YOU DO IT?
YOU GUYS ARE JUST WASTIN' YOUR TIME! LEE BENSON, THE DISTRICT ATTORNEY, WON'T EVER SEND ME OVER THE ROAD!
WHAT'S THAT ABOUT LEE BENSON?
WE WAS KIDS TOGETHER-- I SAVED HIS LIFE ONCE--- HE WON'T FORGET THAT! HE'S MY PAL!
3
AND WHEN DISTRICT ATTORNEY BENSON ARRIVES AT HIS OFFICE IN ANSWER TO THE BATMAN'S SUMMONS...
AND HERE'S THE EVIDENCE THAT WILL HELP YOU CONVICT JOE DOLAN AND HIS MOB!
JOE DOLAN! BATMAN, YOU'VE JUST GIVEN ME THE TOUGHEST ASSIGNMENT OF MY LIFE!
IF IT WASN'T FOR DOLAN, I WOULDN'T BE ALIVE TODAY! HOW CAN I ASK THE STATE TO TAKE HIS LIFE?
IT'S YOUR DUTY, BENSON---DOLAN MAY HAVE BEEN DECENT WHEN YOU WERE KIDS TOGETHER, BUT HE'S A MENACE TO SOCIETY NOW!

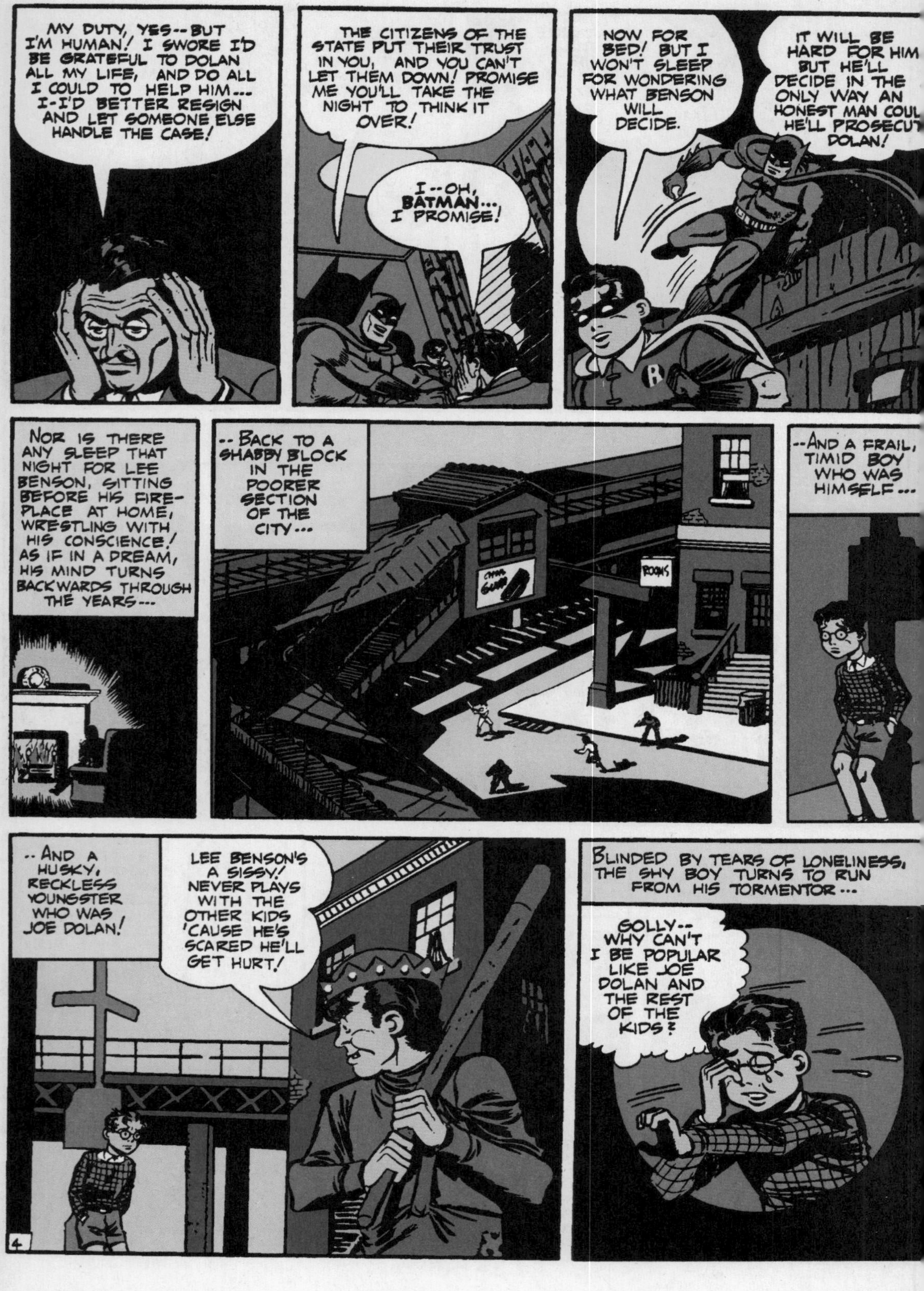

MY DUTY, YES--BUT I'M HUMAN! I SWORE I'D BE GRATEFUL TO DOLAN ALL MY LIFE, AND DO ALL I COULD TO HELP HIM... I-I'D BETTER RESIGN AND LET SOMEONE ELSE HANDLE THE CASE!
THE CITIZENS OF THE STATE PUT THEIR TRUST IN YOU, AND YOU CAN'T LET THEM DOWN! PROMISE ME YOU'LL TAKE THE NIGHT TO THINK IT OVER!
I--OH, BATMAN... I PROMISE!
NOW FOR BED! BUT I WON'T SLEEP FOR WONDERING WHAT BENSON WILL DECIDE.
IT WILL BE HARD FOR HIM BUT HE'LL DECIDE IN THE ONLY WAY AN HONEST MAN COUL HE'LL PROSECUT DOLAN!
NOR IS THERE ANY SLEEP THAT NIGHT FOR LEE BENSON, SITTING BEFORE HIS FIRE-PLACE AT HOME, WRESTLING WITH HIS CONSCIENCE! AS IF IN A DREAM, HIS MIND TURNS BACKWARDS THROUGH THE YEARS---
--BACK TO A SHABBY BLOCK IN THE POORER SECTION OF THE CITY---
ROOMS
--AND A FRAIL, TIMID BOY WHO WAS HIMSELF...
--AND A HUSKY, RECKLESS YOUNGSTER WHO WAS JOE DOLAN!
LEE BENSON'S A SISSY! NEVER PLAYS WITH THE OTHER KIDS 'CAUSE HE'S SCARED HE'LL GET HURT!
4
BLINDED BY TEARS OF LONELINESS, THE SHY BOY TURNS TO RUN FROM HIS TORMENTOR...
GOLLY-- WHY CAN'T I BE POPULAR LIKE JOE DOLAN AND THE REST OF THE KIDS?

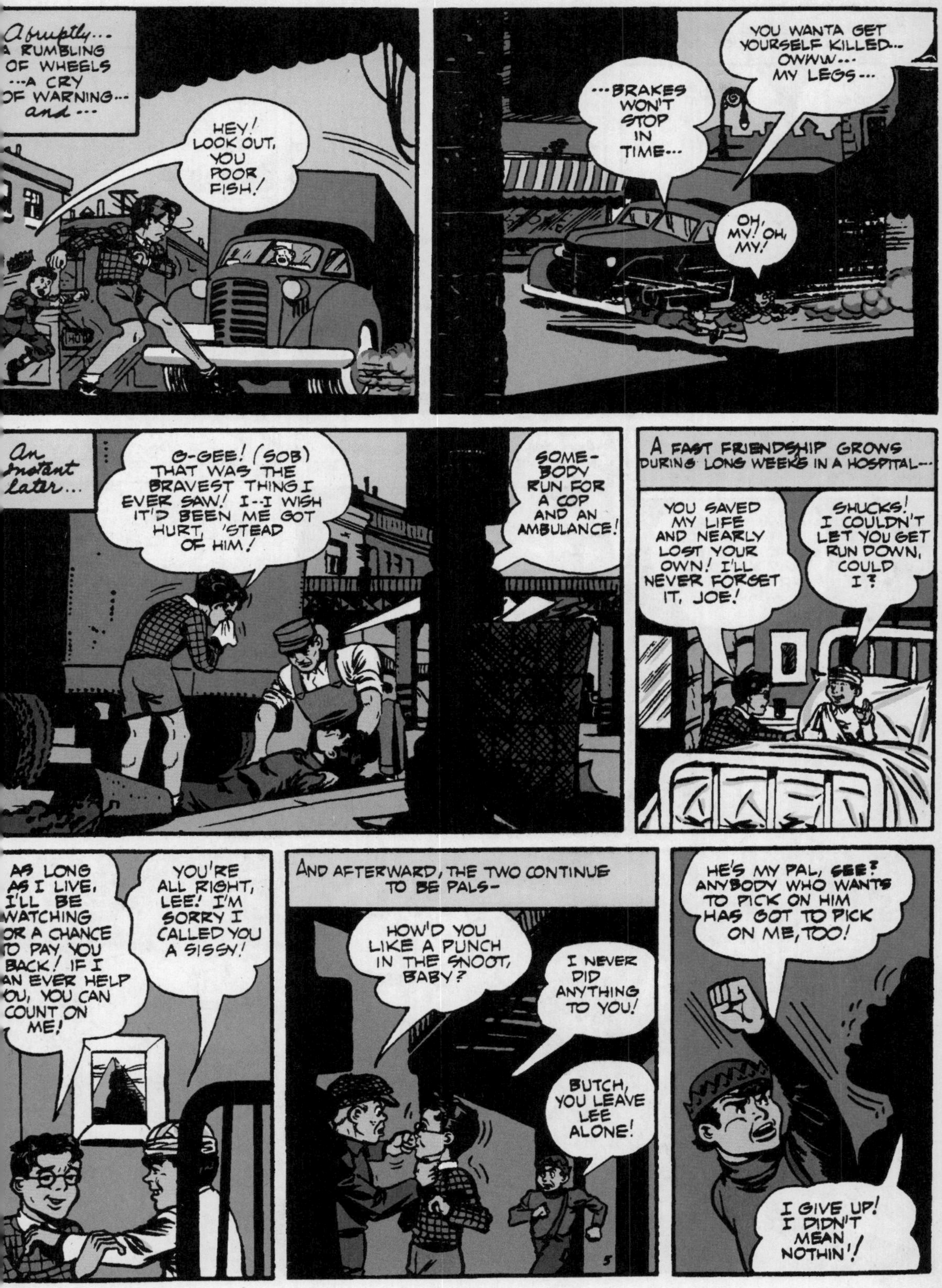
Abruptly... a rumbling of wheels ...a cry of warning... and...
HEY! LOOK OUT, YOU POOR FISH!
...BRAKES WON'T STOP IN TIME...
YOU WANTA GET YOURSELF KILLED... OWWW... MY LEGS...
OH, MY! OH, MY!
An instant later...
G-GEE! (SOB) THAT WAS THE BRAVEST THING I EVER SAW! I--I WISH IT'D BEEN ME GOT HURT, 'STEAD OF HIM!
SOME-BODY RUN FOR A COP AND AN AMBULANCE!
A FAST FRIENDSHIP GROWS DURING LONG WEEKS IN A HOSPITAL---
YOU SAVED MY LIFE AND NEARLY LOST YOUR OWN! I'LL NEVER FORGET IT, JOE!
SHUCKS! I COULDN'T LET YOU GET RUN DOWN, COULD I?
AS LONG AS I LIVE, I'LL BE WATCHING FOR A CHANCE TO PAY YOU BACK! IF I CAN EVER HELP YOU, YOU CAN COUNT ON ME!
YOU'RE ALL RIGHT, LEE! I'M SORRY I CALLED YOU A SISSY!
AND AFTERWARD, THE TWO CONTINUE TO BE PALS-
HOW'D YOU LIKE A PUNCH IN THE SNOOT, BABY?
I NEVER DID ANYTHING TO YOU!
BUTCH, YOU LEAVE LEE ALONE!
5
HE'S MY PAL, SEE? ANYBODY WHO WANTS TO PICK ON HIM HAS GOT TO PICK ON ME, TOO!
I GIVE UP! I DIDN'T MEAN NOTHIN'!

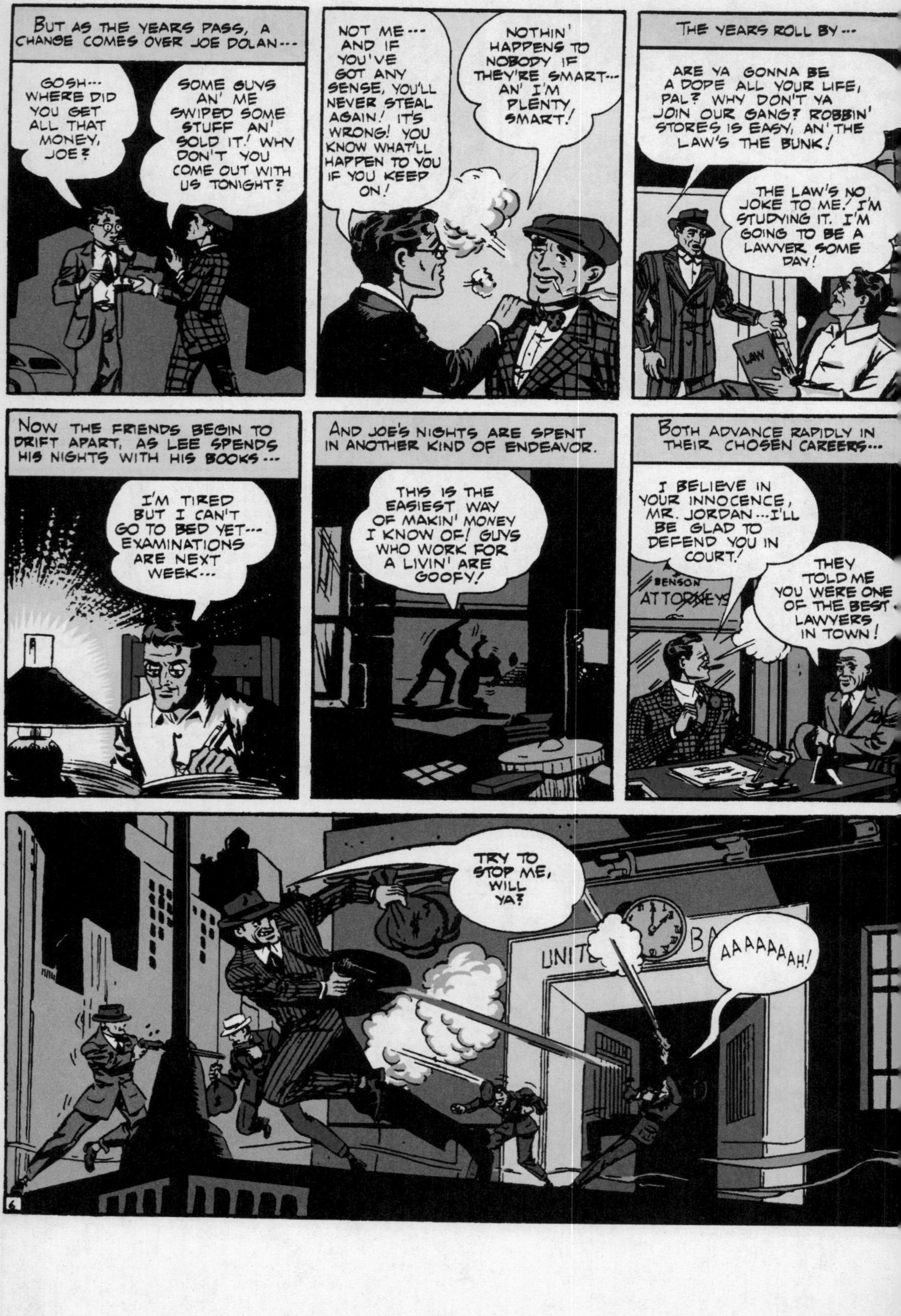
BUT AS THE YEARS PASS, A CHANGE COMES OVER JOE DOLAN...
GOSH... WHERE DID YOU GET ALL THAT MONEY, JOE?
SOME GUYS AN' ME SWIPED SOME STUFF AN' SOLD IT! WHY DON'T YOU COME OUT WITH US TONIGHT?
NOT ME... AND IF YOU'VE GOT ANY SENSE, YOU'LL NEVER STEAL AGAIN! IT'S WRONG! YOU KNOW WHAT'LL HAPPEN TO YOU IF YOU KEEP ON!
NOTHIN' HAPPENS TO NOBODY IF THEY'RE SMART... AN' I'M PLENTY SMART!
THE YEARS ROLL BY...
ARE YA GONNA BE A DOPE ALL YOUR LIFE, PAL? WHY DON'T YA JOIN OUR GANG? ROBBIN' STORES IS EASY, AN' THE LAW'S THE BUNK!
THE LAW'S NO JOKE TO ME! I'M STUDYING IT. I'M GOING TO BE A LAWYER SOME DAY!
LAW
NOW THE FRIENDS BEGIN TO DRIFT APART, AS LEE SPENDS HIS NIGHTS WITH HIS BOOKS...
I'M TIRED BUT I CAN'T GO TO BED YET... EXAMINATIONS ARE NEXT WEEK...
AND JOE'S NIGHTS ARE SPENT IN ANOTHER KIND OF ENDEAVOR.
THIS IS THE EASIEST WAY OF MAKIN' MONEY I KNOW OF! GUYS WHO WORK FOR A LIVIN' ARE GOOFY!
BOTH ADVANCE RAPIDLY IN THEIR CHOSEN CAREERS...
I BELIEVE IN YOUR INNOCENCE, MR. JORDAN... I'LL BE GLAD TO DEFEND YOU IN COURT!
BENSON
ATTORNEYS
THEY TOLD ME YOU WERE ONE OF THE BEST LAWYERS IN TOWN!
TRY TO STOP ME, WILL YA?
UNIT
BA
AAAAAAAH!
6

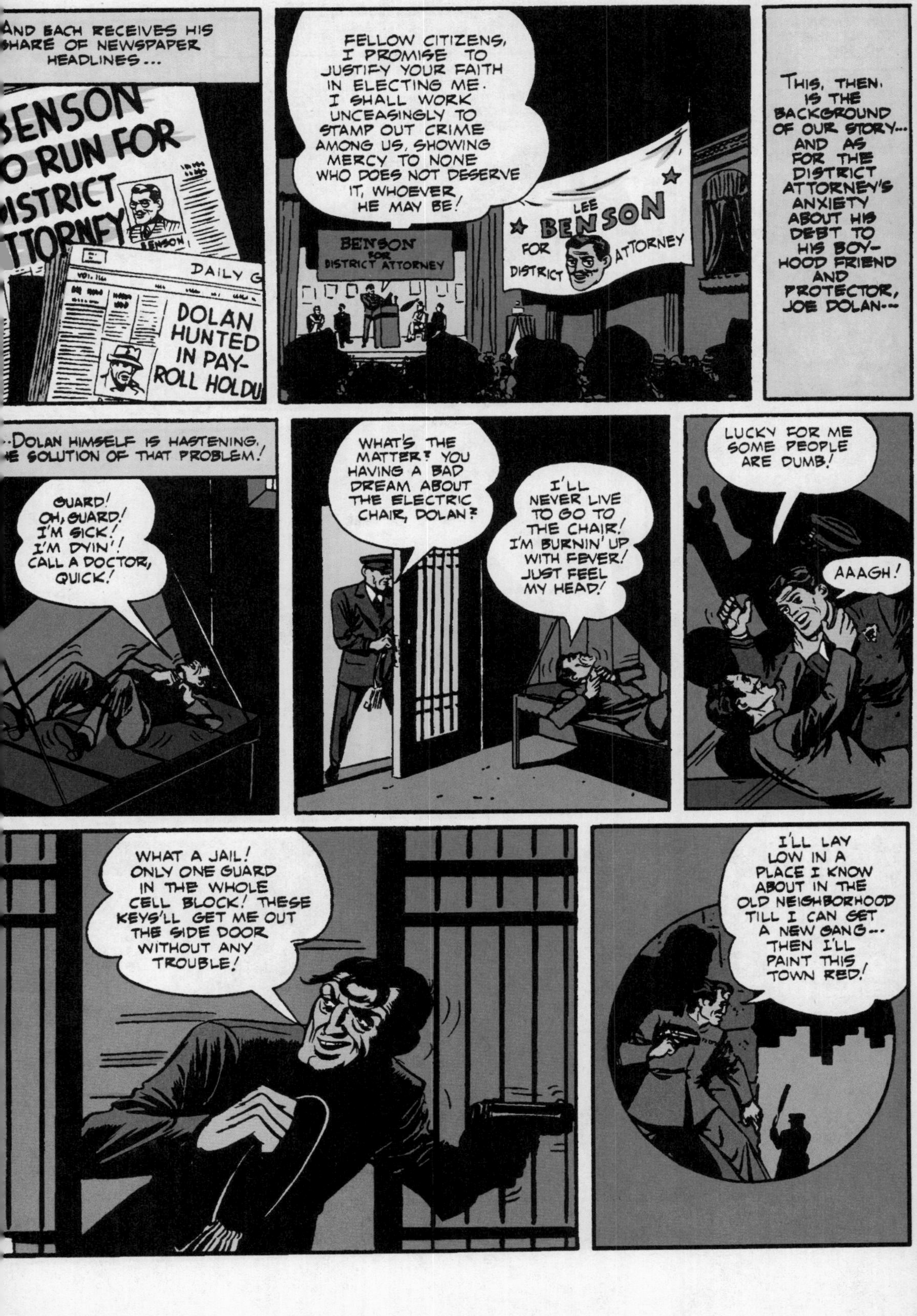
AND EACH RECEIVES HIS SHARE OF NEWSPAPER HEADLINES...
BENSON TO RUN FOR DISTRICT ATTORNEY
BENSON
DAILY G
DOLAN HUNTED IN PAY-ROLL HOLDU
FELLOW CITIZENS, I PROMISE TO JUSTIFY YOUR FAITH IN ELECTING ME. I SHALL WORK UNCEASINGLY TO STAMP OUT CRIME AMONG US, SHOWING MERCY TO NONE WHO DOES NOT DESERVE IT, WHOEVER HE MAY BE!
BENSON FOR DISTRICT ATTORNEY
LEE BENSON FOR DISTRICT ATTORNEY
THIS, THEN, IS THE BACKGROUND OF OUR STORY... AND AS FOR THE DISTRICT ATTORNEY'S ANXIETY ABOUT HIS DEBT TO HIS BOYHOOD FRIEND AND PROTECTOR, JOE DOLAN...
...DOLAN HIMSELF IS HASTENING THE SOLUTION OF THAT PROBLEM!
GUARD! OH, GUARD! I'M SICK! I'M DYIN'! CALL A DOCTOR, QUICK!
WHAT'S THE MATTER? YOU HAVING A BAD DREAM ABOUT THE ELECTRIC CHAIR, DOLAN?
I'LL NEVER LIVE TO GO TO THE CHAIR! I'M BURNIN' UP WITH FEVER! JUST FEEL MY HEAD!
LUCKY FOR ME SOME PEOPLE ARE DUMB!
AAAGH!
WHAT A JAIL! ONLY ONE GUARD IN THE WHOLE CELL BLOCK! THESE KEYS'LL GET ME OUT THE SIDE DOOR WITHOUT ANY TROUBLE!
I'LL LAY LOW IN A PLACE I KNOW ABOUT IN THE OLD NEIGHBORHOOD TILL I CAN GET A NEW GANG... THEN I'LL PAINT THIS TOWN RED!

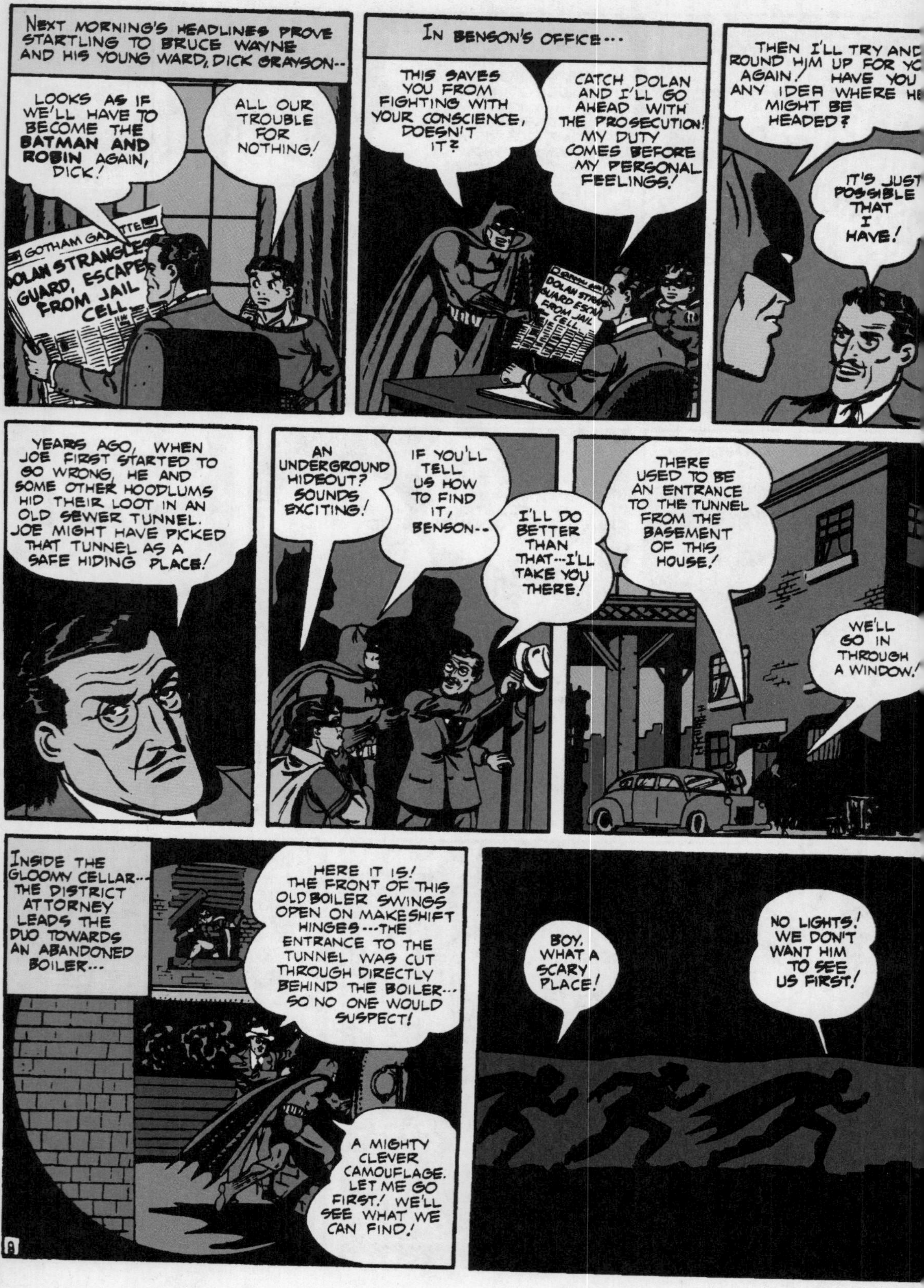

NEXT MORNING'S HEADLINES PROVE STARTLING TO BRUCE WAYNE AND HIS YOUNG WARD, DICK GRAYSON--
LOOKS AS IF WE'LL HAVE TO BECOME THE **BATMAN AND ROBIN** AGAIN, DICK!
GOTHAM GAZETTE
DOLAN STRANGLES GUARD, ESCAPES FROM JAIL CELL
ALL OUR TROUBLE FOR NOTHING!
IN BENSON'S OFFICE...
THIS SAVES YOU FROM FIGHTING WITH YOUR CONSCIENCE, DOESN'T IT?
CATCH DOLAN AND I'LL GO AHEAD WITH THE PROSECUTION! MY DUTY COMES BEFORE MY PERSONAL FEELINGS!
THEN I'LL TRY AND ROUND HIM UP FOR YO AGAIN! HAVE YOU ANY IDEA WHERE HE MIGHT BE HEADED?
IT'S JUST POSSIBLE THAT I HAVE!
YEARS AGO, WHEN JOE FIRST STARTED TO GO WRONG, HE AND SOME OTHER HOODLUMS HID THEIR LOOT IN AN OLD SEWER TUNNEL. JOE MIGHT HAVE PICKED THAT TUNNEL AS A SAFE HIDING PLACE!
AN UNDERGROUND HIDEOUT? SOUNDS EXCITING!
IF YOU'LL TELL US HOW TO FIND IT, BENSON--
I'LL DO BETTER THAN THAT---I'LL TAKE YOU THERE!
THERE USED TO BE AN ENTRANCE TO THE TUNNEL FROM THE BASEMENT OF THIS HOUSE!
WE'LL GO IN THROUGH A WINDOW!
INSIDE THE GLOOMY CELLAR... THE DISTRICT ATTORNEY LEADS THE DUO TOWARDS AN ABANDONED BOILER...
HERE IT IS! THE FRONT OF THIS OLD BOILER SWINGS OPEN ON MAKESHIFT HINGES---THE ENTRANCE TO THE TUNNEL WAS CUT THROUGH DIRECTLY BEHIND THE BOILER... SO NO ONE WOULD SUSPECT!
A MIGHTY CLEVER CAMOUFLAGE. LET ME GO FIRST! WE'LL SEE WHAT WE CAN FIND!
8
BOY, WHAT A SCARY PLACE!
NO LIGHTS! WE DON'T WANT HIM TO SEE US FIRST!

MEANWHILE, IN A CAVERN-LIKE RECESS OF THE TUNNEL---

THIS IS WORSE'N JAIL! THE ONLY GOOD THING ABOUT IT IS I CAN LEAVE WHENEVER I WANT! BAH! THIS SOLITAIRE IS GETTIN' ON ME NERVES!

DISTANT SOUNDS MAKE THE FUGITIVE INSTANTLY ALERT---

WHAT'S THAT?... PROBABLY RATS---BUT I BETTER MAKE SURE!

CREEPING INTO THE TUNNEL, THE JITTERY DOLAN SPIES A SHADOWY SILHOUETTE---

CAN'T SEE INTO THAT DARKNESS. WHO'S THERE? SPEAK UP, OR I'LL BLAST YA!

BENSON MAKES A FORLORN ATTEMPT TO REASON WITH HIS ONE-TIME FRIEND---

IT'S LEE BENSON, JOE! SURRENDER AND I'LL GUARANTEE YOU'LL HAVE A FAIR TRIAL!

I'M AFRAID HE WON'T LIKE YOUR PROPOSITION!

WHAT? BENSON?

BENSON! YOU DOUBLE-CROSSING HEEL! I SHOULDA LET THAT TRUCK RUN OVER YOU!

LIE FLAT! HE'S GOT THE UPPER HAND RIGHT NOW!

I'M HIT!

THIS IS NO PICNIC!

Z-I-N-G

BLASTING LEAD COVERS THE RETREAT OF THE DESPERATE FUGITIVE CRIMINAL---

GOT TO GET OUTA HERE! EVEN IF I'VE KILLED HIM, BENSON MIGHT'VE TOLD THE COPS ABOUT THIS PLACE!

THIS TOWN'S GETTIN' TOO HOT FOR ME! I BETTER TAKE IT ON THE LAM TILL THINGS COOL DOWN!

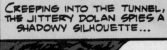

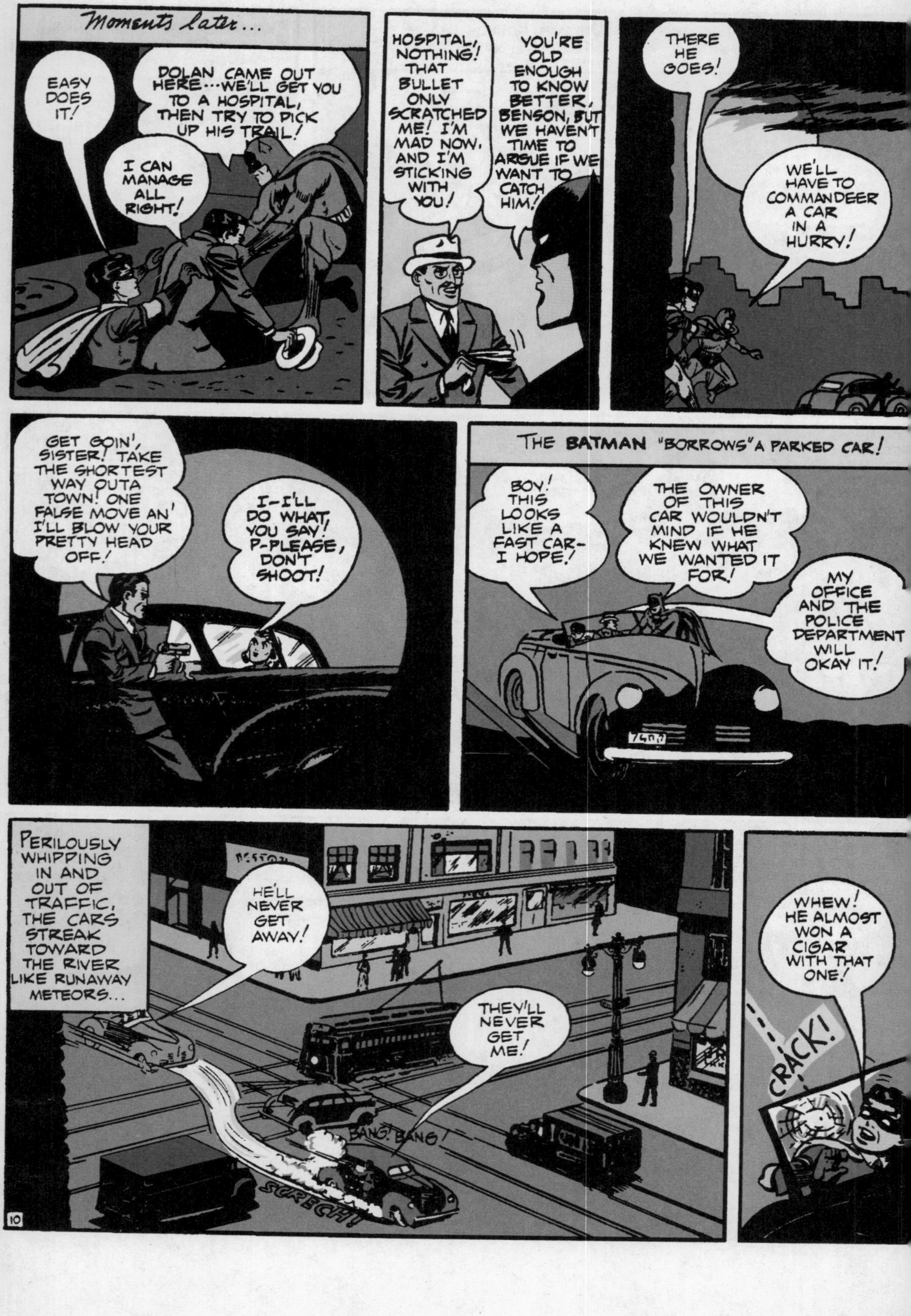
Moments later...
EASY DOES IT!
DOLAN CAME OUT HERE...WE'LL GET YOU TO A HOSPITAL, THEN TRY TO PICK UP HIS TRAIL!
I CAN MANAGE ALL RIGHT!
HOSPITAL, NOTHING! THAT BULLET ONLY SCRATCHED ME! I'M MAD NOW, AND I'M STICKING WITH YOU!
YOU'RE OLD ENOUGH TO KNOW BETTER, BENSON, BUT WE HAVEN'T TIME TO ARGUE IF WE WANT TO CATCH HIM!
THERE HE GOES!
WE'LL HAVE TO COMMANDEER A CAR IN A HURRY!
GET GOIN', SISTER! TAKE THE SHORTEST WAY OUTA TOWN! ONE FALSE MOVE AN' I'LL BLOW YOUR PRETTY HEAD OFF!
I-I'LL DO WHAT YOU SAY! P-PLEASE, DON'T SHOOT!
THE BATMAN "BORROWS" A PARKED CAR!
BOY! THIS LOOKS LIKE A FAST CAR- I HOPE!
THE OWNER OF THIS CAR WOULDN'T MIND IF HE KNEW WHAT WE WANTED IT FOR!
MY OFFICE AND THE POLICE DEPARTMENT WILL OKAY IT!
PERILOUSLY WHIPPING IN AND OUT OF TRAFFIC, THE CARS STREAK TOWARD THE RIVER LIKE RUNAWAY METEORS...
HE'LL NEVER GET AWAY!
THEY'LL NEVER GET ME!
BANG! BANG!
SCREECH!
10
WHEW! HE ALMOST WON A CIGAR WITH THAT ONE!
CRACK!

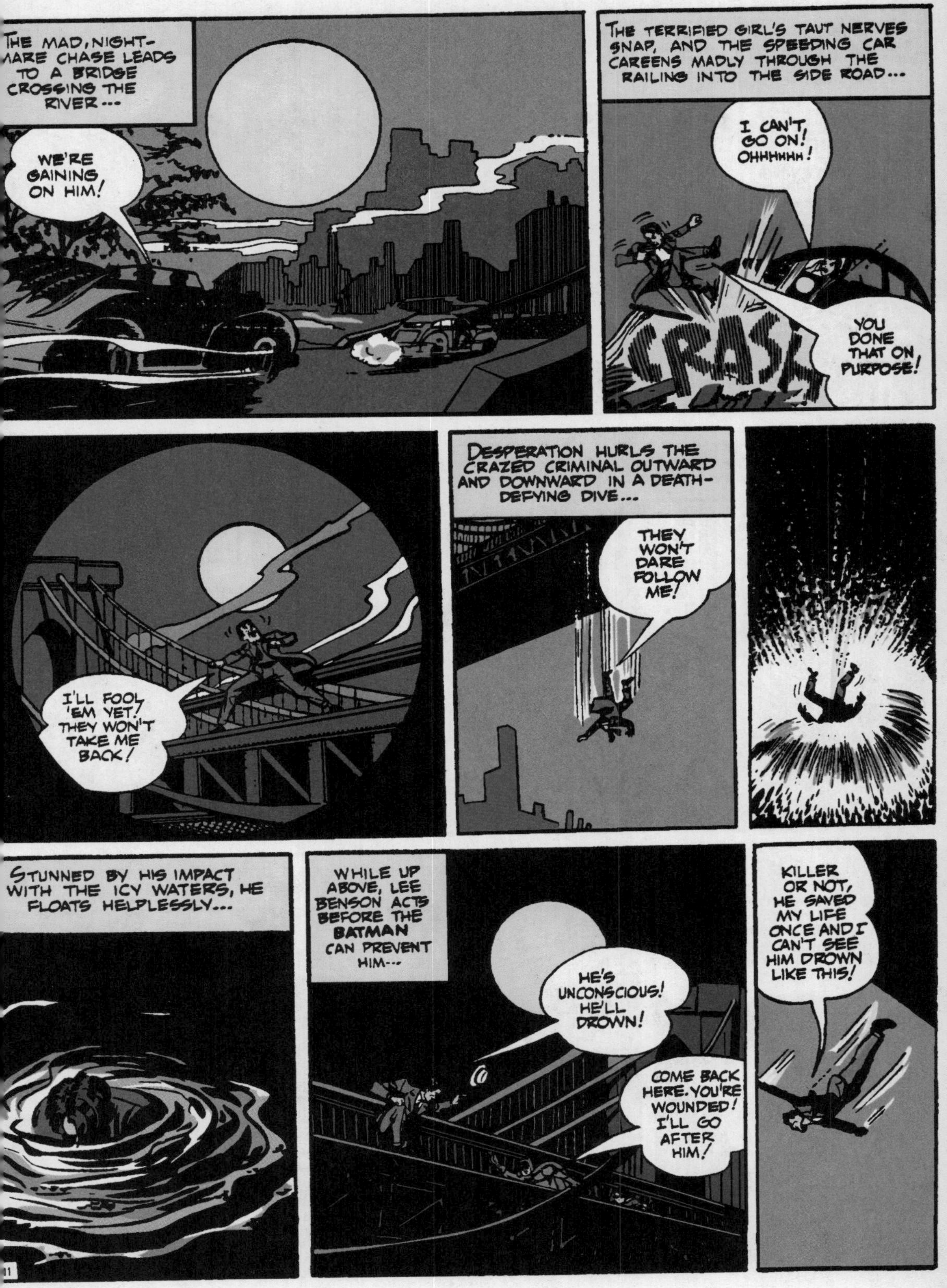
THE MAD, NIGHT-MARE CHASE LEADS TO A BRIDGE CROSSING THE RIVER...
WE'RE GAINING ON HIM!
THE TERRIFIED GIRL'S TAUT NERVES SNAP, AND THE SPEEDING CAR CAREENS MADLY THROUGH THE RAILING INTO THE SIDE ROAD...
I CAN'T GO ON! OHHHHHH!
CRASH
YOU DONE THAT ON PURPOSE!
I'LL FOOL 'EM YET! THEY WON'T TAKE ME BACK!
DESPERATION HURLS THE CRAZED CRIMINAL OUTWARD AND DOWNWARD IN A DEATH-DEFYING DIVE...
THEY WON'T DARE FOLLOW ME!
STUNNED BY HIS IMPACT WITH THE ICY WATERS, HE FLOATS HELPLESSLY...
WHILE UP ABOVE, LEE BENSON ACTS BEFORE THE BATMAN CAN PREVENT HIM...
HE'S UNCONSCIOUS! HE'LL DROWN!
COME BACK HERE. YOU'RE WOUNDED! I'LL GO AFTER HIM!
KILLER OR NOT, HE SAVED MY LIFE ONCE AND I CAN'T SEE HIM DROWN LIKE THIS!
11

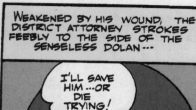

WEAKENED BY HIS WOUND, THE DISTRICT ATTORNEY STROKES FEEBLY TO THE SIDE OF THE SENSELESS DOLAN···

I'LL SAVE HIM ···OR DIE TRYING!

AND TWO MANTLED FIGURES PLUMMET SWIFTLY TO HIS AID···

THEY'LL NEVER GET TO SHORE WITHOUT HELP!

THIS IS THE HIGHEST DIVE I EVER WANT TO MAKE!

BUT SUPERHUMAN EFFORT DRIVES LEE BENSON BEYOND THE LIMITS OF ORDINARY STRENGTH—

HUH? WHERE AM I? WHO'S GOT HOLD OF ME?

IT'S LEE··· YOUR OLD CHUM-- REMEMBER WHEN YOU SAVED MY LIFE?

NOW··· WE'RE EVEN! I DON'T OWE YOU ANYTHING!

BUT I OWE YOU SOMETHIN', COPPER!

OH, WOULDN'T I?

JOE! YOU···YOU WOULDN'T!

YOU'RE JUST THE KIND OF SISSY THAT WOULD REMEMBER OLD TIMES! BUT ME, I'M TOUGH! I ONLY WORRY ABOUT MYSELF! AFTER THIS HITS YOU, YOU WON'T GO PUTTIN' THE BATMAN ON MY TRAIL NO MORE!

IN HIS BLIND FRENZY, THE KILLER DOES NOT SEE THE CHARGING AGENTS OF HIS DOOM···

ANOTHER SECOND WILL BE TOO LATE!

MAYBE THIS PIECE OF DRIFTWOOD WILL HELP!

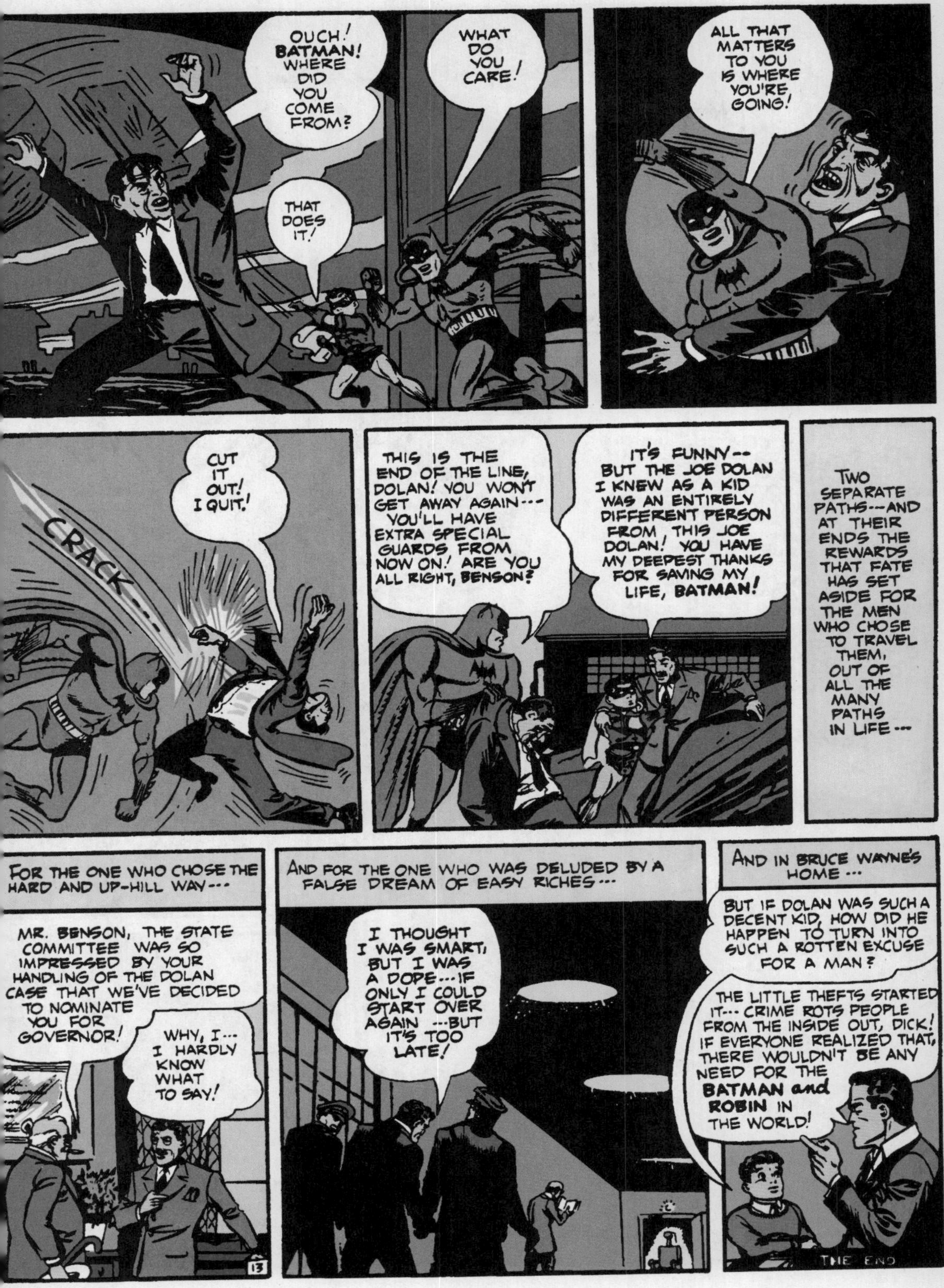
OUCH! BATMAN! WHERE DID YOU COME FROM?
WHAT DO YOU CARE!
THAT DOES IT!
ALL THAT MATTERS TO YOU IS WHERE YOU'RE GOING!
CUT IT OUT! I QUIT!
CRACK---
THIS IS THE END OF THE LINE, DOLAN! YOU WON'T GET AWAY AGAIN--- YOU'LL HAVE EXTRA SPECIAL GUARDS FROM NOW ON! ARE YOU ALL RIGHT, BENSON?
IT'S FUNNY-- BUT THE JOE DOLAN I KNEW AS A KID WAS AN ENTIRELY DIFFERENT PERSON FROM THIS JOE DOLAN! YOU HAVE MY DEEPEST THANKS FOR SAVING MY LIFE, BATMAN!
TWO SEPARATE PATHS---AND AT THEIR ENDS THE REWARDS THAT FATE HAS SET ASIDE FOR THE MEN WHO CHOSE TO TRAVEL THEM, OUT OF ALL THE MANY PATHS IN LIFE---
FOR THE ONE WHO CHOSE THE HARD AND UP-HILL WAY---
MR. BENSON, THE STATE COMMITTEE WAS SO IMPRESSED BY YOUR HANDLING OF THE DOLAN CASE THAT WE'VE DECIDED TO NOMINATE YOU FOR GOVERNOR!
WHY, I--- I HARDLY KNOW WHAT TO SAY!
13
AND FOR THE ONE WHO WAS DELUDED BY A FALSE DREAM OF EASY RICHES---
I THOUGHT I WAS SMART, BUT I WAS A DOPE--- IF ONLY I COULD START OVER AGAIN ---BUT IT'S TOO LATE!
AND IN BRUCE WAYNE'S HOME---
BUT IF DOLAN WAS SUCH A DECENT KID, HOW DID HE HAPPEN TO TURN INTO SUCH A ROTTEN EXCUSE FOR A MAN?
THE LITTLE THEFTS STARTED IT--- CRIME ROTS PEOPLE FROM THE INSIDE OUT, DICK! IF EVERYONE REALIZED THAT, THERE WOULDN'T BE ANY NEED FOR THE BATMAN and ROBIN IN THE WORLD!
THE END

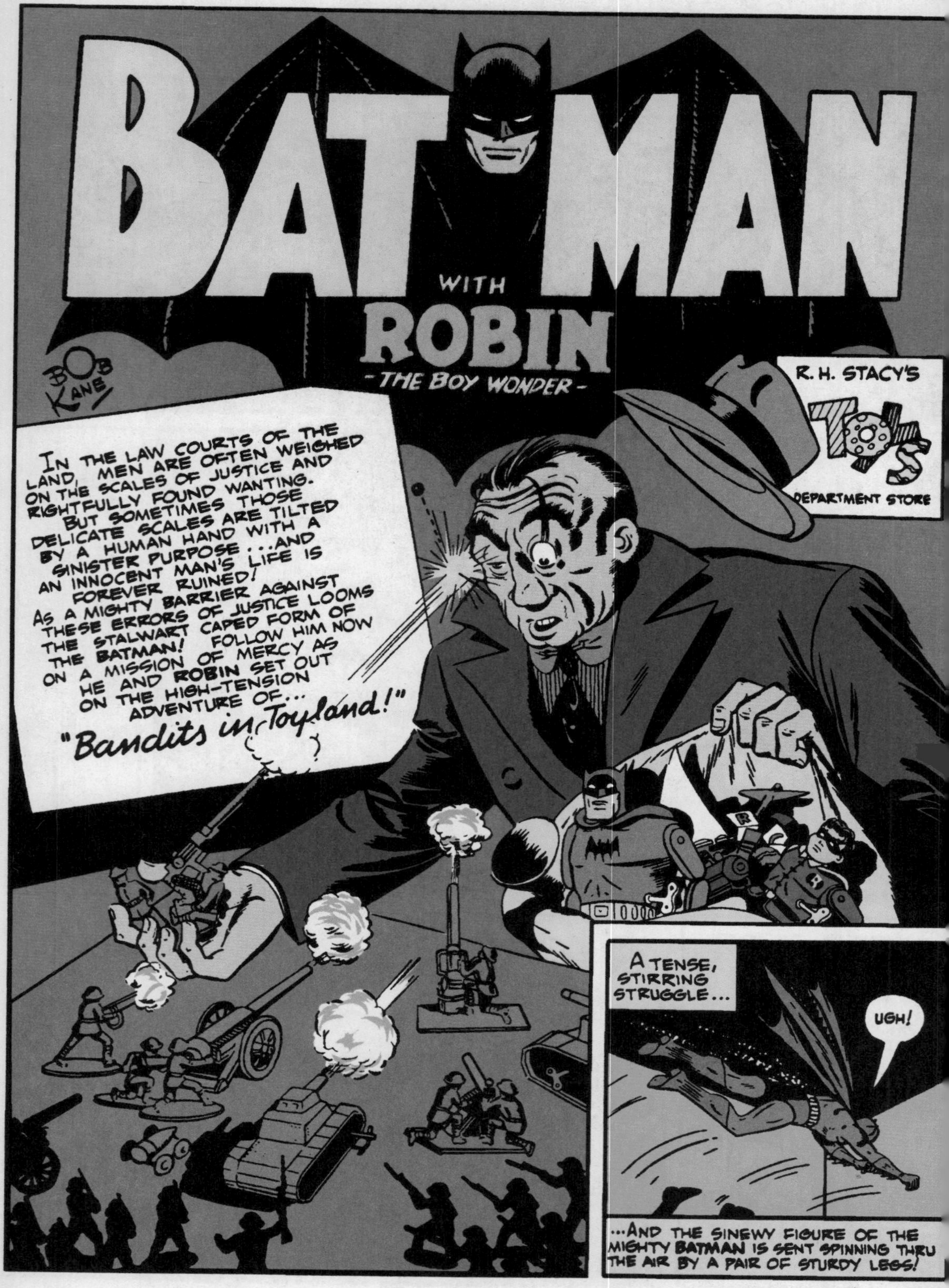
BATMAN
WITH
ROBIN
-THE BOY WONDER-
BOB KANE
R. H. STACY'S
TOYS
DEPARTMENT STORE
IN THE LAW COURTS OF THE LAND, MEN ARE OFTEN WEIGHED ON THE SCALES OF JUSTICE AND RIGHTFULLY FOUND WANTING. BUT SOMETIMES THOSE DELICATE SCALES ARE TILTED BY A HUMAN HAND WITH A SINISTER PURPOSE ...AND AN INNOCENT MAN'S LIFE IS FOREVER RUINED! AS A MIGHTY BARRIER AGAINST THESE ERRORS OF JUSTICE LOOMS THE STALWART CAPED FORM OF THE BATMAN! FOLLOW HIM NOW ON A MISSION OF MERCY AS HE AND ROBIN SET OUT ON THE HIGH-TENSION ADVENTURE OF...
"Bandits in Toyland!"
A TENSE, STIRRING STRUGGLE...
UGH!
...AND THE SINEWY FIGURE OF THE MIGHTY BATMAN IS SENT SPINNING THRU THE AIR BY A PAIR OF STURDY LEGS!

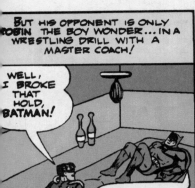

BUT HIS OPPONENT IS ONLY ROBIN THE BOY WONDER... IN A WRESTLING DRILL WITH A MASTER COACH!

WELL, I BROKE THAT HOLD, BATMAN!

GOOD WORK, ROBIN! NOW LET'S TACKLE SOME OTHER EXERCISE! PRACTICE MAKES PERFECT, YOU KNOW!

YES, PRACTICE MAKES PERFECT! THAT IS THE SECRET BEHIND THE DARING DEEDS AND PHENOMENAL FEATS OF THE TWIN FOES OF CRIME!

A BRISK SHOWER, AND THE DYNAMIC DUO DRESS FOR THEIR EVERYDAY ROLES OF PLAYBOY BRUCE WAYNE AND HIS YOUNG WARD, DICK GRAYSON!

LOOK AT THOSE HEADLINES, BRUCE! SOME GANG IS ROBBING KIDS OF THEIR TOYS!

THE CHEAP CROOKS! NEXT THING THEY'LL BE STEALING PENNIES FROM BLIND MEN!

BOLD HEADLINES CONJURE UP A PUZZLING CRIME PICTURE!

GOTHAM GAZETTE — NIGHT EDITION

TOY BEAR STOLEN FROM NURSERY – A MYSTERY...

LATE EDITION

YOUNGSTER ROBBED OF MECHANICAL MULE

SKATING DOLL STOLEN FROM CARRIAGE

HMM...THE POLICE SAY ONE OF THOSE THUGS MIGHT BE A MEMBER OF "MUSCLES" MALONE'S GANG!

BUT WHY SHOULD A BIG SHOT LIKE "MUSCLES" BE STEALING TOYS? THAT'S NOT LIKE... WAIT A MINUTE--- THERE'S THE DOOR BELL!

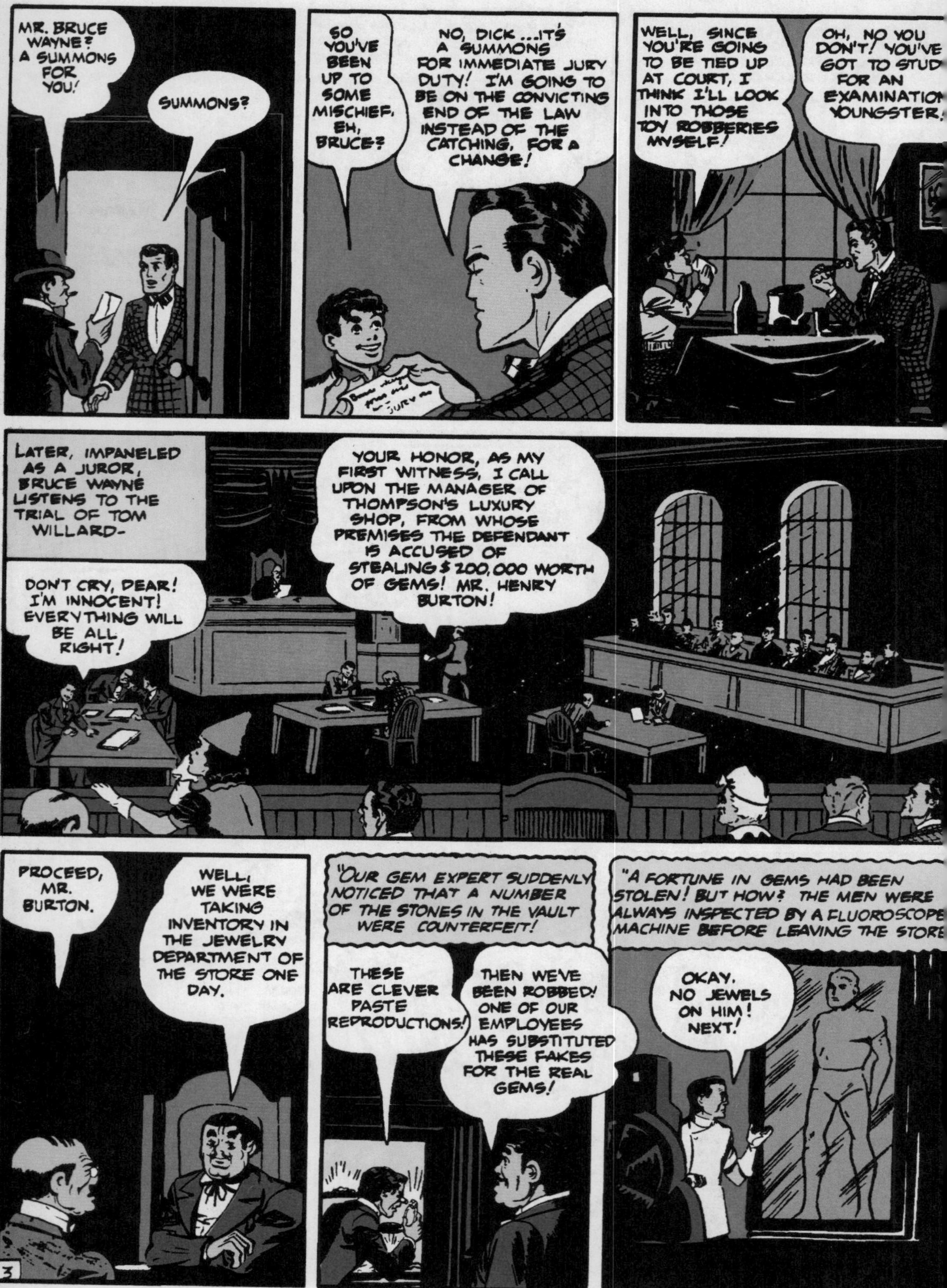
MR. BRUCE WAYNE? A SUMMONS FOR YOU!
SUMMONS?
SO YOU'VE BEEN UP TO SOME MISCHIEF, EH, BRUCE?
NO, DICK ...IT'S A SUMMONS FOR IMMEDIATE JURY DUTY! I'M GOING TO BE ON THE CONVICTING END OF THE LAW INSTEAD OF THE CATCHING, FOR A CHANGE!
WELL, SINCE YOU'RE GOING TO BE TIED UP AT COURT, I THINK I'LL LOOK INTO THOSE TOY ROBBERIES MYSELF!
OH, NO YOU DON'T! YOU'VE GOT TO STUD FOR AN EXAMINATIO YOUNGSTER.
LATER, IMPANELED AS A JUROR, BRUCE WAYNE LISTENS TO THE TRIAL OF TOM WILLARD-
YOUR HONOR, AS MY FIRST WITNESS, I CALL UPON THE MANAGER OF THOMPSON'S LUXURY SHOP, FROM WHOSE PREMISES THE DEFENDANT IS ACCUSED OF STEALING $200,000 WORTH OF GEMS! MR. HENRY BURTON!
DON'T CRY, DEAR! I'M INNOCENT! EVERYTHING WILL BE ALL RIGHT!
PROCEED, MR. BURTON.
WELL, WE WERE TAKING INVENTORY IN THE JEWELRY DEPARTMENT OF THE STORE ONE DAY.
3
"OUR GEM EXPERT SUDDENLY NOTICED THAT A NUMBER OF THE STONES IN THE VAULT WERE COUNTERFEIT!
THESE ARE CLEVER PASTE REPRODUCTIONS!
THEN WE'VE BEEN ROBBED! ONE OF OUR EMPLOYEES HAS SUBSTITUTED THESE FAKES FOR THE REAL GEMS!
"A FORTUNE IN GEMS HAD BEEN STOLEN! BUT HOW? THE MEN WERE ALWAYS INSPECTED BY A FLUOROSCOPE MACHINE BEFORE LEAVING THE STORE
OKAY. NO JEWELS ON HIM! NEXT!

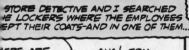

"...STORE DETECTIVE AND I SEARCHED THE LOCKERS WHERE THE EMPLOYEES KEPT THEIR COATS—AND IN ONE OF THEM..."

HERE ARE SOME OF THOSE JEWELS, MR. BURTON!

AHA! TOM WILLARD'S LOCKER! HE MUST HAVE BEEN ROBBING US FOR MONTHS!

OBVIOUSLY, WILLARD HID THE GEMS IN HIS JACKET DURING BUSINESS HOURS!

THANK YOU, MR. BURTON! THAT WILL BE ALL!

THAT FELLOW DOESN'T LOOK LIKE A CROOK! NICE WIFE, TOO! NO, A JOB LIKE THIS WOULD REQUIRE A CLEVER GANG OF ORGANIZED THIEVES!

SUDDENLY, BRUCE'S ATTENTION IS ATTRACTED BY A PAIR OF FAMILIAR FACES AMONG THE SPECTATORS...

PATSY DAY AND JOHNNY TEAL.. MEMBERS OF "MUSCLES" MALONE'S GANG! WONDER WHAT THEY'RE JOKING ABOUT? I'LL SOON FIND OUT!

KEEN EYES EFFORTLESSLY TRANSLATE THOSE FURTIVELY MOVING MOUTHS ... FOR BRUCE WAYNE ...THE BATMAN... IS AN ACCOMPLISHED LIP-READER!

SAY, JOHNNY, THAT WILLARD KID LOOKS HOOKED, DON'T HE?

YEAH, THE BIG BOSS FRAMED HIM GOOD!

SO MY HUNCH IS RIGHT! BUT HOW CAN I PREVENT THE LAW FROM MAKING A GRAVE ERROR?

LATER, IN THE JURY ROOM, TWELVE GOOD MEN AND TRUE DECIDE THE FATE OF A FELLOW MAN!

THE THIRD BALLOT... AND IT'S STILL ELEVEN FOR GUILTY AND ONE AGAINST! GENTLEMEN, WE CAN'T GO HOME UNTIL WE REACH A VERDICT. WHO'S HOLDING OUT?

I AM! I THINK WILLARD WAS FRAMED! HOW COULD HE HAVE MANAGED TO SNEAK ALL THOSE GEMS OUT OF THE STORE?

THE ARGUMENT WAXES FURIOUSLY UNTIL DUSK!

TIME FOR DINNER, GENTLEMEN! THEN YOU'LL HAVE TO BE LOCKED UP FOR THE NIGHT AT A HOTEL!

ALL WAYNE'S FAULT! WE'RE KEPT AWAY FROM OUR FAMILIES, JUST BECAUSE HE'S STUBBORN!

HMPH! A LOT THESE WEALTHY PLAYBOYS KNOW ABOUT LAW!

THAT NIGHT, AT BRUCE WAYNE'S HOTEL ROOM...

WHEW! THOSE FELLOWS THINK I'M CRAZY! BUT THAT MAN'S INNOCENT, I KNOW! AND I ONLY HAVE UNTIL MORNING TO PROVE IT!

MINUTES LATER, A MANTLED FIGURE SWINGS OUT INTO THE NIGHT ON AN ERRAND OF JUSTICE— THE BATMAN!

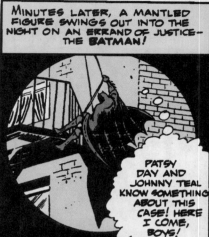

PATSY DAY AND JOHNNY TEAL KNOW SOMETHING ABOUT THIS CASE! HERE I COME, BOYS!

MEANWHILE, YOUNG ROBIN BECOMES RESTLESS...

THAT'S ENOUGH STUDYING! I'M GOING OUT TO SEE WHAT "MUSCLES" MALONE HAS TO DO WITH THOSE TOY ROBBERIES! WON'T BRUCE BE SURPRISED IF I SOLVE THIS CASE MYSELF!

CLICK!

AT MALONE'S HEADQUARTERS...

C'MON, GUYS! FIRST STOP'S THE VAN COURTLEY HOME!

AH! THERE THEY ARE! I'LL TRAIL THEM IN THE BATMOBILE!

LATER... AT THE VAN COURTLEY RESIDENCE...

THERE'S A TOY AROUND HERE THAT I WANT... A LITTLE TANK! WHERE IS IT?

I DON'T KNOW! I'M THE BUTLER— THE FAMILY IS OUT. I...I BELIEVE THE TOY YOU MENTION WAS LEFT AT THE PLAYGROUND NEARBY!

A SUDDEN NOISE AT THE WINDOW... AND INTO THE ROOM PLUNGES THE LAUGHING BOY WONDER...

HEY, "MUSCLES"! LOOK OUT!

OLD MEN AND KIDS...THAT'S WHO YOU MUGGS TACKLE! WELL...

...HOW DO YOU LIKE THIS LITTLE BOY?

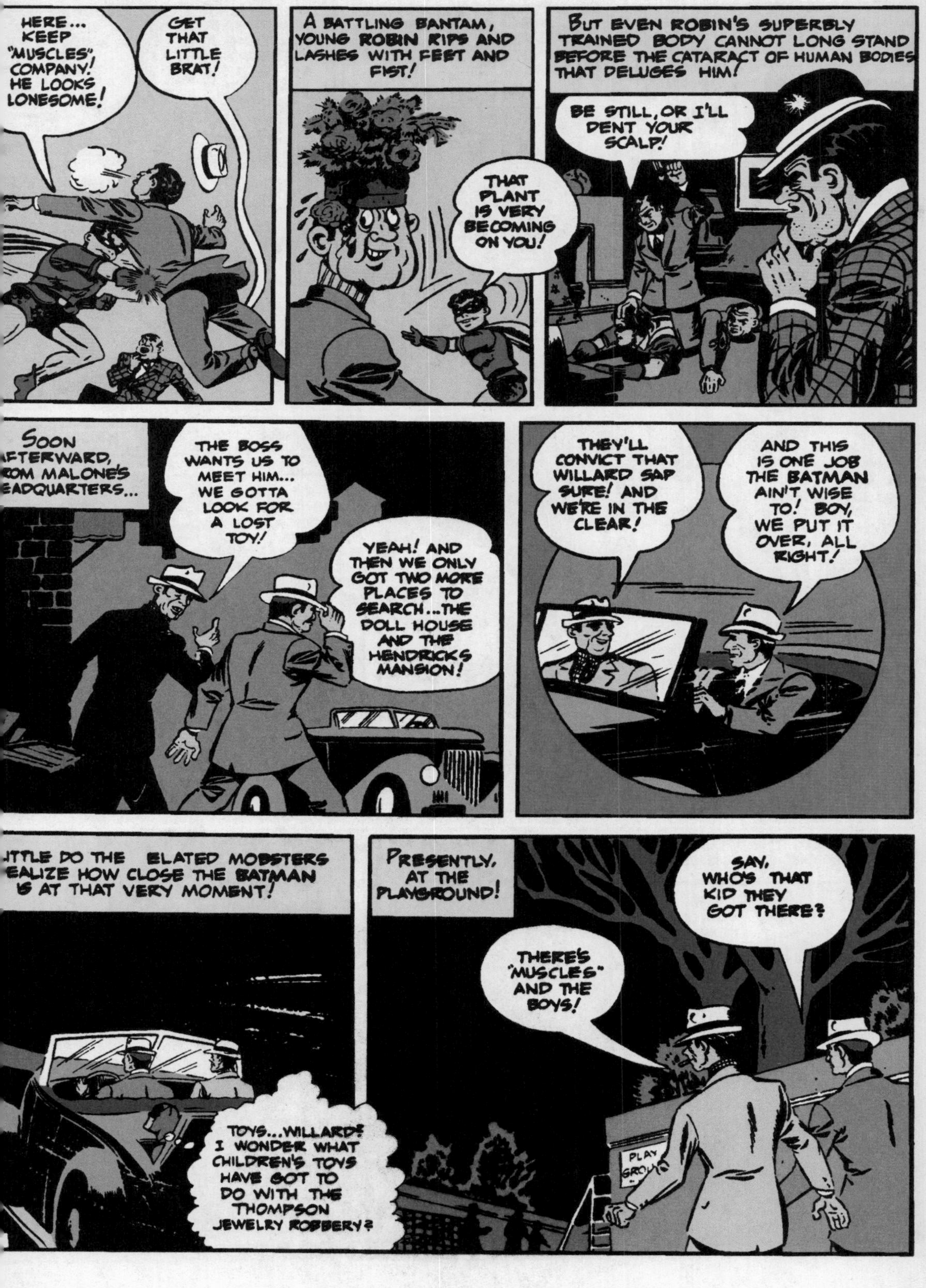
HERE... KEEP "MUSCLES" COMPANY! HE LOOKS LONESOME!
GET THAT LITTLE BRAT!
A BATTLING BANTAM, YOUNG ROBIN RIPS AND LASHES WITH FEET AND FIST!
THAT PLANT IS VERY BECOMING ON YOU!
BUT EVEN ROBIN'S SUPERBLY TRAINED BODY CANNOT LONG STAND BEFORE THE CATARACT OF HUMAN BODIES THAT DELUGES HIM!
BE STILL, OR I'LL DENT YOUR SCALP!
SOON FTERWARD, ROM MALONE'S EADQUARTERS...
THE BOSS WANTS US TO MEET HIM... WE GOTTA LOOK FOR A LOST TOY!
YEAH! AND THEN WE ONLY GOT TWO MORE PLACES TO SEARCH...THE DOLL HOUSE AND THE HENDRICKS MANSION!
THEY'LL CONVICT THAT WILLARD SAP SURE! AND WE'RE IN THE CLEAR!
AND THIS IS ONE JOB THE BATMAN AIN'T WISE TO! BOY, WE PUT IT OVER, ALL RIGHT!
ITTLE DO THE ELATED MOBSTERS EALIZE HOW CLOSE THE BATMAN IS AT THAT VERY MOMENT!
TOYS...WILLARD? I WONDER WHAT CHILDREN'S TOYS HAVE GOT TO DO WITH THE THOMPSON JEWELRY ROBBERY?
PRESENTLY, AT THE PLAYGROUND!
SAY, WHO'S THAT KID THEY GOT THERE?
THERE'S "MUSCLES" AND THE BOYS!
PLAY

LET'S FINISH THIS PEST NOW!

NAW! MUSCLES SAYS HE'S GONNA SEND THE BATMAN A SPECIAL PRESENT OF HIS PAL! ALL WRAPPED UP IN TAR AND FEATHERS!

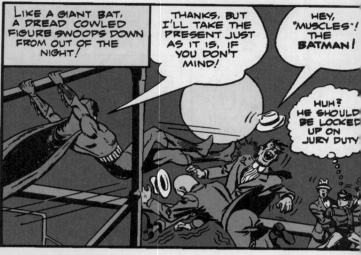

LIKE A GIANT BAT, A DREAD COWLED FIGURE SWOOPS DOWN FROM OUT OF THE NIGHT!

THANKS, BUT I'LL TAKE THE PRESENT JUST AS IT IS, IF YOU DON'T MIND!

HEY, "MUSCLES"! THE BATMAN!

HUH? HE SHOULD BE LOCKED UP ON JURY DUTY.

I TOLD YOU TO STUDY, ROBIN, DIDN'T I?

THIS IS MUCH MORE INTERESTING THAN GEOMETRY!

AN ANGRY ROAR CUTS THROUGH THE PLAYGROUND...

WHAT'RE YOU WAITING FOR, YOU FOOLS? IT'S THE BATMAN! GET HIM BEFORE HE GETS US!

UNDAUNTED, THE DYNAMIC DUO MEETS THE CHALLENGE!

THIS IS ONLY A TEMPORARY RESTING PLACE!...

...BECAUSE BROTHER RAT, HERE, WILL HELP YOU!...

...RISE UP IN THE WORLD!

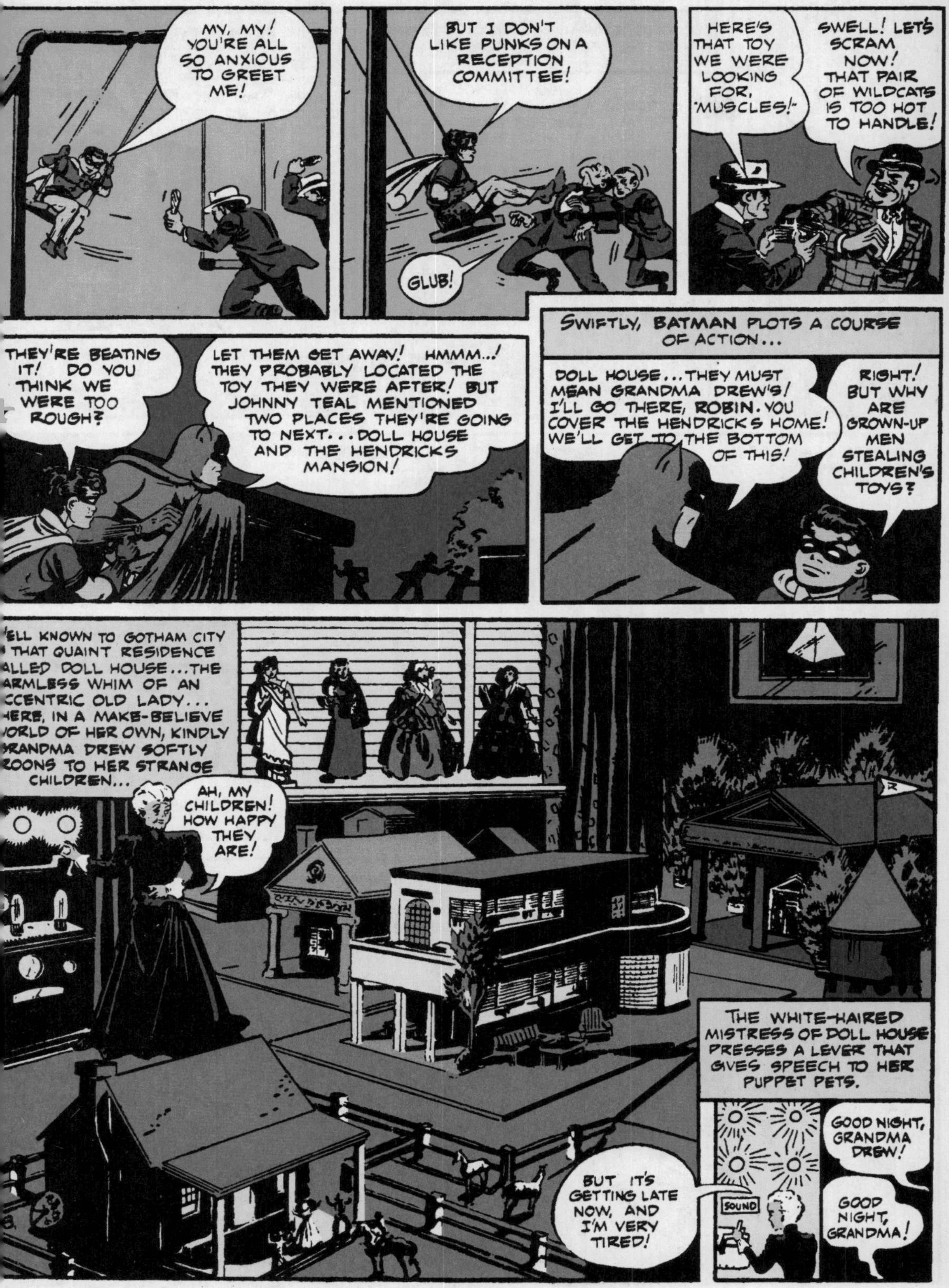
MY, MY! YOU'RE ALL SO ANXIOUS TO GREET ME!
BUT I DON'T LIKE PUNKS ON A RECEPTION COMMITTEE!
GLUB!
HERE'S THAT TOY WE WERE LOOKING FOR, "MUSCLES!"
SWELL! LET'S SCRAM NOW! THAT PAIR OF WILDCATS IS TOO HOT TO HANDLE!
THEY'RE BEATING IT! DO YOU THINK WE WERE TOO ROUGH?
LET THEM GET AWAY! HMMM...! THEY PROBABLY LOCATED THE TOY THEY WERE AFTER! BUT JOHNNY TEAL MENTIONED TWO PLACES THEY'RE GOING TO NEXT...DOLL HOUSE AND THE HENDRICKS MANSION!
SWIFTLY, BATMAN PLOTS A COURSE OF ACTION...
DOLL HOUSE...THEY MUST MEAN GRANDMA DREW'S! I'LL GO THERE, ROBIN. YOU COVER THE HENDRICKS HOME! WE'LL GET TO THE BOTTOM OF THIS!
RIGHT! BUT WHY ARE GROWN-UP MEN STEALING CHILDREN'S TOYS?
ELL KNOWN TO GOTHAM CITY THAT QUAINT RESIDENCE ALLED DOLL HOUSE...THE ARMLESS WHIM OF AN CCENTRIC OLD LADY... HERE, IN A MAKE-BELIEVE VORLD OF HER OWN, KINDLY RANDMA DREW SOFTLY ROONS TO HER STRANGE CHILDREN...
AH, MY CHILDREN! HOW HAPPY THEY ARE!
THE WHITE-HAIRED MISTRESS OF DOLL HOUSE PRESSES A LEVER THAT GIVES SPEECH TO HER PUPPET PETS.
BUT IT'S GETTING LATE NOW, AND I'M VERY TIRED!
SOUND
GOOD NIGHT, GRANDMA DREW!
GOOD NIGHT, GRANDMA!

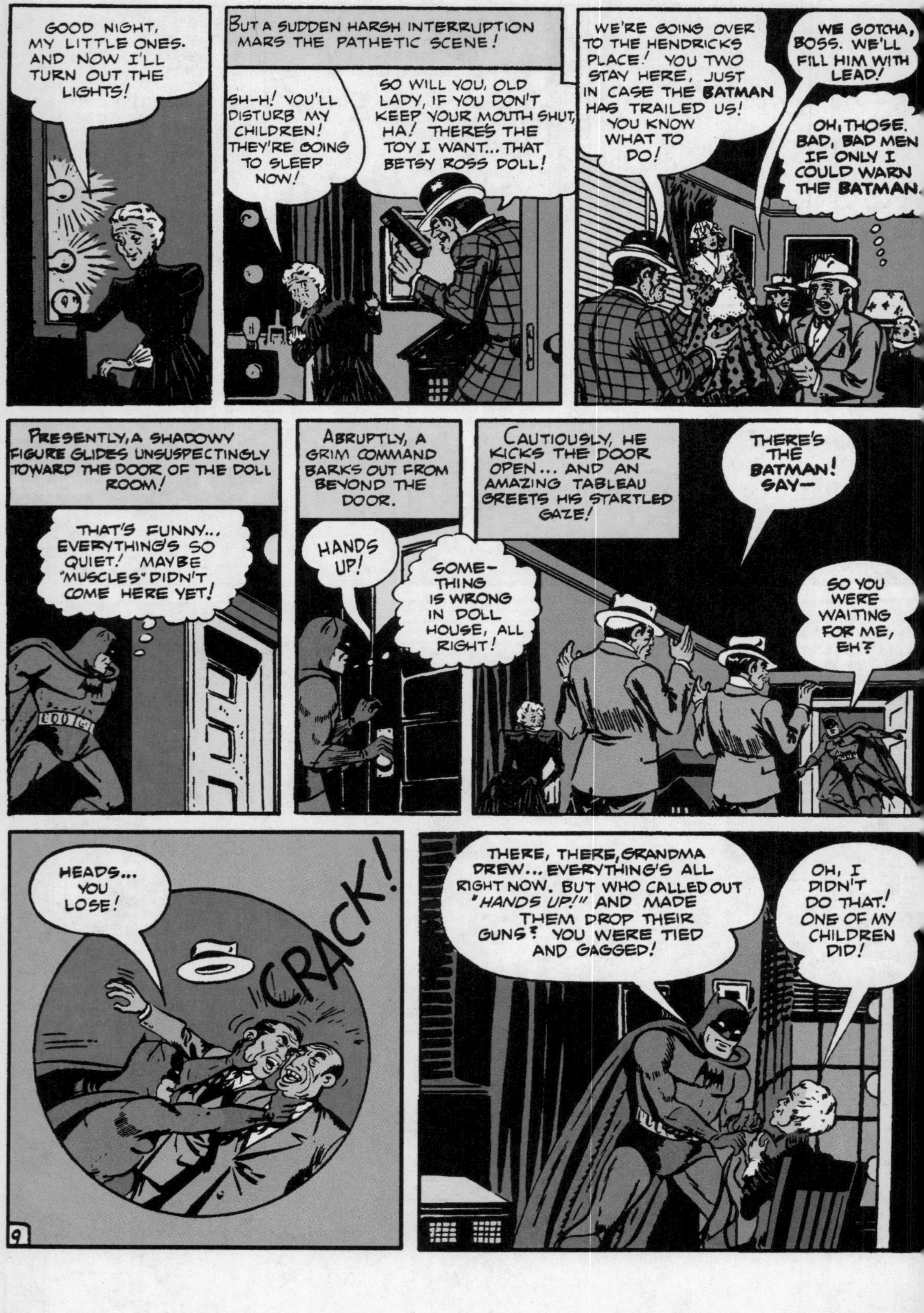
GOOD NIGHT, MY LITTLE ONES. AND NOW I'LL TURN OUT THE LIGHTS!
BUT A SUDDEN HARSH INTERRUPTION MARS THE PATHETIC SCENE!
SH-H! YOU'LL DISTURB MY CHILDREN! THEY'RE GOING TO SLEEP NOW!
SO WILL YOU, OLD LADY, IF YOU DON'T KEEP YOUR MOUTH SHUT, HA! THERE'S THE TOY I WANT... THAT BETSY ROSS DOLL!
WE'RE GOING OVER TO THE HENDRICKS PLACE! YOU TWO STAY HERE, JUST IN CASE THE BATMAN HAS TRAILED US! YOU KNOW WHAT TO DO!
WE GOTCHA, BOSS. WE'LL FILL HIM WITH LEAD!
OH, THOSE. BAD, BAD MEN IF ONLY I COULD WARN THE BATMAN.
PRESENTLY, A SHADOWY FIGURE GLIDES UNSUSPECTINGLY TOWARD THE DOOR OF THE DOLL ROOM!
THAT'S FUNNY... EVERYTHING'S SO QUIET! MAYBE "MUSCLES" DIDN'T COME HERE YET!
ABRUPTLY, A GRIM COMMAND BARKS OUT FROM BEYOND THE DOOR.
HANDS UP!
SOME-THING IS WRONG IN DOLL HOUSE, ALL RIGHT!
CAUTIOUSLY, HE KICKS THE DOOR OPEN... AND AN AMAZING TABLEAU GREETS HIS STARTLED GAZE!
THERE'S THE BATMAN! SAY—
SO YOU WERE WAITING FOR ME, EH?
HEADS... YOU LOSE!
CRACK!
THERE, THERE, GRANDMA DREW... EVERYTHING'S ALL RIGHT NOW. BUT WHO CALLED OUT "HANDS UP!" AND MADE THEM DROP THEIR GUNS? YOU WERE TIED AND GAGGED!
OH, I DIDN'T DO THAT! ONE OF MY CHILDREN DID!
9

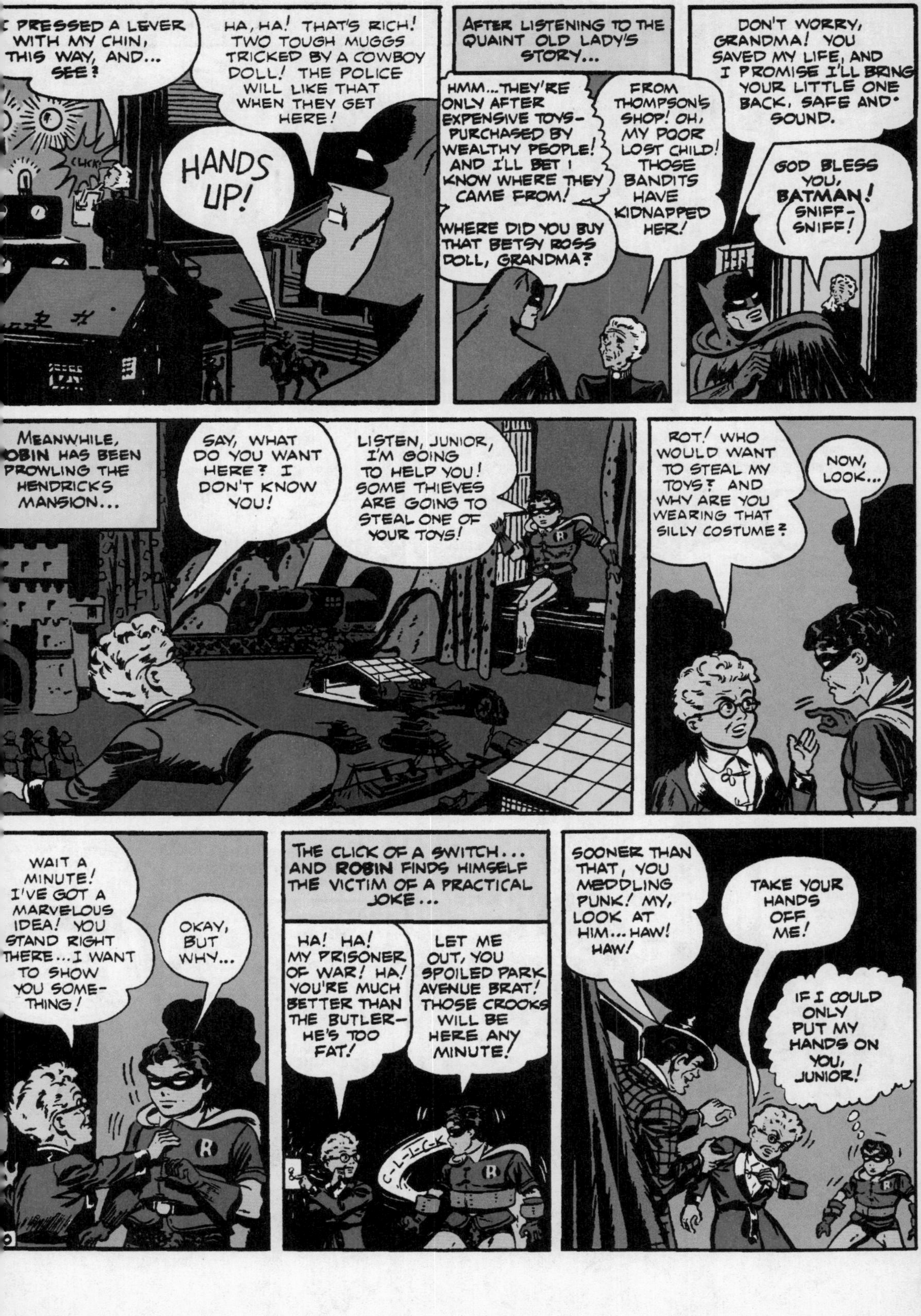
I PRESSED A LEVER WITH MY CHIN, THIS WAY, AND... SEE?
HA, HA! THAT'S RICH! TWO TOUGH MUGGS TRICKED BY A COWBOY DOLL! THE POLICE WILL LIKE THAT WHEN THEY GET HERE!
CLICK
HANDS UP!
AFTER LISTENING TO THE QUAINT OLD LADY'S STORY...
HMM...THEY'RE ONLY AFTER EXPENSIVE TOYS-PURCHASED BY WEALTHY PEOPLE! AND I'LL BET I KNOW WHERE THEY CAME FROM!
WHERE DID YOU BUY THAT BETSY ROSS DOLL, GRANDMA?
FROM THOMPSON'S SHOP! OH, MY POOR LOST CHILD! THOSE BANDITS HAVE KIDNAPPED HER!
DON'T WORRY, GRANDMA! YOU SAVED MY LIFE, AND I PROMISE I'LL BRING YOUR LITTLE ONE BACK, SAFE AND SOUND.
GOD BLESS YOU, BATMAN! SNIFF-SNIFF!
MEANWHILE, ROBIN HAS BEEN PROWLING THE HENDRICKS MANSION...
SAY, WHAT DO YOU WANT HERE? I DON'T KNOW YOU!
LISTEN, JUNIOR, I'M GOING TO HELP YOU! SOME THIEVES ARE GOING TO STEAL ONE OF YOUR TOYS!
ROT! WHO WOULD WANT TO STEAL MY TOYS? AND WHY ARE YOU WEARING THAT SILLY COSTUME?
NOW, LOOK...
WAIT A MINUTE! I'VE GOT A MARVELOUS IDEA! YOU STAND RIGHT THERE...I WANT TO SHOW YOU SOME-THING!
OKAY, BUT WHY...
THE CLICK OF A SWITCH... AND ROBIN FINDS HIMSELF THE VICTIM OF A PRACTICAL JOKE...
HA! HA! MY PRISONER OF WAR! HA! YOU'RE MUCH BETTER THAN THE BUTLER-HE'S TOO FAT!
C-L-I-C-K
LET ME OUT, YOU SPOILED PARK AVENUE BRAT! THOSE CROOKS WILL BE HERE ANY MINUTE!
SOONER THAN THAT, YOU MEDDLING PUNK! MY, LOOK AT HIM... HAW! HAW!
TAKE YOUR HANDS OFF ME!
IF I COULD ONLY PUT MY HANDS ON YOU, JUNIOR!

COME ON KID, TALK! WHERE'S THAT TOY SUBMARINE YOUR FATHER BOUGHT YOU?

OUCH! YOU'RE HURTING ME! IT...IT WAS RETURNED TO THE STORE BECAUSE IT DIDN'T WORK!

A HUMAN PROJECTILE SUDDENLY HURTLES INTO THE ROOM...

LET'S PLAY, PUNKS...YOU LIKE TOYS SO MUCH!

I'LL PLUG YOU ONCE AND FOR ALL, BATMAN!

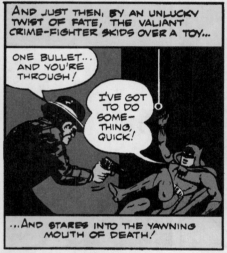

AND JUST THEN, BY AN UNLUCKY TWIST OF FATE, THE VALIANT CRIME-FIGHTER SKIDS OVER A TOY...

ONE BULLET... AND YOU'RE THROUGH!

I'VE GOT TO DO SOMETHING, QUICK!

...AND STARES INTO THE YAWNING MOUTH OF DEATH!

SHREWD, ROVING EYES SWIFTLY FOCUS ON AN OBJECT OVERHEAD... THEN, A LIGHTNING PULL AT A CORD AND...

HEY! WHAT'S HAPPENING?

JUNIOR'S PARACHUTE TROOPS, "MUSCLES!" A LITTLE INVASION!

ALERTLY, ROBIN ADDS SOUND EFFECTS TO THE MINIATURE BATTLE!

HA! HA!

BLANK CARTRIDGES - I THOUGHT SO!

LET ME OUT OF HERE...IT'S A BLITZ!

BOOM!

THE ENEMY HAS RETREATED! ROBIN IS FREED!

NOW I KNOW HOW THE GEMS GOT OUT OF THE THOMPSON STORE! AND THE BIG BOSS MUST BE SOMEONE WHO HAS A LIST OF ALL CUSTOMERS!

THEY'RE GOING THERE NOW FOR JUNIOR'S TOY. THAT REMINDS ME... WAIT A SECOND!

HELP! SOMEBODY RELEASE ME! HELP!

OKAY, BATMAN, LET'S GO! JUNIOR DOESN'T LIKE SOME OF HIS OWN MEDICINE..

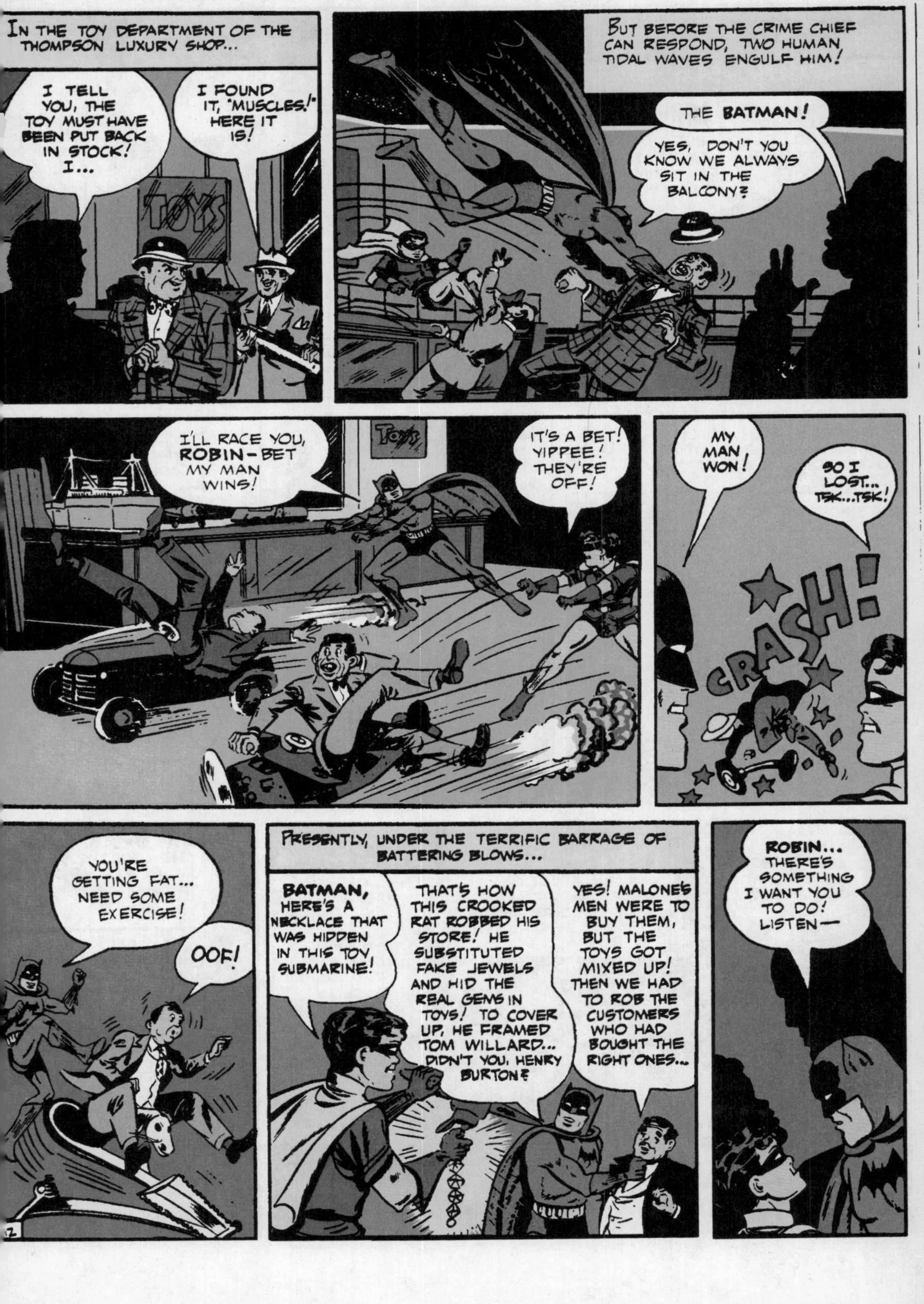

IN THE TOY DEPARTMENT OF THE THOMPSON LUXURY SHOP...
I TELL YOU, THE TOY MUST HAVE BEEN PUT BACK IN STOCK! I...
I FOUND IT, "MUSCLES!" HERE IT IS!
TOYS
BUT BEFORE THE CRIME CHIEF CAN RESPOND, TWO HUMAN TIDAL WAVES ENGULF HIM!
THE BATMAN!
YES, DON'T YOU KNOW WE ALWAYS SIT IN THE BALCONY?
I'LL RACE YOU, ROBIN-BET MY MAN WINS!
TOYS
IT'S A BET! YIPPEE! THEY'RE OFF!
MY MAN WON!
SO I LOST... TSK...TSK!
CRASH!
YOU'RE GETTING FAT... NEED SOME EXERCISE!
OOF!
PRESENTLY, UNDER THE TERRIFIC BARRAGE OF BATTERING BLOWS...
BATMAN, HERE'S A NECKLACE THAT WAS HIDDEN IN THIS TOY SUBMARINE!
THAT'S HOW THIS CROOKED RAT ROBBED HIS STORE! HE SUBSTITUTED FAKE JEWELS AND HID THE REAL GEMS IN TOYS! TO COVER UP, HE FRAMED TOM WILLARD... DIDN'T YOU, HENRY BURTON?
YES! MALONE'S MEN WERE TO BUY THEM, BUT THE TOYS GOT MIXED UP! THEN WE HAD TO ROB THE CUSTOMERS WHO HAD BOUGHT THE RIGHT ONES...
ROBIN... THERE'S SOMETHING I WANT YOU TO DO! LISTEN—

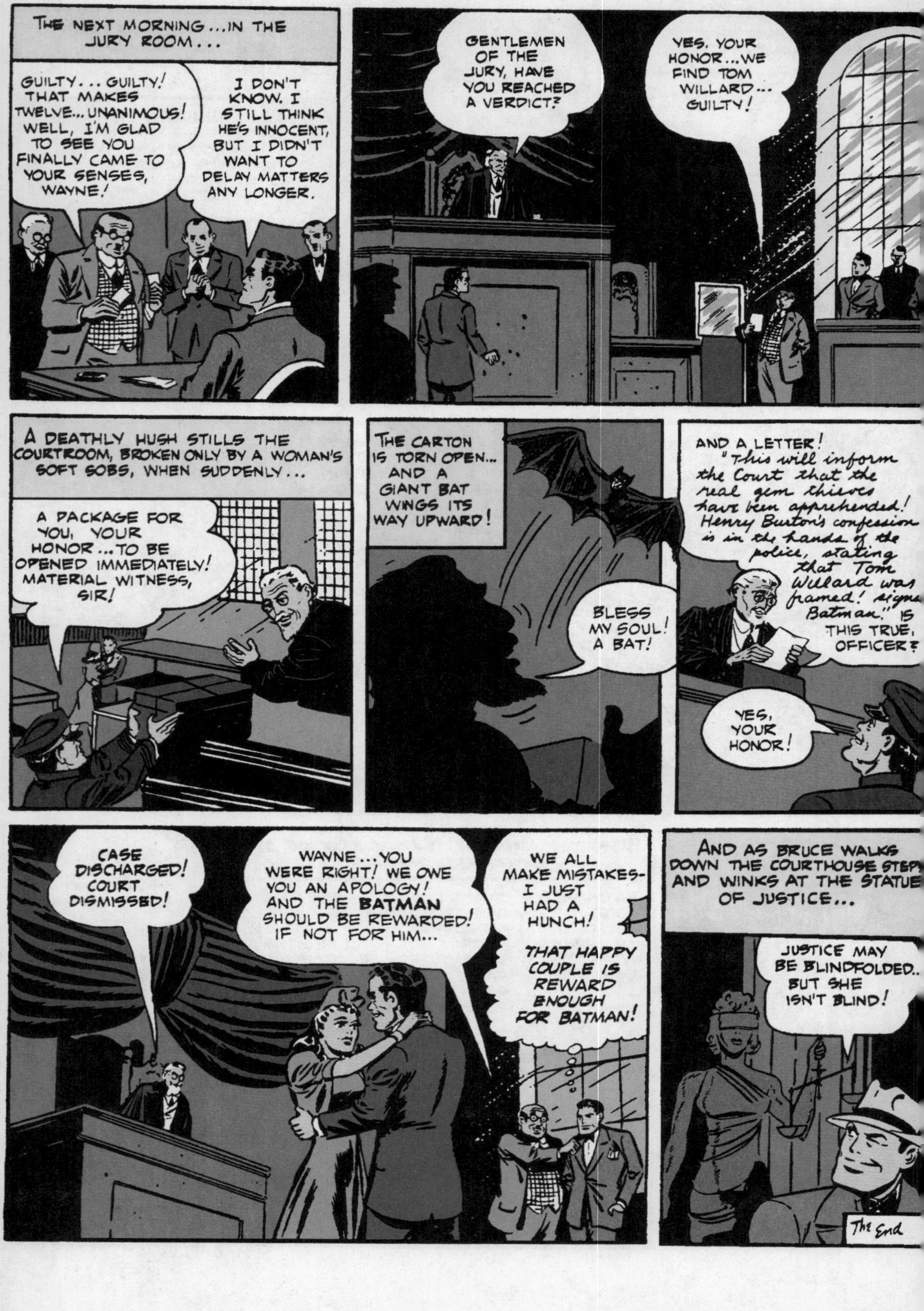
THE NEXT MORNING...IN THE JURY ROOM...
GUILTY... GUILTY! THAT MAKES TWELVE... UNANIMOUS! WELL, I'M GLAD TO SEE YOU FINALLY CAME TO YOUR SENSES, WAYNE!
I DON'T KNOW. I STILL THINK HE'S INNOCENT, BUT I DIDN'T WANT TO DELAY MATTERS ANY LONGER.
GENTLEMEN OF THE JURY, HAVE YOU REACHED A VERDICT?
YES, YOUR HONOR...WE FIND TOM WILLARD... GUILTY!
A DEATHLY HUSH STILLS THE COURTROOM, BROKEN ONLY BY A WOMAN'S SOFT SOBS, WHEN SUDDENLY...
A PACKAGE FOR YOU, YOUR HONOR...TO BE OPENED IMMEDIATELY! MATERIAL WITNESS, SIR!
THE CARTON IS TORN OPEN... AND A GIANT BAT WINGS ITS WAY UPWARD!
BLESS MY SOUL! A BAT!
AND A LETTER! "This will inform the Court that the real gem thieves have been apprehended! Henry Burton's confession is in the hands of the police, stating that Tom Willard was framed! signed Batman." IS THIS TRUE, OFFICER?
YES, YOUR HONOR!
CASE DISCHARGED! COURT DISMISSED!
WAYNE...YOU WERE RIGHT! WE OWE YOU AN APOLOGY! AND THE BATMAN SHOULD BE REWARDED! IF NOT FOR HIM...
WE ALL MAKE MISTAKES- I JUST HAD A HUNCH!
THAT HAPPY COUPLE IS REWARD ENOUGH FOR BATMAN!
AND AS BRUCE WALKS DOWN THE COURTHOUSE STEPS AND WINKS AT THE STATUE OF JUSTICE...
JUSTICE MAY BE BLINDFOLDED... BUT SHE ISN'T BLIND!
The End

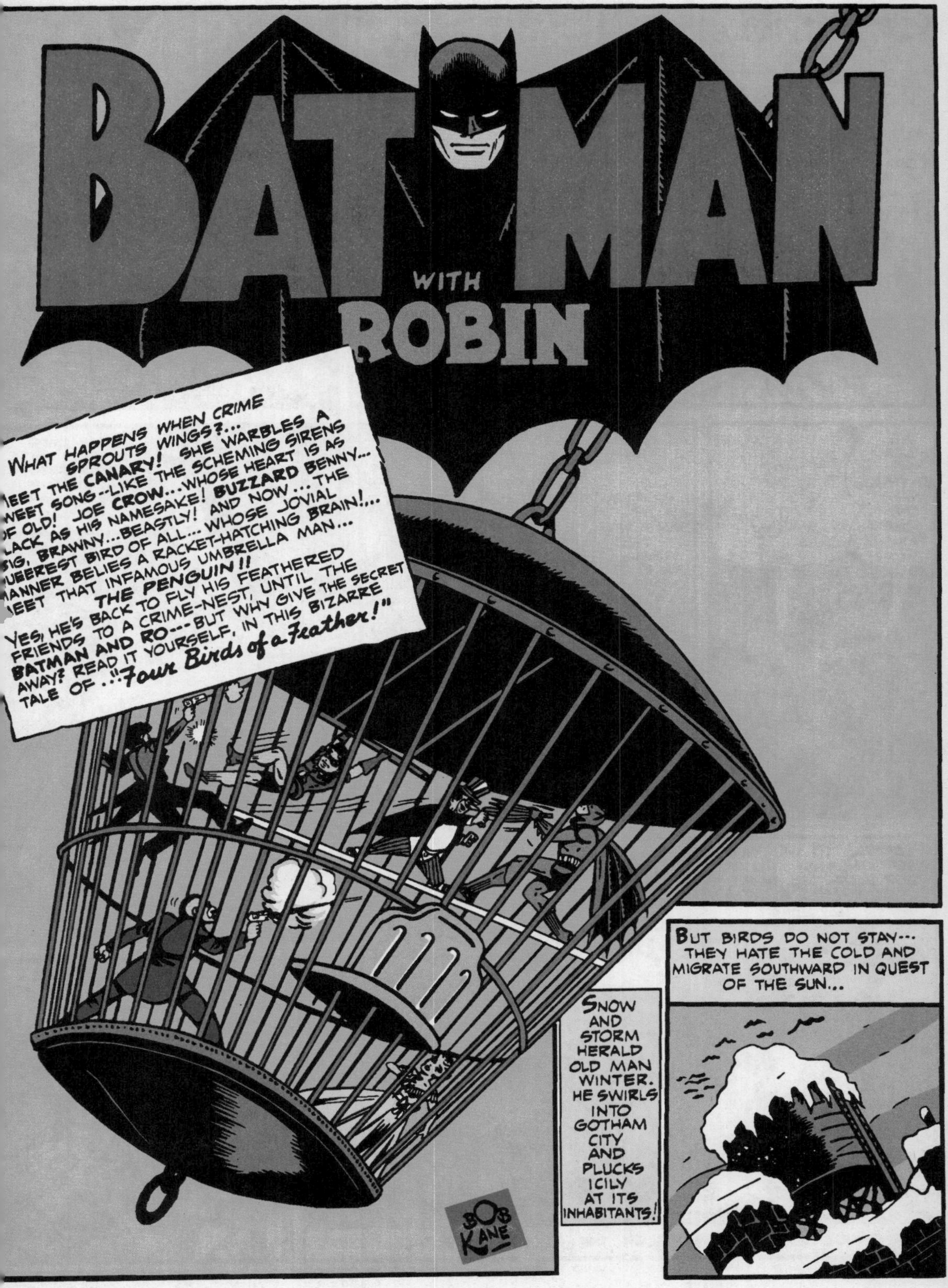
BATMAN
WITH
ROBIN
WHAT HAPPENS WHEN CRIME SPROUTS WINGS?... MEET THE CANARY! SHE WARBLES A WEET SONG--LIKE THE SCHEMING SIRENS OF OLD! JOE CROW...WHOSE HEART IS AS LACK AS HIS NAMESAKE! BUZZARD BENNY... BIG, BRAWNY...BEASTLY! AND NOW... THE UEEREST BIRD OF ALL... WHOSE JOVIAL MANNER BELIES A RACKET-HATCHING BRAIN!... MEET THAT INFAMOUS UMBRELLA MAN... THE PENGUIN!!
YES, HE'S BACK TO FLY HIS FEATHERED FRIENDS TO A CRIME-NEST, UNTIL THE BATMAN AND RO--- BUT WHY GIVE THE SECRET AWAY? READ IT YOURSELF, IN THIS BIZARRE TALE OF ..!! "Four Birds of a Feather!"
BOB KANE
SNOW AND STORM HERALD OLD MAN WINTER. HE SWIRLS INTO GOTHAM CITY AND PLUCKS ICILY AT ITS INHABITANTS!
BUT BIRDS DO NOT STAY--- THEY HATE THE COLD AND MIGRATE SOUTHWARD IN QUEST OF THE SUN...

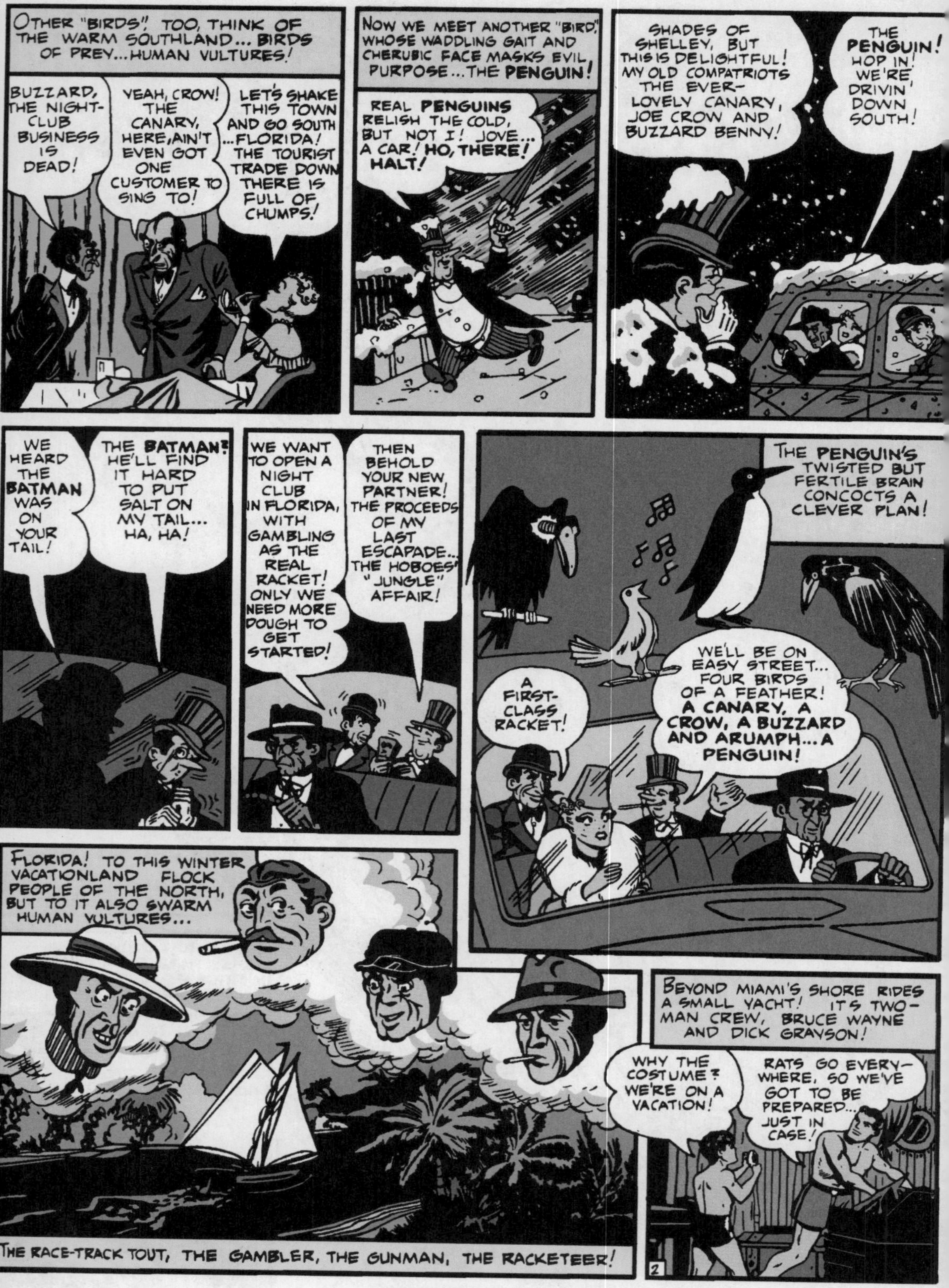
OTHER "BIRDS", TOO, THINK OF THE WARM SOUTHLAND... BIRDS OF PREY...HUMAN VULTURES!
BUZZARD, THE NIGHT-CLUB BUSINESS IS DEAD!
YEAH, CROW! THE CANARY, HERE, AIN'T EVEN GOT ONE CUSTOMER TO SING TO!
LET'S SHAKE THIS TOWN AND GO SOUTH ...FLORIDA! THE TOURIST TRADE DOWN THERE IS FULL OF CHUMPS!
NOW WE MEET ANOTHER "BIRD", WHOSE WADDLING GAIT AND CHERUBIC FACE MASKS EVIL PURPOSE...THE PENGUIN!
REAL PENGUINS RELISH THE COLD, BUT NOT I! JOVE... A CAR! HO, THERE! HALT!
SHADES OF SHELLEY, BUT THIS IS DELIGHTFUL! MY OLD COMPATRIOTS THE EVER-LOVELY CANARY, JOE CROW AND BUZZARD BENNY!
THE PENGUIN! HOP IN! WE'RE DRIVIN' DOWN SOUTH!
WE HEARD THE BATMAN WAS ON YOUR TAIL!
THE BATMAN? HE'LL FIND IT HARD TO PUT SALT ON MY TAIL... HA, HA!
WE WANT TO OPEN A NIGHT CLUB IN FLORIDA, WITH GAMBLING AS THE REAL RACKET! ONLY WE NEED MORE DOUGH TO GET STARTED!
THEN BEHOLD YOUR NEW PARTNER! THE PROCEEDS OF MY LAST ESCAPADE... THE HOBOES' "JUNGLE" AFFAIR!
THE PENGUIN'S TWISTED BUT FERTILE BRAIN CONCOCTS A CLEVER PLAN!
A FIRST-CLASS RACKET!
WE'LL BE ON EASY STREET... FOUR BIRDS OF A FEATHER! A CANARY, A CROW, A BUZZARD AND ARUMPH... A PENGUIN!
FLORIDA! TO THIS WINTER VACATIONLAND FLOCK PEOPLE OF THE NORTH, BUT TO IT ALSO SWARM HUMAN VULTURES...
THE RACE-TRACK TOUT, THE GAMBLER, THE GUNMAN, THE RACKETEER!
BEYOND MIAMI'S SHORE RIDES A SMALL YACHT! IT'S TWO-MAN CREW, BRUCE WAYNE AND DICK GRAYSON!
WHY THE COSTUME? WE'RE ON A VACATION!
RATS GO EVERY-WHERE, SO WE'VE GOT TO BE PREPARED... JUST IN CASE!
2

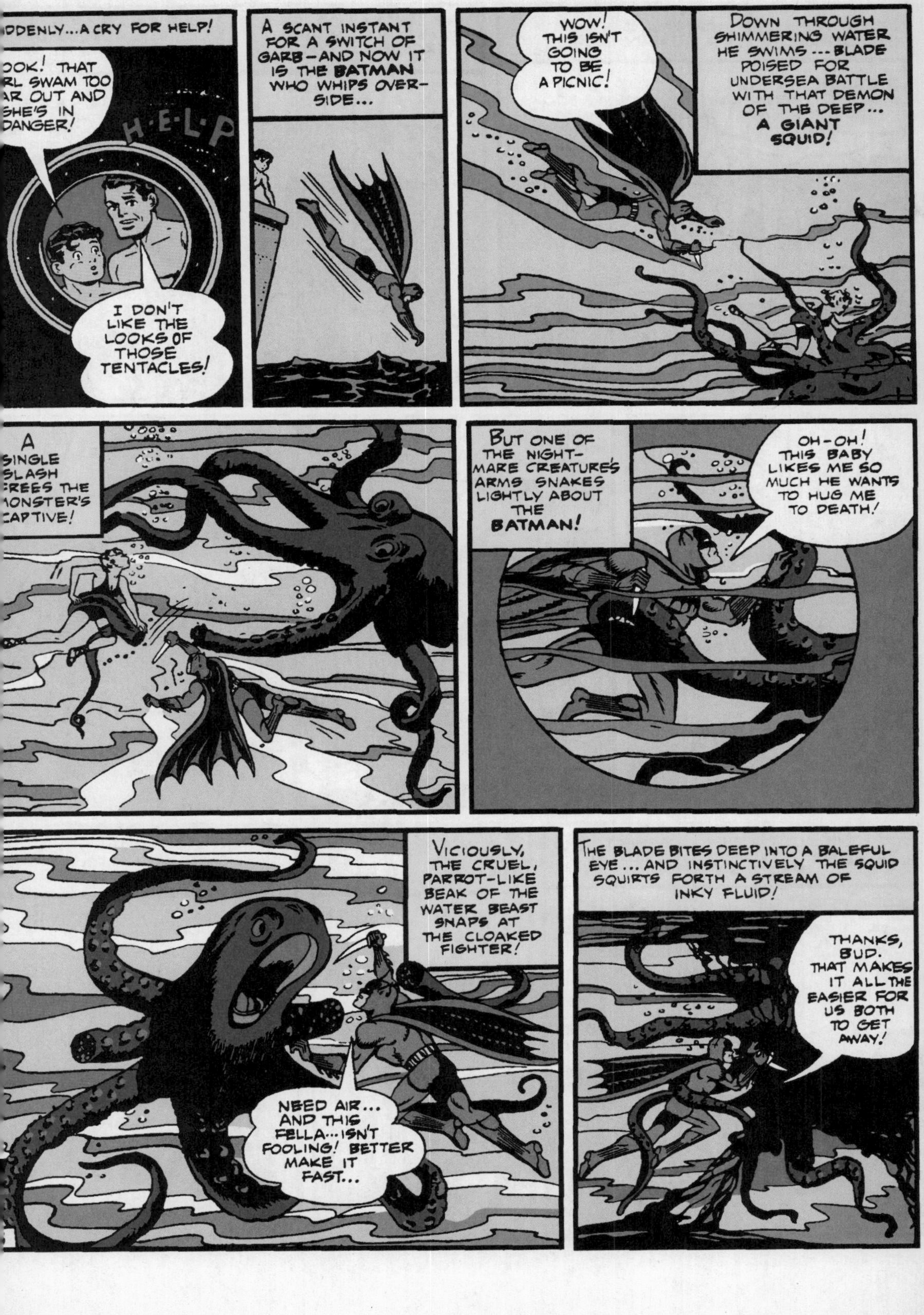

...DDENLY...A CRY FOR HELP!
...OOK! THAT ...RL SWAM TOO ...AR OUT AND SHE'S IN DANGER!
H-E-L-P
I DON'T LIKE THE LOOKS OF THOSE TENTACLES!
A SCANT INSTANT FOR A SWITCH OF GARB—AND NOW IT IS THE BATMAN WHO WHIPS OVER-SIDE...
WOW! THIS ISN'T GOING TO BE A PICNIC!
DOWN THROUGH SHIMMERING WATER HE SWIMS ... BLADE POISED FOR UNDERSEA BATTLE WITH THAT DEMON OF THE DEEP... A GIANT SQUID!
A SINGLE ...LASH ...REES THE ...ONSTER'S ...APTIVE!
BUT ONE OF THE NIGHT-MARE CREATURE'S ARMS SNAKES LIGHTLY ABOUT THE BATMAN!
OH-OH! THIS BABY LIKES ME SO MUCH HE WANTS TO HUG ME TO DEATH!
VICIOUSLY, THE CRUEL, PARROT-LIKE BEAK OF THE WATER BEAST SNAPS AT THE CLOAKED FIGHTER!
NEED AIR... AND THIS FELLA...ISN'T FOOLING! BETTER MAKE IT FAST...
THE BLADE BITES DEEP INTO A BALEFUL EYE... AND INSTINCTIVELY THE SQUID SQUIRTS FORTH A STREAM OF INKY FLUID!
THANKS, BUD. THAT MAKES IT ALL THE EASIER FOR US BOTH TO GET AWAY!

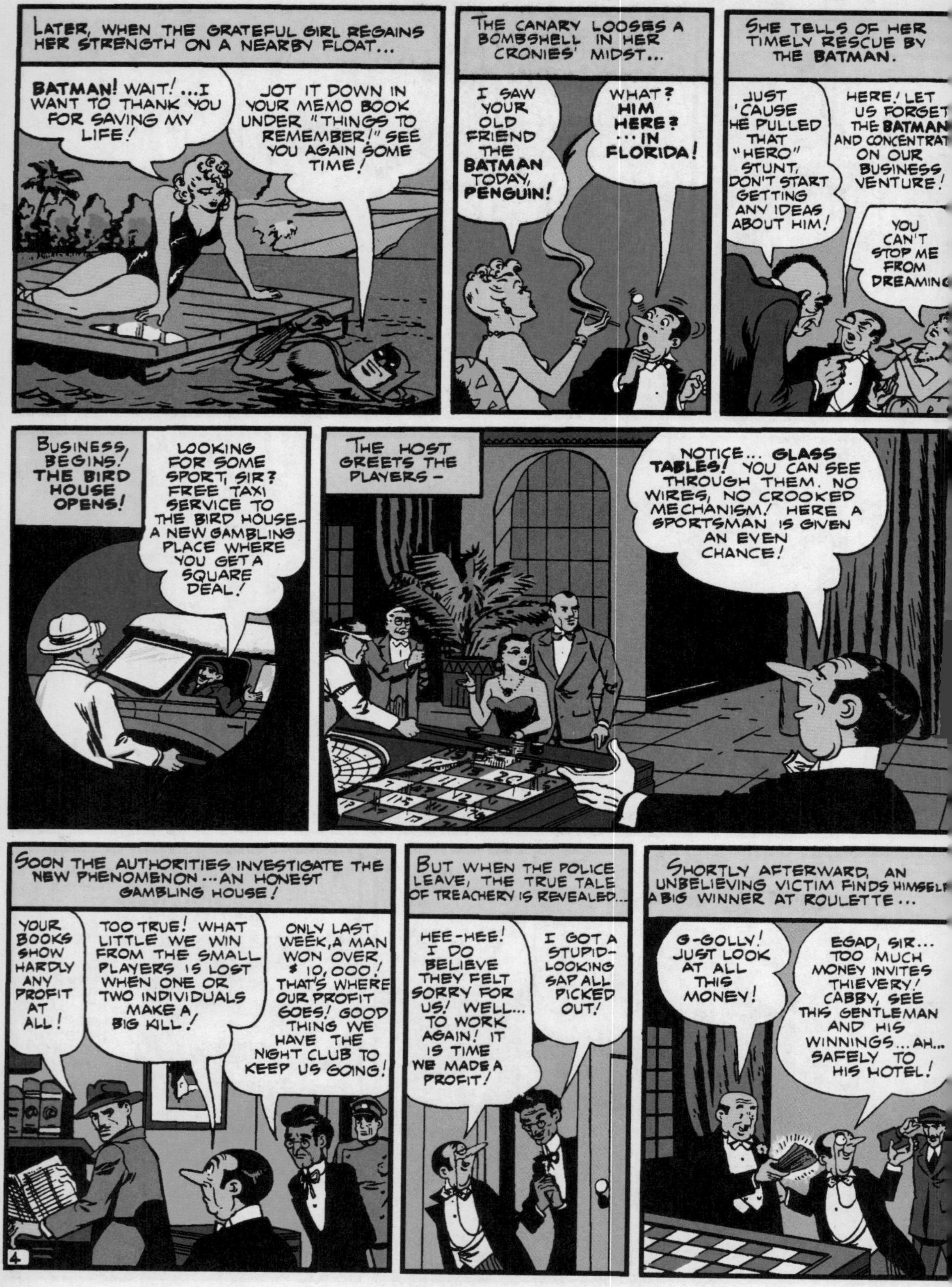
LATER, WHEN THE GRATEFUL GIRL REGAINS HER STRENGTH ON A NEARBY FLOAT...
BATMAN! WAIT! ...I WANT TO THANK YOU FOR SAVING MY LIFE!
JOT IT DOWN IN YOUR MEMO BOOK UNDER "THINGS TO REMEMBER!" SEE YOU AGAIN SOME TIME!
THE CANARY LOOSES A BOMBSHELL IN HER CRONIES' MIDST...
I SAW YOUR OLD FRIEND THE BATMAN TODAY, PENGUIN!
WHAT? HIM HERE? ...IN FLORIDA!
SHE TELLS OF HER TIMELY RESCUE BY THE BATMAN.
JUST 'CAUSE HE PULLED THAT "HERO" STUNT, DON'T START GETTING ANY IDEAS ABOUT HIM!
HERE! LET US FORGET THE BATMAN AND CONCENTRAT ON OUR BUSINESS VENTURE!
YOU CAN'T STOP ME FROM DREAMING
BUSINESS BEGINS! THE BIRD HOUSE OPENS!
LOOKING FOR SOME SPORT, SIR? FREE TAXI SERVICE TO THE BIRD HOUSE- A NEW GAMBLING PLACE WHERE YOU GET A SQUARE DEAL!
THE HOST GREETS THE PLAYERS -
NOTICE... GLASS TABLES! YOU CAN SEE THROUGH THEM. NO WIRES, NO CROOKED MECHANISM! HERE A SPORTSMAN IS GIVEN AN EVEN CHANCE!
SOON THE AUTHORITIES INVESTIGATE THE NEW PHENOMENON...AN HONEST GAMBLING HOUSE!
YOUR BOOKS SHOW HARDLY ANY PROFIT AT ALL!
TOO TRUE! WHAT LITTLE WE WIN FROM THE SMALL PLAYERS IS LOST WHEN ONE OR TWO INDIVIDUALS MAKE A BIG KILL!
ONLY LAST WEEK, A MAN WON OVER $10,000! THAT'S WHERE OUR PROFIT GOES! GOOD THING WE HAVE THE NIGHT CLUB TO KEEP US GOING!
4
BUT WHEN THE POLICE LEAVE, THE TRUE TALE OF TREACHERY IS REVEALED...
HEE-HEE! I DO BELIEVE THEY FELT SORRY FOR US! WELL... TO WORK AGAIN! IT IS TIME WE MADE A PROFIT!
I GOT A STUPID-LOOKING SAP ALL PICKED OUT!
SHORTLY AFTERWARD, AN UNBELIEVING VICTIM FINDS HIMSELF A BIG WINNER AT ROULETTE...
G-GOLLY! JUST LOOK AT ALL THIS MONEY!
EGAD, SIR... TOO MUCH MONEY INVITES THIEVERY! CABBY, SEE THIS GENTLEMAN AND HIS WINNINGS...AH... SAFELY TO HIS HOTEL!

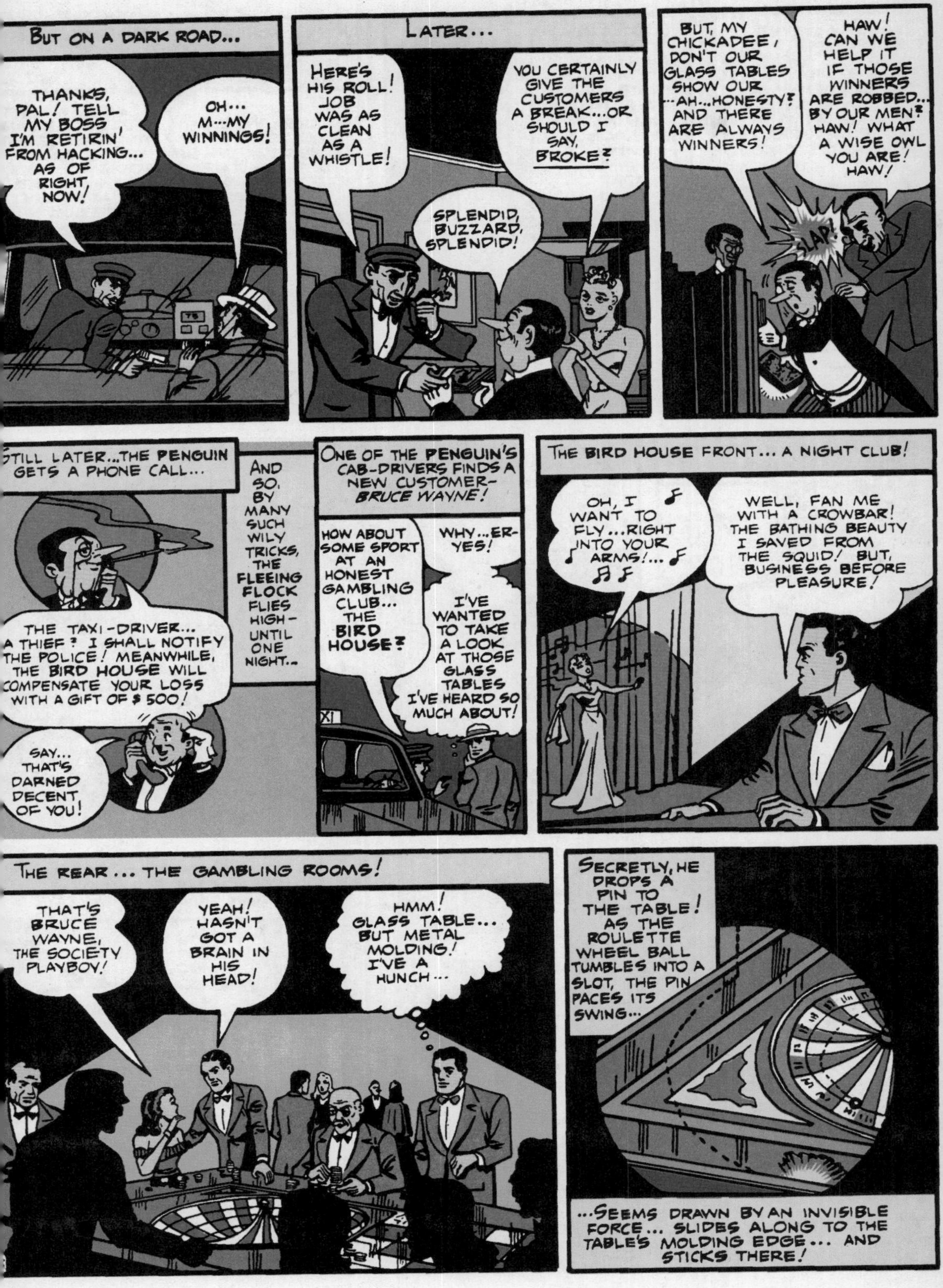
BUT ON A DARK ROAD...
THANKS, PAL! TELL MY BOSS I'M RETIRIN' FROM HACKING... AS OF RIGHT NOW!
OH... M...MY WINNINGS!
LATER...
HERE'S HIS ROLL! JOB WAS AS CLEAN AS A WHISTLE!
SPLENDID, BUZZARD, SPLENDID!
YOU CERTAINLY GIVE THE CUSTOMERS A BREAK...OR SHOULD I SAY, BROKE?
BUT, MY CHICKADEE, DON'T OUR GLASS TABLES SHOW OUR ...AH...HONESTY? AND THERE ARE ALWAYS WINNERS!
HAW! CAN WE HELP IT IF THOSE WINNERS ARE ROBBED... BY OUR MEN? HAW! WHAT A WISE OWL YOU ARE! HAW!
SLAP!
STILL LATER...THE PENGUIN GETS A PHONE CALL...
THE TAXI-DRIVER... A THIEF? I SHALL NOTIFY THE POLICE! MEANWHILE, THE BIRD HOUSE WILL COMPENSATE YOUR LOSS WITH A GIFT OF $ 500!
SAY... THAT'S DARNED DECENT OF YOU!
AND SO, BY MANY SUCH WILY TRICKS, THE FLEEING FLOCK FLIES HIGH - UNTIL ONE NIGHT..
ONE OF THE PENGUIN'S CAB-DRIVERS FINDS A NEW CUSTOMER- BRUCE WAYNE!
HOW ABOUT SOME SPORT AT AN HONEST GAMBLING CLUB... THE BIRD HOUSE?
WHY...ER- YES!
I'VE WANTED TO TAKE A LOOK AT THOSE GLASS TABLES I'VE HEARD SO MUCH ABOUT!
THE BIRD HOUSE FRONT... A NIGHT CLUB!
OH, I WANT TO FLY...RIGHT INTO YOUR ARMS!...
WELL, FAN ME WITH A CROWBAR! THE BATHING BEAUTY I SAVED FROM THE SQUID! BUT, BUSINESS BEFORE PLEASURE!
THE REAR ... THE GAMBLING ROOMS!
THAT'S BRUCE WAYNE, THE SOCIETY PLAYBOY!
YEAH! HASN'T GOT A BRAIN IN HIS HEAD!
HMM! GLASS TABLE... BUT METAL MOLDING! I'VE A HUNCH...
SECRETLY, HE DROPS A PIN TO THE TABLE! AS THE ROULETTE WHEEL BALL TUMBLES INTO A SLOT, THE PIN PACES ITS SWING...
...SEEMS DRAWN BY AN INVISIBLE FORCE... SLIDES ALONG TO THE TABLE'S MOLDING EDGE... AND STICKS THERE!

VERY CLEVER! ELECTRO-MAGNETS IN THE MOLDING! THE STEEL BALL IS DRAWN INTO THE ROULETTE SLOT, DIRECTLY IN LINE WITH THE MAGNET THAT THE CROUPIER SENDS CURRENT THROUGH!

GOT A NEW CLUCK PICKED OUT TONIGHT! BRUCE WAYNE, A PLAYBOY. YOU KNOW THE KIND... PLENTY OF MONEY BUT SHORT ON BRAINS!

SOUNDS FASCINATING. THINK I'LL TODDLE ALONG, TOO, AND WATCH YOU... AH... TAKE HIM!

AFTER A WONDERING BRUCE NOTES THAT THE CROUPIER PERMITS HIM TO WIN A LARGE SUM...

MR. WAYNE, THE HOUSE WOULD LIKE YOUR ADDRESS...FOR THE RECORD OF YOUR WINNINGS, OF COURSE!

WELL, WELL! BUZZARD BENNY AND JOE CROW— THESE BIRDS BODE NO GOOD! I'LL GIVE THEM THE ADDRESS OF MY TEMPORARY ROOM IN TOWN!

BRUCE MAKES A HASTY CALL TO DICK GRAYSON...

...AND THEY PROBABLY WANT TO LIFT MY WINNINGS!

THEY WANTED YOUR ADDRESS SO THEY CAN BEAT YOU HOME AND WAIT FOR YOU! NICE PEOPLE!

LATER... FROM THE BROODING SHADOWS OF BRUCE'S PENTHOUSE...

Y... YES, SIR!

REACH FOR A CLOUD, CHUM!

THEN, FLASHING FROM CONCEALMENT, COMES A CATAPULTING, COLORFUL FIGURE... ROBIN!

I'M GOING INSIDE TO PHONE THE POLICE!

SURPRISED?

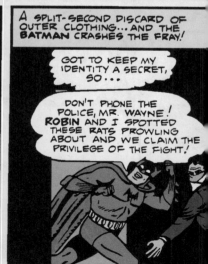

A SPLIT-SECOND DISCARD OF OUTER CLOTHING... AND THE BATMAN CRASHES THE FRAY!

GOT TO KEEP MY IDENTITY A SECRET, SO...

DON'T PHONE THE POLICE, MR. WAYNE! ROBIN AND I SPOTTED THESE RATS PROWLING ABOUT AND WE CLAIM THE PRIVILEGE OF THE FIGHT!

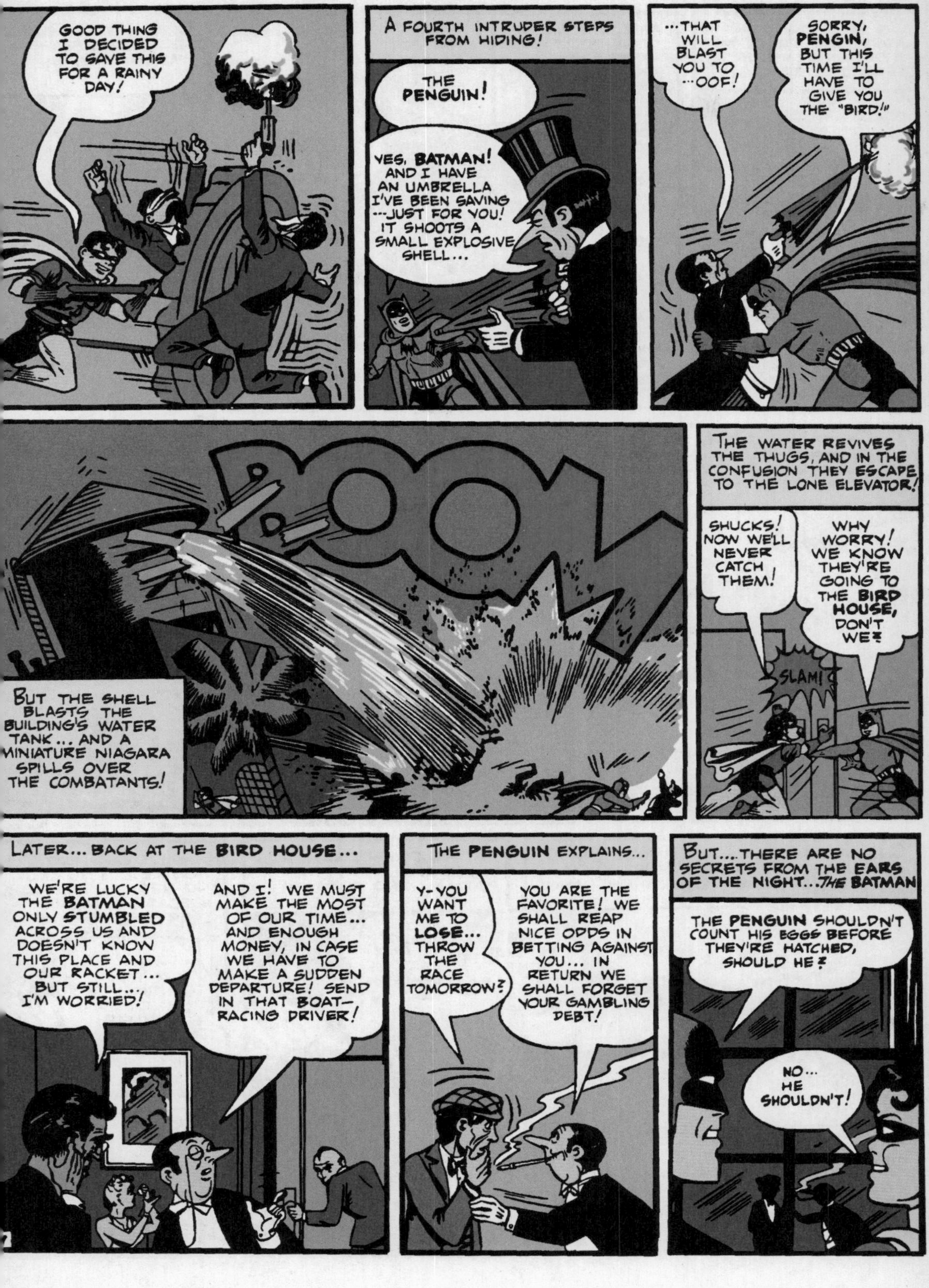
GOOD THING I DECIDED TO SAVE THIS FOR A RAINY DAY!
A FOURTH INTRUDER STEPS FROM HIDING!
THE PENGUIN!
YES, BATMAN! AND I HAVE AN UMBRELLA I'VE BEEN SAVING --JUST FOR YOU! IT SHOOTS A SMALL EXPLOSIVE SHELL...
...THAT WILL BLAST YOU TO ...OOF!
SORRY, PENGIN, BUT THIS TIME I'LL HAVE TO GIVE YOU THE "BIRD!"
BOOM
BUT THE SHELL BLASTS THE BUILDING'S WATER TANK... AND A MINIATURE NIAGARA SPILLS OVER THE COMBATANTS!
THE WATER REVIVES THE THUGS, AND IN THE CONFUSION THEY ESCAPE TO THE LONE ELEVATOR!
SHUCKS! NOW WE'LL NEVER CATCH THEM!
WHY WORRY! WE KNOW THEY'RE GOING TO THE BIRD HOUSE, DON'T WE?
SLAM!
LATER... BACK AT THE BIRD HOUSE...
WE'RE LUCKY THE BATMAN ONLY STUMBLED ACROSS US AND DOESN'T KNOW THIS PLACE AND OUR RACKET... BUT STILL... I'M WORRIED!
AND I! WE MUST MAKE THE MOST OF OUR TIME... AND ENOUGH MONEY, IN CASE WE HAVE TO MAKE A SUDDEN DEPARTURE! SEND IN THAT BOAT-RACING DRIVER!
THE PENGUIN EXPLAINS...
Y-YOU WANT ME TO LOSE... THROW THE RACE TOMORROW?
YOU ARE THE FAVORITE! WE SHALL REAP NICE ODDS IN BETTING AGAINST YOU... IN RETURN WE SHALL FORGET YOUR GAMBLING DEBT!
BUT.... THERE ARE NO SECRETS FROM THE EARS OF THE NIGHT... THE BATMAN
THE PENGUIN SHOULDN'T COUNT HIS EGGS BEFORE THEY'RE HATCHED, SHOULD HE?
NO... HE SHOULDN'T!

THE DAY OF THE OUTBOARD STEEPLECHASE RACE THAT A CERTAIN DRIVER IS DESTINED NEVER TO SEE!
OH-H-H!
LATER...THE BOATS JOCKEY INTO THE STARTING LINE... AND THEN... THEY'RE OFF... AT SIXTY MILES PER HOUR!
FROM A CAR ON SHORE THE PENGUIN SPIES A FAMILIAR FIGURE!
EGAD! THE BATMAN... SUBSTITUTING FOR OUR MAN!
AND INDEED IT IS THE BATMAN WHOSE CRAFT LEAPS HIGH OVER THE SLANTING PLATFORM FOR THE LEADING JUMP!
HOLDING THE SCANT LEAD, THE OUTBOARD ROCKETS OVER CHOPPY WATERS... THROUGH THE NEXT HAZARD... A SHEET OF ROARING FLAME!
ON WHIP THE BOATS, AT A MILE-A-MINUTE CLIP... 'ROUND HAIR-PIN TURNS... OVER MORE JUMPS, THEN ...THE FINAL HAZARD!
C'MON, BATMAN!
THE BATMAN'S BOAT BULLETS THROUGH A BRICK WALL ...TO WIN!
8
AT THE FINISH LINE... A BULLET DRILLS PAST THE BATMAN AND SMASHES INTO THE WOOD!
THE PENGUIN WON'T LIKE TH--- UH? A BULLET!
LOOK! IN THAT CAR...THE PENGUIN AND HIS CREW! LET'S GO AND GET 'EM!
Z-I-N-G
YOU'LL GET HURT! THEY'RE OUT TO KILL... AND BESIDES ... ER...TH BOAT CAN ONLY CARRY ONE PERSON!
CUT THE SENTIMENT! I CAN RIDE A SURFBOARD, CAN'T I? C'MON.. WHILE WE'RE ARGUING, THEY'RE GETTING AWAY!

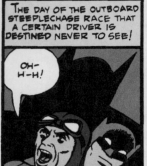

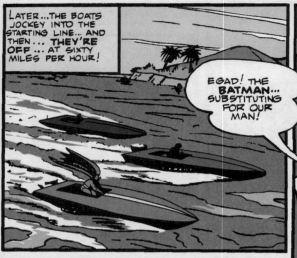

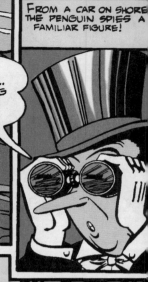

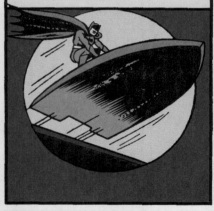

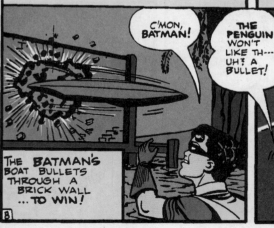

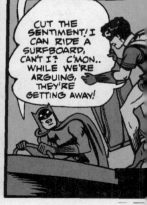

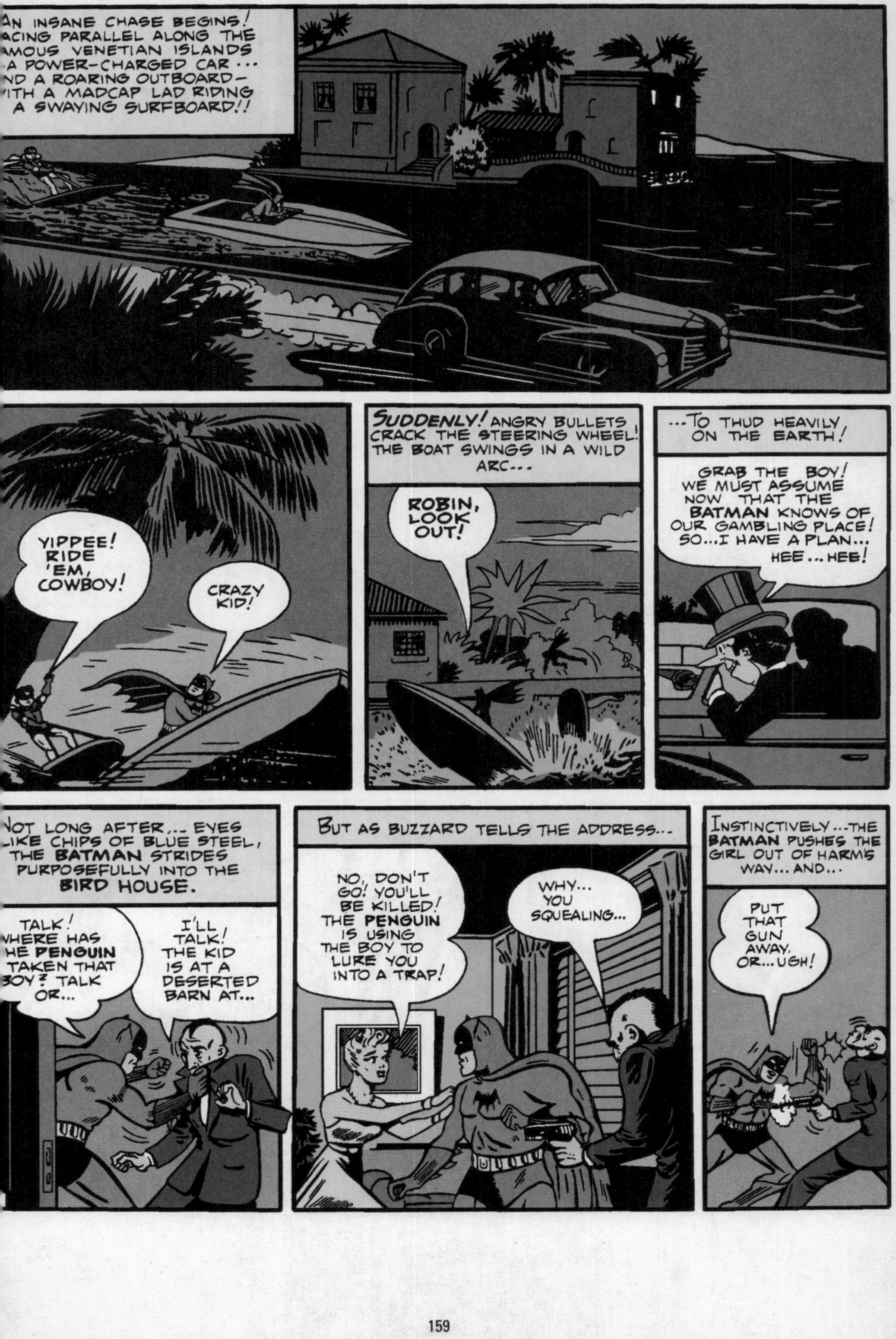
AN INSANE CHASE BEGINS! ACING PARALLEL ALONG THE AMOUS VENETIAN ISLANDS A POWER-CHARGED CAR... ND A ROARING OUTBOARD—VITH A MADCAP LAD RIDING A SWAYING SURFBOARD!!
YIPPEE! RIDE 'EM, COWBOY!
CRAZY KID!
SUDDENLY! ANGRY BULLETS CRACK THE STEERING WHEEL! THE BOAT SWINGS IN A WILD ARC...
ROBIN, LOOK OUT!
...TO THUD HEAVILY ON THE EARTH!
GRAB THE BOY! WE MUST ASSUME NOW THAT THE BATMAN KNOWS OF OUR GAMBLING PLACE! SO...I HAVE A PLAN... HEE...HEE!
NOT LONG AFTER... EYES LIKE CHIPS OF BLUE STEEL, THE BATMAN STRIDES PURPOSEFULLY INTO THE BIRD HOUSE.
TALK! WHERE HAS HE PENGUIN TAKEN THAT BOY? TALK OR...
I'LL TALK! THE KID IS AT A DESERTED BARN AT...
BUT AS BUZZARD TELLS THE ADDRESS...
NO, DON'T GO! YOU'LL BE KILLED! THE PENGUIN IS USING THE BOY TO LURE YOU INTO A TRAP!
WHY... YOU SQUEALING...
INSTINCTIVELY...THE BATMAN PUSHES THE GIRL OUT OF HARM'S WAY... AND...
PUT THAT GUN AWAY, OR...UGH!

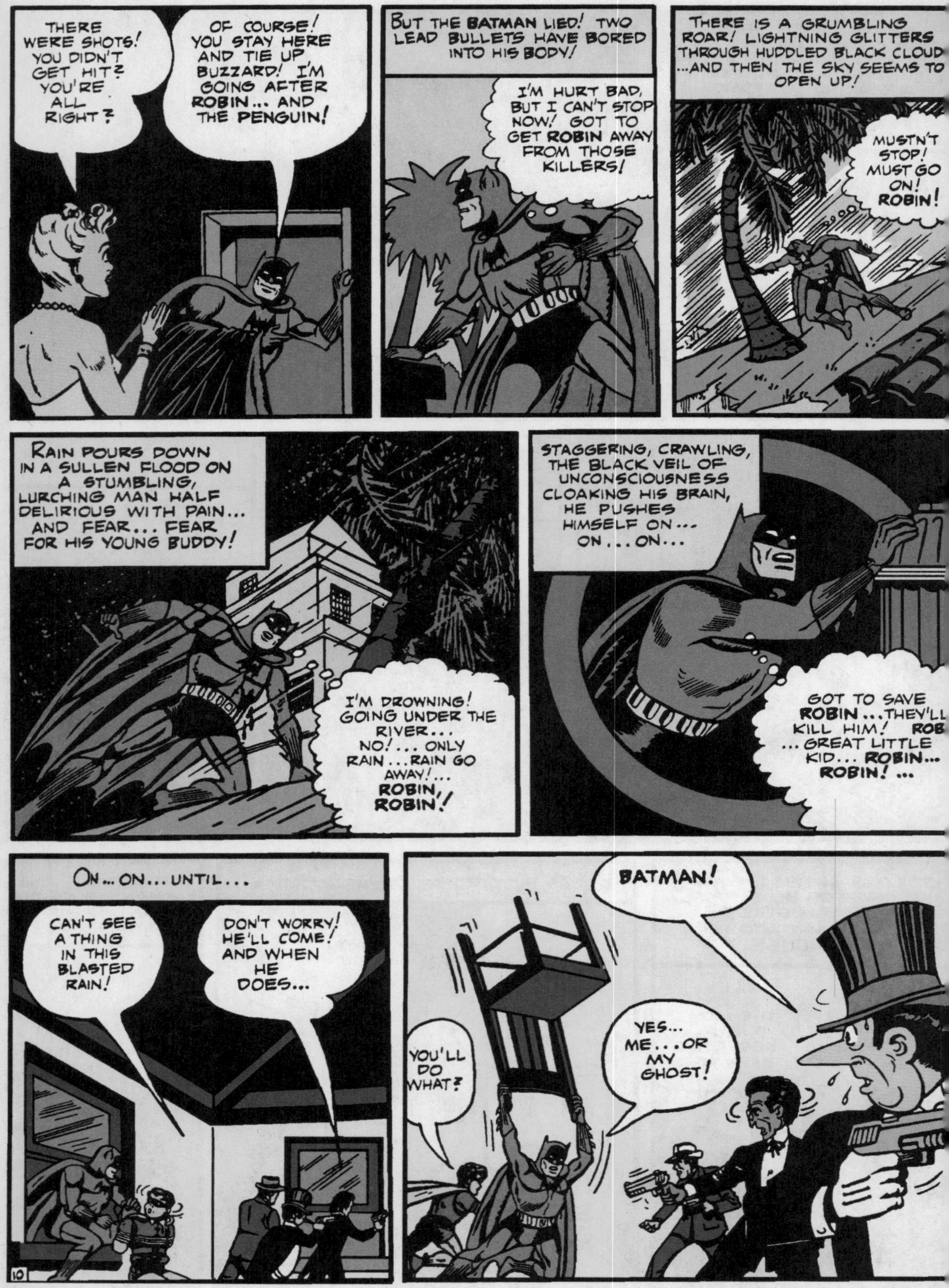
THERE WERE SHOTS! YOU DIDN'T GET HIT? YOU'RE ALL RIGHT?
OF COURSE! YOU STAY HERE AND TIE UP BUZZARD! I'M GOING AFTER ROBIN... AND THE PENGUIN!
BUT THE BATMAN LIED! TWO LEAD BULLETS HAVE BORED INTO HIS BODY!
I'M HURT BAD, BUT I CAN'T STOP NOW! GOT TO GET ROBIN AWAY FROM THOSE KILLERS!
THERE IS A GRUMBLING ROAR! LIGHTNING GLITTERS THROUGH HUDDLED BLACK CLOUD ...AND THEN THE SKY SEEMS TO OPEN UP!
MUSTN'T STOP! MUST GO ON! ROBIN!
RAIN POURS DOWN IN A SULLEN FLOOD ON A STUMBLING, LURCHING MAN HALF DELIRIOUS WITH PAIN... AND FEAR... FEAR FOR HIS YOUNG BUDDY!
I'M DROWNING! GOING UNDER THE RIVER... NO!... ONLY RAIN... RAIN GO AWAY!... ROBIN, ROBIN!
STAGGERING, CRAWLING, THE BLACK VEIL OF UNCONSCIOUSNESS CLOAKING HIS BRAIN, HE PUSHES HIMSELF ON... ON... ON...
GOT TO SAVE ROBIN ...THEY'LL KILL HIM! ROB ...GREAT LITTLE KID... ROBIN... ROBIN! ...
ON... ON... UNTIL...
CAN'T SEE A THING IN THIS BLASTED RAIN!
DON'T WORRY! HE'LL COME! AND WHEN HE DOES...
10
BATMAN!
YOU'LL DO WHAT?
YES... ME... OR MY GHOST!

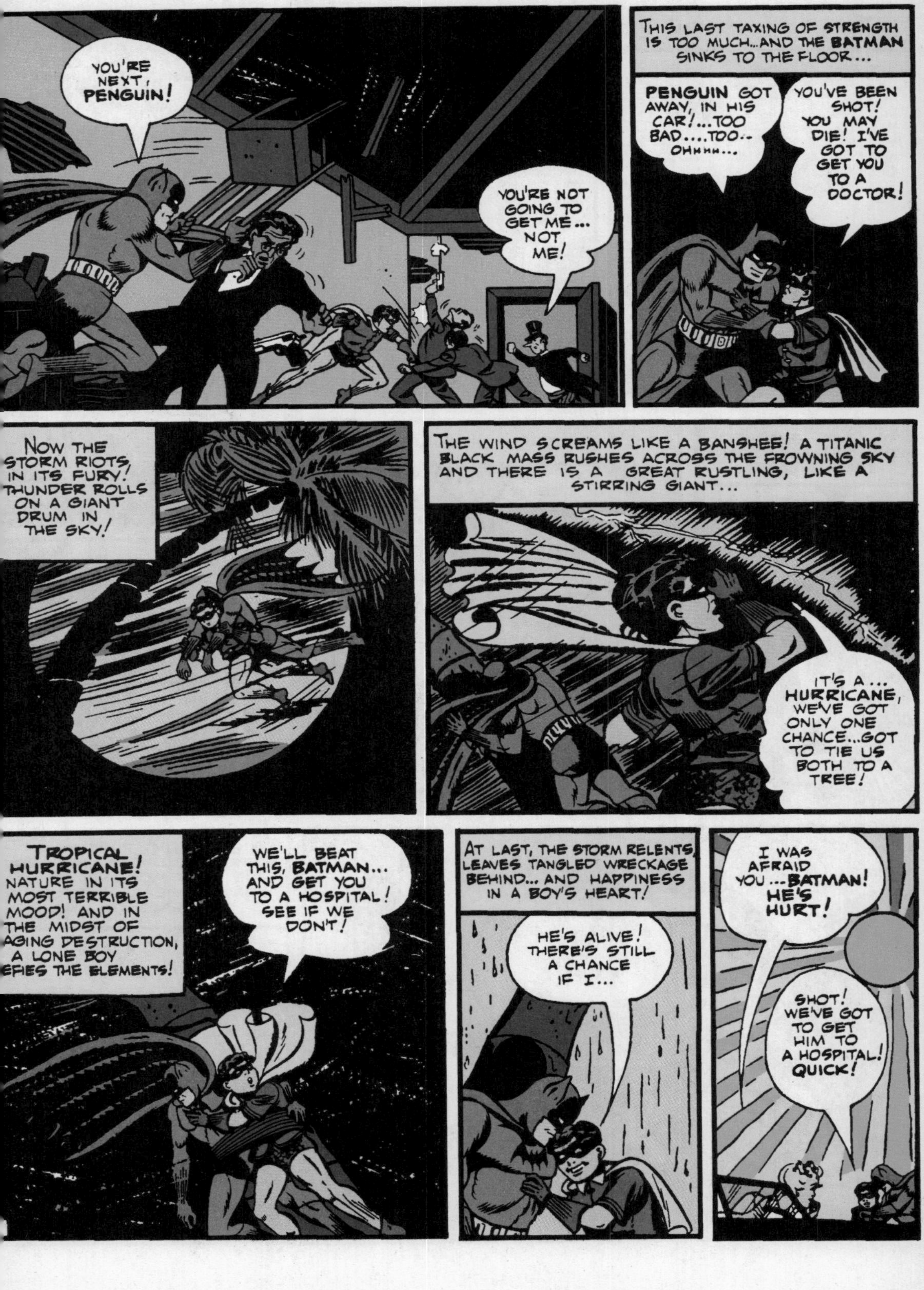
YOU'RE NEXT, PENGUIN!
YOU'RE NOT GOING TO GET ME... NOT ME!
THIS LAST TAXING OF STRENGTH IS TOO MUCH...AND THE BATMAN SINKS TO THE FLOOR...
PENGUIN GOT AWAY, IN HIS CAR!...TOO BAD....TOO.. OHHHHH....
YOU'VE BEEN SHOT! YOU MAY DIE! I'VE GOT TO GET YOU TO A DOCTOR!
NOW THE STORM RIOTS IN ITS FURY! THUNDER ROLLS ON A GIANT DRUM IN THE SKY!
THE WIND SCREAMS LIKE A BANSHEE! A TITANIC BLACK MASS RUSHES ACROSS THE FROWNING SKY AND THERE IS A GREAT RUSTLING, LIKE A STIRRING GIANT...
IT'S A... HURRICANE, WE'VE GOT ONLY ONE CHANCE...GOT TO TIE US BOTH TO A TREE!
TROPICAL HURRICANE! NATURE IN ITS MOST TERRIBLE MOOD! AND IN THE MIDST OF AGING DESTRUCTION, A LONE BOY EFIES THE ELEMENTS!
WE'LL BEAT THIS, BATMAN... AND GET YOU TO A HOSPITAL! SEE IF WE DON'T!
AT LAST, THE STORM RELENTS, LEAVES TANGLED WRECKAGE BEHIND... AND HAPPINESS IN A BOY'S HEART!
HE'S ALIVE! THERE'S STILL A CHANCE IF I...
I WAS AFRAID YOU...BATMAN! HE'S HURT!
SHOT! WE'VE GOT TO GET HIM TO A HOSPITAL! QUICK!

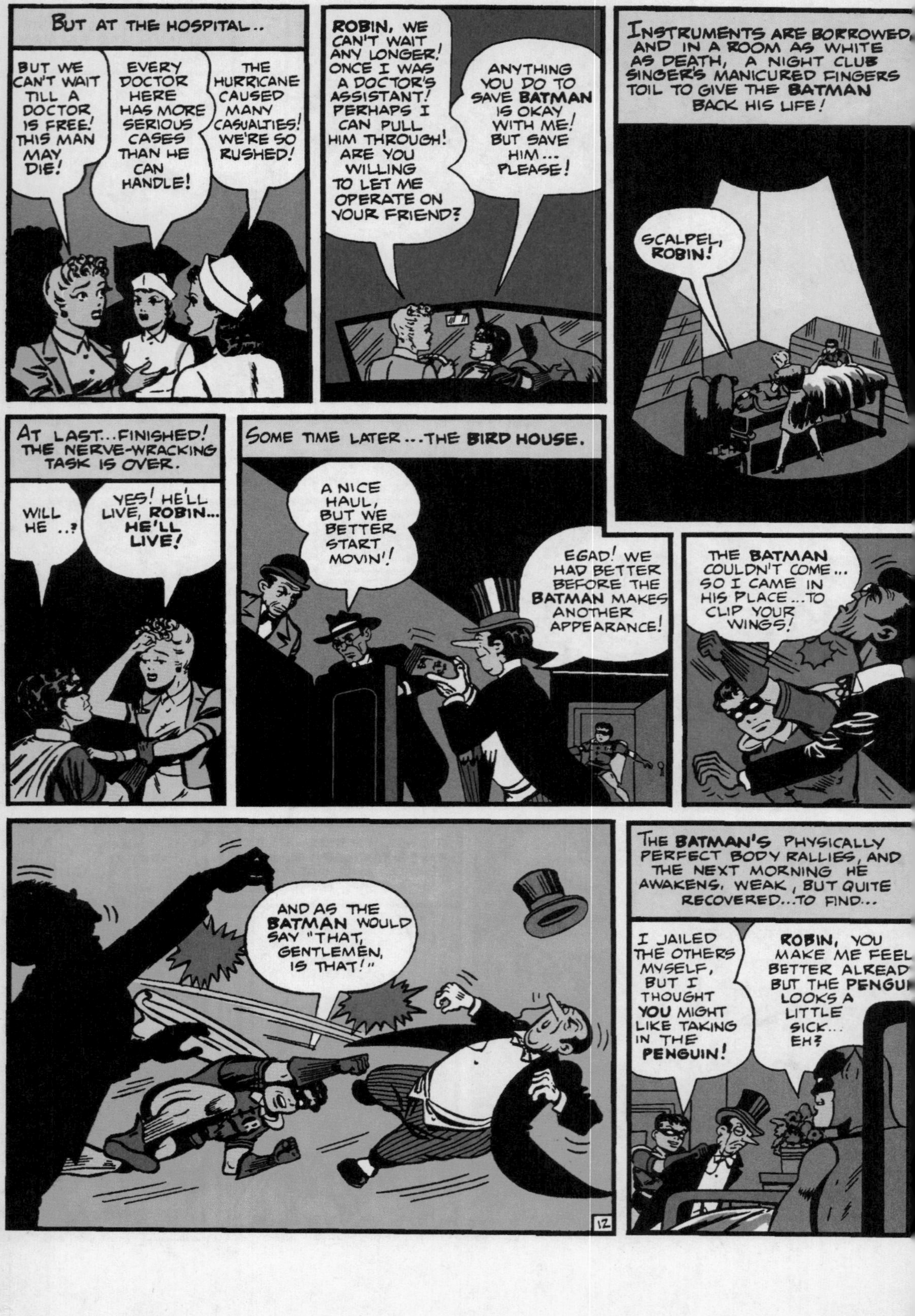
BUT AT THE HOSPITAL..
BUT WE CAN'T WAIT TILL A DOCTOR IS FREE! THIS MAN MAY DIE!
EVERY DOCTOR HERE HAS MORE SERIOUS CASES THAN HE CAN HANDLE!
THE HURRICANE CAUSED MANY CASUALTIES! WE'RE SO RUSHED!
ROBIN, WE CAN'T WAIT ANY LONGER! ONCE I WAS A DOCTOR'S ASSISTANT! PERHAPS I CAN PULL HIM THROUGH! ARE YOU WILLING TO LET ME OPERATE ON YOUR FRIEND?
ANYTHING YOU DO TO SAVE BATMAN IS OKAY WITH ME! BUT SAVE HIM... PLEASE!
INSTRUMENTS ARE BORROWED, AND IN A ROOM AS WHITE AS DEATH, A NIGHT CLUB SINGER'S MANICURED FINGERS TOIL TO GIVE THE BATMAN BACK HIS LIFE!
SCALPEL, ROBIN!
AT LAST...FINISHED! THE NERVE-WRACKING TASK IS OVER.
WILL HE ..?
YES! HE'LL LIVE, ROBIN... HE'LL LIVE!
SOME TIME LATER... THE BIRD HOUSE.
A NICE HAUL, BUT WE BETTER START MOVIN'!
EGAD! WE HAD BETTER BEFORE THE BATMAN MAKES ANOTHER APPEARANCE!
THE BATMAN COULDN'T COME... SO I CAME IN HIS PLACE...TO CLIP YOUR WINGS!
AND AS THE BATMAN WOULD SAY "THAT, GENTLEMEN, IS THAT!"
12
THE BATMAN'S PHYSICALLY PERFECT BODY RALLIES, AND THE NEXT MORNING HE AWAKENS, WEAK, BUT QUITE RECOVERED...TO FIND...
I JAILED THE OTHERS MYSELF, BUT I THOUGHT YOU MIGHT LIKE TAKING IN THE PENGUIN!
ROBIN, YOU MAKE ME FEEL BETTER ALREAD BUT THE PENGU LOOKS A LITTLE SICK... EH?

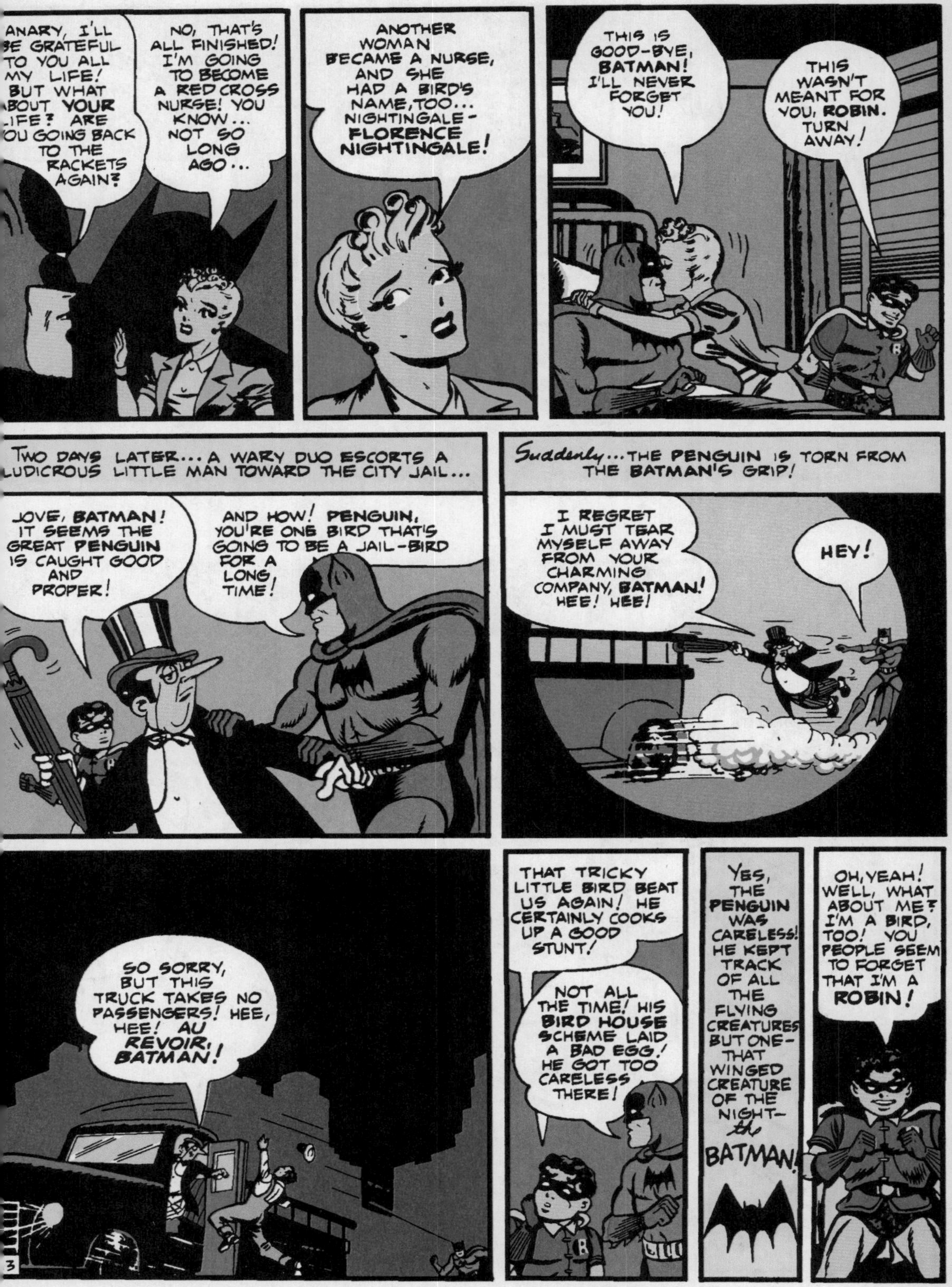
ANARY, I'LL BE GRATEFUL TO YOU ALL MY LIFE! BUT WHAT ABOUT YOUR LIFE? ARE OU GOING BACK TO THE RACKETS AGAIN?
NO, THAT'S ALL FINISHED! I'M GOING TO BECOME A RED CROSS NURSE! YOU KNOW... NOT SO LONG AGO...
ANOTHER WOMAN BECAME A NURSE, AND SHE HAD A BIRD'S NAME, TOO... NIGHTINGALE- FLORENCE NIGHTINGALE!
THIS IS GOOD-BYE, BATMAN! I'LL NEVER FORGET YOU!
THIS WASN'T MEANT FOR YOU, ROBIN. TURN AWAY!
TWO DAYS LATER... A WARY DUO ESCORTS A LUDICROUS LITTLE MAN TOWARD THE CITY JAIL...
JOVE, BATMAN! IT SEEMS THE GREAT PENGUIN IS CAUGHT GOOD AND PROPER!
AND HOW! PENGUIN, YOU'RE ONE BIRD THAT'S GOING TO BE A JAIL-BIRD FOR A LONG TIME!
Suddenly... THE PENGUIN IS TORN FROM THE BATMAN'S GRIP!
I REGRET I MUST TEAR MYSELF AWAY FROM YOUR CHARMING COMPANY, BATMAN! HEE! HEE!
HEY!
SO SORRY, BUT THIS TRUCK TAKES NO PASSENGERS! HEE, HEE! AU REVOIR, BATMAN!
3
THAT TRICKY LITTLE BIRD BEAT US AGAIN! HE CERTAINLY COOKS UP A GOOD STUNT!
NOT ALL THE TIME! HIS BIRD HOUSE SCHEME LAID A BAD EGG! HE GOT TOO CARELESS THERE!
YES, THE PENGUIN WAS CARELESS! HE KEPT TRACK OF ALL THE FLYING CREATURES BUT ONE- THAT WINGED CREATURE OF THE NIGHT- the BATMAN!
OH, YEAH! WELL, WHAT ABOUT ME? I'M A BIRD, TOO! YOU PEOPLE SEEM TO FORGET THAT I'M A ROBIN!

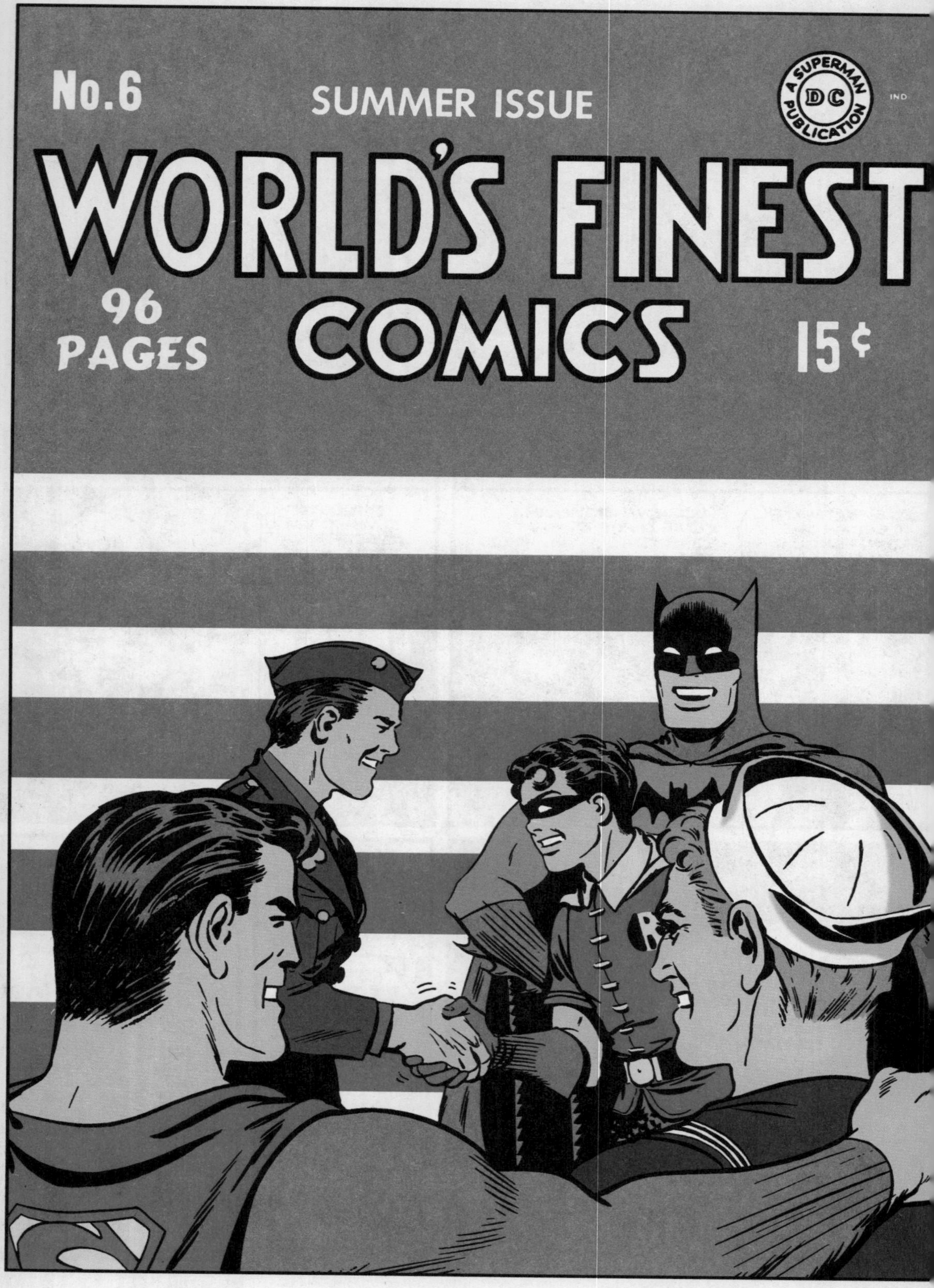
No.6
SUMMER ISSUE
A SUPERMAN DC PUBLICATION
IND
WORLD'S FINEST COMICS
96 PAGES
15¢

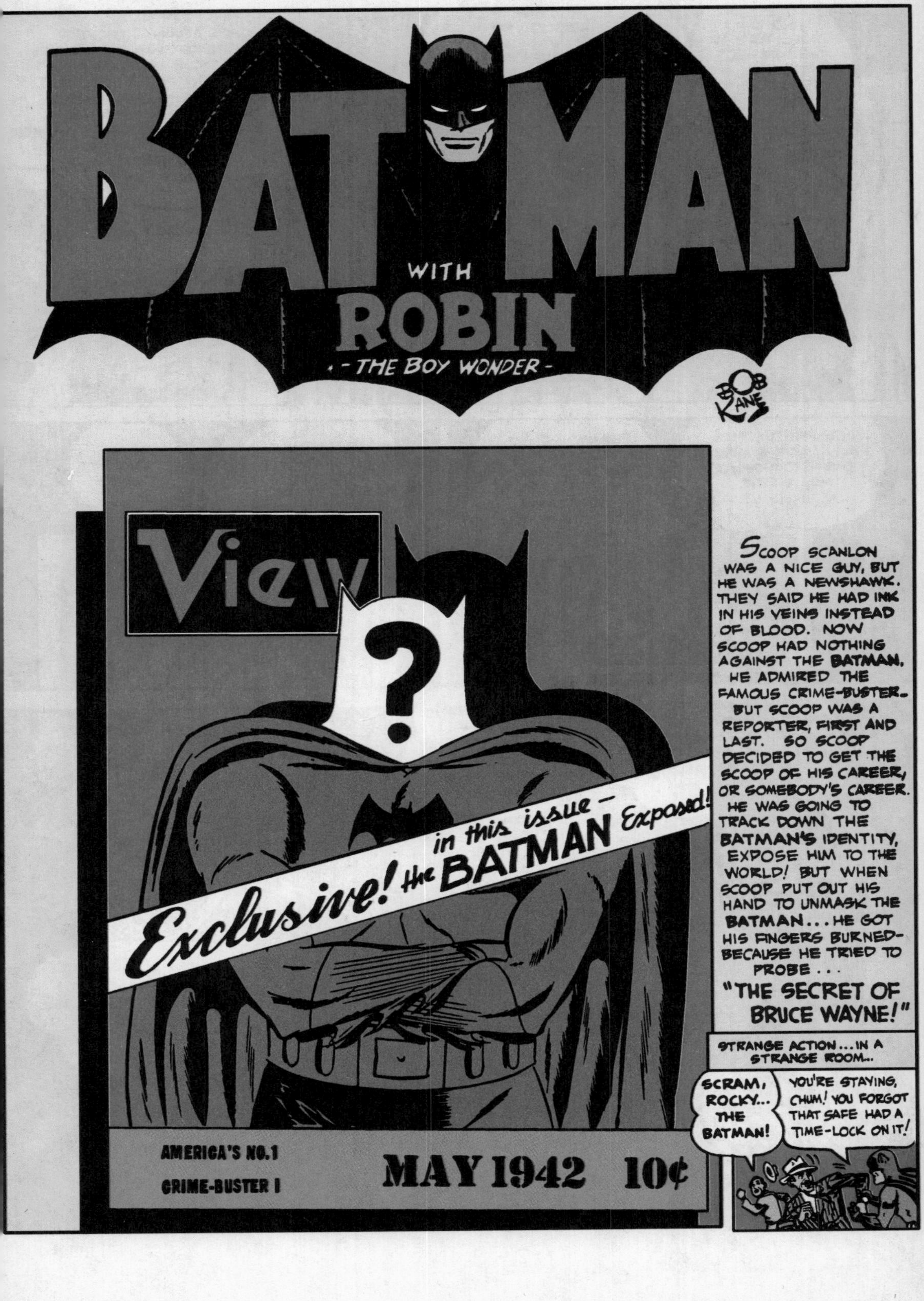
BATMAN
WITH
ROBIN
-THE BOY WONDER-
BOB KANE
View
Exclusive! in this issue— the BATMAN Exposed!
AMERICA'S NO.1
CRIME-BUSTER !
MAY 1942 10¢
SCOOP SCANLON WAS A NICE GUY, BUT HE WAS A NEWSHAWK. THEY SAID HE HAD INK IN HIS VEINS INSTEAD OF BLOOD. NOW SCOOP HAD NOTHING AGAINST THE BATMAN. HE ADMIRED THE FAMOUS CRIME-BUSTER- BUT SCOOP WAS A REPORTER, FIRST AND LAST. SO SCOOP DECIDED TO GET THE SCOOP OF HIS CAREER, OR SOMEBODY'S CAREER. HE WAS GOING TO TRACK DOWN THE BATMAN'S IDENTITY, EXPOSE HIM TO THE WORLD! BUT WHEN SCOOP PUT OUT HIS HAND TO UNMASK THE BATMAN... HE GOT HIS FINGERS BURNED- BECAUSE HE TRIED TO PROBE...
"THE SECRET OF BRUCE WAYNE!"
STRANGE ACTION... IN A STRANGE ROOM...
SCRAM, ROCKY... THE BATMAN!
YOU'RE STAYING, CHUM! YOU FORGOT THAT SAFE HAD A TIME-LOCK ON IT!

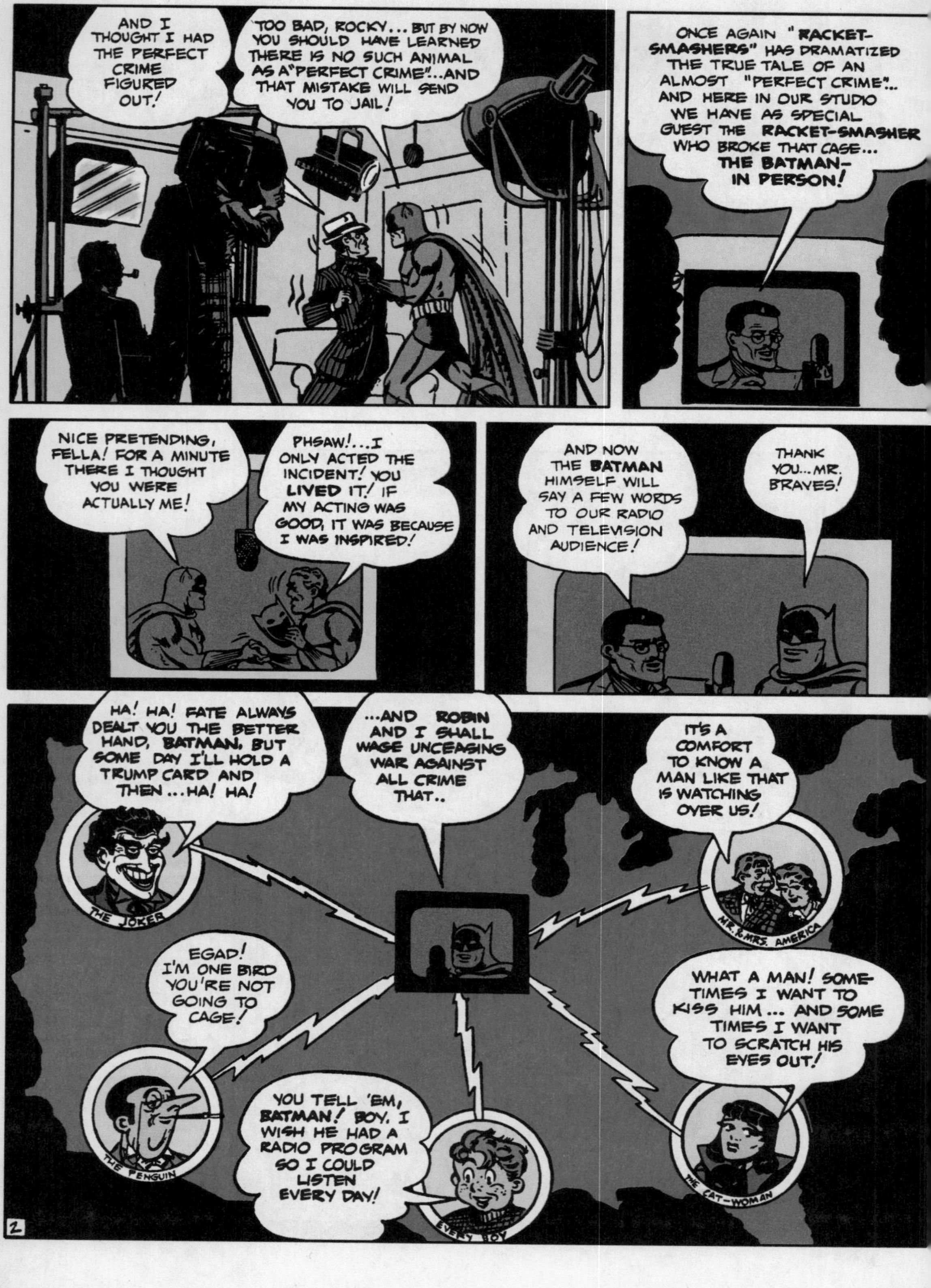
AND I THOUGHT I HAD THE PERFECT CRIME FIGURED OUT!
TOO BAD, ROCKY... BUT BY NOW YOU SHOULD HAVE LEARNED THERE IS NO SUCH ANIMAL AS A "PERFECT CRIME"...AND THAT MISTAKE WILL SEND YOU TO JAIL!
ONCE AGAIN "RACKET-SMASHERS" HAS DRAMATIZED THE TRUE TALE OF AN ALMOST "PERFECT CRIME"... AND HERE IN OUR STUDIO WE HAVE AS SPECIAL GUEST THE RACKET-SMASHER WHO BROKE THAT CASE... THE BATMAN-IN PERSON!
NICE PRETENDING, FELLA! FOR A MINUTE THERE I THOUGHT YOU WERE ACTUALLY ME!
PHSAW!...I ONLY ACTED THE INCIDENT! YOU LIVED IT! IF MY ACTING WAS GOOD, IT WAS BECAUSE I WAS INSPIRED!
AND NOW THE BATMAN HIMSELF WILL SAY A FEW WORDS TO OUR RADIO AND TELEVISION AUDIENCE!
THANK YOU... MR. BRAVES!
HA! HA! FATE ALWAYS DEALT YOU THE BETTER HAND, BATMAN, BUT SOME DAY I'LL HOLD A TRUMP CARD AND THEN...HA! HA!
...AND ROBIN AND I SHALL WAGE UNCEASING WAR AGAINST ALL CRIME THAT..
IT'S A COMFORT TO KNOW A MAN LIKE THAT IS WATCHING OVER US!
THE JOKER
MR. & MRS. AMERICA
EGAD! I'M ONE BIRD YOU'RE NOT GOING TO CAGE!
WHAT A MAN! SOMETIMES I WANT TO KISS HIM... AND SOMETIMES I WANT TO SCRATCH HIS EYES OUT!
YOU TELL 'EM, BATMAN! BOY, I WISH HE HAD A RADIO PROGRAM SO I COULD LISTEN EVERY DAY!
THE PENGUIN
EVERY BOY
THE CAT-WOMAN
2

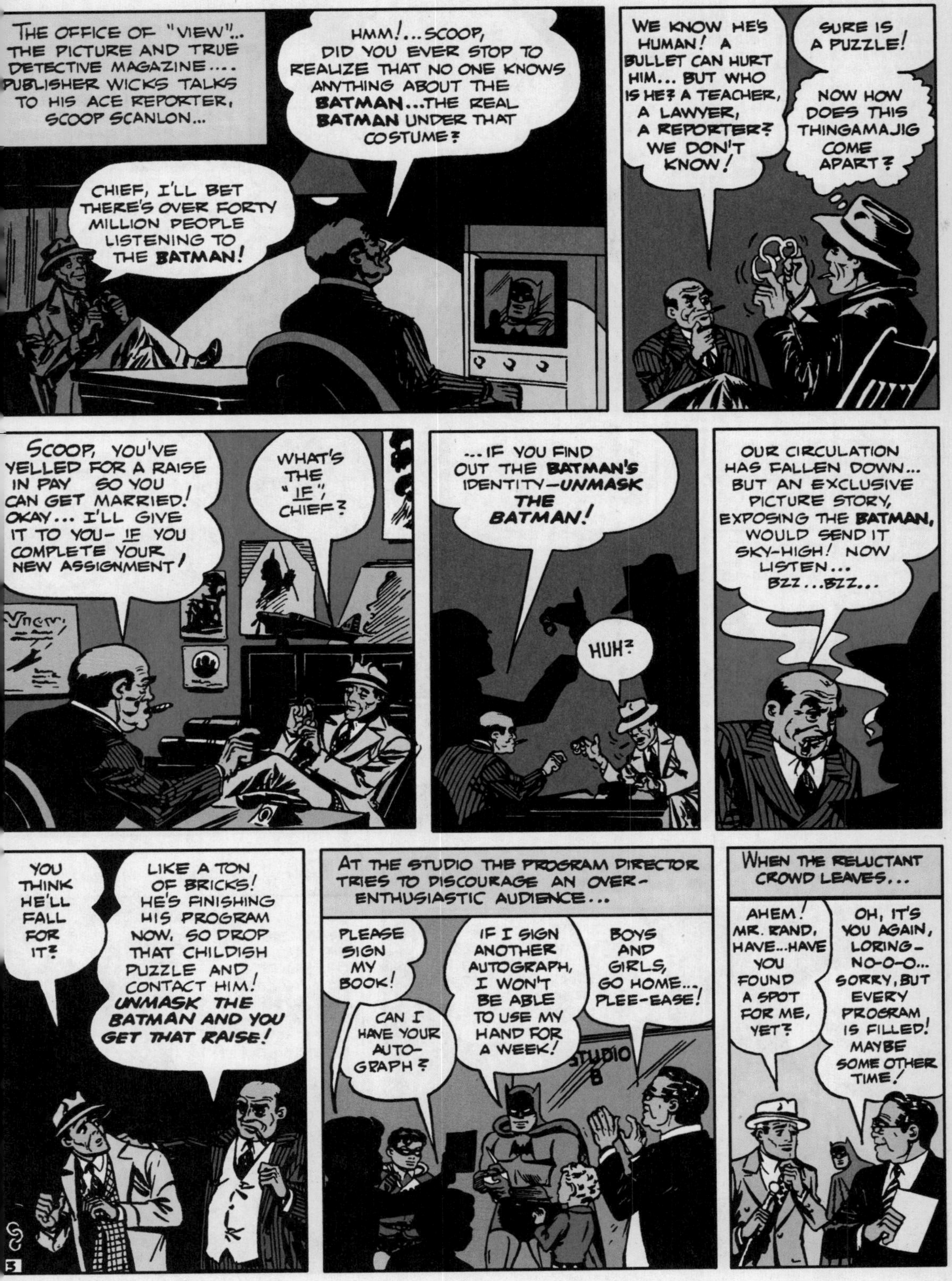
THE OFFICE OF "VIEW"... THE PICTURE AND TRUE DETECTIVE MAGAZINE.... PUBLISHER WICKS TALKS TO HIS ACE REPORTER, SCOOP SCANLON...
HMM!...SCOOP, DID YOU EVER STOP TO REALIZE THAT NO ONE KNOWS ANYTHING ABOUT THE **BATMAN**...THE REAL **BATMAN** UNDER THAT COSTUME?
CHIEF, I'LL BET THERE'S OVER FORTY MILLION PEOPLE LISTENING TO THE **BATMAN**!
WE KNOW HE'S HUMAN! A BULLET CAN HURT HIM... BUT WHO IS HE? A TEACHER, A LAWYER, A REPORTER? WE DON'T KNOW!
SURE IS A PUZZLE!
NOW HOW DOES THIS THINGAMAJIG COME APART?
SCOOP, YOU'VE YELLED FOR A RAISE IN PAY SO YOU CAN GET MARRIED! OKAY... I'LL GIVE IT TO YOU- IF YOU COMPLETE YOUR NEW ASSIGNMENT!
WHAT'S THE "IF", CHIEF?
...IF YOU FIND OUT THE **BATMAN'S** IDENTITY-**UNMASK THE BATMAN!**
HUH?
OUR CIRCULATION HAS FALLEN DOWN... BUT AN EXCLUSIVE PICTURE STORY, EXPOSING THE **BATMAN**, WOULD SEND IT SKY-HIGH! NOW LISTEN... BZZ...BZZ...
YOU THINK HE'LL FALL FOR IT?
LIKE A TON OF BRICKS! HE'S FINISHING HIS PROGRAM NOW. SO DROP THAT CHILDISH PUZZLE AND CONTACT HIM! ***UNMASK THE BATMAN AND YOU GET THAT RAISE!***
AT THE STUDIO THE PROGRAM DIRECTOR TRIES TO DISCOURAGE AN OVER-ENTHUSIASTIC AUDIENCE...
PLEASE SIGN MY BOOK!
CAN I HAVE YOUR AUTO-GRAPH?
IF I SIGN ANOTHER AUTOGRAPH, I WON'T BE ABLE TO USE MY HAND FOR A WEEK!
BOYS AND GIRLS, GO HOME... PLEE-EASE!
STUDIO 8
WHEN THE RELUCTANT CROWD LEAVES...
AHEM! MR. RAND, HAVE...HAVE YOU FOUND A SPOT FOR ME, YET?
OH, IT'S YOU AGAIN, LORING-NO-O-O... SORRY, BUT EVERY PROGRAM IS FILLED! MAYBE SOME OTHER TIME!
3

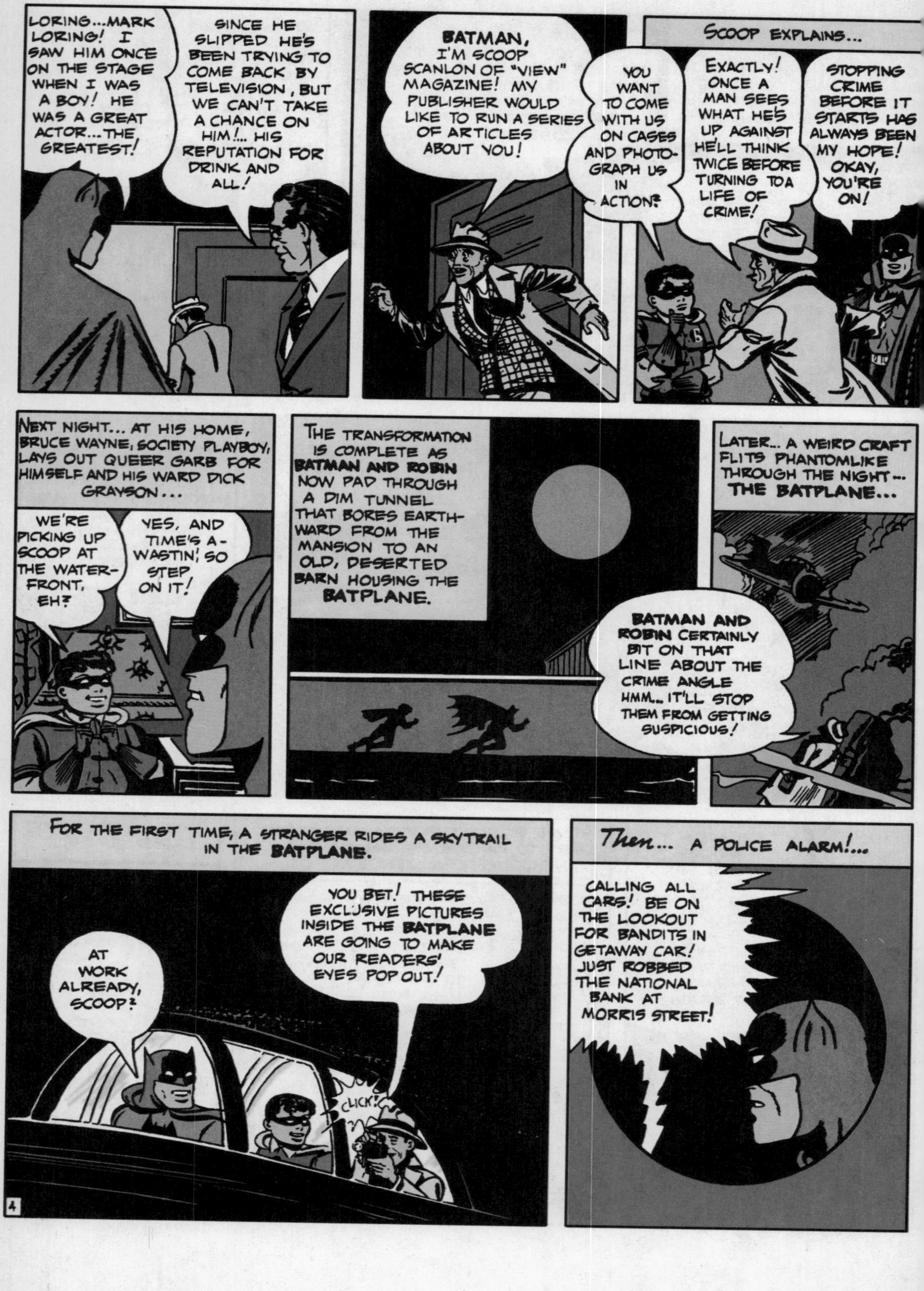
LORING...MARK LORING! I SAW HIM ONCE ON THE STAGE WHEN I WAS A BOY! HE WAS A GREAT ACTOR...THE GREATEST!
SINCE HE SLIPPED HE'S BEEN TRYING TO COME BACK BY TELEVISION, BUT WE CAN'T TAKE A CHANCE ON HIM!... HIS REPUTATION FOR DRINK AND ALL!
BATMAN, I'M SCOOP SCANLON OF "VIEW" MAGAZINE! MY PUBLISHER WOULD LIKE TO RUN A SERIES OF ARTICLES ABOUT YOU!
SCOOP EXPLAINS...
YOU WANT TO COME WITH US ON CASES AND PHOTOGRAPH US IN ACTION?
EXACTLY! ONCE A MAN SEES WHAT HE'S UP AGAINST HE'LL THINK TWICE BEFORE TURNING TO A LIFE OF CRIME!
STOPPING CRIME BEFORE IT STARTS HAS ALWAYS BEEN MY HOPE! OKAY, YOU'RE ON!
NEXT NIGHT... AT HIS HOME, BRUCE WAYNE, SOCIETY PLAYBOY, LAYS OUT QUEER GARB FOR HIMSELF AND HIS WARD DICK GRAYSON...
WE'RE PICKING UP SCOOP AT THE WATER-FRONT, EH?
YES, AND TIME'S A-WASTIN', SO STEP ON IT!
THE TRANSFORMATION IS COMPLETE AS BATMAN AND ROBIN NOW PAD THROUGH A DIM TUNNEL THAT BORES EARTHWARD FROM THE MANSION TO AN OLD, DESERTED BARN HOUSING THE BATPLANE.
LATER... A WEIRD CRAFT FLITS PHANTOMLIKE THROUGH THE NIGHT... THE BATPLANE...
BATMAN AND ROBIN CERTAINLY BIT ON THAT LINE ABOUT THE CRIME ANGLE HMM... IT'LL STOP THEM FROM GETTING SUSPICIOUS!
FOR THE FIRST TIME, A STRANGER RIDES A SKYTRAIL IN THE BATPLANE.
AT WORK ALREADY, SCOOP?
YOU BET! THESE EXCLUSIVE PICTURES INSIDE THE BATPLANE ARE GOING TO MAKE OUR READERS' EYES POP OUT!
CLICK!
4
THEN... A POLICE ALARM!...
CALLING ALL CARS! BE ON THE LOOKOUT FOR BANDITS IN GETAWAY CAR! JUST ROBBED THE NATIONAL BANK AT MORRIS STREET!

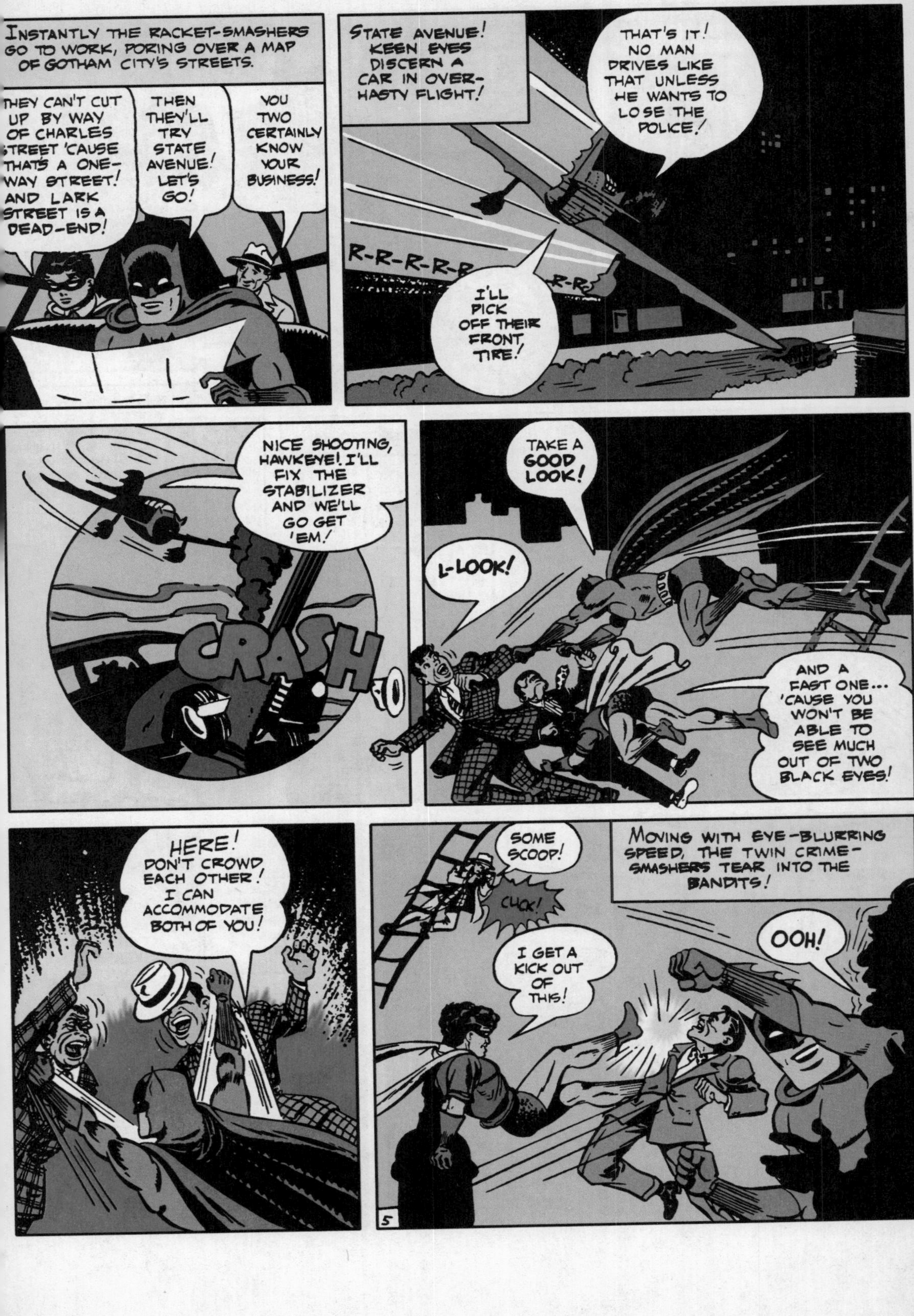
INSTANTLY THE RACKET-SMASHERS GO TO WORK, PORING OVER A MAP OF GOTHAM CITY'S STREETS.
THEY CAN'T CUT UP BY WAY OF CHARLES STREET 'CAUSE THAT'S A ONE-WAY STREET! AND LARK STREET IS A DEAD-END!
THEN THEY'LL TRY STATE AVENUE! LET'S GO!
YOU TWO CERTAINLY KNOW YOUR BUSINESS!
STATE AVENUE! KEEN EYES DISCERN A CAR IN OVER-HASTY FLIGHT!
THAT'S IT! NO MAN DRIVES LIKE THAT UNLESS HE WANTS TO LOSE THE POLICE!
R-R-R-R-R
R-R
I'LL PICK OFF THEIR FRONT TIRE!
NICE SHOOTING, HAWKEYE! I'LL FIX THE STABILIZER AND WE'LL GO GET 'EM!
CRASH
TAKE A GOOD LOOK!
L-LOOK!
AND A FAST ONE... 'CAUSE YOU WON'T BE ABLE TO SEE MUCH OUT OF TWO BLACK EYES!
HERE! DON'T CROWD EACH OTHER! I CAN ACCOMMODATE BOTH OF YOU!
SOME SCOOP!
CLICK!
MOVING WITH EYE-BLURRING SPEED, THE TWIN CRIME-SMASHERS TEAR INTO THE BANDITS!
OOH!
I GET A KICK OUT OF THIS!
5

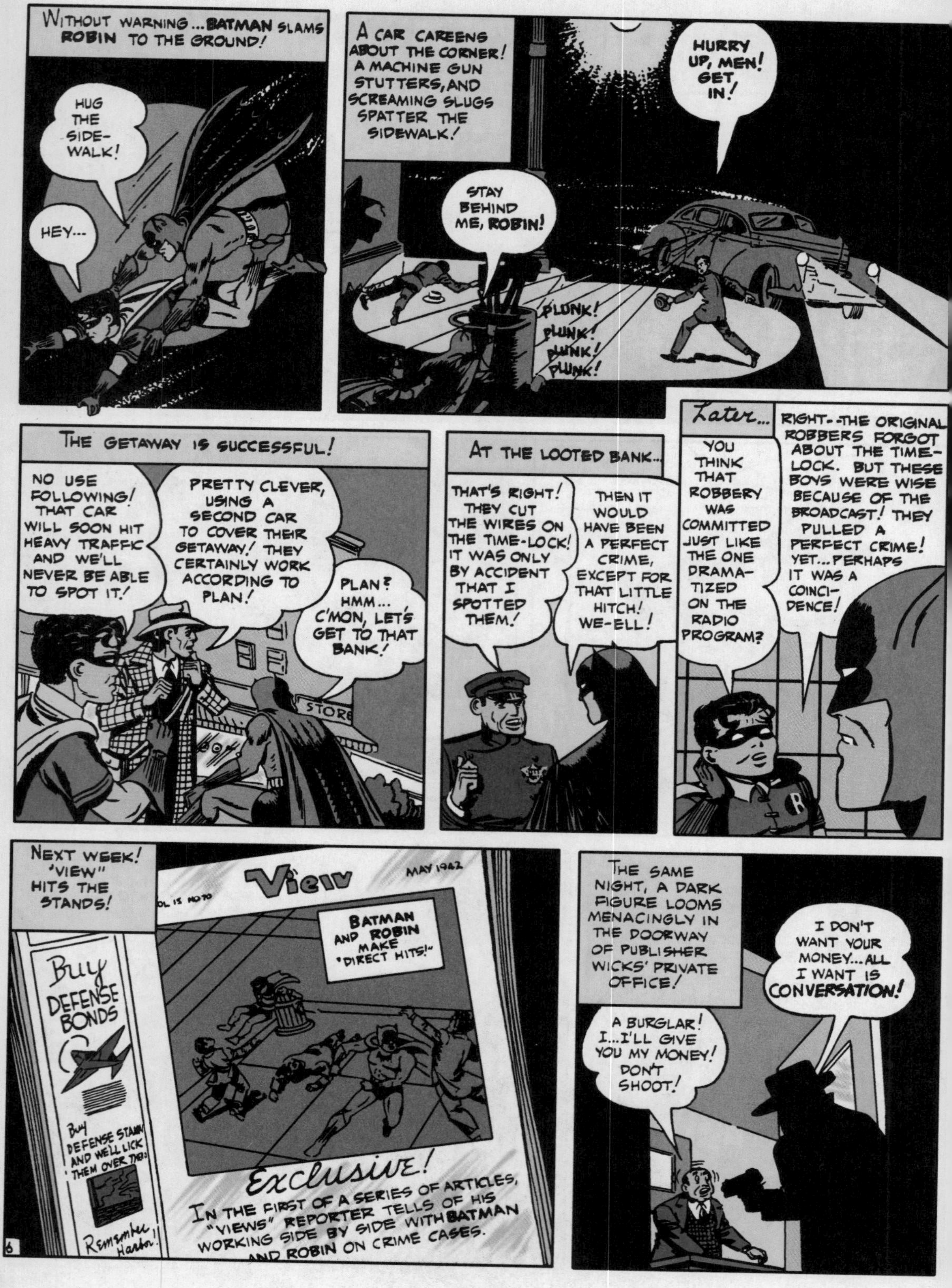
WITHOUT WARNING... BATMAN SLAMS ROBIN TO THE GROUND!
HUG THE SIDE-WALK!
HEY...
A CAR CAREENS ABOUT THE CORNER! A MACHINE GUN STUTTERS, AND SCREAMING SLUGS SPATTER THE SIDEWALK!
HURRY UP, MEN! GET IN!
STAY BEHIND ME, ROBIN!
PLUNK! PLUNK! PLUNK! PLUNK!
THE GETAWAY IS SUCCESSFUL!
NO USE FOLLOWING! THAT CAR WILL SOON HIT HEAVY TRAFFIC AND WE'LL NEVER BE ABLE TO SPOT IT!
PRETTY CLEVER, USING A SECOND CAR TO COVER THEIR GETAWAY! THEY CERTAINLY WORK ACCORDING TO PLAN!
PLAN? HMM... C'MON, LET'S GET TO THAT BANK!
STORE
AT THE LOOTED BANK...
THAT'S RIGHT! THEY CUT THE WIRES ON THE TIME-LOCK! IT WAS ONLY BY ACCIDENT THAT I SPOTTED THEM!
THEN IT WOULD HAVE BEEN A PERFECT CRIME, EXCEPT FOR THAT LITTLE HITCH! WE-ELL!
Later...
YOU THINK THAT ROBBERY WAS COMMITTED JUST LIKE THE ONE DRAMA-TIZED ON THE RADIO PROGRAM?
RIGHT--THE ORIGINAL ROBBERS FORGOT ABOUT THE TIME-LOCK. BUT THESE BOYS WERE WISE BECAUSE OF THE BROADCAST! THEY PULLED A PERFECT CRIME! YET... PERHAPS IT WAS A COINCI-DENCE!
NEXT WEEK! "VIEW" HITS THE STANDS!
View
MAY 1942
BATMAN AND ROBIN MAKE "DIRECT HITS!"
Exclusive!
IN THE FIRST OF A SERIES OF ARTICLES, "VIEWS" REPORTER TELLS OF HIS WORKING SIDE BY SIDE WITH BATMAN AND ROBIN ON CRIME CASES.
Buy DEFENSE BONDS
Buy DEFENSE STAMPS AND WE'LL LICK THEM OVER THERE
Remember Harbor!
6
THE SAME NIGHT, A DARK FIGURE LOOMS MENACINGLY IN THE DOORWAY OF PUBLISHER WICKS' PRIVATE OFFICE!
A BURGLAR! I...I'LL GIVE YOU MY MONEY! DON'T SHOOT!
I DON'T WANT YOUR MONEY... ALL I WANT IS CONVERSATION!

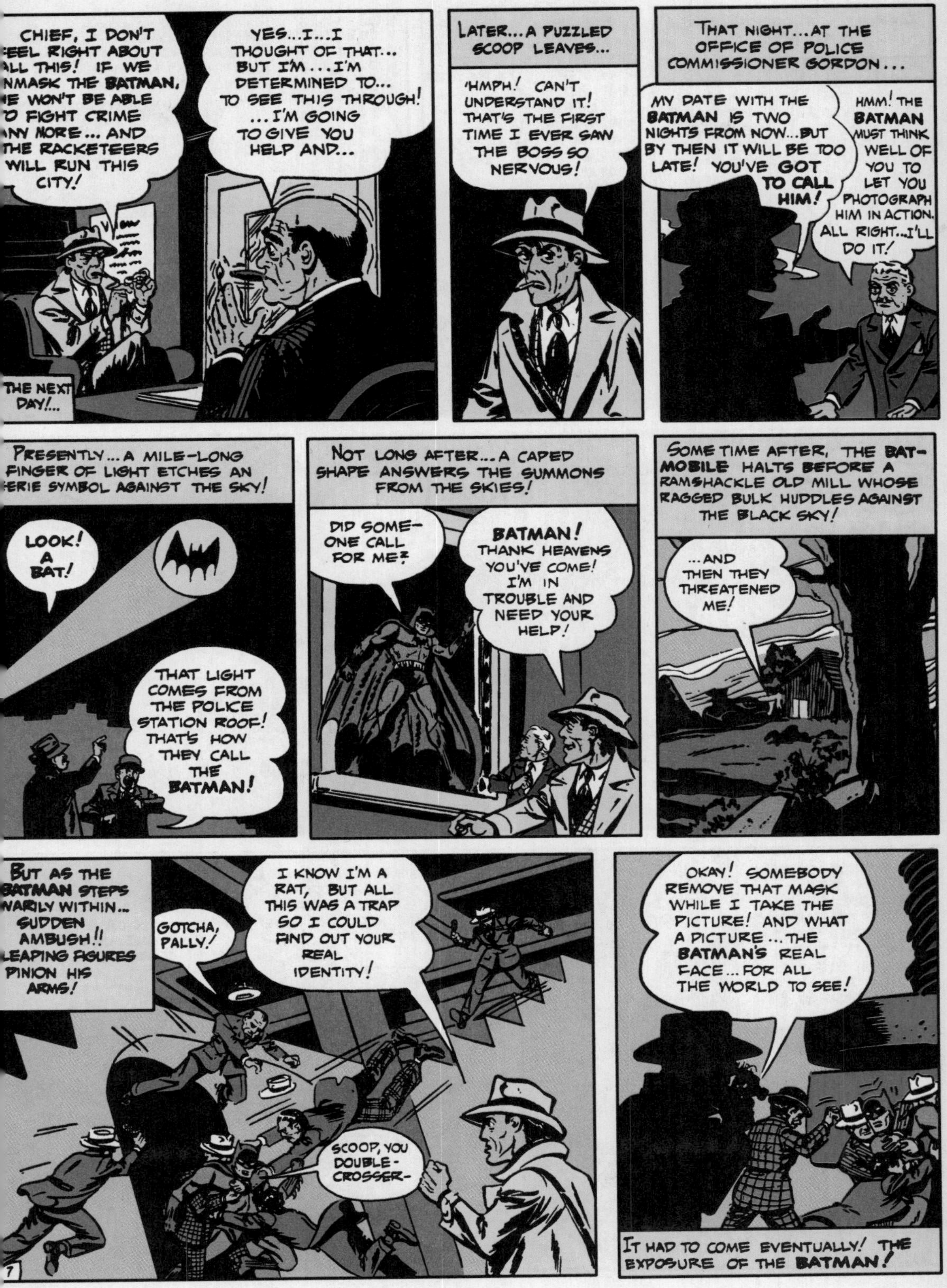
CHIEF, I DON'T EEL RIGHT ABOUT LL THIS! IF WE NMASK THE BATMAN, E WON'T BE ABLE O FIGHT CRIME NY MORE... AND THE RACKETEERS WILL RUN THIS CITY!
YES... I... I THOUGHT OF THAT... BUT I'M... I'M DETERMINED TO... TO SEE THIS THROUGH! ... I'M GOING TO GIVE YOU HELP AND...
THE NEXT DAY!...
LATER... A PUZZLED SCOOP LEAVES...
'HMPH! CAN'T UNDERSTAND IT! THAT'S THE FIRST TIME I EVER SAW THE BOSS SO NERVOUS!
THAT NIGHT... AT THE OFFICE OF POLICE COMMISSIONER GORDON...
MY DATE WITH THE BATMAN IS TWO NIGHTS FROM NOW... BUT BY THEN IT WILL BE TOO LATE! YOU'VE GOT TO CALL HIM!
HMM! THE BATMAN MUST THINK WELL OF YOU TO LET YOU PHOTOGRAPH HIM IN ACTION. ALL RIGHT... I'LL DO IT!
PRESENTLY... A MILE-LONG FINGER OF LIGHT ETCHES AN ERIE SYMBOL AGAINST THE SKY!
LOOK! A BAT!
THAT LIGHT COMES FROM THE POLICE STATION ROOF! THAT'S HOW THEY CALL THE BATMAN!
NOT LONG AFTER... A CAPED SHAPE ANSWERS THE SUMMONS FROM THE SKIES!
DID SOME-ONE CALL FOR ME?
BATMAN! THANK HEAVENS YOU'VE COME! I'M IN TROUBLE AND NEED YOUR HELP!
SOME TIME AFTER, THE BAT-MOBILE HALTS BEFORE A RAMSHACKLE OLD MILL WHOSE RAGGED BULK HUDDLES AGAINST THE BLACK SKY!
...AND THEN THEY THREATENED ME!
BUT AS THE BATMAN STEPS WARILY WITHIN... SUDDEN AMBUSH!! LEAPING FIGURES PINION HIS ARMS!
GOTCHA, PALLY!
I KNOW I'M A RAT, BUT ALL THIS WAS A TRAP SO I COULD FIND OUT YOUR REAL IDENTITY!
SCOOP, YOU DOUBLE-CROSSER-
7
OKAY! SOMEBODY REMOVE THAT MASK WHILE I TAKE THE PICTURE! AND WHAT A PICTURE... THE BATMAN'S REAL FACE... FOR ALL THE WORLD TO SEE!
IT HAD TO COME EVENTUALLY! THE EXPOSURE OF THE BATMAN!

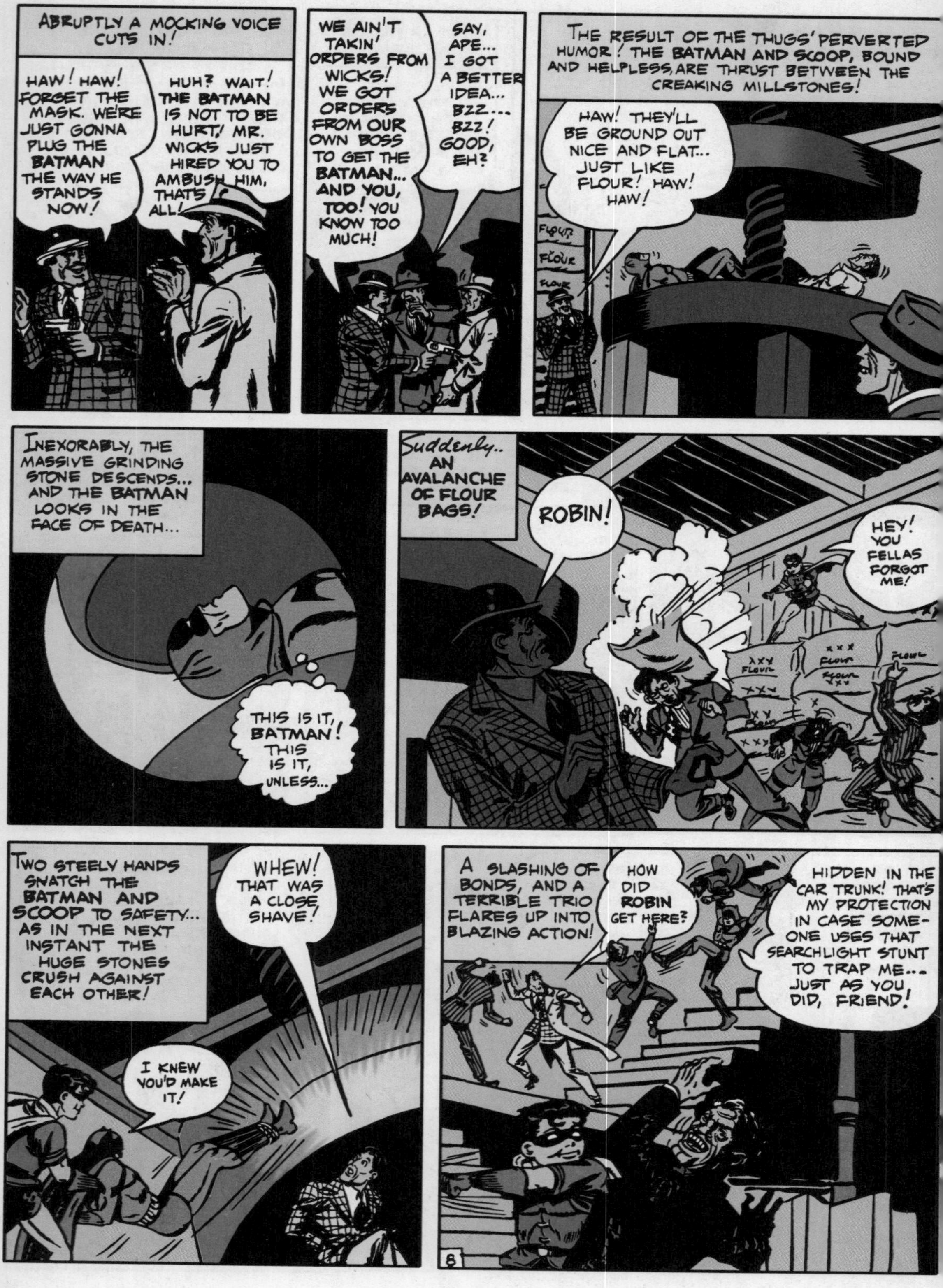

ABRUPTLY A MOCKING VOICE CUTS IN!
HAW! HAW! FORGET THE MASK. WE'RE JUST GONNA PLUG THE BATMAN THE WAY HE STANDS NOW!
HUH? WAIT! THE BATMAN IS NOT TO BE HURT! MR. WICKS JUST HIRED YOU TO AMBUSH HIM, THAT'S ALL!
WE AIN'T TAKIN' ORDERS FROM WICKS! WE GOT ORDERS FROM OUR OWN BOSS TO GET THE BATMAN... AND YOU, TOO! YOU KNOW TOO MUCH!
SAY, APE... I GOT A BETTER IDEA... BZZ... BZZ! GOOD, EH?
THE RESULT OF THE THUGS' PERVERTED HUMOR! THE BATMAN AND SCOOP, BOUND AND HELPLESS, ARE THRUST BETWEEN THE CREAKING MILLSTONES!
HAW! THEY'LL BE GROUND OUT NICE AND FLAT... JUST LIKE FLOUR! HAW! HAW!
FLOUR
FLOUR
FLOUR
INEXORABLY, THE MASSIVE GRINDING STONE DESCENDS... AND THE BATMAN LOOKS IN THE FACE OF DEATH...
THIS IS IT, BATMAN! THIS IS IT, UNLESS...
Suddenly.. AN AVALANCHE OF FLOUR BAGS!
ROBIN!
HEY! YOU FELLAS FORGOT ME!
FLOUR
FLOUR
FLOUR
FLOUR
TWO STEELY HANDS SNATCH THE BATMAN AND SCOOP TO SAFETY... AS IN THE NEXT INSTANT THE HUGE STONES CRUSH AGAINST EACH OTHER!
WHEW! THAT WAS A CLOSE SHAVE!
I KNEW YOU'D MAKE IT!
A SLASHING OF BONDS, AND A TERRIBLE TRIO FLARES UP INTO BLAZING ACTION!
HOW DID ROBIN GET HERE?
HIDDEN IN THE CAR TRUNK! THAT'S MY PROTECTION IN CASE SOME-ONE USES THAT SEARCHLIGHT STUNT TO TRAP ME... JUST AS YOU DID, FRIEND!
8

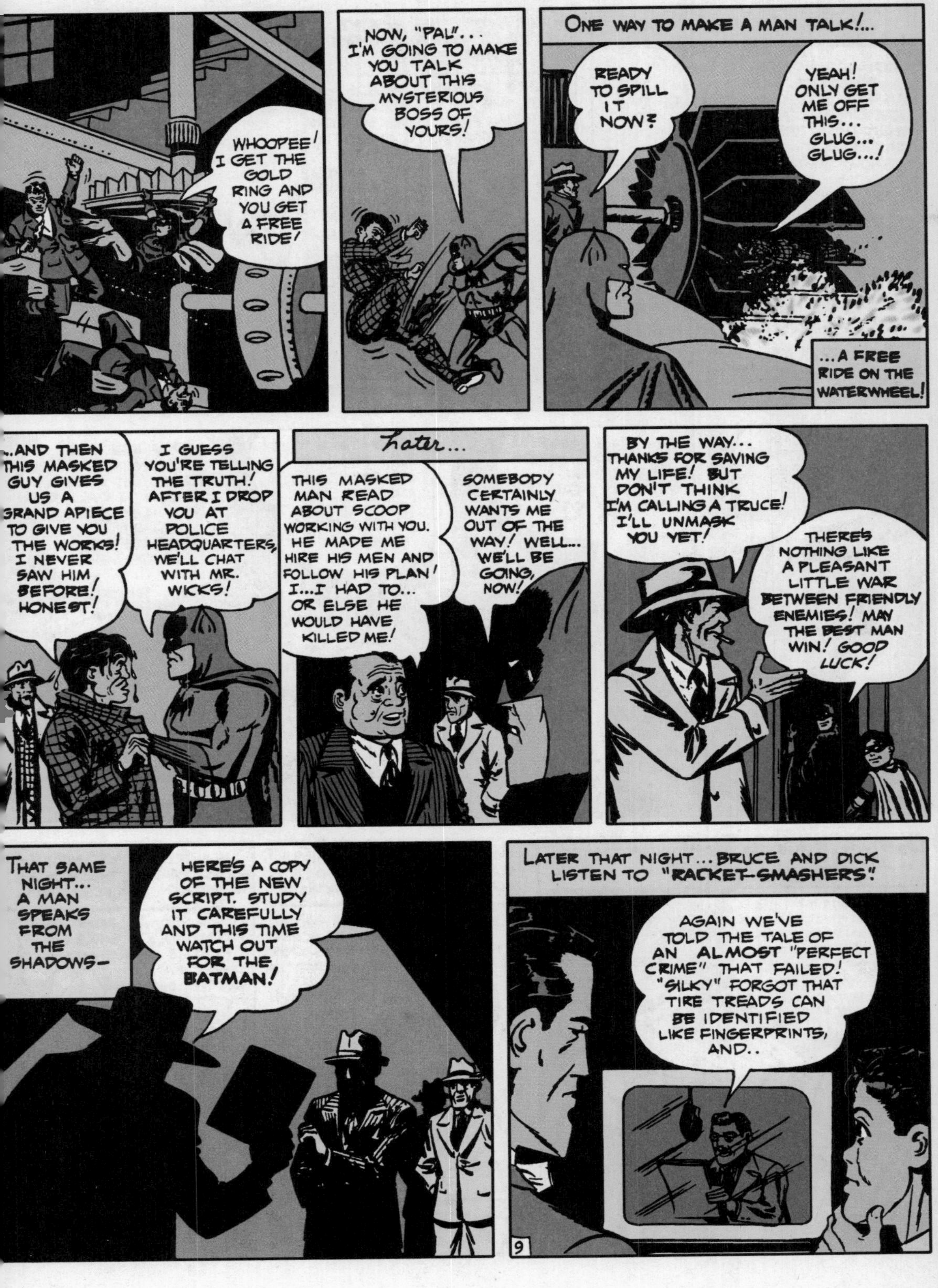

WHOOPEE! I GET THE GOLD RING AND YOU GET A FREE RIDE!
NOW, "PAL!"... I'M GOING TO MAKE YOU TALK ABOUT THIS MYSTERIOUS BOSS OF YOURS!
ONE WAY TO MAKE A MAN TALK!...
READY TO SPILL IT NOW?
YEAH! ONLY GET ME OFF THIS... GLUG... GLUG...!
...A FREE RIDE ON THE WATERWHEEL!
..AND THEN THIS MASKED GUY GIVES US A GRAND APIECE TO GIVE YOU THE WORKS! I NEVER SAW HIM BEFORE! HONEST!
I GUESS YOU'RE TELLING THE TRUTH! AFTER I DROP YOU AT POLICE HEADQUARTERS, WE'LL CHAT WITH MR. WICKS!
Later...
THIS MASKED MAN READ ABOUT SCOOP WORKING WITH YOU. HE MADE ME HIRE HIS MEN AND FOLLOW HIS PLAN! I...I HAD TO... OR ELSE HE WOULD HAVE KILLED ME!
SOMEBODY CERTAINLY WANTS ME OUT OF THE WAY! WELL... WE'LL BE GOING, NOW!
BY THE WAY... THANKS FOR SAVING MY LIFE! BUT DON'T THINK I'M CALLING A TRUCE! I'LL UNMASK YOU YET!
THERE'S NOTHING LIKE A PLEASANT LITTLE WAR BETWEEN FRIENDLY ENEMIES! MAY THE BEST MAN WIN! GOOD LUCK!
THAT SAME NIGHT... A MAN SPEAKS FROM THE SHADOWS—
HERE'S A COPY OF THE NEW SCRIPT. STUDY IT CAREFULLY AND THIS TIME WATCH OUT FOR THE BATMAN!
LATER THAT NIGHT... BRUCE AND DICK LISTEN TO "RACKET-SMASHERS"!
AGAIN WE'VE TOLD THE TALE OF AN ALMOST "PERFECT CRIME" THAT FAILED! "SILKY" FORGOT THAT TIRE TREADS CAN BE IDENTIFIED LIKE FINGERPRINTS, AND..
9

Panel 1 (The Next Day..):

THE NEXT DAY..

LOOK! A ROBBERY PULLED EXACTLY AS IT WAS DRAMATIZED OVER "RACKET-SMASHERS" THE OTHER NIGHT... BUT THIS TIME WITHOUT MISTAKES!

THAT CLINCHES IT! THIS IS NO COINCIDENCE! PUT ON YOUR DUDS! WE'VE GOT WORK TO DO!

Panel 2:

FIRST STOP! THE SCRIPT WRITER OF "RACKET-SMASHERS," MR. BRENT!

WHERE DO YOU GET THE MATERIAL FOR YOUR SCRIPTS?

POLICE RECORDS! POLICE CHIEFS COOPERATE WITH US! I GET INSIDE INFORMATION! BUT WHAT BUSINESS IS IT OF YOURS?

Panel 3:

NEXT STOP! THE PROGRAM DIRECTOR, MR. RAND!

YOU SAY THE SCRIPTS ARE GIVEN TO THE ACTORS A WEEK IN ADVANCE?

THIS IS A TELEVISION PROGRAM! OUR ACTORS CAN'T READ FROM SCRIPTS! ONLY THE ANNOUNCER, GRAVES, DOES THAT... AND HE'S GIVEN THE SCRIPT THE DAY BEFORE WE GO ON!

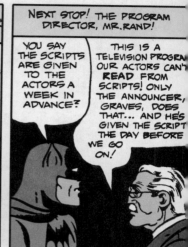

Panel 4:

LORING AGAIN! NO... I'M SORRY, BUT THERE'S NO OPENING YET!

PLEASE, I MUST HAVE WORK... OTHERWISE, I MUST SELL MY OLD COSTUMES AND...

Panel 5:

HERE, TAKE THIS! OH, IT'S NOT CHARITY! JUST A LOAN... TILL YOU GET A BIG PART AGAIN!

GOD BLESS YOU, SIR! I'M INDEBTED TO YOU! IF EVER I CAN SERVE YOU IN SOME WAY, DO NOT HESITATE TO CALL ON ME!

Panel 6:

AND WHILE THE BATMAN INVESTIGATES... SO DOES ANOTHER..

THIS FILE ON THE BATMAN SHOULD GIVE ME PLENTY OF DOPE! THE JOKER... THE PENGUIN... WHAT A PAIR! WONDER WHERE THEY ARE NOW?

Panel 7:

AS SCOOP SCANS THE FILES, SUDDENLY A QUEER FACT COMES TO HIS ATTENTION!

THIS PLAYBOY, BRUCE WAYNE... HE'S BEEN ON THE SCENE OF SEVERAL CASES! "THE SUPERSTITION MURDERS" "THE CASE OF THE PROPHETIC CRIMES." I WONDER NOW!

Panel 8:

THE MORE THE ACE NEWS-HOUND READS, THE MORE HE BECOMES CONVINCED THAT...

BRUCE WAYNE MUST BE THE BATMAN! I'M SURE OF IT! WHY IS HE ALWAYS AROUND IN CASES THAT INVOLVE BATMAN? WHY? THERE'S ONLY ONE POSSIBLE ANSWER!

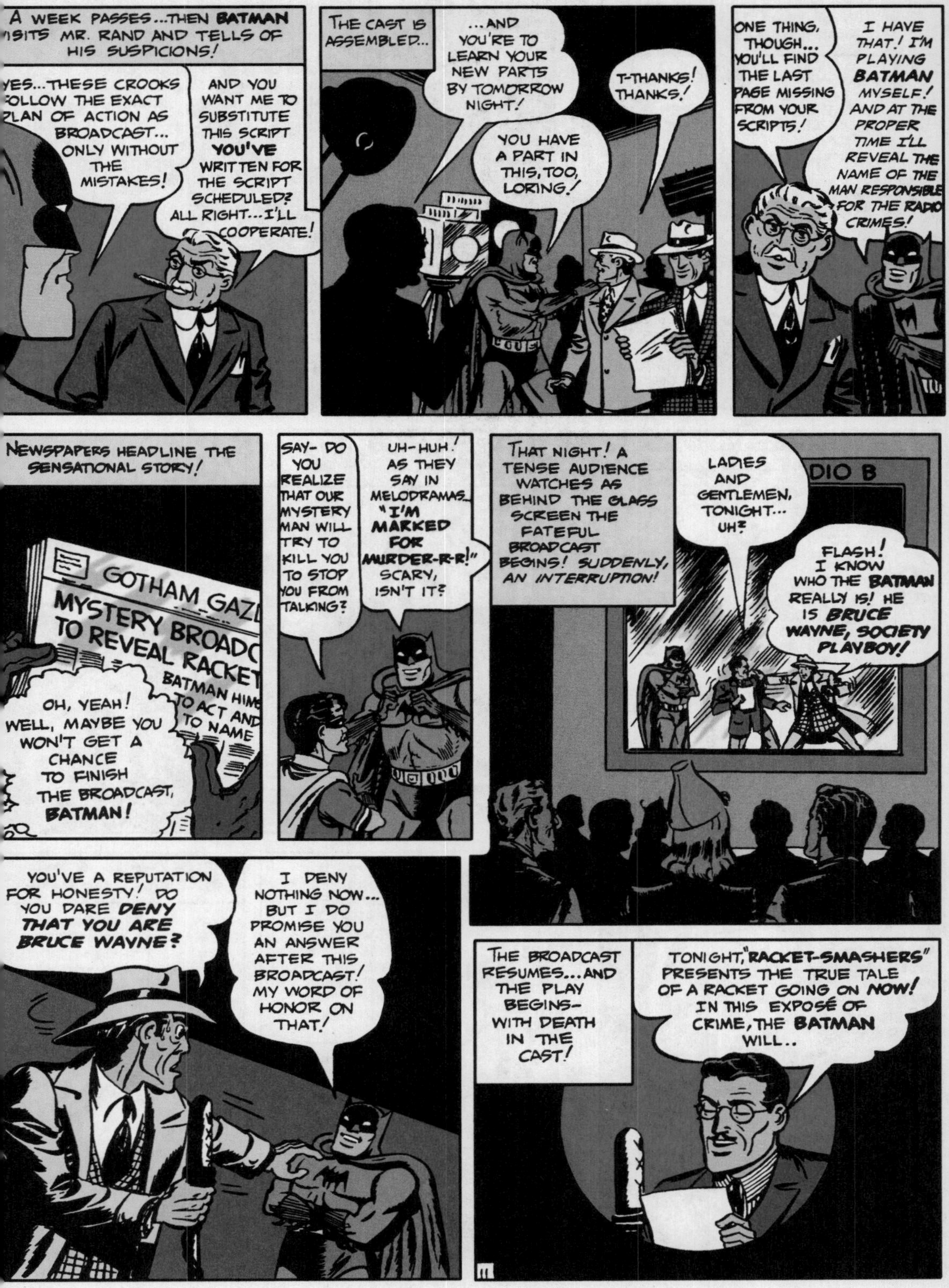
A WEEK PASSES...THEN BATMAN VISITS MR. RAND AND TELLS OF HIS SUSPICIONS!
YES...THESE CROOKS FOLLOW THE EXACT PLAN OF ACTION AS BROADCAST... ONLY WITHOUT THE MISTAKES!
AND YOU WANT ME TO SUBSTITUTE THIS SCRIPT YOU'VE WRITTEN FOR THE SCRIPT SCHEDULED? ALL RIGHT...I'LL COOPERATE!
THE CAST IS ASSEMBLED...
...AND YOU'RE TO LEARN YOUR NEW PARTS BY TOMORROW NIGHT!
T-THANKS! THANKS!
YOU HAVE A PART IN THIS, TOO, LORING!
ONE THING, THOUGH... YOU'LL FIND THE LAST PAGE MISSING FROM YOUR SCRIPTS!
I HAVE THAT! I'M PLAYING BATMAN MYSELF! AND AT THE PROPER TIME I'LL REVEAL THE NAME OF THE MAN RESPONSIBLE FOR THE RADIO CRIMES!
NEWSPAPERS HEADLINE THE SENSATIONAL STORY!
GOTHAM GAZ
MYSTERY BROADC
TO REVEAL RACKET
BATMAN HIM
TO ACT AND
TO NAME
OH, YEAH! WELL, MAYBE YOU WON'T GET A CHANCE TO FINISH THE BROADCAST, BATMAN!
SAY- DO YOU REALIZE THAT OUR MYSTERY MAN WILL TRY TO KILL YOU TO STOP YOU FROM TALKING?
UH-HUH! AS THEY SAY IN MELODRAMAS, "I'M MARKED FOR MURDER-R-R!" SCARY, ISN'T IT?
THAT NIGHT! A TENSE AUDIENCE WATCHES AS BEHIND THE GLASS SCREEN THE FATEFUL BROADCAST BEGINS! SUDDENLY, AN INTERRUPTION!
DIO B
LADIES AND GENTLEMEN, TONIGHT... UH?
FLASH! I KNOW WHO THE BATMAN REALLY IS! HE IS BRUCE WAYNE, SOCIETY PLAYBOY!
YOU'VE A REPUTATION FOR HONESTY! DO YOU DARE DENY THAT YOU ARE BRUCE WAYNE?
I DENY NOTHING NOW... BUT I DO PROMISE YOU AN ANSWER AFTER THIS BROADCAST! MY WORD OF HONOR ON THAT!
THE BROADCAST RESUMES...AND THE PLAY BEGINS- WITH DEATH IN THE CAST!
TONIGHT, "RACKET-SMASHERS" PRESENTS THE TRUE TALE OF A RACKET GOING ON NOW! IN THIS EXPOSÉ OF CRIME, THE BATMAN WILL..
11

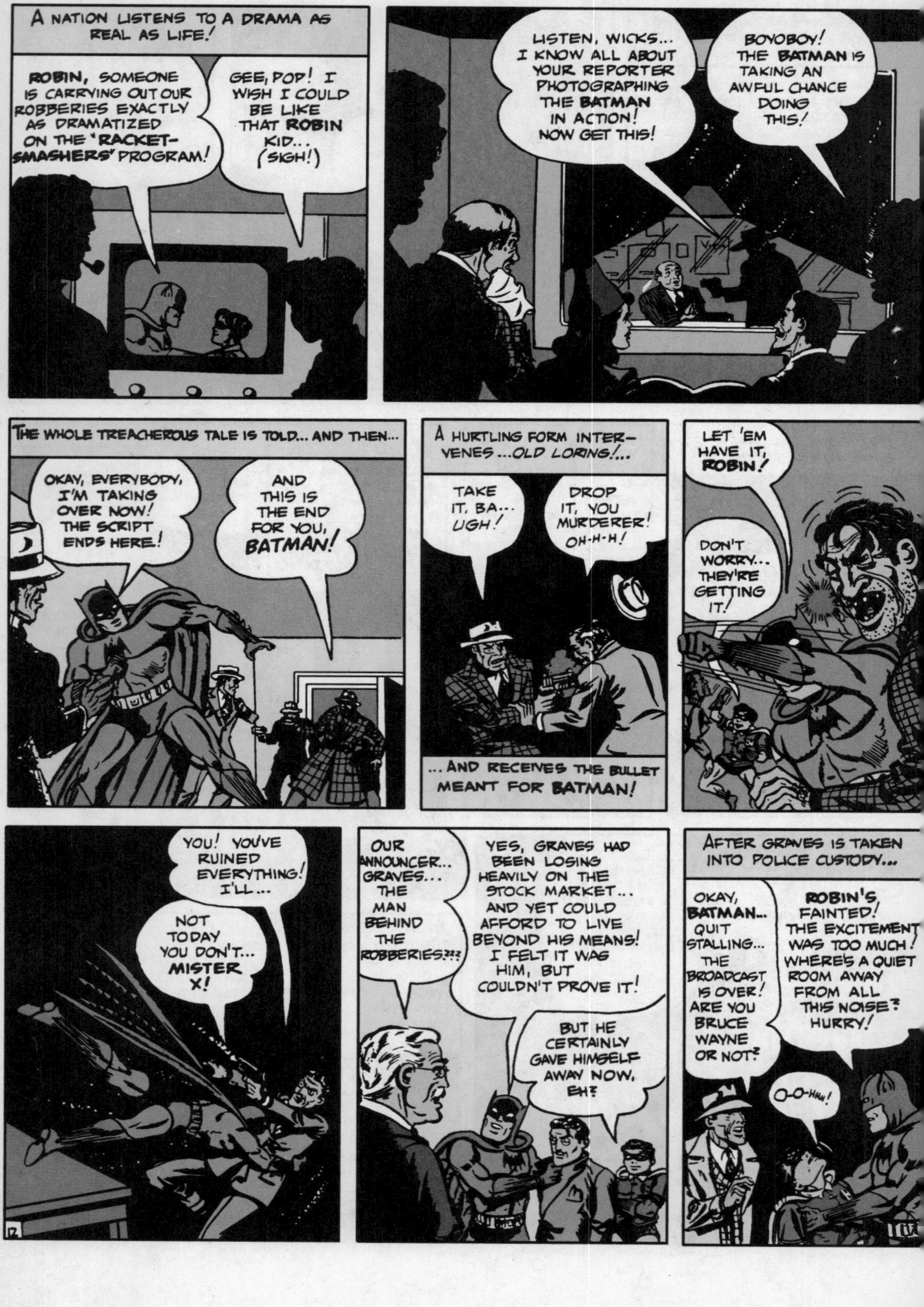
A NATION LISTENS TO A DRAMA AS REAL AS LIFE!
ROBIN, SOMEONE IS CARRYING OUT OUR ROBBERIES EXACTLY AS DRAMATIZED ON THE 'RACKET-SMASHERS' PROGRAM!
GEE, POP! I WISH I COULD BE LIKE THAT ROBIN KID... (SIGH!)
LISTEN, WICKS... I KNOW ALL ABOUT YOUR REPORTER PHOTOGRAPHING THE BATMAN IN ACTION! NOW GET THIS!
BOYOBOY! THE BATMAN IS TAKING AN AWFUL CHANCE DOING THIS!
THE WHOLE TREACHEROUS TALE IS TOLD... AND THEN...
OKAY, EVERYBODY, I'M TAKING OVER NOW! THE SCRIPT ENDS HERE!
AND THIS IS THE END FOR YOU, BATMAN!
A HURTLING FORM INTERVENES ...OLD LORING!...
TAKE IT, BA... UGH!
DROP IT, YOU MURDERER! OH-H-H!
...AND RECEIVES THE BULLET MEANT FOR BATMAN!
LET 'EM HAVE IT, ROBIN!
DON'T WORRY... THEY'RE GETTING IT!
YOU! YOU'VE RUINED EVERYTHING! I'LL ...
NOT TODAY YOU DON'T... MISTER X!
OUR ANNOUNCER... GRAVES... THE MAN BEHIND THE ROBBERIES???
YES, GRAVES HAD BEEN LOSING HEAVILY ON THE STOCK MARKET... AND YET COULD AFFORD TO LIVE BEYOND HIS MEANS! I FELT IT WAS HIM, BUT COULDN'T PROVE IT!
BUT HE CERTAINLY GAVE HIMSELF AWAY NOW, EH?
AFTER GRAVES IS TAKEN INTO POLICE CUSTODY...
OKAY, BATMAN... QUIT STALLING... THE BROADCAST IS OVER! ARE YOU BRUCE WAYNE OR NOT?
ROBIN'S FAINTED! THE EXCITEMENT WAS TOO MUCH! WHERE'S A QUIET ROOM AWAY FROM ALL THIS NOISE? HURRY!
O-O-HHH!

BUT ONCE IN THE LONELY, QUIET ROOM...

FAST THINKING, KID, BUT THAT PHONEY FAINT ISN'T GOING TO STOP SCOOP FOR LONG!

SHH! THEY MIGHT HEAR YOU!

LOOK! LORING!

HE HEARD EVERYTHING!

DON'T WORRY, MR. WAYNE... YOUR SECRET WILL GO TO THE GRAVE WITH ME! THAT BULLET... IT HIT ME...I WON'T LIVE LONG...CAME HERE TO DIE BY MYSELF!

ALWAYS THOUGHT WHEN I DIED IT WOULD BE AFTER PLAYING MY GREATEST ROLE... BUT MY LAST ROLE'S A BIT PART... A WALK-ON!

LORING... I'LL GIVE YOU THE CHANCE TO PLAY A ROLE... A TOUGH ONE! ROBIN, STALL THEM OUTSIDE A MINUTE!

WHERE'S THE BATMAN? IS HE TRYING TO RUN OUT ON US?

UH-NO... HE'S SPEAKING WITH A FRIEND— HE'LL BE OUT IN A MINUTE!

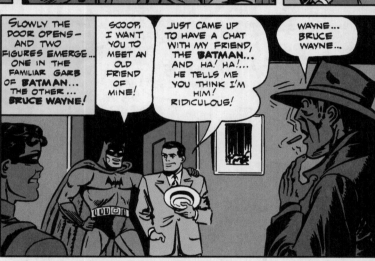

SLOWLY THE DOOR OPENS— AND TWO FIGURES EMERGE... ONE IN THE FAMILIAR GARB OF BATMAN... THE OTHER... BRUCE WAYNE!

SCOOP, I WANT YOU TO MEET AN OLD FRIEND OF MINE!

JUST CAME UP TO HAVE A CHAT WITH MY FRIEND, THE BATMAN... AND HA! HA!... HE TELLS ME YOU THINK I'M HIM! RIDICULOUS!

WAYNE... BRUCE WAYNE...

OKAY! I KNOW WHEN I'M LICKED! I WONDER WHO YOU REALLY ARE?

SH-H-H! DON'T TELL ANYBODY... BUT I'M REALLY THE JOKER!

HA! HA! SAY, BATMAN HOW ABOUT A RIDE IN YOUR BATMOBILE?

AFTER A SWIFT RACE TO THE WAYNE HOUSE..

LORING...YOU DID IT! VOICE, WALK, EVERYTHING! SORRY THAT ONLY ROBIN AND MYSELF WERE A MERE AUDIENCE OF TWO TO APPRECIATE IT!

BETTER THAN PLAYING TO AN EMPTY HOUSE... AND I DID PLAY MY GREATEST ROLE AFTER ALL ... PROUD I DID IT, TOO.. PLAYED A HERO'S ROLE!

CURTAIN COMING DOWN NOW! MY CUE TO GO... EXIT SMILING... AAAHHH!

IT'S AS IF HIS DYING GIVES LIFE TO ME! ON HIS GRAVESTONE I'LL HAVE CARVED "HUMBLY IN LIFE HE PLAYED THE PROUDEST OF ALL ROLES... MAN"!

HE'S DEAD... AND YOUR SECRET IS SAFE!

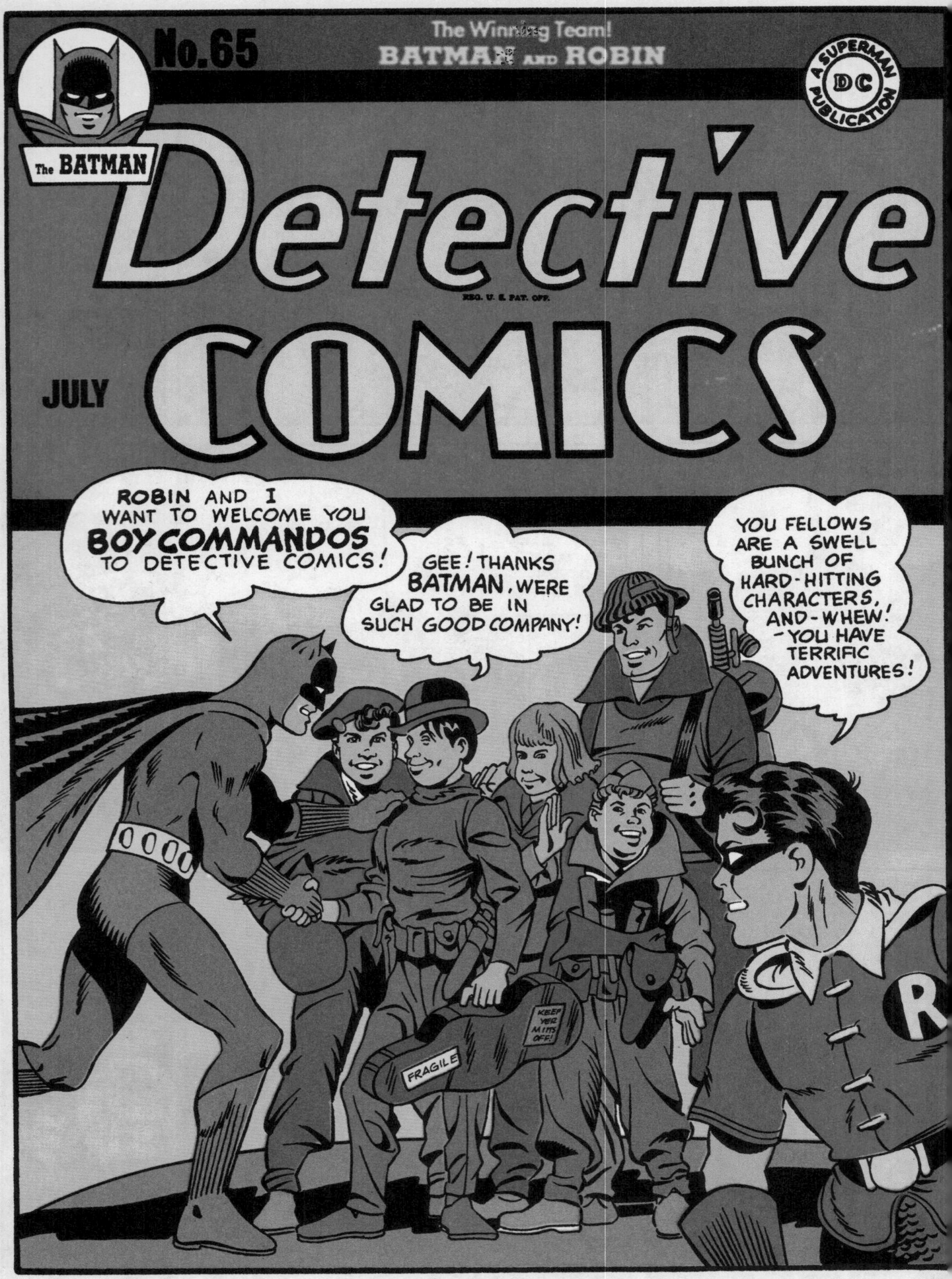
No.65
The Winning Team!
BATMAN AND ROBIN
A SUPERMAN DC PUBLICATION
The BATMAN
Detective
REG. U. S. PAT. OFF.
JULY
COMICS
ROBIN AND I WANT TO WELCOME YOU BOY COMMANDOS TO DETECTIVE COMICS!
GEE! THANKS BATMAN, WERE GLAD TO BE IN SUCH GOOD COMPANY!
YOU FELLOWS ARE A SWELL BUNCH OF HARD-HITTING CHARACTERS, AND-WHEW! -YOU HAVE TERRIFIC ADVENTURES!
KEEP YER MITS OFF!
FRAGILE
R

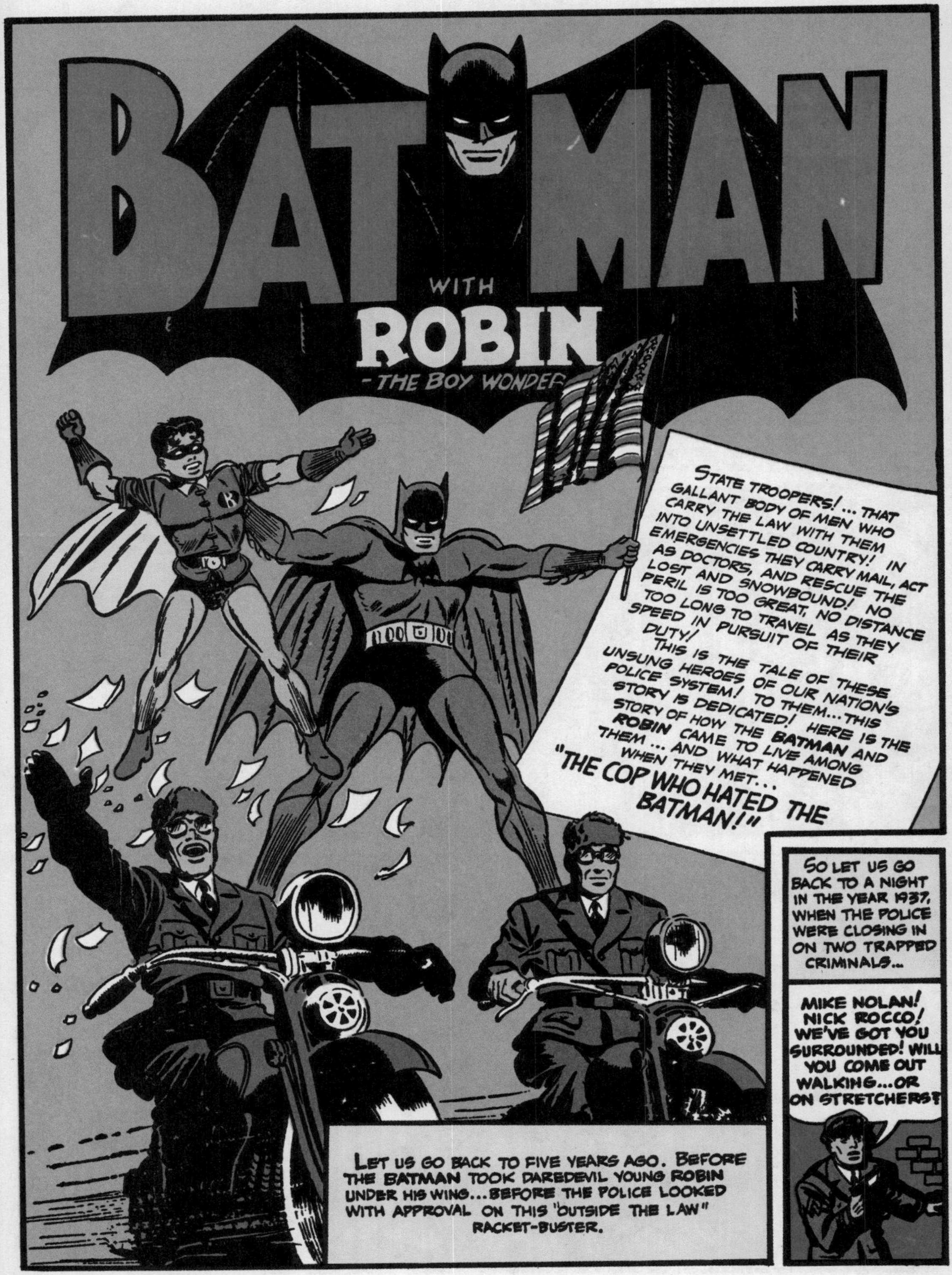
BATMAN
WITH
ROBIN
-THE BOY WONDER
STATE TROOPERS!... THAT GALLANT BODY OF MEN WHO CARRY THE LAW WITH THEM INTO UNSETTLED COUNTRY! IN EMERGENCIES THEY CARRY MAIL, ACT AS DOCTORS, AND RESCUE THE LOST AND SNOWBOUND! NO PERIL IS TOO GREAT, NO DISTANCE TOO LONG TO TRAVEL AS THEY SPEED IN PURSUIT OF THEIR DUTY!
THIS IS THE TALE OF THESE UNSUNG HEROES OF OUR NATION'S POLICE SYSTEM! TO THEM... THIS STORY IS DEDICATED! HERE IS THE STORY OF HOW THE BATMAN AND ROBIN CAME TO LIVE AMONG THEM ... AND WHAT HAPPENED WHEN THEY MET...
"THE COP WHO HATED THE BATMAN!"
LET US GO BACK TO FIVE YEARS AGO. BEFORE THE BATMAN TOOK DAREDEVIL YOUNG ROBIN UNDER HIS WING... BEFORE THE POLICE LOOKED WITH APPROVAL ON THIS "OUTSIDE THE LAW" RACKET-BUSTER.
SO LET US GO BACK TO A NIGHT IN THE YEAR 1937, WHEN THE POLICE WERE CLOSING IN ON TWO TRAPPED CRIMINALS...
MIKE NOLAN! NICK ROCCO! WE'VE GOT YOU SURROUNDED! WILL YOU COME OUT WALKING...OR ON STRETCHERS?

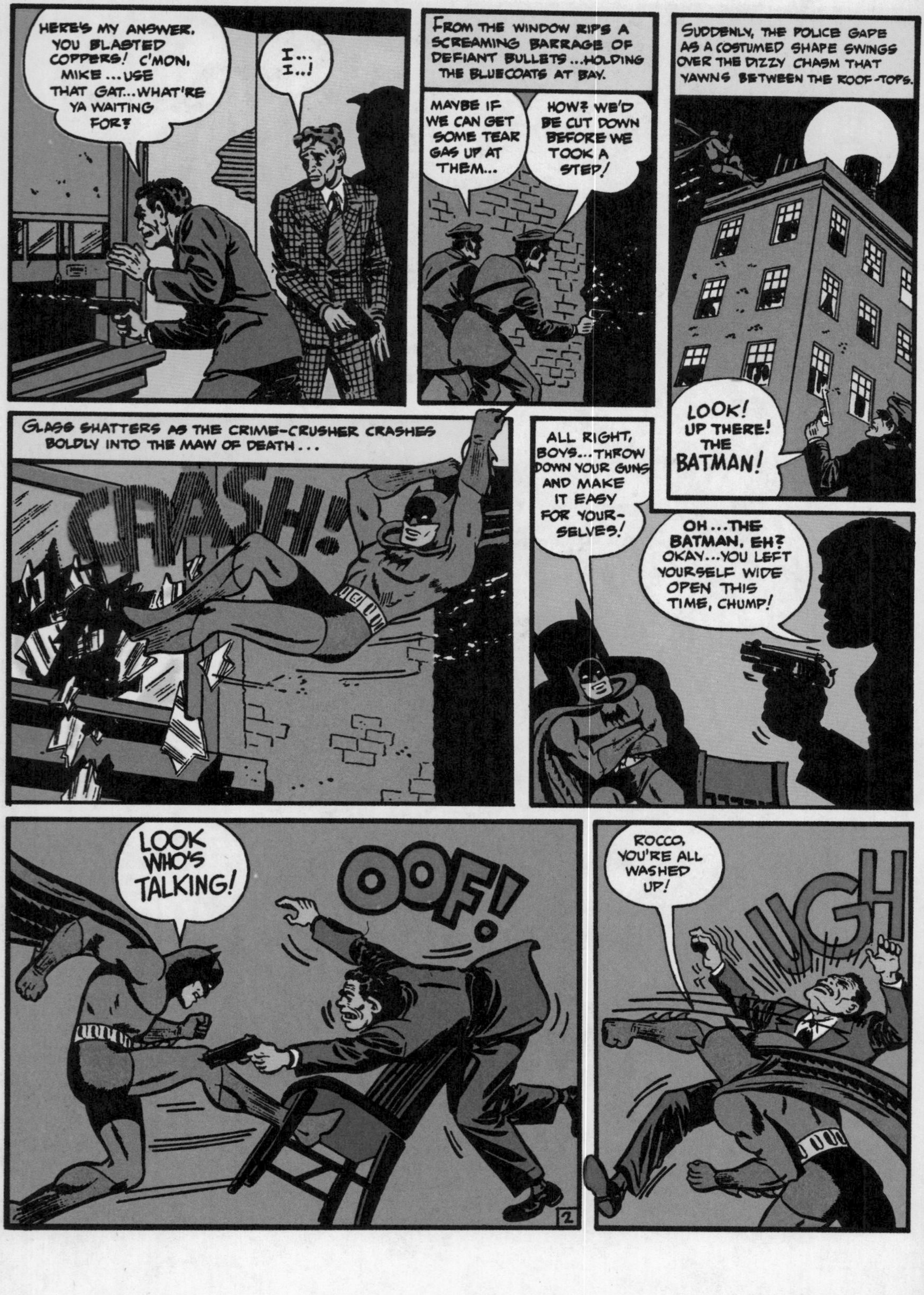
HERE'S MY ANSWER. YOU BLASTED COPPERS! C'MON, MIKE...USE THAT GAT...WHAT'RE YA WAITING FOR?
I... I...!
FROM THE WINDOW RIPS A SCREAMING BARRAGE OF DEFIANT BULLETS...HOLDING THE BLUECOATS AT BAY.
MAYBE IF WE CAN GET SOME TEAR GAS UP AT THEM...
HOW? WE'D BE CUT DOWN BEFORE WE TOOK A STEP!
SUDDENLY, THE POLICE GAPE AS A COSTUMED SHAPE SWINGS OVER THE DIZZY CHASM THAT YAWNS BETWEEN THE ROOF-TOPS.
LOOK! UP THERE! THE BATMAN!
GLASS SHATTERS AS THE CRIME-CRUSHER CRASHES BOLDLY INTO THE MAW OF DEATH...
CRASH!
ALL RIGHT, BOYS...THROW DOWN YOUR GUNS AND MAKE IT EASY FOR YOURSELVES!
OH...THE BATMAN, EH? OKAY...YOU LEFT YOURSELF WIDE OPEN THIS TIME, CHUMP!
LOOK WHO'S TALKING!
OOF!
2
ROCCO, YOU'RE ALL WASHED UP!
UGH

YOU'RE NEXT, NOLAN!

I'LL BE GLAD TO GO! I'M TIRED OF HIDING IN ALLEYS... AND I NEVER WANTED ANY PART OF COP KILLINGS!

I NEVER WANTED TO BE A CRIMINAL. I'M GOING TO MAKE A COMPLETE CONFESSION... TELL EVERYTHING ABOUT NICK AND ME!

DOWNSTAIRS, POLICE HOLD THEIR BREATH AND LISTEN! IT IS DEATHLY STILL! THEN... A SINGLE SHOT CRACKS THE SILENCE! IT IS LIKE THE CRACK OF DOOM. TERRIBLE ...FINAL!

SOME-THING'S HAPPENED! C'MON!

BANG!

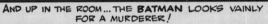

AND UP IN THE ROOM... THE **BATMAN** LOOKS VAINLY FOR A MURDERER!

ROCCO SHOT HIM! BUT WHERE DID HE DISAPPEAR TO SO QUICKLY?

OH-OH! POLICE! I'D BETTER MAKE TRACKS! I'M STILL ON THE OUTS BECAUSE I'M WORKING OUTSIDE THE LAW.

THUMP! THUMP!

LOOK! NOLAN! AND THERE GOES THE BATMAN!

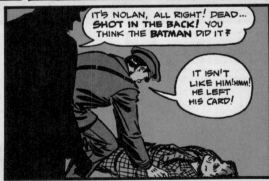

IT'S NOLAN, ALL RIGHT! DEAD... **SHOT IN THE BACK!** YOU THINK THE **BATMAN** DID IT?

IT ISN'T LIKE HIM! HMM! HE LEFT HIS CARD!

Mike Rocco got away! Mike Nolan didn't!

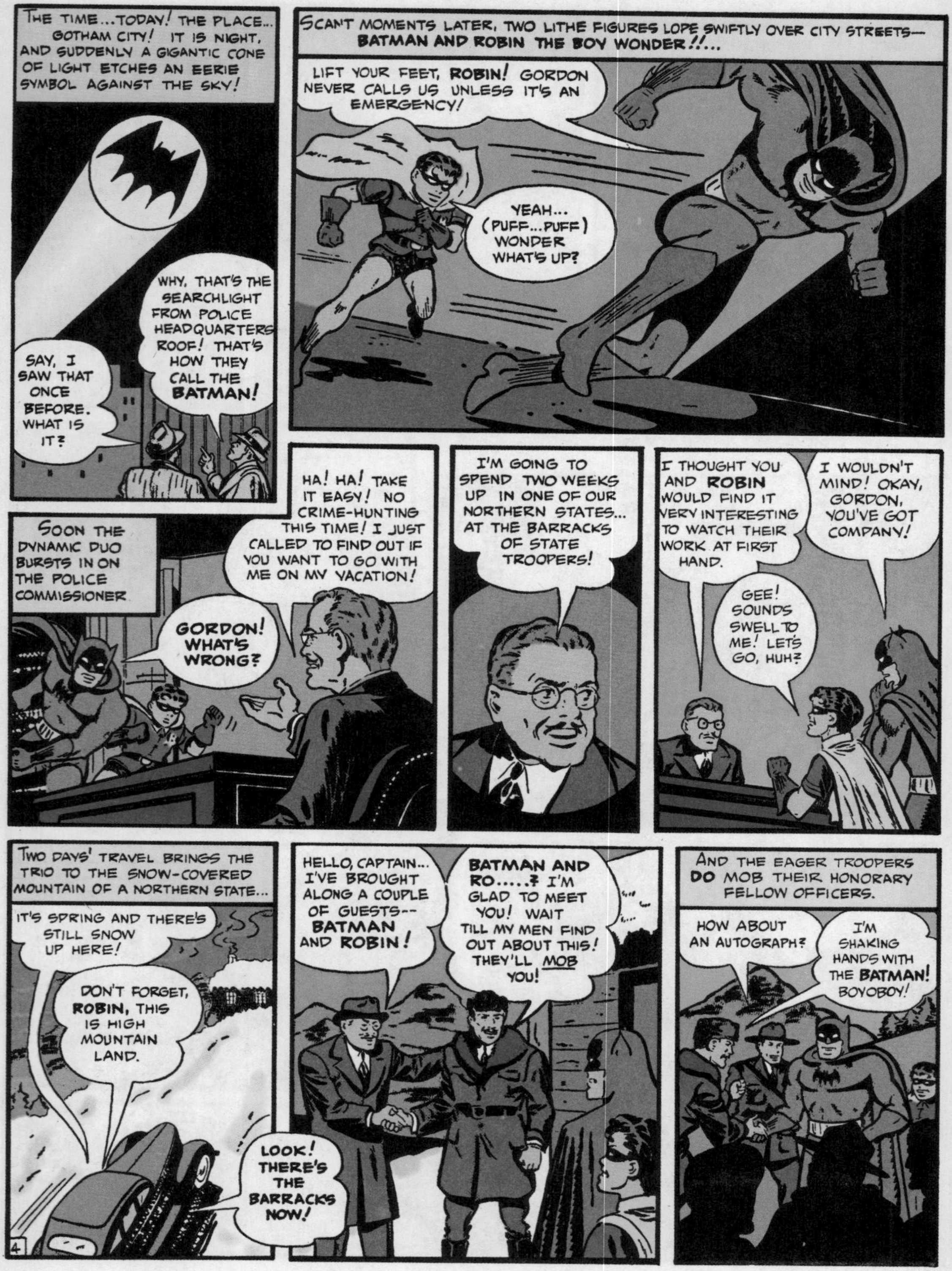
THE TIME...TODAY! THE PLACE... GOTHAM CITY! IT IS NIGHT, AND SUDDENLY A GIGANTIC CONE OF LIGHT ETCHES AN EERIE SYMBOL AGAINST THE SKY!
SAY, I SAW THAT ONCE BEFORE. WHAT IS IT?
WHY, THAT'S THE SEARCHLIGHT FROM POLICE HEADQUARTERS ROOF! THAT'S HOW THEY CALL THE BATMAN!
SCANT MOMENTS LATER, TWO LITHE FIGURES LOPE SWIFTLY OVER CITY STREETS— BATMAN AND ROBIN THE BOY WONDER!!...
LIFT YOUR FEET, ROBIN! GORDON NEVER CALLS US UNLESS IT'S AN EMERGENCY!
YEAH... (PUFF...PUFF) WONDER WHAT'S UP?
SOON THE DYNAMIC DUO BURSTS IN ON THE POLICE COMMISSIONER
GORDON! WHAT'S WRONG?
HA! HA! TAKE IT EASY! NO CRIME-HUNTING THIS TIME! I JUST CALLED TO FIND OUT IF YOU WANT TO GO WITH ME ON MY VACATION!
I'M GOING TO SPEND TWO WEEKS UP IN ONE OF OUR NORTHERN STATES... AT THE BARRACKS OF STATE TROOPERS!
I THOUGHT YOU AND ROBIN WOULD FIND IT VERY INTERESTING TO WATCH THEIR WORK AT FIRST HAND.
I WOULDN'T MIND! OKAY, GORDON, YOU'VE GOT COMPANY!
GEE! SOUNDS SWELL TO ME! LET'S GO, HUH?
TWO DAYS' TRAVEL BRINGS THE TRIO TO THE SNOW-COVERED MOUNTAIN OF A NORTHERN STATE...
IT'S SPRING AND THERE'S STILL SNOW UP HERE!
DON'T FORGET, ROBIN, THIS IS HIGH MOUNTAIN LAND.
LOOK! THERE'S THE BARRACKS NOW!
4
HELLO, CAPTAIN... I'VE BROUGHT ALONG A COUPLE OF GUESTS-- BATMAN AND ROBIN!
BATMAN AND RO.....? I'M GLAD TO MEET YOU! WAIT TILL MY MEN FIND OUT ABOUT THIS! THEY'LL MOB YOU!
AND THE EAGER TROOPERS DO MOB THEIR HONORARY FELLOW OFFICERS.
HOW ABOUT AN AUTOGRAPH?
I'M SHAKING HANDS WITH THE BATMAN! BOYOBOY!

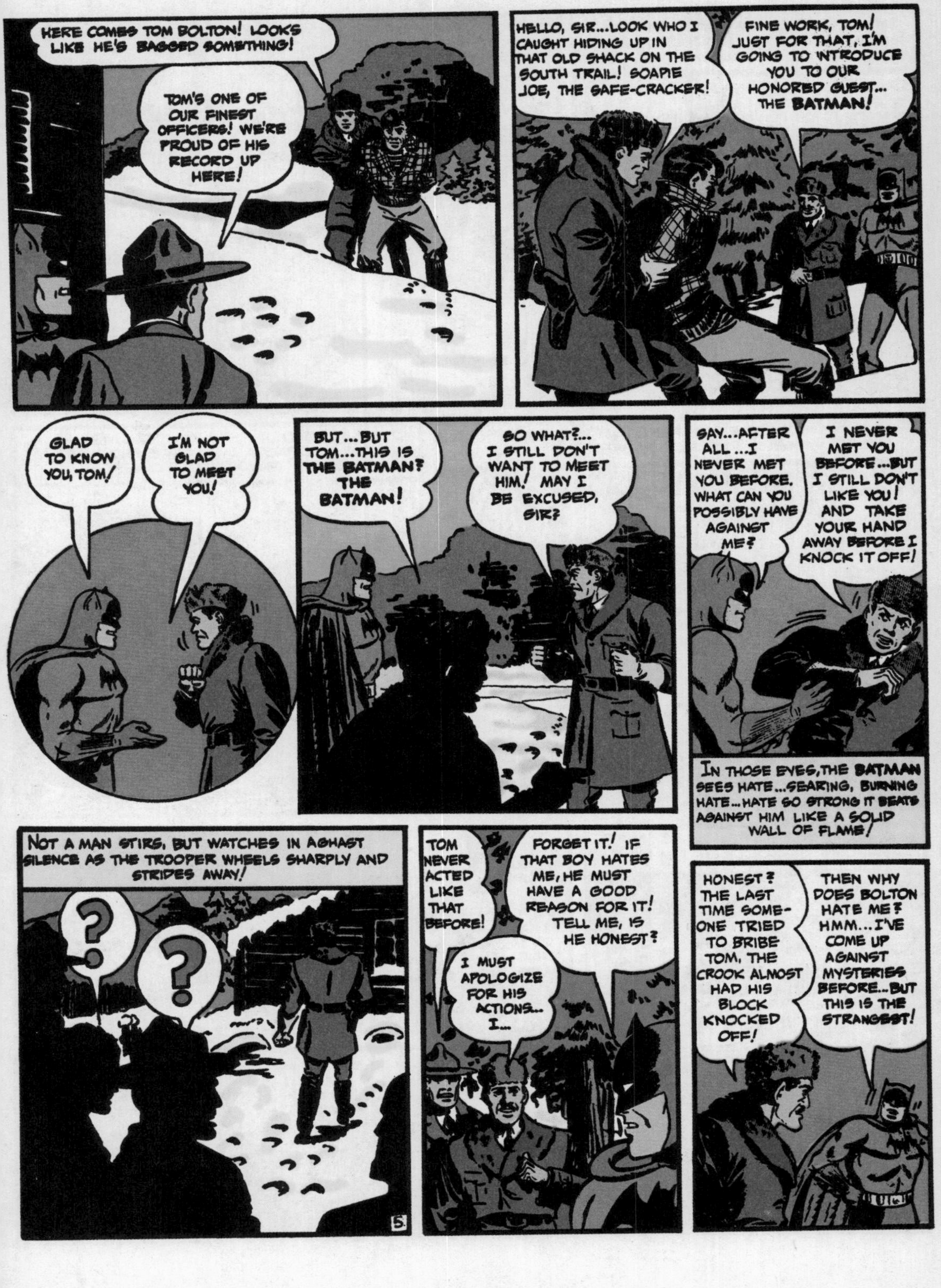
HERE COMES TOM BOLTON! LOOKS LIKE HE'S BAGGED SOMETHING!
TOM'S ONE OF OUR FINEST OFFICERS! WE'RE PROUD OF HIS RECORD UP HERE!
HELLO, SIR...LOOK WHO I CAUGHT HIDING UP IN THAT OLD SHACK ON THE SOUTH TRAIL! SOAPIE JOE, THE SAFE-CRACKER!
FINE WORK, TOM! JUST FOR THAT, I'M GOING TO INTRODUCE YOU TO OUR HONORED GUEST... THE BATMAN!
GLAD TO KNOW YOU, TOM!
I'M NOT GLAD TO MEET YOU!
BUT...BUT TOM...THIS IS THE BATMAN? THE BATMAN!
SO WHAT?... I STILL DON'T WANT TO MEET HIM! MAY I BE EXCUSED, SIR?
SAY...AFTER ALL...I NEVER MET YOU BEFORE. WHAT CAN YOU POSSIBLY HAVE AGAINST ME?
I NEVER MET YOU BEFORE...BUT I STILL DON'T LIKE YOU! AND TAKE YOUR HAND AWAY BEFORE I KNOCK IT OFF!
IN THOSE EYES, THE BATMAN SEES HATE...SEARING, BURNING HATE...HATE SO STRONG IT BEATS AGAINST HIM LIKE A SOLID WALL OF FLAME!
NOT A MAN STIRS, BUT WATCHES IN AGHAST SILENCE AS THE TROOPER WHEELS SHARPLY AND STRIDES AWAY!
?
?
5.
TOM NEVER ACTED LIKE THAT BEFORE!
FORGET IT! IF THAT BOY HATES ME, HE MUST HAVE A GOOD REASON FOR IT! TELL ME, IS HE HONEST?
I MUST APOLOGIZE FOR HIS ACTIONS... I...
HONEST? THE LAST TIME SOME-ONE TRIED TO BRIBE TOM, THE CROOK ALMOST HAD HIS BLOCK KNOCKED OFF!
THEN WHY DOES BOLTON HATE ME? HMM...I'VE COME UP AGAINST MYSTERIES BEFORE...BUT THIS IS THE STRANGEST!

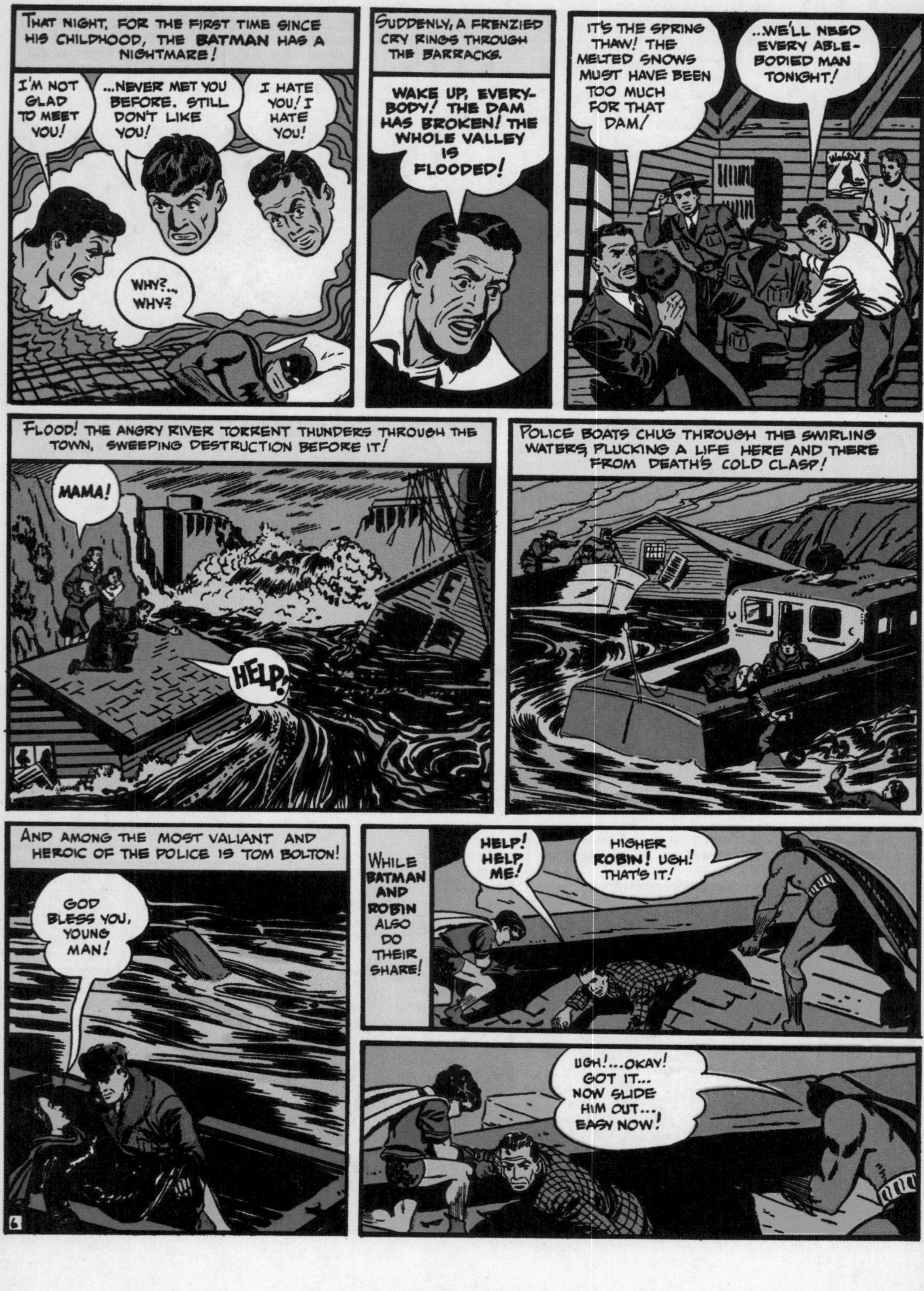

THAT NIGHT, FOR THE FIRST TIME SINCE HIS CHILDHOOD, THE BATMAN HAS A NIGHTMARE!
I'M NOT GLAD TO MEET YOU!
...NEVER MET YOU BEFORE. STILL DON'T LIKE YOU!
I HATE YOU! I HATE YOU!
WHY?... WHY?
SUDDENLY, A FRENZIED CRY RINGS THROUGH THE BARRACKS.
WAKE UP, EVERYBODY! THE DAM HAS BROKEN! THE WHOLE VALLEY IS FLOODED!
IT'S THE SPRING THAW! THE MELTED SNOWS MUST HAVE BEEN TOO MUCH FOR THAT DAM!
...WE'LL NEED EVERY ABLE-BODIED MAN TONIGHT!
FLOOD! THE ANGRY RIVER TORRENT THUNDERS THROUGH THE TOWN, SWEEPING DESTRUCTION BEFORE IT!
MAMA!
HELP!
POLICE BOATS CHUG THROUGH THE SWIRLING WATERS, PLUCKING A LIFE HERE AND THERE FROM DEATH'S COLD CLASP!
AND AMONG THE MOST VALIANT AND HEROIC OF THE POLICE IS TOM BOLTON!
GOD BLESS YOU, YOUNG MAN!
6
WHILE BATMAN AND ROBIN ALSO DO THEIR SHARE!
HELP! HELP ME!
HIGHER ROBIN! UGH! THAT'S IT!
UGH!...OKAY! GOT IT... NOW SLIDE HIM OUT... EASY NOW!

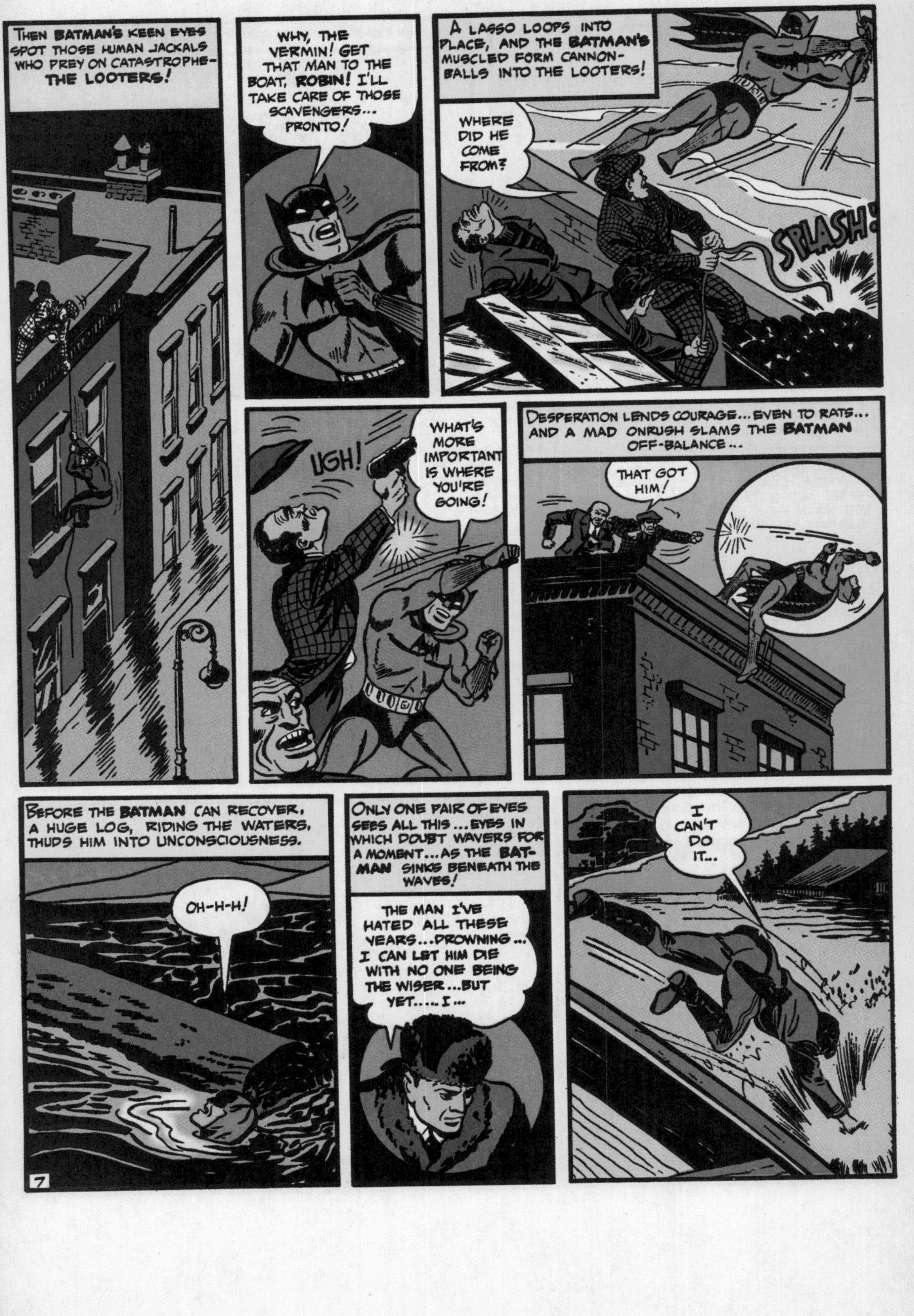
THEN BATMAN'S KEEN EYES SPOT THOSE HUMAN JACKALS WHO PREY ON CATASTROPHE- THE LOOTERS!
WHY, THE VERMIN! GET THAT MAN TO THE BOAT, ROBIN! I'LL TAKE CARE OF THOSE SCAVENGERS... PRONTO!
A LASSO LOOPS INTO PLACE, AND THE BATMAN'S MUSCLED FORM CANNON-BALLS INTO THE LOOTERS!
WHERE DID HE COME FROM?
SPLASH!
UGH!
WHAT'S MORE IMPORTANT IS WHERE YOU'RE GOING!
DESPERATION LENDS COURAGE... EVEN TO RATS... AND A MAD ONRUSH SLAMS THE BATMAN OFF-BALANCE...
THAT GOT HIM!
BEFORE THE BATMAN CAN RECOVER, A HUGE LOG, RIDING THE WATERS, THUDS HIM INTO UNCONSCIOUSNESS.
OH-H-H!
7
ONLY ONE PAIR OF EYES SEES ALL THIS... EYES IN WHICH DOUBT WAVERS FOR A MOMENT... AS THE BAT-MAN SINKS BENEATH THE WAVES!
THE MAN I'VE HATED ALL THESE YEARS... DROWNING... I CAN LET HIM DIE WITH NO ONE BEING THE WISER... BUT YET..... I...
I CAN'T DO IT...

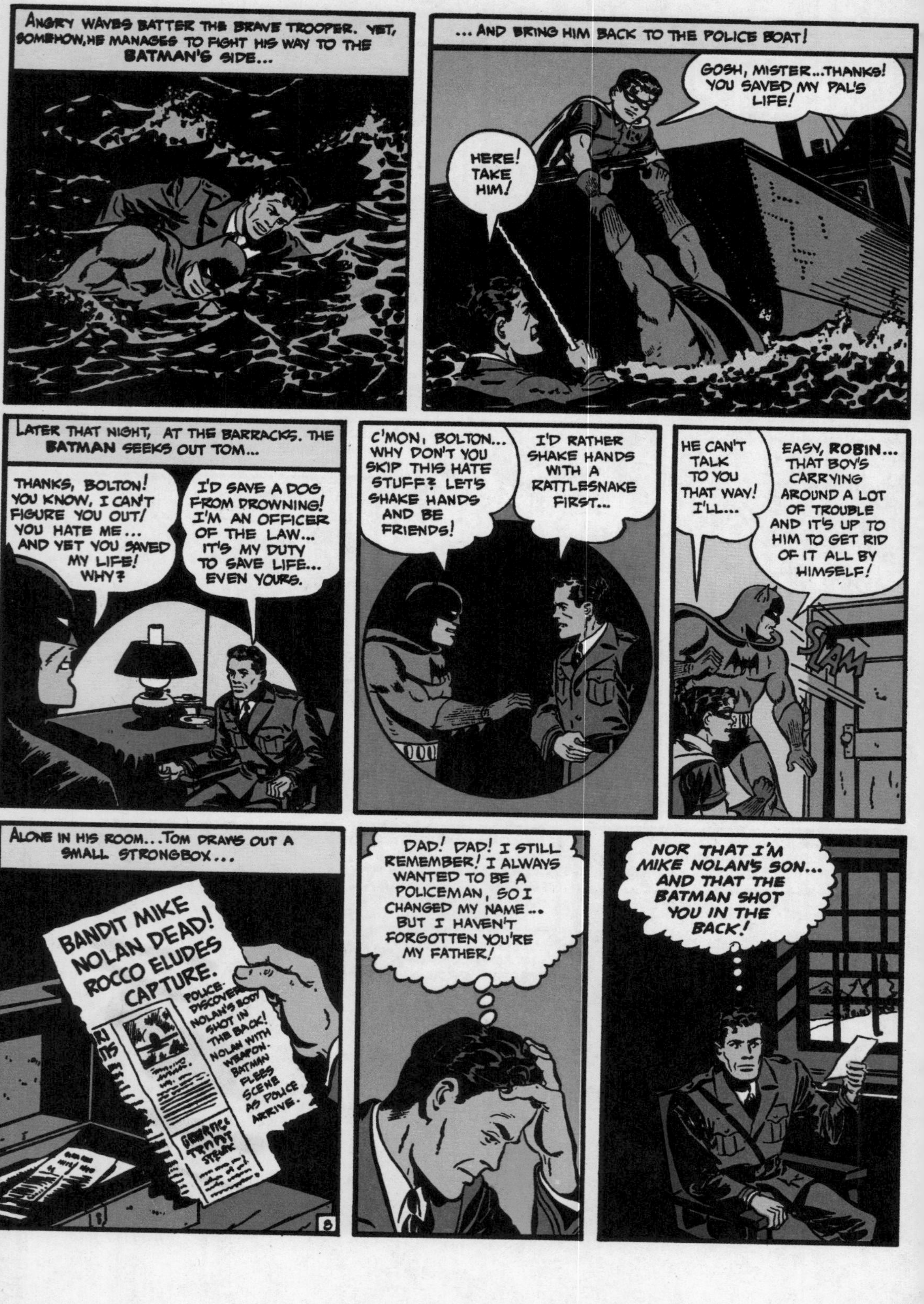
ANGRY WAVES BATTER THE BRAVE TROOPER. YET, SOMEHOW, HE MANAGES TO FIGHT HIS WAY TO THE BATMAN'S SIDE...
... AND BRING HIM BACK TO THE POLICE BOAT!
GOSH, MISTER...THANKS! YOU SAVED MY PAL'S LIFE!
HERE! TAKE HIM!
LATER THAT NIGHT, AT THE BARRACKS. THE BATMAN SEEKS OUT TOM...
THANKS, BOLTON! YOU KNOW, I CAN'T FIGURE YOU OUT! YOU HATE ME... AND YET YOU SAVED MY LIFE! WHY?
I'D SAVE A DOG FROM DROWNING! I'M AN OFFICER OF THE LAW... IT'S MY DUTY TO SAVE LIFE... EVEN YOURS.
C'MON, BOLTON... WHY DON'T YOU SKIP THIS HATE STUFF? LET'S SHAKE HANDS AND BE FRIENDS!
I'D RATHER SHAKE HANDS WITH A RATTLESNAKE FIRST...
HE CAN'T TALK TO YOU THAT WAY! I'LL...
EASY, ROBIN... THAT BOY'S CARRYING AROUND A LOT OF TROUBLE AND IT'S UP TO HIM TO GET RID OF IT ALL BY HIMSELF!
SLAM
ALONE IN HIS ROOM...TOM DRAWS OUT A SMALL STRONGBOX...
BANDIT MIKE NOLAN DEAD! ROCCO ELUDES CAPTURE.
POLICE DISCOVER NOLAN'S BODY SHOT IN THE BACK! NOLAN WITH WEAPON. BATMAN FLEES SCENE AS POLICE ARRIVE.
8
DAD! DAD! I STILL REMEMBER! I ALWAYS WANTED TO BE A POLICEMAN, SO I CHANGED MY NAME... BUT I HAVEN'T FORGOTTEN YOU'RE MY FATHER!
NOR THAT I'M MIKE NOLAN'S SON... AND THAT THE BATMAN SHOT YOU IN THE BACK!

THE NEXT DAY... AS THE TROOPERS HOLD DAILY TARGET PRACTICE...

PANGGG!

C'MON, BATMAN, LET'S SEE HOW YOU CAN HANDLE A GUN!

OH... I SEE... MY MARKSMANSHIP TEST! OKAY!

IN THE BATMAN'S EXPERT HAND, THE GUN ROARS... AND SIX BULLETS HIT THE TARGET DEAD CENTER!

PANG! PANG! PANG! PANG! PANG! PANG!

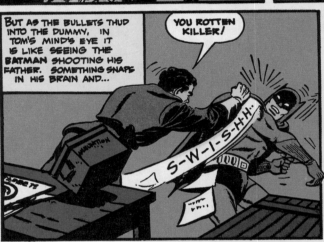

BUT AS THE BULLETS THUD INTO THE DUMMY, IN TOM'S MIND'S EYE IT IS LIKE SEEING THE BATMAN SHOOTING HIS FATHER. SOMETHING SNAPS IN HIS BRAIN AND...

YOU ROTTEN KILLER!

S-W-I-S-H-H...

BOLTON! YOU'RE UNDER ARREST FOR STRIKING A BROTHER OFFICER!

THE COWARD! LET ME TAKE OFF MY BADGE AND FIGHT IT OUT WITH HIM, MAN TO MAN!

ALL RIGHT, TOM... IF ONLY A FIGHT WILL SATISFY YOU... I'LL FIGHT YOU!

A CLEARING IS MADE... THE TWO OPPONENTS SQUARE OFF... AND THE BATTLE BEGINS!

THE FIRST THING A BOXER LEARNS IS TO USE CAUTION!

I'LL TEAR YOUR H... OH!

SKIP THE ADVICE! C'MON... FIGHT!

RELUCTANT BUT GRIM, THE DEADLY FIGHTING MACHINE THAT IS THE BATMAN BEGINS TO CRACK HOME WITH DYNAMITE FISTS!

OKAY... I HATE TO DO THIS... BUT YOU ASKED FOR IT!

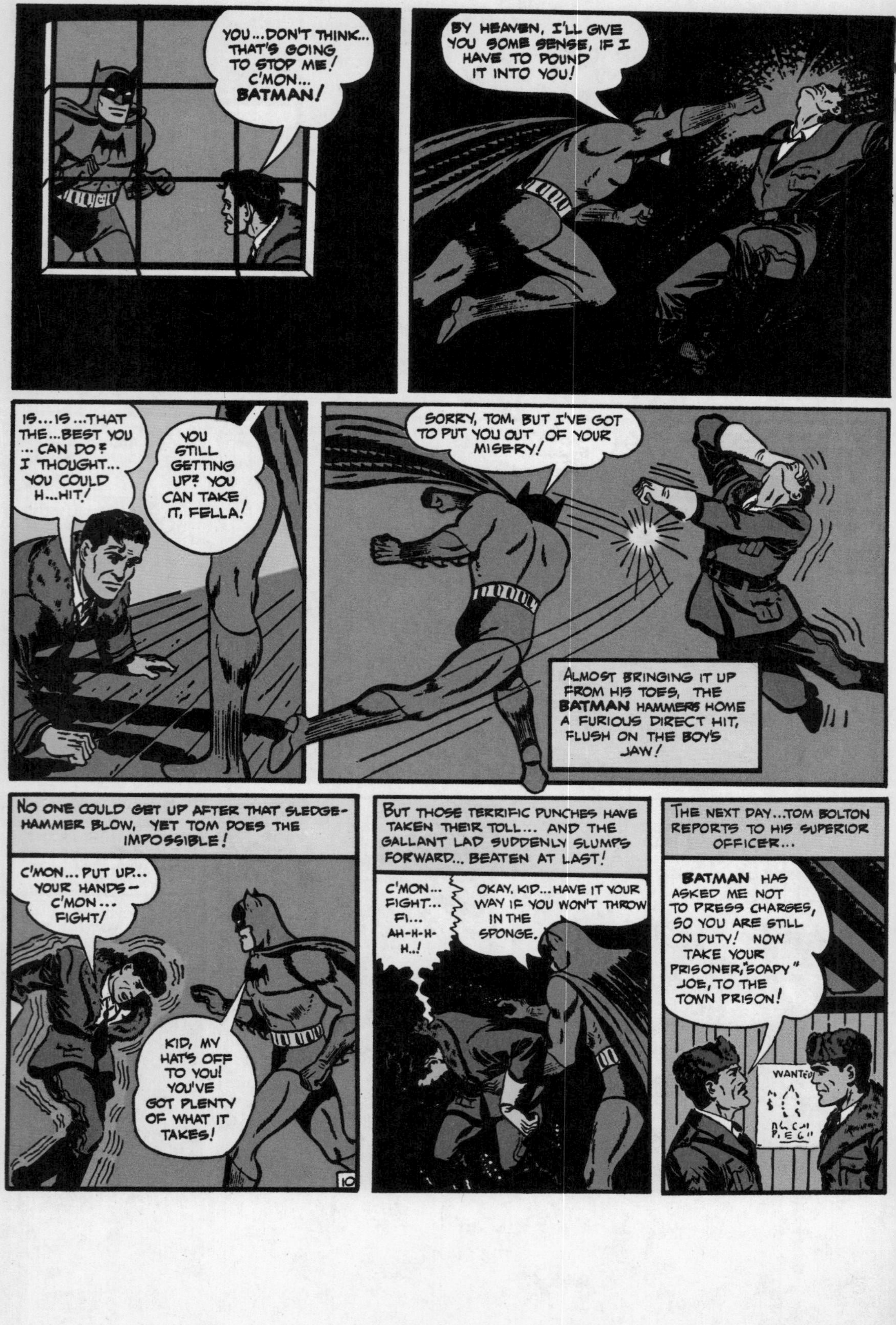
YOU...DON'T THINK... THAT'S GOING TO STOP ME! C'MON... BATMAN!
BY HEAVEN, I'LL GIVE YOU SOME SENSE, IF I HAVE TO POUND IT INTO YOU!
IS...IS...THAT THE...BEST YOU ...CAN DO? I THOUGHT... YOU COULD H...HIT!
YOU STILL GETTING UP? YOU CAN TAKE IT, FELLA!
SORRY, TOM, BUT I'VE GOT TO PUT YOU OUT OF YOUR MISERY!
ALMOST BRINGING IT UP FROM HIS TOES, THE BATMAN HAMMERS HOME A FURIOUS DIRECT HIT, FLUSH ON THE BOY'S JAW!
NO ONE COULD GET UP AFTER THAT SLEDGE-HAMMER BLOW, YET TOM DOES THE IMPOSSIBLE!
C'MON...PUT UP... YOUR HANDS- C'MON... FIGHT!
KID, MY HAT'S OFF TO YOU! YOU'VE GOT PLENTY OF WHAT IT TAKES!
10
BUT THOSE TERRIFIC PUNCHES HAVE TAKEN THEIR TOLL... AND THE GALLANT LAD SUDDENLY SLUMPS FORWARD... BEATEN AT LAST!
C'MON... FIGHT... FI... AH-H-H-H..!
OKAY, KID...HAVE IT YOUR WAY IF YOU WON'T THROW IN THE SPONGE.
THE NEXT DAY...TOM BOLTON REPORTS TO HIS SUPERIOR OFFICER...
BATMAN HAS ASKED ME NOT TO PRESS CHARGES, SO YOU ARE STILL ON DUTY! NOW TAKE YOUR PRISONER, "SOAPY" JOE, TO THE TOWN PRISON!
WANTED

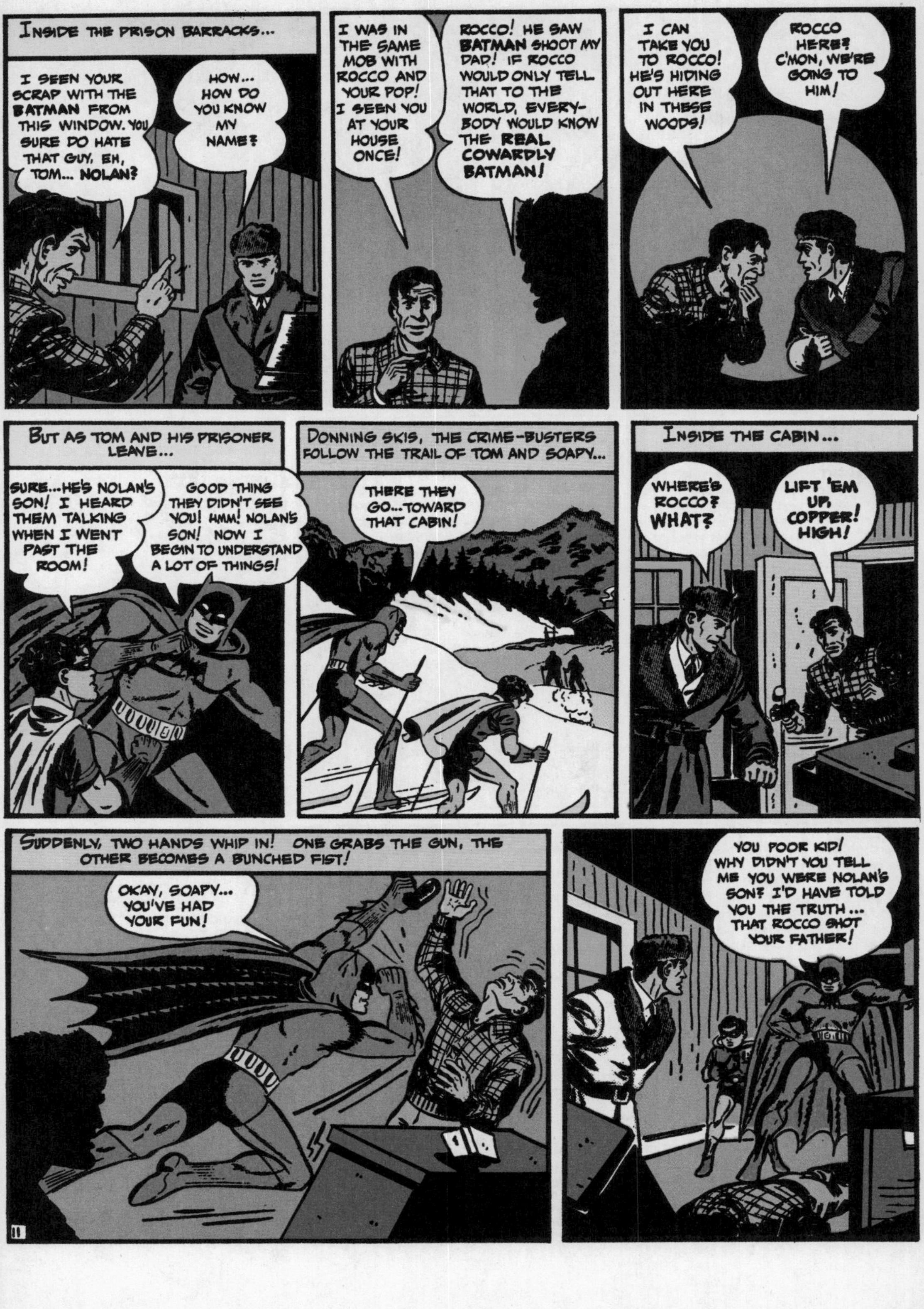

INSIDE THE PRISON BARRACKS...
I SEEN YOUR SCRAP WITH THE BATMAN FROM THIS WINDOW. YOU SURE DO HATE THAT GUY, EH, TOM... NOLAN?
HOW... HOW DO YOU KNOW MY NAME?
I WAS IN THE SAME MOB WITH ROCCO AND YOUR POP! I SEEN YOU AT YOUR HOUSE ONCE!
ROCCO! HE SAW BATMAN SHOOT MY DAD! IF ROCCO WOULD ONLY TELL THAT TO THE WORLD, EVERYBODY WOULD KNOW THE REAL COWARDLY BATMAN!
I CAN TAKE YOU TO ROCCO! HE'S HIDING OUT HERE IN THESE WOODS!
ROCCO HERE? C'MON, WE'RE GOING TO HIM!
BUT AS TOM AND HIS PRISONER LEAVE...
SURE...HE'S NOLAN'S SON! I HEARD THEM TALKING WHEN I WENT PAST THE ROOM!
GOOD THING THEY DIDN'T SEE YOU! HMM! NOLAN'S SON! NOW I BEGIN TO UNDERSTAND A LOT OF THINGS!
DONNING SKIS, THE CRIME-BUSTERS FOLLOW THE TRAIL OF TOM AND SOAPY...
THERE THEY GO...TOWARD THAT CABIN!
INSIDE THE CABIN...
WHERE'S ROCCO? WHAT?
LIFT 'EM UP, COPPER! HIGH!
SUDDENLY, TWO HANDS WHIP IN! ONE GRABS THE GUN, THE OTHER BECOMES A BUNCHED FIST!
OKAY, SOAPY... YOU'VE HAD YOUR FUN!
11
YOU POOR KID! WHY DIDN'T YOU TELL ME YOU WERE NOLAN'S SON? I'D HAVE TOLD YOU THE TRUTH... THAT ROCCO SHOT YOUR FATHER!

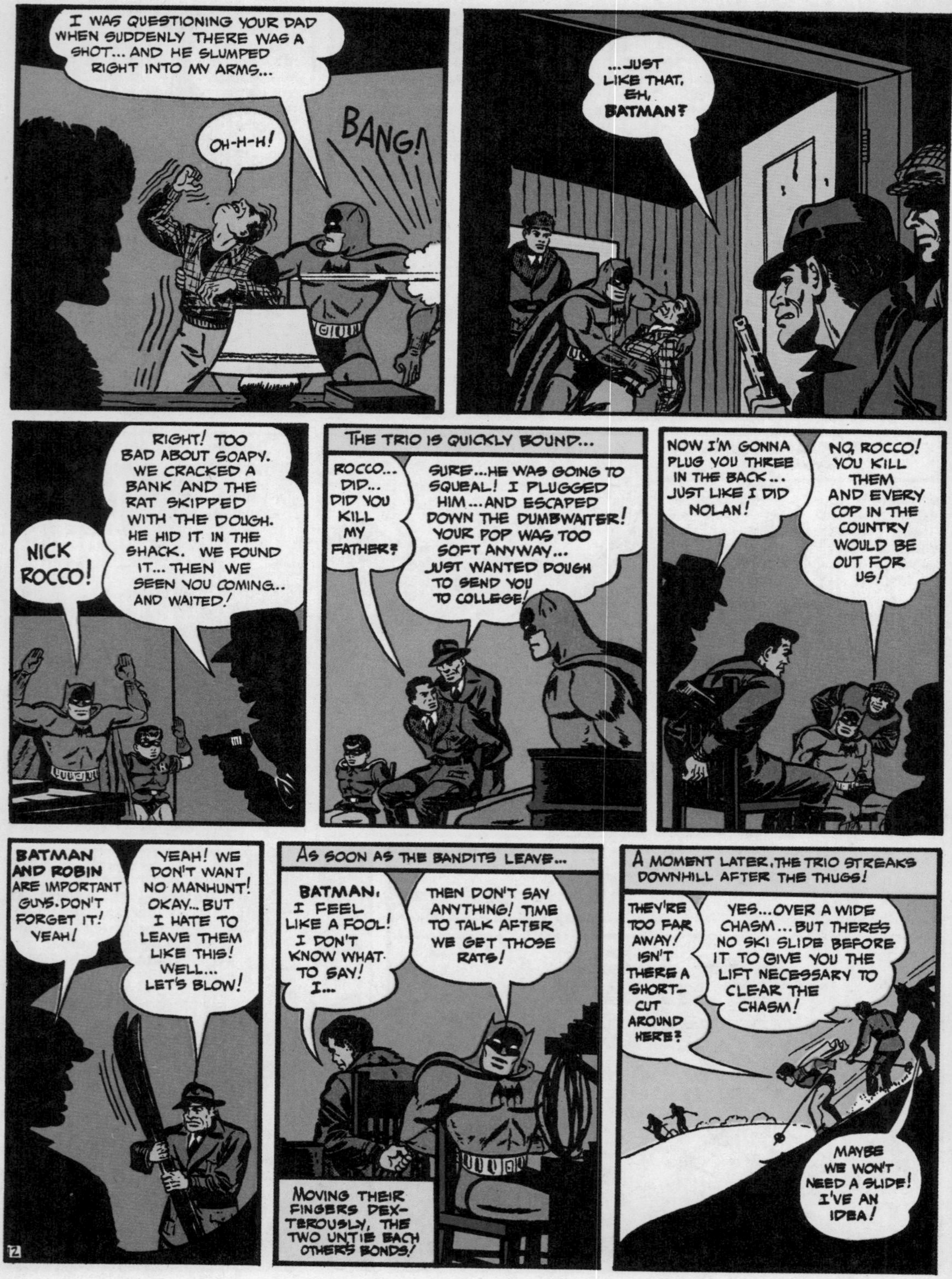
I WAS QUESTIONING YOUR DAD WHEN SUDDENLY THERE WAS A SHOT... AND HE SLUMPED RIGHT INTO MY ARMS...
OH-H-H!
BANG!
...JUST LIKE THAT, EH, BATMAN?
NICK ROCCO!
RIGHT! TOO BAD ABOUT SOAPY. WE CRACKED A BANK AND THE RAT SKIPPED WITH THE DOUGH. HE HID IT IN THE SHACK. WE FOUND IT... THEN WE SEEN YOU COMING... AND WAITED!
THE TRIO IS QUICKLY BOUND...
ROCCO... DID... DID YOU KILL MY FATHER?
SURE...HE WAS GOING TO SQUEAL! I PLUGGED HIM...AND ESCAPED DOWN THE DUMBWAITER! YOUR POP WAS TOO SOFT ANYWAY... JUST WANTED DOUGH TO SEND YOU TO COLLEGE!
NOW I'M GONNA PLUG YOU THREE IN THE BACK... JUST LIKE I DID NOLAN!
NO, ROCCO! YOU KILL THEM AND EVERY COP IN THE COUNTRY WOULD BE OUT FOR US!
BATMAN AND ROBIN ARE IMPORTANT GUYS. DON'T FORGET IT! YEAH!
YEAH! WE DON'T WANT NO MANHUNT! OKAY... BUT I HATE TO LEAVE THEM LIKE THIS! WELL... LET'S BLOW!
AS SOON AS THE BANDITS LEAVE...
BATMAN, I FEEL LIKE A FOOL! I DON'T KNOW WHAT TO SAY! I...
THEN DON'T SAY ANYTHING! TIME TO TALK AFTER WE GET THOSE RATS!
MOVING THEIR FINGERS DEXTEROUSLY, THE TWO UNTIE EACH OTHER'S BONDS!
A MOMENT LATER, THE TRIO STREAKS DOWNHILL AFTER THE THUGS!
THEY'RE TOO FAR AWAY! ISN'T THERE A SHORT-CUT AROUND HERE?
YES...OVER A WIDE CHASM... BUT THERE'S NO SKI SLIDE BEFORE IT TO GIVE YOU THE LIFT NECESSARY TO CLEAR THE CHASM!
MAYBE WE WON'T NEED A SLIDE! I'VE AN IDEA!

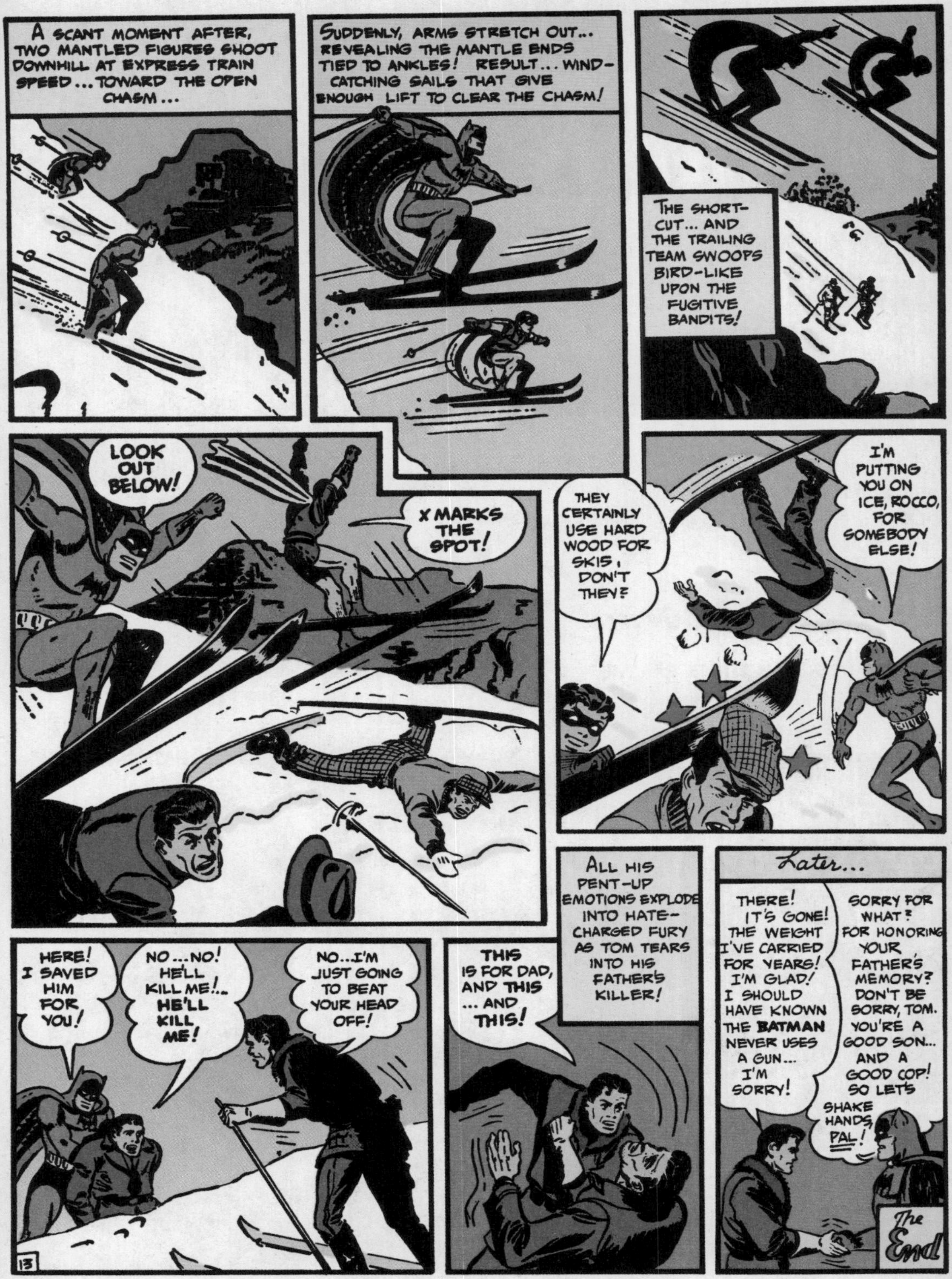
A SCANT MOMENT AFTER, TWO MANTLED FIGURES SHOOT DOWNHILL AT EXPRESS TRAIN SPEED... TOWARD THE OPEN CHASM...
SUDDENLY, ARMS STRETCH OUT... REVEALING THE MANTLE ENDS TIED TO ANKLES! RESULT... WIND-CATCHING SAILS THAT GIVE ENOUGH LIFT TO CLEAR THE CHASM!
THE SHORT-CUT... AND THE TRAILING TEAM SWOOPS BIRD-LIKE UPON THE FUGITIVE BANDITS!
LOOK OUT BELOW!
X MARKS THE SPOT!
THEY CERTAINLY USE HARD WOOD FOR SKIS, DON'T THEY?
I'M PUTTING YOU ON ICE, ROCCO, FOR SOMEBODY ELSE!
HERE! I SAVED HIM FOR YOU!
NO...NO! HE'LL KILL ME!.. HE'LL KILL ME!
NO...I'M JUST GOING TO BEAT YOUR HEAD OFF!
13
THIS IS FOR DAD, AND THIS ... AND THIS!
ALL HIS PENT-UP EMOTIONS EXPLODE INTO HATE-CHARGED FURY AS TOM TEARS INTO HIS FATHER'S KILLER!
Later...
THERE! IT'S GONE! THE WEIGHT I'VE CARRIED FOR YEARS! I'M GLAD! I SHOULD HAVE KNOWN THE BATMAN NEVER USES A GUN... I'M SORRY!
SORRY FOR WHAT? FOR HONORING YOUR FATHER'S MEMORY? DON'T BE SORRY, TOM. YOU'RE A GOOD SON... AND A GOOD COP! SO LET'S SHAKE HANDS, PAL!
The End